Research Culture in Architecture

Cornelie Leopold
Christopher Robeller
Ulrike Weber (Eds.)

Research Culture in Architecture

Cross-Disciplinary Collaboration

Birkhäuser
Basel

Contents

CONTENTS

Preface

Georg Vrachliotis

Is it possible to talk about architectural research without first talking about architecture? History has shown that opinions differ on this point and the current situation still appears confusing. Some claim that every architectural field trip is research. Others claim that the design process itself implies research. Still others explain with a blinking eye their own everyday office life as research. In addition to all the current debates that have taken place about what is covered by the term *research* in the field of architecture, a long-locked door opens: it is about the great possibility of repositioning and redefining oneself as a school of architecture in sociopolitical terms. So, could the question of what research could mean in the field of architecture not also open up a new discussion about the relations between schools of architecture and society?

A narrative of the present often sounds like a great story of loss. First, universities no longer seem to be the central political corrective for society. Half a century after '68, with all its optimism, and related academic reforms, the university as once so proud intellectual bloom of free thought and social criticism seems somewhat wilted. The creative will (Gestaltungswillen) seems to have been replaced by a soberly appearing administrative power, idealism has given way to innovation. Secondly, universities currently seem to be busy trying to find a way out of the supposed credibility crisis of their own institutional history. The ideal of objectivity and rationality is confronted with an increasingly popular performative relativism. The authority of expertise and science, even the belief in the power of the factual – they are (once again) in a state of transition. And thirdly, with the integration of artificial intelligence in everyday life, a new kind of data empiricism has gained in social acceptance, through which creativity and fantasy – as two of the great historical genres in the history of ideas – are increasingly questioned. One speaks of the beginning of the transhuman age. No matter how powerful certain applications and tools can actually be, there is no doubt about it: The history of architecture is not only a history of design, but also a history of fear – of the power of technology and industry, of over-regulation by norms and laws, or of the loss of social relevance. But instead of practicing defensive rhetoric and hiding behind any notion of autonomy, it might be a matter of gaining cultural and political access to society through research.

According to the first thesis, architectural research only becomes socially relevant when it succeeds in questioning – and overcoming – the traditional claim to autonomy of architecture.

Hence the liveliness and explosive force that a discussion about architecture can unfold. Understood in this way, it is – in the same sense as language – the symbolic expression of general human behavior and a response to existential demands. No matter which aspects of the built environment and society are explored, architecture always touches on questions of existence. To a certain extent, this may be the conservative core of the discipline. Yet architecture is not a universal principle, as one could hastily conclude from it, but an ideal of civil society, whose social, technological and political value must be repeatedly renegotiated and questioned. Architecture is therefore always also a political demand that concerns of social interest be negotiated spatially. According to the second thesis, architectural research always becomes politically relevant when it succeeds in opening up discursive potential.

At present, forms of society, ways of thinking, and modes of existence are emerging that cannot be told without the computer. Data-based processes of encoding, transcoding, and recoding spaces, objects, shapes, surfaces, materials – even the human body – are leading to recursive processes of a comprehensive datafication of society, thereby calling into question traditional cultural, political, and economic value systems and systems of production. What we will remember in the future and in which form depends on who organizes and controls the storage media, and in which medium our individual and collective experiences are transported and passed on. Information fragments will be continuously generated, stored, retrieved, updated, and resaved – a seemingly endless cycle of coding and recoding history and the present. What is copied onto thousands of computers, reproduced, and becomes part of our everyday world through constant repetition, stabilizes itself and finally becomes a cultural sediment of the system. More and more, social, political, and ethical questions of global dimension are dominating the discussion, in which established structures of order in modern Western societies are dismantled and reconfigured. The accelerated datafication of society is challenging the cornerstones of traditional sovereignty and collective forms of cooperation. This calls into question long-established cultural, political, and economic value and production systems. Forms of technological restlessness arise, which require not only new hypothetical and critical thinking, but also alternative approaches for shaping our future data-driven society.

The conference *Research Culture in Architecture* gave the chance to reflect and discuss those actual issues. This resulting book presents some important research topics in a cross-disciplinary research approach in architecture.

Introduction

Cornelie Leopold, Christopher Robeller, and Ulrike Weber

In times of High Gothic Leonardo Fibonacci of Pisa (ca. 1180–after 1240) already had an impact on the theory and practice of geometry and therefore contributed to geometry as a science. Gothic architects were artists and structural engineers at the same time; geometry determined their artistic practice. But was architecture a science, too? Architectural research was done in the fields of structures and construction by studying collapsing buildings to find their conditions and limitations. Nevertheless, written knowledge was transferred in many different ways. What knowledge Gothic architects actually had, we do not know today, because they themselves did not write. The Gothic period not only symbolizes the complexity of architecture and architectural knowledge, but also the current state of architectural research. Today, it is still difficult to define research in architecture or architectural research. On the one hand it is thought that architects aren't researching because they apply or develop. Then again, how could architecture have been developed from its beginning until today without research?

Not only architects are researching architectural subjects. A lot of researchers come from other disciplines with different research cultures. Hence, research approaches as well as research achievements are different. They are published in journals of each discipline, often not knowing from each other; some are not even published, as they were done in offices and not labeled as research. In many areas of architectural research, the methodological, scientific work has long been established. These include, for example, the theory of architecture and history, but also the engineering disciplines of structures and building technology. The core discipline, architectural design, on the other hand, faces special challenges. The design process refers to many involved disciplines such as construction, materials science, building physics, manufacturing technology, computer science, geometry, aesthetics, sociology, philosophy, and history. For architecture it is essential that these disciplines do not remain separate in their consideration, but interlock in the planning, design, and implementation of architecture. This is probably one of the reasons why scientific work in the field of design is different compared to other fields.

Architecture today faces new challenges through digitalization and the building industry. In this area of digital technology, a community of research architects has developed rapidly and successfully in the past few years, which is reflected in the development of new conference series such as RobArch (Robotic Fabrication in Architecture, Art, and Design), AAG (Advances in Architectural Geometry) and FABRICATE (Digital Fabrication). New research areas of architectural technology have developed in recent decades. An important driving force for this are extended planning possibilities by the direct integration of processes in the areas of fabrication, statics, and building physics into the architectural design. Algorithmic solutions are also increasingly being developed for complex tasks in the area of spatial and urban planning. In contrast to classical architectural design, designing such computer programs and parametric models inevitably requires an analytic-methodical formulation of parameters and processes, which at the same time provides the basis for scientific exploitation and communication of the results. However, this research community is not too well connected with many other areas of architectural research, such as social sciences, urbanism, or building energy.

In this publication research in architecture is taken for granted. It shows that research is part of architectural offices, bringing together different research fields, methods, and current changes in architectural research. It reviews their research approaches in terms of their relevance to architectural design and discusses the increasing diffusion of digital and parametric design methods. It is based on the 2018 research conference entitled *Research Culture in Architecture: International Conference on Cross-Disciplinary Collaboration in Architecture*, held at fatuk, the Faculty of Architecture of the Technische Universität Kaiserslautern, Germany. Researchers from different disciplines in both theory and practice had to discuss their research approaches and show their impact on architectural design. The aim was to stimulate a cross-disciplinary dialogue across the various fields that are relevant for architectural research in order to discuss the different perspectives on architecture as a whole.

This publication is focused on six research topics, both digital and analog: Digitalization and Robotics, Timber Construction, Architectural Practice and Research, Design Methods, Sustainability, and Architectural Space.

Digitalization and Robotics
As one of the challenges today, digitalization takes a big part of the conference's publication. In the first chapter, Christian Derix (Woods Bagot SuperSpace, Sydney), gives a brief history of computer-aided design methods in architecture. In contrast to a large amount of research in digital design methods, which is often at the intersection of architecture and engineering, such as digital fabrication or structural engineering, this chapter sets a particular focus on the origins and successive developments of digital methods

and algorithms for the analysis, generation, and optimization of spaces, both at the level of urban planning and architectural design. In which direction or directions will the profession of the architect develop? For some participants, the future architect seems to be a protagonist of parameters; for others the profession as it is today will be obsolete and for a third party, both visions will be part of the future depending on the building type. The role of data and automation in architectural design had been discussed by the conference participants. In the discussion of Christian Derix's contribution, Michael Hensel pointed out the difference between data and information. To get information as a basis for designing, data, which is unstructured at first, has to become structured through interventions like questions. Data can be structured by design, and the design process can transform data into information. For these transformations, abstraction processes are important to achieve operational working methods and to make the step from data to information and finally generate relevant knowledge as a research result for architecture.

Sigrid Brell-Cokcan (RWTH Aachen, Germany) presented advances in manufacturing processes, through robots for design and construction. While previous research in this field had shown precise prefabrication of parts through robots and CNC machines, new research presents approaches such as autonomous and interactive strategies, addressing the special context of on-site building construction. Dynamic and autonomous applications can react to unexpected and unplanned situations, as they often occur on building construction sites, or to certain unpredictable imprecisions of building materials, which are not as accurate as, for example, the components in the mechanical engineering of machines. Another important part of robotics in general and construction robotics research in particular is robot-human interaction. This also touches on the questions of digitalization and its effects on society, work environments, and the economy.

Timber Construction

Building with wood is one of the key areas of research and teaching at the Faculty of Architecture at the Technische Universität Kaiserslautern. In modern building construction, timber and digital technology are connected particularly closely. The weight-to-strength ratio of wood is outstanding and makes it ideal for prefabricated structures, which benefit from high-tech factory technology, achieving a level of precision that is currently not possible for in situ construction methods. For such prefabricated structures, it is particularly important that they can be assembled easily, quickly, and precisely, which makes the topic of smart connectors a very active area of research and innovation.

As one of the oldest building materials, wood is currently seeing a renaissance in architecture and architectural research. This is both due to its ecological aspects, such as CO_2 storage in wood products and buildings, but also due to the particular design possibilities that timber construction offers. Compared to other materials, timber can be cut into precise and complex 3-D shapes, including elaborate joint geometries, with comparably little energy, time, and cost.

Our articles on timber construction cover a wide range of topics, ranging from the design and fabrication for timber construction, a special section for robotics in timber construction, and engineering-focused methods for timber construction. The research includes not only particularly material-efficient innovative free-form and lightweight structures, but also research for the optimization of regularly shaped building structures. The presented innovations range from new, CNC-fabricated shell structures (Bannwart) to new wood materials for building construction (Silbermann et al.), innovative joining methods (Garufi et al., Klopfer et al.), and recycling-sourced building components (Poteschkin et al.), all the way to autonomous construction techniques, which incorporate the components of a building into the kinematics of the structure (Leder et al.).

Digital prefabrication technology such as CNC joinery and cutting machines have been readily available in timber construction companies around the world for a few decades now. These machines are capable of producing highly precise and differentiated building components (Bannwart) or joints (Garufi et al.), however it has been difficult for architects to take advantage of these new design possibilities. This was partially due to a lack of sufficient software connecting architects with the machines, but it was also due to lack of education about such fabrication technology, which often remains hidden in remote factories.

At the same time, CNC fabrication can be seen as an intermediate technology on the way to on-site robotics, which has established itself as a separate research field in digital timber construction. Our articles focused on timber robotics (Thoma et al., Al Bahar et al., Leder et al.) are already looking ahead to the next generation of machines. In contrast to the highly specialized timber CNC machines, Robots such as the KUKA 6-axis industrial manipulators are universal machines that can carry out a variety of tasks. They are mass-produced in much larger quantities, designed by much larger development teams, and therefore typically are much cheaper. Eventually, this may even open up highly futuristic scenarios such as the distributed construction robotics presented by Leder et al. – a particularly interesting subject.

Architectural Practice and Research
Even though universities have their specialized research fields, they are increasingly under pressure and compared in their research achievements. This means: How many third-party funds are raised during a year and how

many PhD students are starting their research? But what is very often neglected is that the research culture in architecture is different than in most other disciplines. To become a university professor, it is necessary to have a built portfolio but not necessarily a PhD. Still, very few architects enroll for doctoral studies, and most of them do their research in a theoretical or historical subject. Therefore, this chapter illustrates that research has always been a part of architectural practice, but as mentioned above is not labeled as research and therefore is not published. In fact, research in architectural offices is conducted in a disciplinary and interdisciplinary manner and with very new approaches investigating new design methods (Ooms, Cannaerts, and Hoffmann) as well as sustainability problems (Greub).

Furthermore, Michael Hensel (Vienna University of Technology, previously Oslo School of Architecture and Design, Norway) emphasizes the importance of various forms of scientific exchange and cooperation in an interdisciplinary field such as architecture. He also presents various doctoral procedures, that is, the "industrial PhD," which are already successfully practiced in Norway and in particular make it possible to connect practices and universities. On the sidelines, moreover, traditional themes of architecture such as preservation (Ooms) or exhibiting architecture (Greub) are shown in a new manner.

Whether digital or analog, in many architectural offices research is part of the practice and has always been combined with practice. Moreover, as it was common 100 years ago, it is still common practice today for architects, and even more necessary, to work together in an interdisciplinary manner, that is, with civil engineers, psychologists, computer scientists, robotic scientists, and biologists. Collaboration has now become immensely more complex as a result of increasing specialization. Digital methods offer solutions to structure and master complexity.

Design Methods

Architectural design is seen as the core of architecture and precedes the realizing procedures of architecture. Thinking on design methods, presented in chapter four, gives therefore a foundation for research in this core area of architecture. The efforts to bring the processes of designing in architecture onto structured and substantiated foundations were shown in various approaches in architectural design.

Design methodologies that include the users of the built environment in relation to the space configuration via questionnaires, space syntax and space grammar analyses (Schütz), behavioral observations, and experiments in real environments as well as virtual reality had been presented in their interdisciplinary research approaches between architects and psychologists (Emo). The research of Toni Kotnik indicates that along with the changes through digital tools to digital design thinking, mathematics plays an active part in design development. Architecture as a science of structures is based on mathematics as the general science of structures. Mathematics serves as a mediator between the disciplines and as a central element in the integration of external knowledge into the architectural design process.

The importance of physical, artistic procedures, working by hand in three-dimensional space with different materials, were explored in design experiments and presented in their results, also in their roles in design teaching (Kraus et al.). Other authors used artistic procedures as a reference to model digital design procedures with the aim to better understand the interrelationship among artistic approaches and digital design methods (Meyer and Garrido). Eventually, Chinese landscape architecture had been analyzed in its historical cultural context and related to the space concept behind it (Liu et al.).

The problem was discussed that research in their area of specialization often remains isolated and the link between them, especially with the core area of architecture, is missed. Methodological approaches in architectural design, based on sociological, psychological, and mathematical methods, can convey these missing linkages.

Sustainability

As the world is suffering from the rapidly changing climate, the question how the architectural field could help is discussed in the chapter on sustainability. Today, the construction industry still raises a lot of environmental problems and is one of the most resource-intensive industries. Meanwhile highly technical approaches are debatable as they have a high amount of embodied energy and are very often not recyclable or even pollutive. Sustainable architecture could be developed in different ways. Building with ecological and recyclable building material is one possibility, minimizing the energy and material consumption by following the constructive and structural logic in architecture, or using a design and construction which is adapted to its environment and climate are others. In contrast to highly technical sustainable design approaches, Eike Roswag-Klinge (Technische Universität Berlin, Natural Building Lab) researches recycle-capable architecture and experiments with traditional construction materials such as clay and wood in worldwide self-construction projects. The use of recycled material (Greub, Ooms) reduces the amount of new materials and of their embodied energy. New construction methods show how energy could either be saved (Dijoux et al.) or even be generated through new materials (Aden et al.). Eventually, cities are becoming more and more densified with rising temperatures. Facade greening could help to improve the urban climate (Polster et al.) and is another way in an ecological future.

Architectural Space

Studies on perception, spatial abilities, space cognition, and spatial knowledge of architects as well as on required abilities and new tools for architectural design are included in the chapter on architectural space in the first part on perception and visualization. To identify patterns of visual attention characteristics for architects was the purpose of an interdisciplinary research by architects and psycholinguists (Mertins et al.). They found differences in spatial cognition between architects and nonarchitects. These results should be taken into account, because spatial perception of architects differs from that of the users they are designing for. Another cross-disciplinary research, bridging cognitive sciences and design theory, focused on the nature of spatial ability in architecture and how these necessary abilities could be improved (Gerber et al.). New tools by augmented and virtual reality technologies are studied in another paper according to their potential for architectural design and visualization (Tan et al.). The second part of the chapter thematizes the human body and its relationship to architectural space. Based on theories of embodiment, experiments had been conducted to find the possibilities of influencing the user's emotions through architectural space and design objects (Ferreira et al.). The methodology and results show a mostly neglected approach to study the emotional experience of architectural space. Bernard Tschumi's theoretical considerations, if the experience of space determines the space of experience, were the background for studies on relationships between the human body and architectural space. Contemporary dance had been used in the research as a tool to highlight and amplify the effects of architectural spaces on the human body (Voigt). Performance art methods had been used to gain insights into embodied experiences in space with the aim to enrich knowledge on spatial qualities (Vroman et al.).

The research in this field could help discover how architecture is conditioning people with emotions. These approaches contribute to an architecture, considering all senses of the participants and users.

Conclusions

The wide range of the presented research topics shows the importance of interdisciplinary work and exchange between the individual areas of research. A collaborative effort is necessary to tackle the complex challenge of research and innovation at the core discipline of architectural design, with its manifold facets ranging from human and social sciences to material and technical aspects. The conference and this book aim at negotiating the disparate and fragmented research approaches in architecture with its multifaceted aspects. All of the individual disciplines require specialist knowledge, which makes communication and exchange across the disciplines complicated and often leads to the separation of the research fields.

Among the questions discussed was the not always simple, but extremely promising integration of architectural research in teaching. To be able to use software does not necessarily require great knowledge; on the other hand, a very great knowledge is needed in order to master them and be able to develop new and customized solutions, which is highly important to the creative and individual process of architectural design. In this balancing act are universities, which have to ask to what extent they want to and can convey skills in the digital field. Should the digital part in architectural education increase? And if so, in which direction should it be developed: digital analysis, digital designing, or digital fabrication? Which other competencies are then to be neglected? Or should these topics rather be covered by specialized postgraduate courses? But does this widen the gap between the architectural fields? After all, the rapid digitalization of one of the most traditional duties in architecture is reminiscent of becoming aware of social responsibility and facing it.

Technological advances have always influenced architecture and the building construction heavily, such as the introduction of machine technology in the age of industrialization. Mass production has had a great effect on ornament and individuality of details, buildings, and structures. The age of digital information technology bears great potential to reconnect the specialized, fragmented profession that building has become through common interfaces and languages. This affects not only production but also planning tools, and there is undoubtedly a trend toward the automation of simple tasks through software and algorithms. For the architect, such powerful tools may bring back great control over the complexity that modern building designs require. However, the increased complexity and new possibilities of modern design tools are yet to be integrated into the legislative framework and education of architects.

A research culture in architecture has to be developed more intensively by awakening cross-disciplinary interest in future-oriented and fundamental research topics, also by deepening these topics in research projects and related PhD studies. Ways to interest and support young scientists in such efforts to develop a research culture that generates also a culture of innovation in architecture should be evaluated. The examples in this book want to present and discuss some approaches in this direction.

Digitally and analogously research will still be the future whether it is done in practice, at universities or in collaboration of both. But unlike in the Gothic period, architects today should publish their research results to make them accessible for other specialists and future research. Cross-disciplinary conferences, such as the RCA, and their publications are a fundamental part of architectural communication and should become regular instruments in the research culture in architecture.

1 Digitalization and Robotics

Paradigm Reversal – Connectionist Technologies for Linear Environments

Christian Derix
Woods Bagot, Sydney, Australia

Abstract — Applications of computing in environmental design practices (architecture, urban design, landscape) are mostly following technological developments. Further, they even amplify the purpose of the field of development where the technology is borrowed from. Hence, architectural computing saw nearly twenty years of form-finding and fabrication, stemming from parametric models developed in industrial design around the end of the 1980s. With the onset of pervasive data harvesting through sensory networks and mobile computing, architecture again is jumping on a bandwagon: utilization and user-centered optimization. AI and machine learning make use of the massive amounts of data collected to optimize all areas of cognitive and behavioral life. Environmental design in industry and academia is following suit and appears to commit to optimize all spatial and social dynamics in buildings and cities. Questions about what to optimize are rarely asked other than known operational and capital domains.

Original research into spatial computing and machine learning did not focus on optimization but sought alternative representations of environments through distributed heuristic computing and big data for design and planning. The field of architectural research appears to be at the crossroads of a possible paradigm reversal, where an early enthusiasm gives way to market demands. This article briefly sketches out the path from a 1990s paradigm shift to a 2020s paradigm reversal based on technological developments and market demands.

Paradigm Shift: Operations Research to Connectionism

While cybernetics originated from operations research (OR) to predict events such as artillery trajectories, British cyberneticians interpreted the disciplines more broadly to include nonmachinic fields and the interaction between multiple machines such as spatial environments in combination with ambient phenomena (Pask 1969) or social dynamics (Price 2003). Despite the embryonic state of computer sciences based on procedural algorithms, an optimistic vision seemed to be graspable: the democratization of planning. All elements of a system – be they spatial, social, environmental, or economic – would act autonomously and coevolve a synergetic outcome that would reflect a balance between everybody's needs. The master build-er – developers, planners, and architects – would become superfluous as people participate in the design of an environment generated by distributed agents from the bottom-up. Society would effectively fold into one layer, overcoming social standing and spatial inequality (fig. 1).

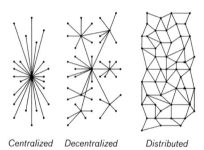

Fig. 1: Spatial Paradigm Shift: from control structure to distributed system – Christopher Alexander's (1965) interpretation of city as a network (© Christopher Alexander)

Centralized   Decentralized   Distributed

Beyond visual analogies to computer science such as Archigram's Computer City or Superstudio's The Continuous Monument, architects in practice would work on designs around that time that built on concepts of spatial autonomy and synergy such as Cedric Price or Hermann Hertzberger. Hertzberger (2014) developed modular spatial systems that assembled into classes of emergent situation-based typologies to give rise to social conditions for manifold uses. This loose-fit principle, which Herzberger called polyvalence, in line with the American systems theorist Simon (1969), afforded an efficient working envi-ronment in which a variety of activities could occur within the same locations (compare that to today's state-of-the-art workplace concepts such as "agile" or "activity-based working," where each type of activity is catered for by a different typology). Hertzberger's preamble was founded on the two assumptions of its time: that the spatial environment is neither simply a linear assembly nor should spaces be programmed for isolated uses or segregated social groups (fig. 2). Many disciplines related to social and spatial sciences were starting to resist the principles of operations research based on the linear analytical approach developed within the general systems theory (van Bertalanffy 1968) during and just after the Second World War, on which cybernetics was based. Christopher Alexander was an architectural theorist who based his concepts on the general systems theory segregating spaces and activities in A Pattern Language (1977) and proposed a linear design process based on analytical discretization in Notes on the Synthesis of Form (1964).

Fig. 2: Office Building Centraal Beheer in Apel-
doorn (1968–72): polyvalent spatial network
generating socially inclusive interaction at the
workplace (© Architectuurstudio Hermann
Hertzberger)

Cybernetics was eventually developed into a second systems theory called
second-order cybernetics (von Foerster 1984, 288–309) based on
"cybernetics of cybernetics," or self-organization. Multiple systems could
coevolve without set goals (nonteleologically), distributing actions across
the systems in parallel rather than sequential processes. Interaction between
systems and parts produce common domains of meaning that represent
knowledge and stability called consensual domains (Maturana 1970). The
conceptual model embodying this paradigm shift developed from procedural
teleological closed system to parallel self-organizing open system was called
connectionism in cognitive sciences. The computational models emerging
in the 1980s to simulate open systems to generate cognitive states were
self-organizing artificial neural networks (ANNs). Teuvo Kohonen's self-organizing feature map (1995) appeared to be the most appropriate model
for spatial classification, since it could process natural numbers, generate
overlapping (polyvalent) categories of features for higher complexity,
and visualize output to a spatial map (Derix and Thum 2000). Derix and
colleagues used SOMs with students and within professional R&D teams
to search for correlations between spatial qualities, user cognition, and
space planning between 2001 and 2014 (Derix and Jagannath 2014). The
research aim of that period was still rooted in the optimistic foundation that
using connectionist and machine-learning models could provide alternative
models of spatial organization to enable citizens and designers to gain independent and rigorous insights to plan socially equitable environments. Data
was sparse but skill was high as no prepackaged code libraries existed that
would hide inner workings from designers. Sparsity of data was made up by
generating sample sets of data or onerous digitization of urban and building
plans (fig. 3).

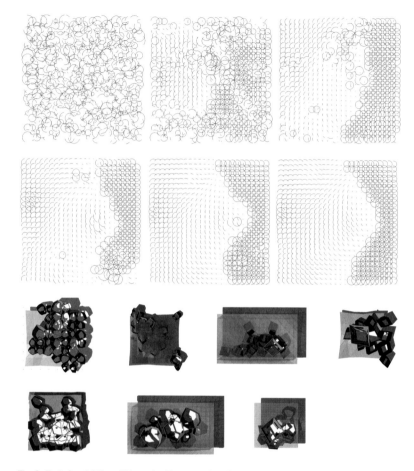

Fig. 3: Early Spatial Neural Networks: Two examples of unsupervised neural networks based on Kohonen's self-organizing feature maps, developed by Derix between 2000 and 2006 for students (top) and a competition for Zaha Hadid architects (bottom) (Derix and Jagannath, 2014)

Market-driven R&D

However, the perceived value of computation – both in practice and academia – at that time was thought to be in form-finding and geometric rationalization through parametric modeling. The purpose for this application of computation was driven by global developers who wanted to differentiate their buildings as iconic brands for quick returns on investment. Hence, most commercial architectural practices and engineers conducted R&D into parametric modeling of shape and its buildability, giving birth to practice-based research conferences such as *Smart Geometry* in 2003.

This strand of quasi-engineering architectural R&D did not apply to spaces or people, neither building organization nor cities. With the exception of rudimentary GIS and the space syntax theory for spatial analysis, no other spatial theory or application of computation to design existed. Machine-learning models and especially AI appeared premature because little data was available to process – a fallacy, as big data could be generated from analytical models such as SUPERSPACE's user-experience analysis for the 2007 National September 11 Memorial Museum in New York (fig. 4) to support the design of the main circulation ramp (Derix et al. 2008).

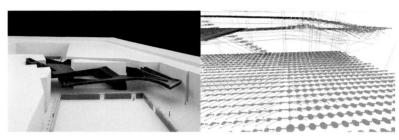

Fig. 4: User Experience Analysis for September 11th Memorial Museum NYC: visitor perception and utilization analysis by SUPERSPACE (then Aedas CDR) in 2007 for architects Davis Brody Bond in New York, generating big data from spatial analysis (© Davis Brody Bond Architects) (left)

In the early years (2004–2010), SUPERSPACE (then Aedas Computational Design Research, or CDR) were the first to pioneer the synthetic approach of spatial analysis with generative computing and would develop a whole host of new algorithmic models and interactive real-time applications for live feedback in design. This coauthoring participatory methodology was researched by Nicholas Negroponte (1970) at MIT in the 1960s when he experimented with "conversations" between designers and machines. But particularly for a professional context, live feedback was vital, as described by Donald Schoen (1983) in the "reflective practitioner."

During those years SUPERSPACE developed fundamental models such as coevolutionary computing for building generation, swarm models for pedestrian agent-based simulations, multicriteria Pareto optimization for urban planning, neural networks and machine-learning models for spatial analysis, 3-D and 4-D interactive visual graph analysis (VGA) for user-experience modeling, social networks for urban planning, and many more. As the only such R&D group in global commercial practice, it was hard to convince clients of the benefits of such an approach, as all the competitors were focusing on parametric modeling for developer-driven iconic form-finding.

The abovementioned models and their synthetic approached outlined by SUPERPSACE are finally gaining traction in architectural practice due to the increased complexity of planning large-scale environments (urban, civic, retail, transport, commercial). Yet their application trends toward the same purpose of the first cybernetics: linear optimization. While SUPERSPACE was testing the convergence of multiple machine-learning models for urban design from 2007 to 2009 on projects like Smart Solutions for Spatial Planning (Derix 2012), it was found that the planning of complex urban environments embodies a lengthy multi-stakeholder process that should not be automated through a single-cycle computing process if complexity and equity are not to be lost (Miranda et al. 2009). However, despite those early findings and testing in practice, current academic and professional R&D seems to ignore the complexity of urban environments and Schoen's observations of the design process by attempting to generate single-cycle large master plans (Schuhmacher 2009; Koenig et al. 2017; Wilson et al. 2019). Of course, it is the market that stipulates such simplistic methods leading to unresolved urban structure and poor environments. In regions of intense urbanization such as Southeast Asia, the endeavor by governments and private developers to mitigate the risk of large investments through feasibility studies for the business case of city-scale master plans appears to warrant superficial responses. Such feasibility studies are fast-paced, mostly low-fee and based on immature planning regimes, creating the perfect conditions for brute-force video-game-style production to churn thousands of unresolved master plan options for quick business case approvals (fig. 5).

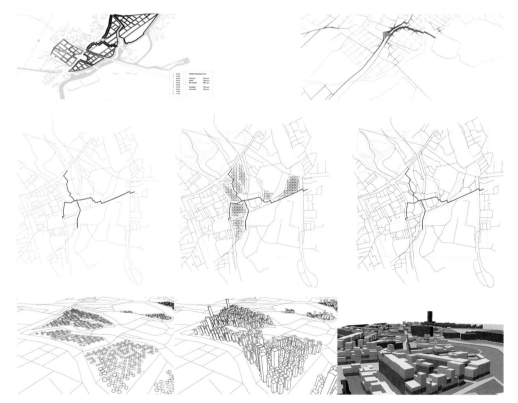

Fig. 5: Smart Solutions for Spatial Planning: the 2008 urban design platform developed by SUPERSPACE (then Aedas CDR) was an open framework with more than 10 software applications, allowing for an open stakeholder engagement across scales of complexity

Paradigm Reversal: Data Science and Control

But the industry is moving on from simply large-scale production to understanding complexity. The original vision of the British cyberneticians has the potential to become reality through contemporary technology such as the cellular parallel computing grids of 5G networks. User and operational performance data for whole cities is harvested to manage the urban system in real time. Yet contemporary machine learning such as ANNs and agent-based modeling requires segmentation of environments and users in order to optimize the experience of discrete end-user groups and places through bespoke controllable procedures. Control as a driver, like in the first cybernetics, is returning predominantly because of the technological opportunity provided by ubiquitous data capture of minute units, allowing for persistent monitoring and individualized response (Derix and Dalton 2016). The architectural market has responded by developing shared spaces programmed with more heterogenous "experiences" for multiple individualized user groups, breaking down traditional sector boundaries and monofunctional building briefs. As a consequence, building environments and privately owned public spaces (POPS) require more efficient management to provide the desired spatial experience mix tailored to multiple parallel user segments at different times of the day, such as airports, street malls, agile workplaces, built-to-rent residential complexes, etc. The mix of users is purposely segregated into finite chunks in order to control their behaviors more minutely, carefully curating monovalent places that array snapshots of experiences into "stories." The contemporary technology-infused equivalent to Hertzberger's polyvalent social workspaces are, for example, WeWork's heavily programmed coworking spaces, where amenities are optimized through data-driven machine-learning models based on individualized utilization predictions (Phelan et al. 2017). Elsewhere, airport and railway stations, universities and retail environments are all planned with multiagent systems (MAS), predicting user typologies from collected online and on-site data (O2O: online to offline), segmenting people into finite types of behaviors and needs that require bespoke programming of spaces for predicted utilization (crowd simulation models based on MAS such as CAST or LEGION; fig. 6). The notion of serendipity originally proposed as a positive effect of computing and self-organization by the British cyberneticians (Reichardt 1968) is about to disappear, as surprise (read "emergence" in computing science vocabulary) is the enemy of programming highly efficient utilization. The original paradigm of nonlinear connectionism is turned on its head into disconnected linearity, where exclusive environments endlessly prescribe predictable experiences for homogenous groups. Alexander Klein's 1928 example of the "frictionless house" (Evans 1997), which he used to illustrate the planning for functional and social segregation in houses, appears to return as a design paradigm (fig. 7).

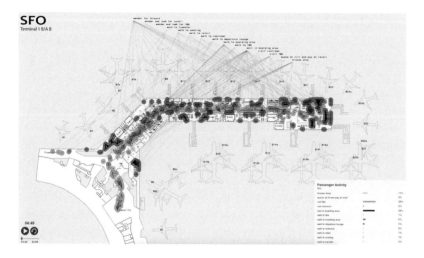

Fig. 6: User Behavior and Journey Simulation: A snapshot of the cognitive multiagent system for spatial affordance modeling by SUPERSPACE developed originally for San Francisco Airport in 2016, used on complex spatial planning projects across Woods Bagot

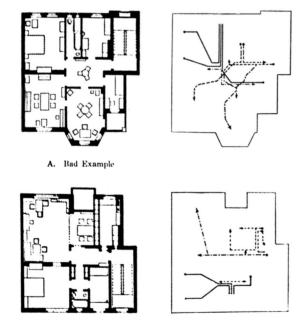

A. Bad Example

B. Good Example

Fig. 7: Functional House for Frictionless Living: Alexander Klein's illustration of 1928 shows social change through spatial planning, segregating uses spatially for optimized experience

Context-free Learning

One of the most applied contemporary models of AI is based on deep learning for pattern recognition: the convolutional neural network (CNN) discretizes images into hierarchical chunks of pixels to identify similarities between the chunks (Schmidhuber 2015). This process is repeated from smaller to larger subdivisions to associate visual features across scales, assembling images from analytical categories of visual relationships much like Christopher Alexander's *A Pattern Language* (1969). CNNs have been utilized recently by architectural and fine arts academics (Lobe.ai n.d.; Kogan n.d.) to generate what can only be described as labels of "images of space," since the models were literally borrowed from Google by using its ML library TensorFlow (Dean et al. 2015), which was developed for image recognition. This approach completely divorces the image of architecture from its context and its many dimensions and can rightly be claimed to be "design by Instagram" (fig. 8).

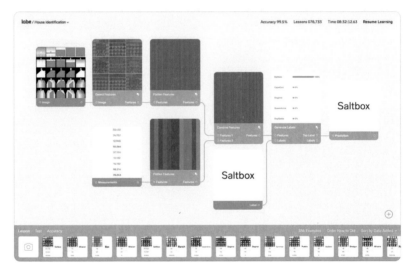

Fig. 8: AI for general image recognition: Google TensorFlow-based image recognition platform Lobe.ai, showcasing multiple uses on their website, including "House Identification" from the workshop Fresh Eyes Open (© Adam Menges, Kat Park, Kyle Steinfeld, and Samantha Walker)

Design without context through visual technology can mislead architects into thinking that experiences can be constructed without empirical knowledge. The Centric Lab, a spin-off from University College London's (UCL) Psychology and Language Sciences, literally interprets neural-firing patterns from fMRI scans of virtual walk-throughs for design strategies of spatial environments. Its research appears to suggest that spatial decisions by way-finding users can be localized in discrete cortical and hippocampal subregions because neural-firing patterns could be related directly to specific spatial features as seen on screen (Epstein et al. 2017).

Conclusions on way-finding behaviors such as the spatial orientation factors of distance, connectivity, and heading direction deviation have long been established through empirical research and spatial analysis (Arthur and Passini 2002; Conroy-Dalton 2003). But the epistemological paradigm resulting from technologies like fMRI or CNNs points to context-free knowledge, where experiences can be constructed from disconnected, discrete snapshots. When experiences are isolated, they can be effectively controlled to optimize behaviors of individuals and operations of places. Empirical research based on the "old" paradigm of self-organization and second-order cybernetics, on the other hand, relates local perception and interaction with a global structure through its local layers, thus giving value to connected places and social ties – an inversion of the twentieth-century paradigms of systems thinking that was adopted by architectural theorists to help design inclusive spatial environments (fig. 9). Because architecture readily adopts other industries' R&D, in particularly digital technologies, without much adaptation, it is those source industries that are increasingly in a position to compete on their terms within the built environment. Facility management will be able to manage interior and commercial design contracts, business consultants expand in urban planning and place-making, engineers consult on spatial and user experiences, software developers encroach on conceptual planning stages, and so on, displacing architects and urban designers from their design turf.

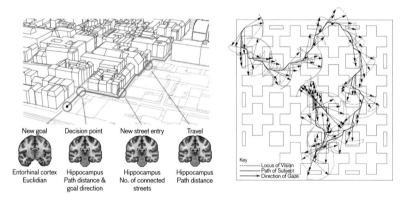

Fig. 9: fMRI v empirical simulation: (left) Epstein et al. (2017) research on spatial navigation using fMRI scans on participants while navigating routes virtually, showing localized 'firing' pattern in the brain; and (right) Conroy-Dalton's (2003) navigation simulation based on empirical research on route choices (© Hugo Spiers and Fiona Zisch [right] & Ruth Conroy-Dalton [left])

Spatial Response

The above discussed models of understanding and designing increasingly complex built environments encode essentially aspatial representations due to technologies borrowed from nonspatial disciplines. Developments in ANNs toward deep learning project a path toward increased fidelity for predictions of narrowly defined knowledge bases trained from data sets of past events (the "rearview mirror" analogy). This evolution from generalization to segmented knowledge makes sense for engineering and efficiency optimization. But for architecture and urban planning as "wicked problems" (Rittel and Webber 1973), the discipline requires less teleological digital models of AI and machine-learning models processing spatial representation rather than images.

The combination is possible when spatial knowledge and computing skills are equally balanced. For his 2009 master's thesis, John Harding developed a multistaged assembly of ANNs that increased the spatial resolution and their associations across classification phases much like current deep-learning ANNs. Across the classification stages (like filters in CNNs) the model would transform the representation of its spatial units according to spatial intent, predominantly using nonvisual syntactical and topological descriptions (Harding and Derix 2010). The model was designed to help curate gallery layouts based on cognitive feature associations of exhibition artifacts, anticipating the concept of deep learning but using spatial cognition. This very technique was still only proposed as late as the *Smart Geometry* 2018 conference by the mathematician Elissa Ross (Smart Geometry 2018) to tackle architectural qualities (fig. 10).

Clearly, there are many other applications of deep learning, AI, and big data in architecture and urban planning such as the Streetchange project by MIT and Harvard (http://streetchange.media.mit.edu) to name but one, yet most often those projects work with existing libraries again released by the large tech firms, employing nonarchitectural representations.

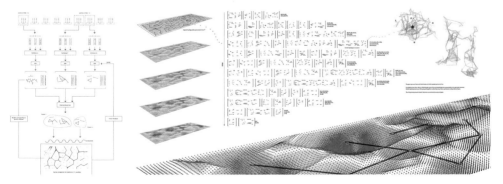

Fig. 10: Artificial Curator: A prototype of deep learning for spatial analysis and layout generation developed by John Harding (Harding and Derix 2010) showing (left) the three stages of classification with decreasing detail like CNNs filters and two stages of generation with topological representations; and (right) the catalogue of spatial associations per layout and over time resulting in weighted partitions per feature space (© John Harding)

At SUPERSPACE, we have developed a series of predominantly city analytics projects using machine learning for urban strategies that are being
used by developers and government clients. Nonconfidential studies include
the comparison of neighborhoods across global cities (fig. 11) done for the
Centre of Tall Buildings and Urban Habitat (CTBUH) (Derix et al. 2018)
and the evaluation of car parking redevelopment for Los Angeles in MoreLA
(fig. 13), which won two honorable mentions in the categories of "Spaces
Places & Cities" and "AI and Data" by *Fast Company*'s World Changing
Ideas Awards 2019 (SUPERSPACE 2019).

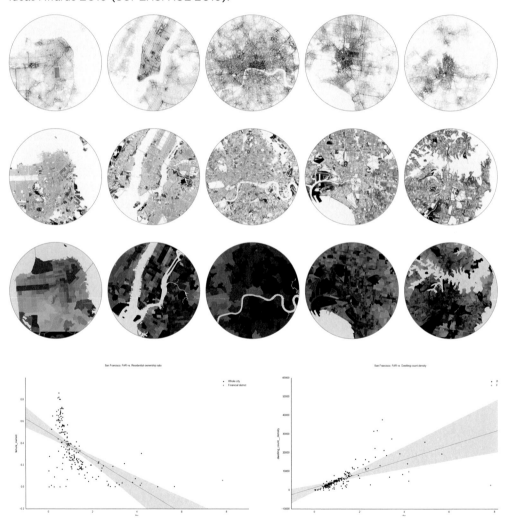

Fig. 11: Local Neighborhoods versus Global Cities: a comparative classification of three neighbor-
hood types across five global cities revealed trends of use and liveability that contradict the concept
of "global indices" for cities (Derix et al., 2018)

Fig. 12: From Strategy to Place: SUPERSPACE develops city-wide analytics using AI for urban strategies and translates those for data-driven master plans and detailed place-making for community benefit (left: location intelligence for a NYC developer 2016; right: neighborhood concept master plan in Sydney 2016)

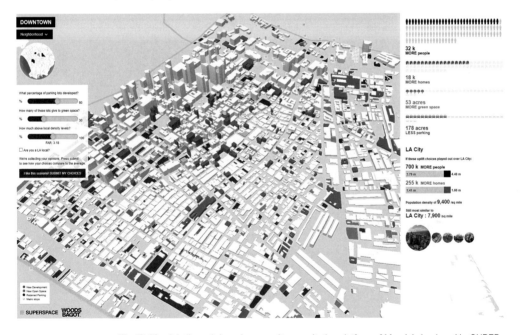

Fig. 13: MoreLA: the web-based community consultation platform of MoreLA developed by SUPERSPACE, incorporating the spatial and social layers of LA neighborhoods and the correlations from machine-learning models that support the user in their decisions on densification and land-use choices

In order to develop models of bespoke architectural nature, architects require the necessary skills for contemporary methods of production: software development literacy and algorithmic spatial thinking. Knowledge of prepackaged scripting software like the Rhino Grasshopper (GH) API are not sufficient to create fundamental architectural digital methodology. When students learn more rigorous software development skills, their interest is generally transformed into a scientific focus for which they will be employed again by developers, business consultants or asset management for the above-stated efficiency optimization purposes. An imbalance in academic curricula and equally professional architectural workflows exists that isolates technological knowledge from spatial thinking (fig. 12).

To overcome this division, collaborative R&D funding might be required to allow industry partners a more equitable role on architectural research grants. Currently, architectural practices can either cofinance architectural research without input on content or fund their own research. Where practices use their own revenue to fund research to remain relevant, they become protective of IP and perversely are accused of protectionism. But currently, practices often don't perceive academic research as relevant to their competitiveness or key issues (Jenkins et al. 2005). For the architectural industry to retain relevance, practices would have to collaborate more closely with academia by helping to define research agendas so that academia can conduct the types of research where it has an advantage over practices, such as fundamental empirical research and some long-term bespoke technological development (Derix 2019).

References

Alexander, Christopher. 1964. *Notes on the Synthesis of Form*. Cambridge, MA: Harvard University Press.

Alexander, Christopher. 1965. "A City Is Not a Tree," *Architectural Forum* 122, no. 1 (April): 58–62.

Alexander, Christopher, Sara Ishikawa, and Murray Silverstein. 1977. *A Pattern Language: Towns, Buildings, Construction*. New York: Oxford University Press.

Arthur, Paul, and Romedi Passini. 2002 [1992]. *Wayfinding: People, Signs, and Architecture*. Ontario: McGraw-Hill.

Conroy-Dalton, Ruth. 2003. "The Secret Is to Follow Your Nose: Route Path Selection and Angularity." *Environment and Behaviour* 35: 107–31.

Conroy-Dalton, Ruth, and Christian Derix. 2016. "User-Experience Typologies of Space." In *The Changing Shape of Practice: Integrating Research and Design in Practice*, edited by Michael U. Hensel and Fredrik Nilsson, 36–46. New York: Routledge.

Dean, Jeff, et al. 2015. "TensorFlow: Large-Scale Machine Learning on Heterogeneous Distributed Systems." Accessed May 13, 2019. TensorFlow.org. Google Research.

Derix, Christian. 2019. "Research between Market and Doctrine." In *Building Research Practices: Connecting Education and Practice through Architectural Research*, edited by Andrea J. Johnson, 35–38. Novato, CA: ORO Editions / AR+D, San Francisco.

Derix, Christian, and Prarthana Jagannath. 2014. "Digital Intuition: Autonomous Classifiers for Spatial Analysis and Empirical Design." *Journal of Space Syntax* 5, no. 2 (Autumn/Winter): 190–215.

Derix, Christian, Åsmund Gamlesæter, and Pablo Miranda. 2008. "3-D Isovists and Spatial Sensations: Two Methods and a Case Study." In *Movement and Orientation in Built Environments: Evaluating Design Rationale and User Cognition*, edited by Saif Haq, Christoph Hölscher, and Sue Torgrude, 67–72. Bremen: SFB/TR 8 (Universität Bremen, Universität Freiburg).

Derix, Christian, Lucy Helme, Fabio Galicia, and Alexander Kachkaev. 2018. "The Data Experience of Local Neighbourhoods in Global Cities." *Landscape Architecture Frontiers* 6, no. 2 (April): 76–92.

Derix, Christian, and Robert Thum. 2000. "Self-Organizing Space: Artificial Neural Network Spaces." In *GA 2000: 3rd Generative Art International Conference,* https://www.generativeart.com.

Epstein, Russell A., Eva Zita Patai, Joshua B. Julian, and Hugo J. Spiers. 2017. "The Cognitive Map in Humans: Spatial Navigation and Beyond." *Nature Neuroscience* 20, no. 11: 1504–13.

Evans, Robin. 1997. *Translation from Drawing to Building and Other Essays.* London: Architectural Association Press.

Harding, John, and Christian Derix. 2010. "Associative Spatial Networks in Architectural Design: Artificial Cognition of Space using Neural Networks with Spectral Graph Theory." In *Design Computing and Cognition 2010*, edited by John S. Gero, 305–23. Dordrecht: Springer.

Hertzberger, Hermann. 2014. "Polyvalence." *Architectural Design* 85, no. 2 (September/October): 106–13.

Jenkins, Paul, Harry Smith, and Soledad Garcia-Ferrari. 2005. *Architecture, Research and the Profession in Scotland*. Edinburgh: RIAS.

Kogan, Gene. n.d. Accessed May 13, 2019. http://genekogan.com.

Kohonen, Teuvo. 1995. *Self-Organizing Maps*. Berlin: Springer.

König, Reinhard, Gerhard Schmitt, Matthias Standfest, Artem Chirkin, and Bernhard Klein. 2017. „Cognitive Computing for Urban Design." In *The Virtual and the Real in Planning and Urban Design: Perspectives, Practices, and Applications*, edited by Claudia Yamu, Alenka Poplin, Oswald Devisch, and Gert De Roo, 93–111. London: Routledge.

Lobe.ai. n.d. Accessed May 13, 2019. https://lobe.ai/examples/.

Maturana, Humberto. 1970. *Biology of Cognition*. Urbana: University of Illinois.

Miranda, Pablo, Christian Derix, Åsmund Gamlesæter, and Lucy Helme. 2009. "Aedas R&D: Global Practices of Computational Design." In *Acadia 09: reForm(): Building a Better Tomorrow*, edited by Russell Loveridge, Douglas Pancoast, and Tristan D'Estrée Sterk, 242–44. Chicago: School of the Art Institute of Chicago.

Negroponte, Nicholas. 1970. *The Architecture Machine: Toward a more Human Environment*. Cambridge, MA: MIT Press.

Pask, Gordon. 1969. "The Architectural Relevance of Cybernetics." *Architectural Design* 39 (September): 494–96.

Phelan, Nicole, Daniel Davis, and Carl Anderson. 2017. "Evaluating Architectural Layouts with Neural Networks." In *SimAUD 2017: Proceedings of the Symposium on Simulation for Architecture and Urban Design*, edited by Michela Turrin, Brady Peters, William O'Brien, Rudi Stouffs, and Timur Dogan, 67–74. San Diego, CA: SCS.

Reichardt, Jasia, ed. 1968. *Cybernetic Serendipity: The Computer and the Arts.* London: Studio International.

Rittel, Horst, and Melvin M. Webber. 1973. *Dilemmas in a General Theory of Planning*. Policy Sciences 4. Amsterdam: Elsevier, 155–69.

Schmidhuber, Jürgen. 2015. "Deep Learning in Neural Networks: An Overview." *Neural Networks* 61 (January): 85–117.

Schön, Donald. 1983. *The Reflective Practitioner: How Professionals Think in Action*. New York: Basic Books.

Schuhmacher, Patrik. 2009. "Parametricism: A New Global Style for Architecture and Urban Design." *Architectural Design* 79, no. 4 (July/August): 14–23.

Simon, Herbert A. 1969. *The Sciences of the Artificial*. Cambridge, MA: MIT Press (3rd ed. 1996).

Smart Geometry. 2018. Accessed May 13, 2019. https://www.smartgeometry.org/sg2018-conference.

SUPERSPACE. 2019. Accessed May 13, 2019. https://superspace.agency/featured/more-la/.

von Bertalanffy, Ludwig. 1968. *General System Theory: Foundations, Development, Applications*. New York: George Braziller.

von Foerster, Heinz. 1984. *Observing Systems*. Seaside, CA: Intersystems Publications.

Wilson, Luc, Jason Danforth, Carlos Cerezo Davila, and Dee Harvey. 2019. "How to Generate a Thousand Master Plans: A Framework for Computational Urban Design." In *SimAUD 2019: Proceedings of the Symposium on Simulation for Architecture and Urban Design*, edited by Siobhan Rockcastle, Tarek Rakha, Carlos Cerezo Davila, Dimitris Papanikolaou, and Tea Zakula, 113–20. San Diego, CA: SCS.

Individualizing Production with DIANA: A Dynamic and Interactive Robotic Assistant for Novel Applications

Sigrid Brell-Cokcan
Chair for Individualized Production, RWTH Aachen University, Germany

Abstract — Architects and designers have always aspired to move beyond the state-of-the-art to create individual, customized objects rather than to mass-produce. Today, innovative machines enable creative minds to finally turn many ideas into reality: Robotic technologies such as CNC-milling and 3-D printing have become increasingly accessible to architects and designers and assist in realizing nearly any imaginable workpiece.

The programming of industrial robots is still commonly static; however, in order to enable the use of robotics in new fields involving construction and mounting applications, these programs need to adapt to their surroundings. Due to their high complexity and unstructured nature, construction can be seen as an ideal testing environment of the universal applicability of robots for a number of reasons: Robot behavior needs to dynamically adjust to environmental constraints, material, and construction tolerances. Lot sizes and repetitiveness of tasks are lower than within most production environments, leading at the moment to a very low utilization of robotics. Most industrial robots are not transportable or mobile enough for usage at the construction site. Due to fluctuation and a low degree of expertise within the workforce, a number of people without a technical background need to be able to use, calibrate, and reprogram a robot for construction tasks.

Research

We therefore propose a new approach toward robot programming. Combining research results from the areas of learning by demonstration with skill and parameter-based robot programming, we redefine the current teaching process and create a Dynamic and Interactive robotic Assistant for Novel

Applications (DIANA). Individualization and customization are becoming increasingly important for all industries. In the case of "structured" fabrication, such developments can be used to fine-tune products to the requirements of the user, realizing lot size one without a significant added effort. Similar technologies in the context of unstructured environments have to go even further by implementing machine intelligence and learning – as their environment is dynamic and changing, the fabrication processes have to constantly and dynamically adjust to new sensor data, while still following a previously set framework of fabrication rules.

In the area of task execution the objectives of the DIANA project focus on the dynamic adaptability of a generated sequence. Within the context of interactive robotic assistance the robot needs to be able to handle human interaction when executing a task, as well as replanning of the execution strategy if environmental changes occur. This also requires an integration of sensor feedback into task execution and into the overall task execution strategy.

In the last three years the capabilities of our approach was demonstrated within various projects of the assembly of small-scale timber structures: At the Hannover Fair in 2016, IP/RWTH Aachen exhibited DIANA with a Sensitive Assembly (fig. 1) installation as one of the KUKA Innovation Award

Fig. 1: DIANA at the KUKA Innovation Award 2016

finalists, using the new KUKA iiwa (intelligent work assistant robot) – a safe robot that "feels" collisions and touch. The robot assembled wooden rod structures, whose shape was set directly by the user – simply by taking the robot at the tip and manually guiding it along the curve to fabricate. During assembly, the robot enabled its compliant/soft mode to assemble rods like a human would do. This also allowed the audience to actively assist the robot by demonstrating directly the mounting position for the rod or to intuitively guide the robot to set geometry or design rules of the structure, rather than executing something solely created according to preprogrammed specifications. Within the 2017 Robodonien project we incorporated a KMR iiwa mobile platform as a work assistant to drive material through a band saw. After the robot grips a timber piece for fabrication, he automatically positions himself to the band saw to cut and mount the piece in a following process step. While streamlining the whole process with a single machine, multiple process steps can be combined accordingly. The user can rewind the robot program simply by touching the robot by hand and pushing the robot's 6th axis backward, or they can control a gripping device by human touch. In our research we refer to this programming technique as *haptic programming* (fig. 2), where process steps can be adapted by the user without using the KUKA teach pendant or an offline computer. Such new methods are important for the construction environment, for a robot cannot use cameras in a dusty environment, and workers may not be able to program or interact with code directly.

Fig. 2: Haptic control of a KUKA iiwa

Apart from such new HMI (human-machine interfaces), we see a great potential in developing new intuitive teaching methods to make robotics, fabrication, and material knowledge more attractive and accessible. We therefore have started an exploratory teaching space on Cloud robotics, in which students can learn, on a software-independent web platform, how to, for example, cut, mill, 3-D-print, etc., with the assistance of industrial robots. The teaching material is embedded in video tutorials; students can choose when, where, and the way they want to be exposed to a deeper material, fabrication, or robotic understanding (fig. 3).

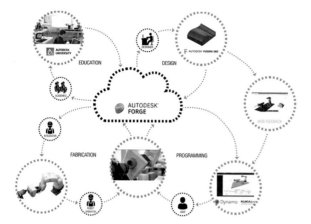

Fig. 3: Concept of Cloud robotics

Conclusion

The construction industry requires robotic assistants to fill the lack of qualified workers with workers who have not been in the focus to the industry. We have to make the construction business more attractive for the digital natives. Here robots can help in the mediation between the digital and physical world.

A further goal in our research will be followed in the "wood workshop of the future," a flexible environment with dynamic robotic assistants, where people and robots can intuitively interact with each other (fig. 4). We therefore see a great potential in mobile robotic platforms to execute multiple individual processes without having to program them offline for each process step or execute them subsequently. Apart from our first attempts with mobile robotics for prefabrication, our new Center for Construction Robotics at the RWTH Aachen Campus was founded in July 2018 to address the digitalization of the construction site of the future.

Fig. 4: Human interaction with a KUKA KMR iiwa

References

Braumann, Johannes, and Sigrid Brell-Cokcan. 2014. "Visual Robot Programming: Linking Design, Simulation, and Fabrication." In *SimAUD 2014: Proceedings of the Symposium on Simulation for Architecture and Urban Design*, edited by David Jason Gerber and Sonny Astani, 118–25. Red Hook: Curran.

Braumann, Johannes, and Sigrid Brell-Cokcan. 2015. "Adaptive Robot Control." In *eCAADe 2015*, edited by Bob Martens et al., 243–50. Vienna: Faculty of Architecture and Regional Planning.

Brell-Cokcan, Sigrid, and Johannes Braumann, eds. 2012. *Robotic Fabrication in Architecture, Art, and Design 2012*. Vienna: Springer.

Brell-Cokcan, Sigrid, and Johannes Braumann. 2013. "Unlocking Robotic Design: Visual Robot Programming for Fabricating Large-Scale Sculptures." In *Rethinking Prototyping: Proceedings of the Design Modelling Symposium Berlin 2013*, edited by Christoph Gengnagel, Axel Kilian, Julien Nembrini, and Fabian Scheurer, 407–16. Berlin: Universität der Künste.

Brell-Cokcan, Sigrid, and Johannes Braumann. 2014. "Robotic Production Immanent Design: Creative Toolpath Design in Micro and Macro Scale." In *Acadia 2014: Design Agency*, edited by David Gerber, Alvin Huang, and Jose Sanchez, 579–88. Cambridge: Riverside Architectural Press.

Brell-Cokcan, Sigrid, Johannes Braumann, Baris Cokcan, and Martin Kleindienst. 2012. "Just-in-Time Design: Developing Parametric Design Tools for Architectural Design." In *Beyond Codes and Pixels: Proceedings of CAADRIA 2012*, edited by Thomas Fischer et al., 455–64. Hong Kong: Association for Computer-Aided Architectural Design Research in Asia.

Stumm, Sven, Johannes Braumann, Martin von Hilchen, and Sigrid Brell-Cokcan. 2016. "On-Site Robotic Construction Assistance for Assembly Using A Priori Knowledge and Human Robot Collaboration." In *Advances in Robot Design and Intelligent Control: Proceedings of the 25th International Conference on Robotics in Alpe-Adria-Danube Region (RAAD 2016)*, edited by Aleksandar Rodić and Theodor Borangiu, 583–92. Cham: Springer.

Stumm, Sven, Sigrid Brell-Cokcan, and Peter Neu. 2017. "Towards Cloud-Informed Robotics." In *34th International Symposium on Automation and Robotics in Construction (ISARC 2017)*, 59–64. New York: Curran.

1.1 Digital Timber Construction

The Gravitational Pavilion: Simplified Node Complexity

Miro Bannwart
Faculty of Architecture and Urban Planning, University of Stuttgart, Germany

Abstract — The gravitational pavilion (fig. 1) was developed in collaboration with the CNC producer Krüsi. The double-curved structure of the pavilion consists of 297 individual CNC-fabricated wood beams. To avoid complex node intersections as well as to reduce fabrication complexity, the crucial parts of the structure nodes were cut out. To make the structure stable and fabricable, a high abstraction from a complex shape to simplified components as well as a two-step assembly logic was worked out. A digital design to fabrication and assembly workflow was developed to accomplish this goal. The results show that the contemporary world of digital fabrication and collaboration of students with industry enables innovative small-scale projects.

Fig. 1: The Gravitational Pavilion (© Bannwart)

Aim and Relevance: A Process of Learning

At the project's beginning stood the wish to be able to design, fabricate, and assemble every physically possible complex shape in wood. To achieve this a process of learning and exploring computation and digital fabrication methods was necessary.

The project together with the preceding development steps are therefore mainly relevant in terms of acquiring digital methods. The question never had been how to develop something completely novel – more complex wood constructions had been built before. The driving question was how to learn methods to enable building every shape in wood.

Beyond this educational value, the system is of potential use for shading roofs, winter gardens, or building extensions. A next step would be to develop an enclosed structure as well as an insulation system. This promises to enlarge the opportunities to deploy this system.

State of the Art and Inspiration

The Landesgartenschau Exhibition Hall (fig. 2) is a beech plywood-plate lightweight structure, with a structural thickness of just 50 mm and spanning over 11 m. A biomimetic approach played an important role in the development of this structure. The plate tessellation of a complex and stable shape as well as the plate connections where inspired by the biological model of sea urchins. The plates and their finger-joint connections were fully robotically fabricated.[1] Sophisticated agent-based modeling approaches as well as a highly accurate robotic fabrication process made this project feasible.

For the project Gravitational Pavilion an agent-based surface tessellation as well as the programming and robotic milling of complex edge-patters were beyond the scope of a student project. Nevertheless, this project inspired and motivated the author of this paper to find solutions beyond conventional wood constructions.

Fig. 2: Landesgartenschau Exhibition Hall ICD/ ITKE, 2014 (© Bannwart)

A further inspiration derived from a small pavilion student project by Jürg Bühren (fig. 3). This reciprocal structure fabricated from straight bar wood on a Hundegger CNC machine demonstrated that smaller pavilions can be built by students. Due to the reciprocal setup the ends of the beams were to a certain degree standing out of the structure. This would make it relatively difficult to cover. It was therefore attempted to develop a structure at a similar scale and simplicity, but using a triangular setup with a smoother surface that could potentially be covered in a more convenient way.

Fig. 3: Jürg Bühren's reciprocal structure 2013 (http://www.parametrismus.com/user-gallery)

Methods

The software Rhinoceros and the visual programming add-on Grasshopper were applied to design the pavilion shape and as well as to generate the fabricable beam geometry. The necessary skills were mainly acquired online, predominantly using YouTube tutorials. To manufacture the generated beam geometry on a CNC machine, cadwork software was used to export machine-readable BTL files.

Results and Development

The world of the Rhino CAD, Grasshopper and its plug-in environment has been explored through many predecessor projects. Important steps toward simple components in complex structures include an investigation of waffle methods which enabled waffle nodes perpendicular to the design surface; the use of the Grasshopper plug-in Kangaroo, which enables the planarization of geometry as parts of complex double-curved systems; and the use of digital fabrication methods including a Kuka robot to mill wood plates. To extend this initial model systems toward pavilion scale, the main questions were how to speed up the relatively slow process of milling the pieces robotically out of plywood and how to develop a system of connecting potentially up to twelve beams at one node. The ability to connect up to twelve beams at one node became necessary with the decision to tesselate the shapes triangularly, which is programmatically a lot simpler than tessellating shapes with planar polygons.

To digitally situate the design optimally in its context in front of the University in Burgdorf, this context was 3-D-scanned precisely by a photogrammetry method. To design the initial triangular mesh in this context, a Grasshopper-Kangaroo mesh relaxation with gravity as one of multiple parameters was combined with a motion-capturing Kinect sensor and an instant structural analysis. This setup allowed the designer to place and impact the system using hand gestures. The results were visualized and evaluated by the Karamba structural analysis, a Grasshopper plug-in. Therefore, the trade-off between a gravitationally and structurally optimized hanging shape and further aesthetic or contextual requirements and constraints caused by user impacts could be played in an interactive way.

To make the production process more efficient, a code was developed that connects all nodes with its neighbors by two beams consisting of planar, and where necessary, parallel sides. This allowed cutting the beams from regular cross sections by a modern CNC machine with a circular saw, which, compared to robotic milling processes, is much faster. If 12 beams (6 planes) meet at one node, the upper side of the plate or beam always meet in one point. The lower offset surfaces (material thickness) do not intersect in one point if the base shape of the structure is irregular double-curved (fig. 4). This highly complex node situation was resolved by cutting out the node, which also reduced the number of cuts and fabrication complexity (fig. 5).

Fig. 4: Node intersection, self-made graphic   Fig. 5: Node cutout (© Bannwart)

On request, the CNC developer Krüsi and the CAD developer cadwork offered to support this project. The beam geometry could be imported into cadwork, which is able to export the beam geometry as machine-readable BTL files, thus storing the geometry as well as the machining data. Krüsi offered to cut the beams on one of their 5-Axis CNC machines. All in all, the beams were cut in three days of production.

A further but no less important reason to connect every node with two parallel beams was the assembly and connection logic. In a first step, each triangle, consisting of three enumerated beams, could be screwed together from the outside using very stable screwing angles. In a second step, the triangles could be screwed together from the gap inside of the triangle (fig. 6). Considering the size of the drill, an on-site beam-by-beam assembly with the triangular system would become very difficult because the beams cover each other in a way that makes it almost impossible to find screwing positions that are physically possible and structurally stable. The use of the two-step connection solved this assembly problem while providing a stable connection.

Using this method, first all triangles were assembled. Second, these triangles were assembled to segments consisting of six to eighteen triangles (fig. 7). In a team of four carpenters and one person documenting the process, the segments could be assembled on-site in one day without a crane or additional scaffolding.

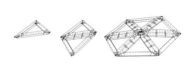 

Fig. 6: Assembly method, self-made graphic   Fig. 7: Segment assembly (© Bannwart)

Stability

The finished structure spanned more than 5 meters with an overall structural thickness of not more than 50 mm. The structure surprised by its high stability: The pavilion could withstand the weight of the five assemblers sitting on top of it. Pulled down by hand at the front bow the slightly flexible structure behaved exactly as predicted by the Karamba analysis during the design process.

Due to its slightly cantilevering shape, the pavilion started to deform slightly during the months after the assembly. Nevertheless, the connection method to screw the beams together allowed enough flexibility to avoid structural failure.

One year after the assembly, it was planned to take down the gravitational pavilion. To give it a second revival, it was suggested to use it for any further projects if anyone within the university context had a creative Idea. Stephan Fricker, a structural engineer and professor in Burgdorf, decided to use the wooden structure as scaffolding for a concrete arch. Luckily the pavilion could be used a second time and enabled a further student project including practical work.

Discussion

Computational methods had been learned within the scope of the Gravitational Pavilion project and at the same time these methods motivated the author of this paper to explore deeper until it was finally possible to build a physical prototype. This experience of learning the field of computation and digital fabrication often reminded us of the words of Buckminster Fuller: "If you want to teach people a new way of thinking, don't bother trying to teach them. Instead, give them a tool, the use of which will lead to new ways of thinking."

It is tempting to equate Fuller's "tool" with the ecosystem of the Rhino and Grasshopper software. This however would be a wrong limitation. Without an online accessible community of people sharing their knowledge in digital design and fabrication, the learning process of acquiring the necessary skills would not have been possible. Therefore, the understanding of the "tool enabling new ways of thinking" has to be enlarged to a net of people in and beyond the academic world, who encourage and help to accomplish projects by sharing their knowledge.

Conclusion

The main driver for the Gravitational Pavilion project was the author's strong affinity to wood construction derived from his background as carpenter.
The structure demonstrates that the contemporary world of digital fabrication and student-industry collaboration can enable innovative small-scale projects.
The abstraction of the complex double-curved shape to highly simplified components greatly reduced the fabrication complexity and fabrication time. Therefore, also the relatively low fabrication costs made the project feasible as a student project.
A further important point to make the structure feasible was the system development from the assembly perspective, which lead to the two-step screwing logic. Without this the structure could not have been assembled.
The fully digital design to fabrication workflow allowed a design process within the exactly 3-D scanned environment. Impacting the design by hand gestures as a part of an interactive design workflow within this 3-D environment allows

architects as well as people unused to CAD programs to have in an intuitive way a very contextual design experience.

From a carpentry and aesthetic perspective, the developed system especially paid off by the uniform wooden visual having reduced elements at the node (fig. 8).

Fig. 8: The finished pavilion (© Bannwart)

Outlook

The main purpose of every roof is to provide shelter. Therefore, developing a watertight enclosure for the structure and – in a next step – insulation would make sense. The main challenge of such a development would be amending the pavilion by adding further elements without losing the structure's basic aesthetics, especially at the cutout node. Moreover, the joining method of the beams may be developed toward a more complex geometrical wood-only joint without any screws. This would be interesting from a geometrical point of view, but may also entail a more complex and time-consuming CNC fabrication. The triangular tessellation is very handy in perspective to the triangle's planarity, but leads as well to the complex node situation that necessarily emerges when more than three planes meet at one node. A hexagonal or polygonal planar tessellation, where at maximum three planes meet at one node can then reduce the node complexity, so that the node's cutout would not be necessary. To learn the way of agent-based planar tessellations is a new adventure.

Acknowledgments

Thanks to Professor Jacques Wüthrich and André Marti who offered a digital fabrication seminar where the Gravitational Pavilion as a student project could be acknowledged. And many thanks to Marcel Duong and Krüsi AG for cutting all the beams on one of their CNC Machines. Thanks to Treppenbau AG for sponsoring the used wood. And finally, thanks a lot to the students and friends who helped to assemble the Gravitational Pavilion.

----

[1] Landesgartenschau Exhibition Hall ICD/ITKE, 2014 Information from: https://icd.uni-stuttgart.de/?p=11173.

Fibrous Joints for Lightweight Segmented Timber Shells

Dominga Garufi[1], Hans Jakob Wagner[1], Simon Bechert[2], Tobias Schwinn[1], Dylan Marx Wood[1], Achim Menges[1], and Jan Knippers[2]
[1] *Institute for Computational Design and Construction (ICD), University of Stuttgart, Germany*
[2] *Institute for Building Structures and Structural Design, University of Stutt-gart, Germany*

Abstract — With fibrous joints for lightweight segmented timber shells we introduce novel techniques for three-dimensional placement and curing of CFRP-Tows within prefabricated plywood plates to create differentiated fibrous bending-resistant timber plate joints. Density, orientation, and position of the fibrous joints can be informed by the calculated local principal tensile forces and dihedral plate angles between 90° and 270° can be achieved, which allows for the gradual integration of various functional and structural aspects into segmented shell structures. After the CFRP tows are placed inside the wood, the matrix can be consolidated in situ via controlled application of electric current without bonding the fibers to the wood. This opens up the possibility of mobile on-site fibrous joining of large-scale structures, as CFRP tows can be cured independently of autoclave sizes. The joints' structural capacity is based on the form stability of the CFRP loops rather than any chemical interface between fibers and plywood plates. This allows the two materials to be separated at the end of the structure's lifetime.

Context

Wood is a natural and sustainable material, which can be highly engineered to serve different purposes in architecture and building industry. Still, state-of-the-art timber constructions possess rather big cross sections and structural heights, resulting in partly unattractive structural design solutions. Big timber cross sections are often not only a consequence of strict fire regulations but also an outcome of the amount of mechanical fasteners that need to be sufficiently placed and spaced.

Segmented timber shells are an example of how timber structures can be built with very slender cross sections and minimal use of material. Through digitally controlled machines and fabrication workflows it is possible to make use of the easy machinability of wood and to achieve differentiation of all parts at high production rates. However, the design freedom of segmented timber shells and their structural capacity is currently still limited by the joinery systems.

Trees that are exposed to harsh environments often have a fibrous growth pattern that deviates from a unidirectional fiber layout to more complex fiber arrangements. These phenomena are usually classified as numerous wooden defects (such as spiraling grain or crossing or interlocking grain; see Hernández and Almeida 2003). As such growth patterns are harmful for timber-processing machinery, they are generally avoided in modern silviculture (see Richter 2015). For a tree however, such complex fiber arrangements are actually a matter of fitness. As an example, they can make trees less prone against failure when bent by winds (see Mattheck and Kubler 1995). For millions of years, trees have evolved to grow in elaborate three-dimensional fibrous arrangements.

A lot of advances have been achieved in the attempt to standardize and homogenize timber as a base material for responsible use of timber for large-scale constructions. Although engineered timber products can overcome the size limitation of tree trunks, limiting factors such as transportation and machine dimensions cannot be easily overcome. As a consequence, timber and engineered wood construction are almost always modular structures and joinery techniques constitute a core aspect of their overall performance. Is it possible to (re)introduce elaborate three-dimensional fibrous arrangements into homogenized wood products to achieve high performative in situ joining techniques?

State of the Art
LANDESGARTENSCHAU 2014 EXHIBITION HALL

Two projects that display novel fabrication strategies and innovative joining techniques of significant contribution are the Landesgartenshau Exhibition Hall by ICD/ITKE (see Schwinn, Krieg, and Menges 2014) and the Interlocked Folded Plate Structure developed at EPFL in Lausanne (see Robeller and Weinand 2015).

The Landesgartenshau Exhibition Hall (LaGa) is characterized as a segmented timber plate shell, designed to carry loads mainly through membrane forces. Its double curvature together with the segments' finger-joint design provide structural stability. Both out-of-plane shear and bending forces are avoided through the shell panelization. According to recent research (Li and Knippers 2015; Wester 2002), plate shell structures with trivalent polyhedral segments are considered kinematically stable, meaning that in such segmented timber shells, bending stiff connections are not a core concern. The main focus of the LaGa Exhibition Hall was therefore to create joints that could resist in-plane shear forces. Nonetheless, in the specific case of 180-degree vertex angles, the kinematic stability of trivalent polyhedral segments is lost. This means that areas where vertex angles are close to 180 degrees need to take small bending moments. Bending moments also appear in segmented shell structures due to inaccuracies during fabrication, uneven load distribution (for example, wind loads) and during the approximation of the desired shell geometry (see Schwinn, Krieg, and Menges 2014). As a result, small bending forces still needed to be accounted for in the LaGa project, which resulted in the introduction of crossing screws. Crossing screws allow the joints to meet building code requirements and take axial and out-of-plane shear as well as small bending forces, but with their rigid size, they also represent a limitation for the plate connection angles.

INTEGRAL MECHANICAL ATTACHMENT
In the Interlocking Folded Plate Structure by the Timber Construction Laboratory IBOIS/EPFL, the use of dovetail joints without discrete fasteners and adhesive bonding is applied to design a folded timber plate structure (see Robeller and Weinand 2015). The dovetail joints are characterized by having a single degree of freedom, meaning that all the relative movements and rotations, apart from a single direction, are blocked. In this way, a bending stiff joint can be achieved without the use of mechanical fasteners or adhesives. However, the singular insertion vectors introduce a new dimension of complexity in respect to the assembly logics of even topologically simple geometries.

HYBRID TIMBER CONSTRUCTION
The Rapid Assembly with Bending-Stabilised Structures (see Gattas et al. 2017) research project consists of a symmetrical arch structure with each arch comprised of seven box segments constructed with 9 mm thick plywood plates. The arch segments were mounted on a flat surface to bind a continuous tensile skin of GFRP onto it.
The project showcases a clear differentiation of structural parts: the glass fiber sheet on the top of the cantilevers is used to mainly resist tensile forces, while the wood pieces on the bottom are pressed together by the acting compression forces. In this project, wood and glass fibers are strongly glued together with epoxy resin, making the recycling of both wood and FRP very energy-intensive.

AUTOMATED FIBER-PLACEMENT TECHNIQUES

Tow steered and tailored fiber-placement techniques are common fabrication techniques used in aerospace industries to build ultra-lightweight structural components using mostly carbon fiber. Both techniques achieve detailed control over the fiber directions. While automated fiber-placement lays the fibers onto a formwork, tailored fiber placement stitches the fiber on a flexible textile base material that can later be wrapped onto multiple shapes. In both scenarios, the design of the fibrous directions is bound to the applied surface.

Research
METHODS

Research on fibrous timber joints puts together findings and advancements of various methods and processes to form a novel material system that offers new possibilities in joining and building of lightweight timber shell structures.

CFRP-Tows are placed into custom-milled grooves and holes inside prefabricated timber segments. This three-dimensional and geometrically controlled fiber placement forms continuous loops that join together wooden segments with a big geometric design solution space.

Computational design methods and bespoke algorithms were developed and used to control and generate geometrically complex fibrous joint geometries within this design solution space. Each fiber's geometry negotiates a multitude of geometric, structural, fabrication, and aesthetic inputs and is the result of a multicriteria optimization.

Custom CNC code-generation tools are used to connect robotic paths directly to the generated three-dimensional path geometries, allowing for the defined translation of digital information into physical reality.

7-axis robotic milling is used for the prefabrication of the timber plates and opens up the possibility of milling, drilling, and cutting from both sides of the timber plates without needing to reposition the pieces.

In situ resistive heat consolidation of CFRP tows is used to cure fibers within the wooden base material. CFRP is conductive and CFRP tows with a constant number of filaments can be heated up to target temperatures by controlled application of current. Wood acts as an insulator for both heat and electricity, which makes it a perfect base material for the efficient, in situ curing of CFRP tows. Resistive heat consolidation was mostly investigated by NASA researchers for deployable structures in space (Schwartz, Jones, and Keller 1963; Naskar and Edie 2006, Sarles and Leo 2008). Solely geometric bonding is used to ensure a tight connection between wood and CFRP. This means that none of the fibers are glued to the wood, neither with the resin matrix nor with additional glue. Although this slightly reduces the joint's structural capability, it comes with two benefits: the fibers can be easily separated from the wood at the end of a structure's lifetime, and the placement of fibers can happen in a dry and clean environment.

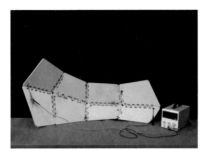

Fig. 1: Controlled application of electric current can be used to consolidate CFRP-tows after joining the timber plates

Fig. 1.1: A custom robotic milling workflow is conceived to enable milling of grooves on both: top and bottom side of the segments

FIBROUS JOINT SYSTEM FOR LIGHTWEIGHT SEGMENTED TIMBER SHELLS

As opposed to compression-only stone vaults, joints in lightweight timber shells need to accommodate a multitude of different forces (see Krieg et al. 2015). While compression forces can be simply transferred through wooden miter joints, tension as well as bending and shear forces are to be considered in the design of a fibrous joint system.

For fibrous joints in lightweight segmented timber shells, two loops of fibers are conceived to connect the wood plates on the top and bottom of the joint – each tying back onto the other side, intertwining with the other in space (fig. 3). While those fibrous loops only take tensile forces (also after curing), their position in space allows them to address a broad spectrum of forces: their position on the top and bottom of the plate makes them an ideal fit to address positive and negative bending moments while their orientation can be adjusted in such way that in-plane shear forces of any direction can be accommodated (fig. 4).

The fibrous joint system furthermore can continuously adjust to dihedral plate angles from 90° to 270° without the need of conceptual, structural, or topological changes. The same flexibility is achievable with variations in joint depth and connector densities. In this way a joint system is achieved where connectors can be positioned where really needed, in various densities, proportions of top/bottom connections, and different orientations (fig. 5).

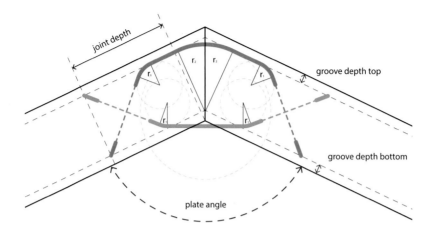

Fig. 2: Section through fibrous joint: Two CFRP loops (green, red) connect top and bottom side of joint. Several parameters need to be considered in the parametric model to adhere to minimum bending radii, sufficient groove, and joint depths.

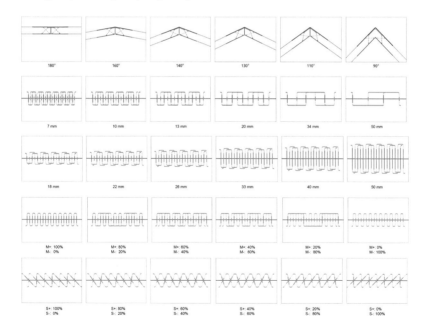

Fig. 3: Matrix of exemplary variations of fibrous joint geometries (from top to bottom): plate angle, density, joint depth, proportion of top/bottom connections, joint orientations

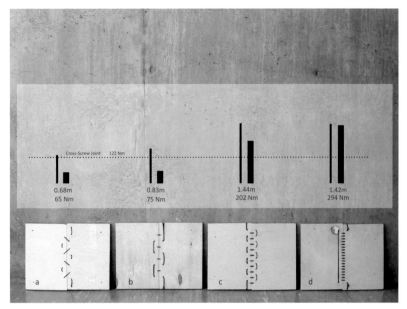

Fig. 4: Relative comparison of differentiated 21 mm plywood plate fibrous joint geometries; the fibers' total length (left bar) and their moment capacity in initial 4-point bending tests (right bar) against a cross-screw sample (10 connections, dotted line): shear forces can be accommodated by the orientation of connections (a) while the joint's moment capacity is not necessarily compromised (b) increasing the number of connections results in higher capacity but longer fibers (c) while the differentiation between top and bottom connections increases the joint's capacity with minimal use of fibers (d).

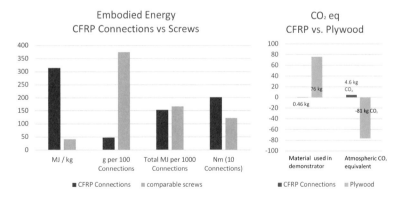

Fig. 5.1: Embodied Energy Carbon Fibre Reinforce Polymer Connections versus Screws (1 g each).
Fig. 5.2: Carbon Dioxide equivalent Carbon Fibre Reinforced Polymer versus Plywood.

DEMONSTRATOR

To demonstrate the capabilities of the joint system, a segmented timber shell was built that cantilevers far beyond its supports, creating high bending forces within the structure. Furthermore, the structure is purposely panelized in quadrilateral faces to further challenge the joint system, as continual creases would theoretically allow the structure to buckle along the joints. As an architectural feature, a set of steps at the right side of the shell illustrates the wide range of dihedral angles that are possible with the joint system (figs. 6 and 7).

Fig. 6: Dihedral curved thin segmented timber structures

Fig. 7: Density, position, and orientation of the fibrous joints are differentiated to accommodate the calculated forces in the shell.

JOINT OPTIMIZATION TECHNIQUES

To better understand the global forces acting on the structure, and to show-case how the fibrous joints can locally react to different stresses, a basic Finite Element Analysis was carried out. For the simulation of the structure the bottom is fixed and a live load is placed on each step. The resulting principal tensile stress directions on the top and bottom faces of each panel then directly inform the generation of 945 bespoke fibrous connections, optimized for minimal use of CFRP. Compared to a regular fibrous joint pattern, 24 percent of fibers are saved (100 m/130 m), while 30 percent more connections can be created in critical areas.

EMBODIED ENERGY ESTIMATIONS

The demonstrator is composed of 35 birch plywood plates with a total weight of 75 kg. Only 460 grams of CFRP were used for the 49 joints. Roughly 105 kg of CO_2 atmospheric equivalent are stored within the wooden base material; the plywood production caused around 24 kg of CO_2 equivalent emissions, whereas the used CFRP caused only around 4.6 kg of CO_2 equivalent emissions. We arrive at a total atmospheric CO_2 equivalent of -76.4 kg (figs. 5 and 6; see Appendix).

Conclusion and Outlook

Advanced timber construction and CFRP composite structures are both fields of continuous research and innovation. With digitally controlled wood manufacturing machines of various sizes, nowadays almost any carpenter can cut and drill grooves into wood with submillimeter precision. The flexible and easily formable pre-impregnated carbon fiber rovings then can be placed manually within these grooves without any additional expensive technological equipment, joining together timber segments through precise and structurally informed three-dimensional fibrous loops. The capacity of these joints still needs to be further investigated, but initial tests indicate promising performance and the successful fabrication of a 1:1 Demonstrator shows the power of the proposed fabrication workflow. Last but not least, the joint system opens up unseen design freedom, enabling the integration of various design aspects into lightweight segmented timber shells.

Acknowledgments

This research was developed as a master thesis within the interdisciplinary environment of the ITECH Master's Program at the University of Stuttgart, dwelling on the expertise of professors and tutors in both architecture and structural engineering.

Appendix

For the embodied energy calculations, we assumed the following values:
- Embodied energy CFRP: 315 MJ/kg (Kara and Manmek 2009)
- Embodied energy steel: ~40 MJ/kg (Hammond and Jones 2008)

For the demonstrator, formed of 35 plywood plates with a total volume of 0.1 m³ and 76 kg, 200 m of 12 k CFRP TowPreg are used for a total of 945 connections in the form of fibrous joints. The weight per meter is approximately 2.3 g, therefore there is around 460 g of CFRP inside the demonstrator which translates to roughly 145 MJ(eq) of embodied energy. These fibrous connections allow for plate angles and bending strengths of the joints that seem hard to match with conventional screws. But as a thought experiment we theorize that we would we able to form each of the 945 connections with a 50 mm long screw of 3.5 mm diameter: assuming a weight of 4 g per screw those would weigh 3.78 kg, having an embodied energy of roughly 158 MJ(eq). Considering the calculation of the total carbon footprint we consider 240 kg CO_2(eq)/m³ for the plywood in fossil CO_2 (emissions caused for the production of the plywood) and 1050 kg CO_2(eq)/m³ biogenic CO_2 (CO_2 stored in the wood) (WISA Product Report 2016). For CFRP we calculate with an estimated 10 kg CO_2/kg CFRP atmospheric equivalent.

In total we calculated:

> +24 kg CO_2 emissions for plywood production (fossil CO_2)
> -105 kg CO_2 stored in plywood (biogenic CO_2)
> +4.6 kg CO_2 emissions for the CFRP connections

Summed up, the demonstrator has an atmospheric CO_2 equivalent of approx. -76.4 kg. The demonstrator therefore eliminates more greenhouse gases than it emits.

References

Gattas, Joe, Yousef Al-Qaryouti, Ting-Uei Lee, and Kim Baber. 2017. "Rapid Assembly with Bending-Stabilised Structures." In *Fabricate: Rethinking Design and Construction*, edited by Achim Menges, Bob Sheil, Ruairi Glynn, and Marilena Skavara, 50–57. London: UCL Press.

Hafner, Anette, Stephan Ott, and Stefan Winter. 2014. "Recycling and End-of-Life Scenarios for Timber Structures." In *Materials and Joints in Timber Structures*, edited by S. Aicher, H. W. Reinhardt, and H. Garrecht, 89–98. RILEM Bookseries 9. Dordrecht: Springer.

Hernández, E. Roger, and Giana Almeida. 2003. "Effects of Wood Density and Interlocked Grain on the Shear Strength of Three Amazonian Tropical Hardwoods." *Wood and Fiber Science* 35, no. 2 (April): 154–66.

Hammond, Geoffrey, and Craig Jones. 2008. "Embodied Energy and Carbon in Construction Materials." *Proceedings of The Institution of Civil Engineers – Energy* 161: 87–98. https://doi.org/10.1680/ener.2008.161.2.87.

Kara, Sami, and Manmek Suphunnika 2009. "Composites: Calculating Their Embodied Energy: Final Report of the Life Cycle Engineering & Management Research Group, University of New South Wales, 2009."

Krieg, Oliver David, et al. 2015. "Biomimetic Lightweight Timber Plate Shells: Computational Integration of Robotic Fabrication, Architectural Geo- metry and Structural Design." In *Advances in Architectural Geometry 2014,* edited by P. Block, J. Knippers, N. Mitra, and W. Wang, 109–25. Cham: Springer.

Li, Jian-Min, and Jan Knippers. 2015. "Segmental Timber Plate Shell for the Landesgartenschau Exhibition Hall in Schwäbisch Gmünd: The Application of Finger Joints in Plate Structures." *International Journal of Space Structures* 30, no. 2: 123–39.

Mattheck, Claus, and Hans Kubler. *Wood: The Internal Optimization of Trees.* 1997. Berlin Heidelberg: Springer.

Naskar, Amit K., and Dan D. Edie. 2006. "Consolidation of Reactive Ultem® Powder-Coated Carbon Fiber Tow for Space Structure Composites by Resistive Heating." *Journal of Composite Materials* 40, no. 20: 1871–83. https://doi.org/10.1177/0021998306061300.

Richter, Christoph. 2015. *Wood Characteristics: Description, Causes, Prevention, Impact on Use and Technological Adaptation*. Cham: Springer.

Robeller, Christopher, and Yves Weinand. 2015. "Interlocking Folded Plate: Integral Me- chanical Attachment for Structural Wood Panels." *International Journal of Space Structures* 30, no. 2: 111–12.

Sarles, Stephen A., and Donald J. Leo. 2008. "Consolidation of U-Nyte® Epoxy-Coated Carbon-Fiber Composites via Temperature-Controlled Resistive Heating." *Journal of Composite Materials* 42, no. 24: 2551–66. https://doi.org/10.1177/0021998308097197.

Schober, Kay-Uwe, et al. 2015. "FRP Reinforcement of Timber Structures." *Construction and Building Materials* 97: 106–18.

Schwartz, S., R. Jones, and L. Keller. 1963. "Ultraviolet and Heat Rigidization of Inflatable Space Structures" In *Aerospace Expandable Structures: Conference Transactions*, 369–80. Washington DC: US National Bureau of Standards.

Schwinn, Tobias, Oliver David Krieg, and Achim Menges. 2014. "Behavioral Strategies, Synthesizing Computation and Robotic Fabrication of Lightweight Tim- ber Plate Structures." In *Acadia 2014: Design Agency*, edited by David Gerber, Alvin Huang, and Jose Sanchez, 177–88. Cambridge: Riverside Architectural Press.

Wester, Ture 2002. "Nature Teaching Structures." *International Journal of Space Structures* 17, no. 2 (September): 135–47.

WISA Plywood Carbon Footprint Report, 2016. Accessed March 2019, https://www.upm.com/siteassets/documents/responsibility/certificate-finder/environmental-product-declaration/carbon-profile-birch-coated.pdf.

Young, S. Song, et al. 2009. "Life Cycle Energy Analysis of Fiber-reinforced Composites." *Composites Part A: Applied Science and Manufacturing* 40, no. 8: 1257–65. https://doi.org/10.1016/j.composite-sa.2009.05.020.

1.2 Robotics in Timber Construction

Towards Distributed In Situ Robotic Timber Construction

Samuel Leder, Ramon Weber, Oliver Bucklin, Dylan Wood, and Achim Menges
Institute of Computational Design and Construction (ICD), University of
Stuttgart, Germany

Abstract — This paper will discuss and explore the impact of creating a new architecture-specific, distributed robotic system for the in situ assembly of timber structures. The system developed is composed of multiple collaborative, single-axis robotic nodes designed to utilize standardized timber struts as a building material and for its locomotion system. The material is therefore not only used in the final built structure but forms an integral part of the robotic system, minimizing its size, weight, and complexity. By codesigning custom robotic builders together with their material assembly system, the tectonic logics and spatial expression of the possible structures are a direct expression of the robotic configuration and building behaviors of the system. The spatial expressions of the proposed robotic system expose new possibilities for timber-based architecture in both design and construction.

Introduction

This paper presents ongoing research on the development of a distributed robotic construction system for in situ, full-scale timber construction. The research is situated in the recent trend in robotic-assisted assembly of timber structures. Although current research has developed highly refined digitally controlled prefabrication methods, on-site construction of architectural systems is still oriented around the human construction worker. Discretely operated machinery, designed originally for factory use, has recently been modified to augment the capabilities of the human construction worker.
In order to tackle the issue of on-site assembly of timber-based architecture, this research proposes a new system composed of multiple minimal single axis robotic nodes explicitly designed to utilize standardized timber struts as a building material and for its locomotion system. The custom robotic builders are codesigned with the assembly logics of the chosen historic building material. The spatial expressions of the proposed robotic assembly system expose new possibilities for timber-based architecture in both design

and construction practice. The tectonic logics and spatial expression of the possible structures are a direct expression of the robotic configuration and building behaviors of the system.

Background
TIMBER PREFABRICATION
For decades the timber industry has been at the forefront of implementing digital fabrication machinery and novel assembly strategies in the construction industry. The implementation of these digitally controlled fabrication strategies has allowed for new design possibilities, more structural performative structures, cost reduction, and greater material efficiency in the realm of timber construction. Large milling machines are now readily available for the precise prefabrication of timber for construction. Generic industrial six-axis robotic arms are also being implemented for milling detailed connections of load-bearing nodes for timber assemblies (see Krieg et al. 2015; and Robeller et al. 2015), and for the prefabrication of large-scale nonregular spatial structures (see Gramazio et al. 2014). Projects such as The Sequential Roof from the ETH showcase the current high standard of robotic prefabrication in including geometric definition, structural performance, robotic constraints, and full automation into the design and planning process (see Apolinarska et al. 2016).

TIMBER ON-SITE FABRICATION
The uniqueness of architectural projects and the ever-changing conditions of on-site assembly and fabrication have led mainly to the implementation of robotic tools in controlled factory environments for precision prefabrication of components. However, classical building techniques with much support from the human worker are still being used for the construction of these structures on-site. Shigeru Ban Architect's Tamedia Office Building in Zurich has recently received attention for its highly structurally innovative use of timber (see Antemann 2014). Yet the project demonstrates how decidedly sophisticated, modern timber structures still follow the rules of manual, human-centered construction methods when assembled on-site.

MOBILE ROBOTICS
Current large-scale, mobile robotic fabrication robots, such as the In Situ Fabricator (Giftthaler et al. 2017) feature a multiaxis robotic manipulator that is combined with a semiautonomous vehicle. The robotic arm is used to automate existing construction tasks, for example bricklaying or spot welding. Automation of tasks currently performed by human construction workers is achieved by a combination of machinery borrowed from other industries. Research on mobile collaborative robotic builders suggests how processes

can be more resilient and responsive when assembled through a small-scale distributed system. Current research has proven the capability of autonomous robotic machines to navigate three-dimensional strut environments (see Yoon 2006). Experimental small-scale robotic systems have focused on simulating the assembly of digital material while maintaining continuous stability (see Melenbrink and Werfel 2018) and on the design of robots that are specific to their material system and construction tasks (see Yablonina and Menger 2017). However, little research has been conducted on systems that can be deployed on construction sites and maintain their building capabilities in these often harsh and unpredictable environments.

Research
In order to tackle the issue of on-site fabrication of timber structures by distributed robotic systems, this research focused initially on the conceptual definition of the system and on the development of an initial working prototype.

ROBOTIC SYSTEM
We present a modular, distributed robotic system that is a combination of struts, nodes, and kinematic chains (fig. 1). The struts are the linear timber beams, which also serve as the building material of the system. The nodes are the robotic components of the system that can rotate, grip, and communicate. Each node consists of one rotating axis with two grippers located on either side that can attach to struts throughout the system. Kinematic chains are formed through both physical and digital coupling of nodes and struts, in order to carry out complex tasks. The entire robotic system is thus a group of nodes, struts, and kinematic chains that all work together in unison.

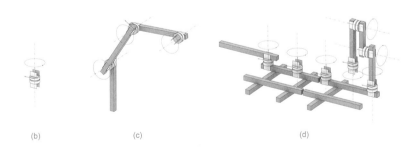

(a)   (b)   (c)   (d)

Fig. 1: Diagrammatic representation of components of the proposed distributed robotic assembly system and the system as a whole

(a) Strut: linear building material, (b) Node: robotic component, (c) Kinematic Chain: combination of struts and nodes, (d) Robotic System: combination of struts, nodes, and kinematic chains

The physical arrangement of the multiaxis kinematic chains specifically relates to their kinematic solution space (fig. 2). Depending on the number and relative orientation of struts and nodes of a kinematic chain, the kinematic solution space of the chain can change from a single point to any point in two-dimensional space to any point in three-dimensional space. Understanding this range of solutions thus becomes important when considering the collaboration between elements of the robotic system. The kinematic solution space becomes increasingly complex when various kinematic chains of digital and/or physical connection work together.

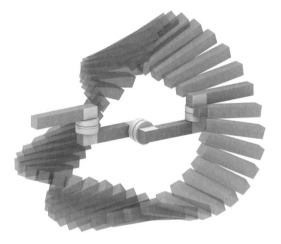

Fig. 2: Three-dimensional working space of
kinematic chain with three nodes and four struts

Using the kinematic solution space of various kinematic chains, complex motions can be achieved through continuously connecting and breaking up chains. The timber struts are therefore not only used in the built structure, but are an integral part of the robotic system, minimizing its complexity. As compared to a generic industrial six-axis robotic arm, the complexity of the robotic node is greatly reduced. By employing smaller building units, the self-weight of the robotic node can be handled by the structure, removing the need of gantry systems that are usually required to increase the working range of industrial robotic arms. Moreover, the small building units and the range in kinematic solutions of the kinematic chains allow for a high range of resolution at which structures can be designed and built.

Assembly Logic

Using the proposed robotic assembly system, this research also investigates processes for autonomously assembling standardized, linear timber struts through collaborative construction behaviors. The tectonic logic of the possible structures are a direct expression of the robotic configuration and collaborative building behaviors of the system (fig. 3).

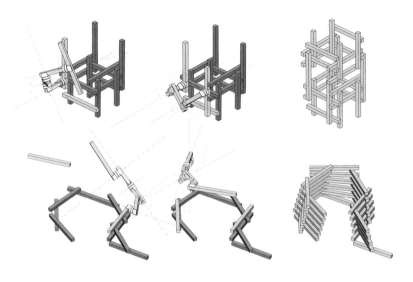

Fig. 3: Digital representation of an assembly sequence of differently configured kinematic chains, each of four nodes and three struts with direct implication on final built structures

Five building behaviors were developed using this robotic system. These behaviors include: *feed strut*, moving building material from a fix point to nodes on the built structure; *locomote*, the motion of nodes on the built structure; *pass strut*, the transfer of building material from one node to another; *change level*, the transition of nodes from one building plane to another; and *place strut*, moving building material to a desired end location. Through the collaboration of many of the single-axis nodes, the behaviors can occur simultaneously and in parallel for the rapid construction of a structure. Using the behaviors of the system, structures are built up layer by layer with the possibility of adding struts linking layers or rotating the plane of the layer itself.

This behavior-based construction logic creates new design opportunities for timber-based architecture relating to issues of density, resolution, and continuity. Structures can gradually adapt from a solid stack to a light frame in a single construction element. Timber struts can be organized in different densities in order to address issues of light and structural depth. Architects can design for both the macro scale and micro scale of a structure as often discussed with additive manufacturing, as struts can be layered in various resolutions to achieve a highly differentiated visual, structural, and architectural performance. Various configurations of kinematic chains can be deployed in the buildup of a structure. This allows for structures that are combinations of different construction typologies, featuring columns, wall elements, and horizontal in-plane assemblies (fig. 4). This in situ construction system would allow variety to emerge from a single fabrication technique as opposed to existing systems where different prefabricated components must be first assembled in a factory and then later assembled on-site.

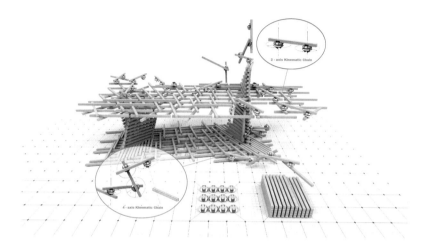

Fig. 4: Digital representation of a large-scale robotic assembly system denoting two different types of kinematic chains that are working simultaneously on the assembly of the structure

Hardware

First tests of functioning low-cost, lightweight, high-torque prototypes of the robotic system have been developed iteratively, combining off-the-shelf gears and ball bearings with custom 3-D-printed ABS parts. Cost was of significance in the prototypes in order to keep with the advantage of robustness from a distributed robotic system – the notion that if one of the robotic nodes fails it can be easily replaced. Reduction in cost also enables the ability to have large numbers of the robotic nodes working in parallel on different construction tasks. Lightness in weight as mentioned earlier would allow for the robotic node to be held by the structure and in turn reduce the complexity of the system. High torque, another factor in the creation of prototypes, is required in order to allow the robotic nodes to lift weights that are much larger than their own.

Prototypes were initially divided between two of the three functionalities of the robotic node: gripping and rotation. Each prototype is actuated by three commercial six-volt continuous rotation servo motors. After successful trials of the two mechanisms, a full prototype was then created with a rotating axis and a custom gripper on either side. Physical studies were conducted using two prototyped nodes and 28 × 28 × 500-millimeter struts that could be passed from one machine to the other (fig. 5). Although the studies revealed initial feasibility, further development of the gripping and rotation mechanisms and the integration of an on-board power supply would be needed in order to fully prove the validity of the system.

The Raspberry Pi platform was chosen for the communication between the robotic nodes. A wireless-enabled Raspberry Pi WO sends signals directly to the motors in order to control their rotations. For execution of the initial studies, a graphical user interface (GUI) was developed using Python within the Raspberry Pi platform in order to manually send rotation values to the motors of the nodes. Raspberry Pi's small size and open hardware serves as the current solution for the control unit for the robotic node.

Fig. 5: Strut passing sequence as seen through two physical prototyped robotic nodes with 28 × 28 × 500-millimeter struts

(a) Two nodes gripped two different fixed struts, (b) left node closes gripper, (c) left node rotates, (d) right node closes gripper, (e) left node opens gripper, (f) right node rotates

Conclusion
DISCUSSION

To overcome its current limitations and challenges of the future, the building industry requires a new generation of construction robots that can be deployed on-site, collaborate as teams at different scales and hierarchies, and respond to their environment. This requires a reimagining of the components and material systems that make up buildings. Showcasing the potential impact of developing architecture-specific robotic systems to create novel types of timber construction tectonics, this paper conceptualizes relevant possibilities to employ on-site distributed, purpose-driven machines for timber construction.

The paper explores a new design paradigm derived from the codesigning of distributed construction robots and a timber assembly system. It conceptualizes a shift from prefabricated, preplanned structures to building autonomously on-site structures with multiple simple, distributed robots. On-site construction can become a less invasive process in which small, relatively inexpensive, distributed robots can react to the environment in which they build. This solution may lend itself to a future construction paradigm where structures can be robotically built or changed adaptively with the arrangement and rearrangement of material.

FUTURE WORK

Future development of the project will explore further architectural potentials derived from the proposed system and will focus on the development of fully functional robotic nodes. Major considerations for their creation will include cost, weight, torque (as related to lifting capacity and gripping strength), communication, and power consumption. The system will be developed in such a way that it is open for incorporating additional functionality for machining and connecting the timber struts during the construction process. A working connection between timber struts would be important to demonstrate the potential for a fully autonomous in situ construction system. In a next step, a large-scale structure will be constructed using four robotic builders in order to demonstrate the architectural potentials of the systems. With this, specific control logics for the automation of numerous machines working toward a common goal will need to be developed.

Acknowledgments

The research was initiated as a part of the Integrative Technologies and Architectural Design Research (ITECH) program at the University of Stuttgart as a master's thesis project from the authors (see Leder and Weber 2018). The authors would like to thank Professor Jan Knippers for his guidance throughout the development of the project.

References

Antemann, David. 2014. "Seven Storey Wood Office Building in Zurich." *Detail*, nos. 1/2: 66–72.

Apolinarska, Aleksandra Anna, Ralph Bärtschi, Reto Furrer, Fabio Gramazio, and Matthias Kohler. 2016. "Mastering the Sequential Roof." *Advances in Architectural Geometry*: 240–59.

Giftthaler, Markus, Timothy Sandy, Kathrin Dörfler, Ian Brooks, Mark Buckingham, Gonzalo Rey, Matthias Kohler, Fabio Gramazio, and Jonas Buchli. 2017. "Mobile Robotic Fabrication at 1:1 Scale: The In Situ Fabricator." *Construction Robotics* 1, nos. 1–4: 3–14.

Gramazio, Fabio, Matthias Kohler, and Jan Willmann. 2014. *The Robotic Touch: How Robots Change Architecture*. Zurich: Park Books.

Krieg, Oliver David, Tobias Schwinn, Achim Menges, Jian-Min Li, Jan Knippers, Annette Schmitt, and Volker Schwieger. 2015. "Biomimetic Lightweight Timber Plate Shells: Computational Integration of Robotic Fabrication, Architectural Geometry and Structural Design." In *Advances in Architectural Geometry 2014*, edited by P. Block, J. Knippers, N. Mitra, and W. Wang, 109–25. Cham: Springer.

Leder, Samuel, and Ramon Weber. 2018. "Distributed Robotic Assembly System for In Situ Timber Construction." Master's thesis, University of Stuttgart.

Melenbrink, Nathan, and Justin Werfel. 2018. "Local Force Cues for Strength and Stability in a Distributed Robotic Construction System." *Swarm Intelligence* 12, no. 2: 129–53.

Robeller, Christopher, Andrea Stitic, Paul Mayencourt, and Yves Weinand. 2014. "Interlocking Folded Plate: Integrated Mechanical Attachment for Structural Wood Panels." *Advances in Architectural Geometry*: 281–94.

Yablonina, Maria, and Achim Menges. 2018. "Towards the Development of Fabrication Machine Species for Filament Materials." *Robotic Fabrication in Architecture, Art and Design*: 152–66.

Yoon, Yeoreum. 2006. "Modular Robots for Making and Climbing 3-D Trusses." PhD diss., Massachusetts Institute of Technology.

Figure Credits

Cooperative Robotic Fabrication of Timber Dowel Assemblies

Andreas Thoma, David Jenny, Matthias Helmreich, Augusto Gandia, Fabio Gramazio, and Matthias Kohler
ETH Zurich, Switzerland

Abstract — This research is developed within the Master of Advanced Studies in Architecture and Digital Fabrication program at ETH Zurich. This paper presents a novel constructive system made solely of wood, enabled by a cooperative robotic fabrication process. The constructive system builds on recent developments in dowel-laminated timber (DLT) as well as advances made in the field of digital fabrication. The paper demonstrates through three experiments how the design space of the dowel-laminated timber constructive system can be expanded, through the implementation of cooperative robotic arms, from purely planar geometries to more complex and curved ones. To connect the individual slats, two types of dowel connectors were tested: the fluted dowel and the dry dowel. The fabrication process employs a large robotic setup allowing for the prefabrication of full-scale building elements and enables a method of in place fabrication that counteracts the inaccuracy buildup that occurs during assembly. Two custom robot end-effectors for gripping and drilling timber slats are also introduced. Finally, a conclusion and outlook as to what the next steps in this research could be are presented.

Introduction

The research presented is developed inside the framework of the Master of Advanced Studies in Architecture and Digital Fabrication at ETH Zurich ("MAS ETH DFAB" n.d.) and is showcased in the Gradual Assemblies project for the Istituto Svizzero in Rome. Over the course of 10 weeks, the 17 students actively participated in the development of the project and its final construction.

Throughout the course, a novel method of layer-based construction and robotic fabrication that aims to enable the digital production of bespoke wood-only assemblies is developed (fig. 1). The construction method builds upon that of the Sequential Roof project (Apolinarska et al. 2016), where short timber slats are layered upon one another and nailed to the layer below. The timber dowel assemblies shift from a method of nail fastening to that of timber dowels, allowing for wood-only assembly.

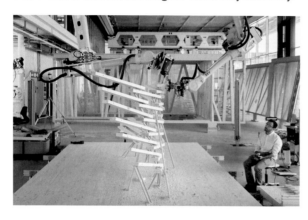

Fig. 1: Cooperative robotic fabrication of a timber dowel assembly

The production of wood-only architectural products such as dowel-laminated timber (DLT) is already widespread in Europe (Smith et al. 2018; Dangel 2016; Sandberg, Bulleit, and Reid 2000; "Holz100" n.d.; "Appenzellerholz" n.d.); they continue to grow in popularity due to their sustainable, economic, and machining properties. Still, these products have a limited design space, as they only allow for the production of planar components as the timber slats are always placed flush upon one another. The dowels in timber-dowel assemblies, however, are dimensioned not only to hold the slats together but also to transfer loads, in turn allowing for the introduction of a gap between the slats. The gap removes the requirement of planarity between slats, thus expanding the system's design space.
Cooperative robotic arms can be employed to efficiently fabricate bespoke spatial timber assemblies. The robotic arm in general allows for material to be supported at a precise position and orientation in space reference- and scaffold-free (Willmann et al. 2016). The second cooperating arm allows for the required connection detailing to be fabricated in place (Thoma et al. 2018; Ariza et al. 2018), reducing inaccuracies that accumulate throughout assembly.

Techniques
CONSTRUCTIVE SYSTEM
The introduction of cooperating robots into the fabrication process allows the timber slats to be spaced from one another, liberating the constructive system of DLT from purely planar geometry. The system is layer-based, consists of solely timber slats and dowels, and requires no additional adhesives or mechanical fasteners.

The assemblies consist of layers of timber slats, which are connected to one another via timber dowels (fig. 2). Each connection between two slats entails a pair of dowels that are orientated at differing angles from one another, mechanically locking the slats in place.

a   b   c   d

Fig. 2: Timber dowel assembly sequence: a. The first timber slat is placed in space. b. The connecting slat is placed. c. Two holes at varying angles are drilled through both slats. d. The connecting dowels are inserted.

The connection between the dowel and the slat is achieved purely through a tight fit friction joint (Blomberg 2006). Both the slats and the dowels are made of typical woods used in construction and can be sourced locally. Beech was the chosen wood for the dowels as it is a strong hard wood and its shrinking and expanding properties can be leveraged to negotiate a loose fit connection during assembly and later a tight fit for structural stiffness. The slats are made of spruce, as it is lightweight, economic, and can be easily machined.

To enable a tight-fit slat-to-dowel connection while considering the assembly process, two types of dowels are tested (fig. 3), the fluted dowel and the dry dowel (Grönquist et al. 2018). Both dowel types enable a tight-fit connection regardless of small inaccuracies occurring in either the dowel or the slat hole from manufacturing. Typically the fluted dowel is used so that glue can be applied throughout the connection without air pockets (see Parker 1959). Here the fluted dowel is used, as they first provide a cavity allowing the beech to compress after being inserted and cut into the surface of the softer spruce slat, thus achieving a tight fit. The dry dowel, on the other hand, is first oven-dried, allowing it to shrink in diameter and be easily inserted into the hole. The dowel then returns to its original diameter by absorbing moisture from its surroundings, forming a tight-fit connection.

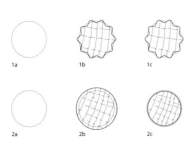

1a   1b   1c

2a   2b   2c

Fig. 3: Diagram of fluted and dry dowel connecting methods. 1a. The dowel hole in the slat. 1b. The fluted dowel profile overlaid with the slat hole. 1c. The fluted dowel after being inserted into the hole. 2a. The dowel hole in the slat. 2b. The dowel profile prior to being dried, overlaid with the slat hole. 2c. The dowel after being oven-dried and inserted into the slat.

FABRICATION METHOD

To fabricate the timber dowel assemblies, the cooperating robots execute three major processes, picking, placing, and in place drilling, which are repeated until the assembly is complete. The process is as follows: firstly, a slat is retrieved by one of the robots from a picking station. The slat is then maneuvered to a defined safe pose above the target pose. The position of the safe pose is parametrically adjusted according to the built members in order to maximize the assembly speed and avoid a collision. The robot then proceeds to move down vertically, placing the slat in its final position and supporting it in space for further processing. A second cooperating robotic arm then proceeds to drill through the robotically supported slat and the already fixed parts to create holes for the dowel connectors. The dowels are then inserted manually, fixing the slat in space. The placing robot can now release the structure and continue with additional slats.

Drilling the holes in place rather than at a different location enables the accuracy required for a tight-fit connection. This is especially important for slat connections that are close to one another, where the dowel connector cannot bend to account for slight inaccuracies in how well the holes line up with each other. In place drilling ensures that all of the holes line up regardless of inaccuracies that occur during prefabricating and positioning the slat, as would be the case if the holes were to be drilled into the slat at a different location than its final position in the structure.

Experimental Setup

MULTI-ROBOTIC PREFABRICATION SETUP

The research applies both manual and physical robotic prototyping, making use of ETH Zurich's Robotic Fabrication Laboratory (RFL). The setup (fig. 4) consists of two overhead six-axis industrial robotic arms, each attached to a base with three axes of movement, x, y, and z. As both robots are mounted to one gantry, they are unable to overtake one another. A timber platform mounted to the ground of the RFL serves as a base on which the timber dowel assemblies are fabricated and fixed using the same dowel connection method as between the individual slats.

END-EFFECTORS

Both robots are equipped with a task-specific end-effector (fig. 5). The robot used for positioning the slats is equipped with a gripping end-effector designed to grip 40 mm thick timber slats while the cooperating robot utilizes a spindle end-effector equipped with a timber drill.

The gripper is designed to grip a timber slat via friction. This is achieved via the implementation of pneumatic grippers with a gripping force of 660 N and sandpaper at the points of contact with the timber slat. The grippers have a total gripping stroke of 20 mm and long, thin gripping fingers allowing them to safely retrieve the slat and subsequently open without obstructing already placed slats either above or below.

The drill end-effector is primarily a spindle and a custom-made drill. The drill itself is made up of number of parts that allow large holes to be drilled into the timber slat at angles as shallow as 20°. To achieve this a pilot drill first enters the timber and acts as a mechanical guide for the Forstner drill to drill the full hole diameter for the dowel connector.[1]

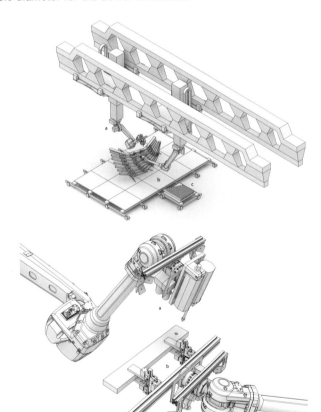

Fig. 4: Multi-robotic prefabrication setup:
a. Industrial robotic arm attached to a gantry
system. b. Timber platform. c. Pickup station.

Fig. 5: Both end-effectors working together
during assembly: a. Spindle end-effector.
b. Gripping end-effector.

Experiments

A first round of preliminary studies were undertaken to validate the constructive system prior to its full-scale implementation. In order to speed up the prototyping and test the validity of the constructive system in general, the first tests were constructed by hand but keeping the robotic process in mind. The detailing and dimensions of the individual members were always in 1:1 as the material properties of wood do not scale; the hygroscopic properties would play a key role in enabling a strong connection between parts.

EXPERIMENT 1: PROOF OF CONCEPT

The first experiment served as a proof of concept to see how the fabrication process would work and test whether the timber dowel assembly showed any structural integrity.

Using a single robot and a gripping end-effector, slats were placed and supported in space via jogging the robot to an arbitrary position after which a person drilled 12 mm holes through multiple slats at varying orientations using a handheld drill. With the aid of a mallet, tight-fitting 12.5 mm fluted dowels were then inserted manually into the holes, thus connecting the slats. The dowels were then cut to be flush with the slat's surface.

This experiment resulted in a stable assembly when bent and twisted by hand, proving that the constructive system in principle works. The gripper, however, did not provide enough support and needed to be adapted for subsequent experiments.

EXPERIMENT 2: FULL-SCALE ARCH

Building on the initial proof of concept, a 3 m tall arch (fig. 6) spanning approximately 3 m was constructed manually with the aid of support jigs. Here the goal was to test the structural integrity of the constructive system at a larger scale and to explore the possible geometric design freedom.

Two people working together constructed the arch in a layer by layer fashion as the robot later would. A plan of the arch was plotted on paper on the ground in 1:1 and acted as a guide for the pair of assembly jigs. The jigs were used alternatingly to support the slats at their respective position in space while a person proceeded to drill the holes required for the dowel connector. Here again, 12.5 mm fluted dowels were inserted into 12 mm holes.

Fig. 6: Full-scale arch after completion

The arch demonstrated a gradient of distributed material and although the individual slats were not as stable as when fixed using a flush connection, it could easily withstand a load of 80 kg hanging from its apex. The connections where dowels exceeded a slenderness ratio of 1:10 proved very weak, supporting little more than their own weight. The force required to hammer in the fluted dowel progressively destroyed the supporting jigs and exerted high amounts of force on the lower and already positioned slats thus shifting their position on occasion by multiple centimeters. This had both a negative effect on the structure's appearance and the assembly procedure, as the holes would no longer line up after one dowel had been inserted, requiring a lot of manual intervention.

EXPERIMENT 3: ROBOTIC FABRICATION OF PERGOLA
The final experiment primarily aimed to merge all of the knowledge gained from previous experimentation with the robotic fabrication process. It also tested the constructive system at an architectural scale and verified whether the use of a dry dowel connection could reduce inaccuracies during assembly when compared to the fluted dowel method.

Using the fabrication method described previously (fig. 7), two robotic arms worked together in conjunction with people to fabricate each element of the Gradual Assemblies pergola. Beech dowels measuring 24.0 mm in diameter[2] were dried in an oven over a period of 24 hours at 103 °C eliminating their moisture content (Grönquist et al. 2018), shrinking them to 23.5 mm in diameter.[3] The holes in both the assembly platform and the slats were drilled at 23.6 mm allowing for a tolerance of 0.1 mm during assembly. Immediately after inserting a dowel, water was sprayed directly onto the dowel, forcing it to expand and form a tight-fit connection with the timber slat. As 0 percent humidity cannot occur in a natural environment, this connection remains permanently a tight fit. To quantify the exact amount of shifting during assembly, pairs of points were measured on each slat for one of the partitions using the RFL tracking system (Stadelmann et al. 2019) throughout the assembly process.

The employment of the dry dowel proved to inflict less force on the slats than the fluted dowel method. The maximum deviation was 8.8 mm for the slats supported on both sides and 19.5 mm for the cantilevering slats (fig. 8). One slat cycle of picking, placing, drilling, and manually connecting with dowels took 10 minutes to complete. At approximately 1 m height, the partitions became unstable and required additional bracing dowels to stiffen the structure.

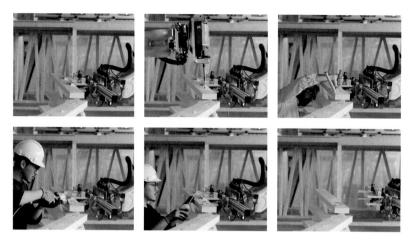

Fig. 7: Step-by-step fabrication process (left to right, top to bottom): 1. A slat is robotically placed at its final position. 2. Holes for the dowel connectors are drilled in place by the cooperating robot. 3. Dry dowels are inserted manually. 4. The dowels are cut to be flush with the slat's surface. 5. Water is applied to the dowels, accelerating their moisture gain and subsequent expansion. 6. The robot releases the slat.

Conclusion

The Gradual Assemblies project, comprising of 22 individual segments, 696 slats, and 2,701 dowels, was successfully produced in Zurich over a period of 19 days and subsequently mounted on-site in Rome. This research in general has opened the design space of DLT to curved surface geometries. Following its installation and inauguration in Rome at the beginning of June 2018, the timber began to show signs of weathering after a few weeks. A few isolated dowel connections, which were executed on-site manually, became dislodged. This is presumably due to the application of solitary dowels rather than pairs, but could also be due to the loss of swelling pressure in the dowels. The persistence of the swelling pressure could be improved by employing densified beechwood (Grönquist et al. 2018). The least curved and most freestanding area of the structure also showed signs of deflection and required additional support to halt the sagging. In order to make a more accurate assessment, the structural performance of this method of construction and the overall accuracy of fabrication needs to be quantified in more detail. During fabrication, the drilling robot induces high amounts of torque on the cooperating robot, thus limiting the maximum slat length. In place milling of the holes rather than in place drilling would, on the one hand, allow for greater slat lengths and, on the other, allow for the fabrication of varying hole sizes and shapes. The spindle used in these experiments had a low amount of torque, which was not ideal for drilling large holes in timber; a more powerful spindle would greatly increase tool life and allow for cleaner holes. The logistics required to process the dowels could be reduced by shifting from shrinkage via oven drying to shrinkage via mechanical compression. This in turn would allow for a swifter and more robot-driven connection process.

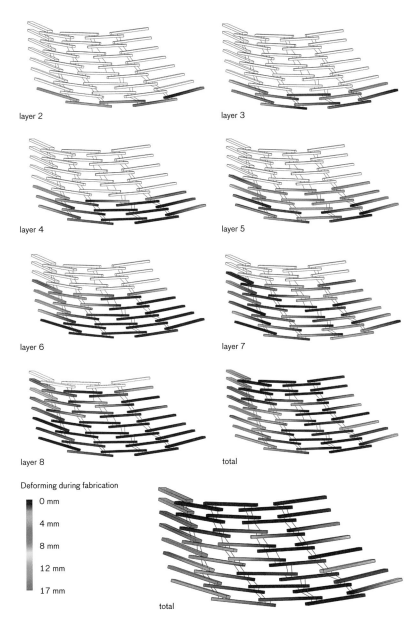

layer 2

layer 3

layer 4

layer 5

layer 6

layer 7

layer 8

total

Deforming during fabrication

0 mm

4 mm

8 mm

12 mm

17 mm

total

Fig. 8: Deviations from original position during assembly

Acknowledgments

The authors thank the MAS program director Hannes Mayer from Gramazio Kohler Research as well as the MAS students Sahar Barzani, Fernando Cena, Georgia Chousou, Alexander Enz, Moon Young Jeong, Frank Lin, Matteo Lomaglio, Ioanna Mitroupolou, Haruna Okawa, Rafael Pastrana, Francisco Regalado, Jetana Ruangjun, Jun Su, Nizar Taha, Yao Wang, Zong-Ru Wu and Angela Yoo. The authors would also like to thank Dr. Mario Rinke, Andrea Biancardi from the Chair of Structural Design, ETH Zurich; Adrian Brändli, Samuel Gross, Anna Schulz Seyring, and Orazio Battaglia from the Istituto Svizzero; Michael Lyrenmann and Philippe Fleischmann from the Robotic Fabrication Laboratory, ETH Zurich; Thomas Schnider, Dr. Robert Jockwer, and Nägeli Holzbau AG. This research was supported by the ETH Zurich, Istituto Svizzero, Gruner AG Basel, and Schilliger Holz.

References

Apolinarska, Aleksandra Anna, Ralph Bärtschi, Reto Furrer, Fabio Gramazio, and Matthias Kohler. "Mastering the 'Sequential Roof' Computational Methods for Integrating Design, Structural Analysis, and Robotic Fabrication." 2016. In *Advances in Architectural Geometry 2016*, edited by Sigrid Adriaenssens, Fabio Gramazio, Matthias Kohler, Achim Menges, and Mark Pauly, 240–58. Zurich: VDF.

"Appenzellerholz." Accessed February 26, 2019. https://www.naegeli-holzbau.ch/appenzellerholz.html.

Ariza, Inés, Ammar Mirjan, Augusto Gandia, Gonzalo Casas, Samuel Cros, Fabio Gramazio, and Matthias Kohler. 2018. "In Place Detailing: Combining 3-D Printing and Robotic Assembly." In *ACADIA 2018: Recalibration: On Imprecision and Infidelity*, edited by Philip Anzalone, Marcella Del Signore, and Andrew J Wit, 312–21. Dover: Acadia Publishing Company.

Blomberg, Jonas. 2006. "Mechanical and Physical Properties of Semi-Isostatically Densified Wood." PhD diss., Luleå University of Technology.

Dangel, Ulrich. 2016. *Turning Point in Timber Construction: A New Economy*. Basel: Birkhäuser.

Grönquist, Philippe, Thomas Schnider, Andreas Thoma, Fabio Gramazio, Matthias Kohler, Ingo Burgert, and Markus Rüggeberg. 2019. "Investigations on Densified Beech Wood for Application as a Swelling Dowel in Timber Joints." *Holzforschung* (January): 1–10. https://doi.org/10.1515/hf-2018-0106.

"Holz100." Accessed February 26, 2019. https://www.thoma.at/holz100/.

"MAS ETH DFAB." Accessed February 26, 2019. https://www.masdfab.com/program.

Parker, H. H. 1959. "Making Wood Dowels." *Popular Mechanics* (June): 957.

Sandberg, L. Bogue, William M Bulleit, and Elizabeth H. Reid. 2000. "Strength and Stiffness of Oak Pegs in Traditional Timber-Frame Joints." *Journal of Structural Engineering* 126 (June): 717–23. https://doi.org/10.1061/(ASCE)0733-9445(2000)126:6(717).

Smith, Ryan E., Gentry Griffin, Talbot Rice, and Benjamin Hagehofer-Daniell. 2018. "Mass Timber: Evaluating Construction Performance." *Architectural Engineering and Design Management* 14, nos. 1–2: 127–38. https://doi.org/10.1080/17452007.2016.1273089.

Stadelmann, Lukas, Timothy Sandy, Andreas Thoma, and Jonas Buchli. 2019. "End-Effector Pose Correction for Versatile Large-Scale Multi-Robotic Systems." *IEEE Robotics and Automation Letters* 4, no. 2 (April): 546–53. https://doi.org/10.1109/LRA.2019.2891499.

Thoma, Andreas, Arash Adel, Matthias Helmreich, Thomas Wehrle, Fabio Gramazio, and Matthias Kohler. 2018. "Robotic Fabrication of Bespoke Timber Frame Modules." In *Robotic Fabrication in Architecture, Art and Design 2018*, edited by Jan Willmann, Philippe Block, Marco Hutter, Kendra Byrne, and Tim Schork, 447–58. Cham: Springer.

Willmann, Jan, Michael Knauss, Tobias Bonwetsch, Aleksandra Anna Apolinarska, Fabio Gramazio, and Matthias Kohler. 2016. "Robotic Timber Construction: Expanding Additive Fabrication to New Dimensions." *Automation in Construction* 61: 16–23. https://doi.org/10.1016/j.autcon.2015.09.011.

Figure Credits

All images © by the authors

---

[1] The 1800 W Suhner spindle has a minimum RPM of 2500. The pilot drill is a 6 mm stepped drill, and the Forstner drill is a custom-turned 23.6 mm HSS Zobo drill coupled with a 150 mm extension.

[2] The dowels were manufactured to 24.0 mm in diameter as this was the closest standard size to the desired 20.0 mm that could be delivered within the given time frame. The accuracy of the diameter was observed to be ± 0.2 mm.

[3] This value also corresponds with the calculated value: 24 (dowel diameter in mm) × 0.00190 (beech wood factor) × 12 (change in humidity percentage) = 0.5472 mm.

Bending-Active Lamination of Robotically Fabricated Timber Elements

Bahar Al Bahar, Abel Groenewolt, Oliver David Krieg, and Achim Menges
Institute for Computational Design and Construction (ICD), University of
Stuttgart, Germany

Abstract — This paper presents a fabrication process that uses elastic bending as both a forming and a clamping process for robotically fabricating curved laminated timber elements. Bending a stack of wooden lamellae that is constrained at its endpoints causes differentiated shortening and lengthening, resulting in pressure between the lamellae. This pressure allows for glue-based lamination without the need for external clamping. This process makes use of the embedded forces resulting from bending, the ability to digitally precompute lengths and positions of wood lamellae, as well as the capability to precisely re-create these positions using an industrial robot arm.

Introduction

Conventional industrial fabrication processes of curved glue-laminated timber rely on external shaping methods such as jigs, formwork, and clamps, and sometimes involve subsequent subtractive milling. Thus, creating a range of unique shapes requires the fabrication of a series of jigs, or at the very least adjustments to an existing jig. This is also true in cases where robotic milling has been utilized as a means of forming curved wood components (Yuan et al. 2016, 203). In contrast, in the method proposed by the authors, jigs and formwork are substituted by robotic elastic bending and positioning, and clamping is replaced by the internal pressure created by controlling the shortening and lengthening of each lamella within one stack of lamellae.

In the proposed fabrication process, an industrial robot holds the end of a stack of wooden strips in place. The elastic bending of a strip with restrained ends results in a shape in energy equilibrium known as the elastica curve (Levien 2008, 4). As the robotic fabrication process does not require the use of any jigs or clamps, a large range of three-dimensional elastica shapes can be created without incurring additional cost or complexity. This project is situated within the broader context of material and process-driven architectural research enabled by computational design and digital fabrication, for which spatial timber structures form a suitable testing platform. As a possible application for the bent elements, a large, three-dimensional assembly is proposed, consisting of components in which the wood fiber directions are aligned at all connection points. Prototypes of the aforementioned elements were built to demonstrate the potential of the proposed system.

Background

Glue-laminated timber, or glulam, is one of the earliest engineered wood products and consists of multiple layers of wood glued together, all with the same grain direction (Hoadley 2001, 242). With an end-to-end and face-to-face joining processes, glulam allows the manufacture of structural elements with dimensions larger than those of the source tree. The production of straight glulam elements typically consists of several steps: drying, strength grading, finger jointing of ends, planing, laminating, and finishing (Ong 2015, 125). In the laminated stage, mechanical presses are often used. However, such presses are limited to the production of straight elements. To form curved elements, lamination processes rely on pressing the lamellae onto a formwork or a jig, and clamping them progressively along their length (Freas and Selbo 1954, 61–64). The time needed for such processes depends on the complexity and size of the jig, the placement of the lamellae and clamps, and on the number of elements that can be created without adjusting the jig. Therefore, despite the possibility of creating curvature, custom glulam elements are most economical when standardized and used in repetition such as in bridges (Ritter 1990, 4).

In comparison, the research presented provides a different approach to forming and pressing, both of which become automated and integrated. The integration between the precision of robotic positioning and the computational precalculation of distinctive elements allows the creation of unique components without increased complexity or extra processes or resources. As a result, fabrication time is reduced while maintaining the freedom of customization. The proposed fabrication method is based on material properties (in particular elasticity) in combination with computational design, bending simulation, and physical prototyping.

Such an integrative approach combining design, material, and processing constraints is not unprecedented, as can be seen in the ancient vernacular mud'hifs of southern Iraq, first constructed 5,000 years ago (Thesiger 1964), or more recently, in Frei Otto's Multihalle in Mannheim (Liddell 2015). Related research into material-based fabrication processes that increase efficiency and design freedom includes the PhD research by Tom Svilans (Svilans et al. 2017), "All Bent Out" (Schwartz et al. 2014), and the master's thesis by Martin Loucka at ICD, University of Stuttgart in 2014 (Loucka et al. 2014).

Another example where material simulation is used to create curved wooden elements is the fabrication method based on hygroscopic properties developed at the University of Stuttgart and ETH Zurich. By using a specific layout of initially flat wooden parts, the laminated elements will self-form to reach a precalculated curvature (Wood et al. 2018).

Contribution

We introduce a fabrication process for the robotic fabrication of bent wooden elements. The central step in this fabrication process consists of bending stacks of wooden lamellae beyond their calculated target elastica curve. Bending a stack of lamellae while holding their ends in such a way that no sliding occurs creates inter-lamella pressure, which is useful for the gluing process. The lamellae are precut to their individual lengths, with alignment holes at precalculated positions where the central lamella is the reference elastica curve. The further away lamellae are from the bending axis, the more they are either lengthened or shortened when the stack is elastically bent. Lamellae on the convex side are lengthened; lamellae on the concave side are shortened. To increase inter-lamella pressure, the outside lamellae are produced slightly shorter than their target length while the inside lamellae are produced slightly longer. In this process, the entire stack is bent such that the lamellae's dowel holes align (fig. 1). Constraining their position while bending exerts pressure toward the reference (central) lamella. In the proposed process, an industrial robot arm bends the lamellae while preventing sliding of the ends of the strips.

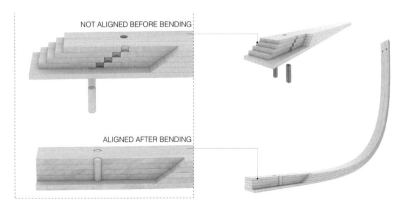

NOT ALIGNED BEFORE BENDING

ALIGNED AFTER BENDING

Fig. 1: In the prefabricated straight lamellae, holes are initially not aligned. After bending the stack of lamellae, the holes do align and dowels can be inserted.

Inter-Lamella Pressure

As the physical properties of a glued joint (as well as curing time) strongly depend on the pressure between parts that are glued together, critical questions
in the fabrication process are how much pressure is built up during bending,
and how is this pressure distributed along the length of the lamellae? In order
to test the effect of bending on pressure between lamellae, five InterLink
402 force-sensitive resistors were placed between two 2 cm lamellae of 2 mm
thickness to monitor the results of unequal lengthening. No twisting was
applied in these tests.

Using an Arduino microcontroller connected to Grasshopper (McNeel
2010), the pressure distribution was visually represented as a curve so that
the measurements could easily be observed during the bending process.
The measurements show that, as expected, pressure between the lamellae
gradually increases while the robot effector causes the lamellae to bend. Due
to natural variation in material properties, certain areas initially showed low or
no pressure, but during the bending process, pressure in all areas gradually
increased, leading to sensor readings in a range from 4.8 to 9.2 Newtons
in the final position (fig. 2). This corresponds to a pressure of approximately
0.038–0.073 N/mm².

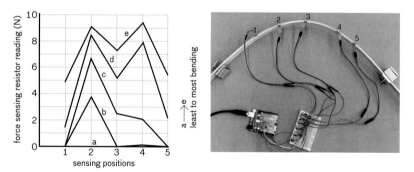

Fig. 2: (Left) Graph showing force-resistive sensor readings from least to most shifting of the holes;
(Right) Measurement setup

Length Control

Based on initial experiments, the authors assume that the proposed process
of bending-active lamination is effective for the production of double-curved
glue-laminated engineered timber due to the ability to precalculate the lengths
and positions of each wooden lamella. This precalculation is based on elastica
curves, which define the design space of this process. Besides the alignment
holes for the dowels, additional holes can be predrilled to facilitate the assembly of finished elements into components as well as the assembly of several
components into a larger structure. Additionally, by alternating the lengths of
the lamellae, finger joints can be created at the ends of the elements.

Precisely controlling the length of the lamellae eliminates the need for subtractive postprocessing such as CNC milling and drilling.

To customize the ends of the components while maintaining the ability to clamp them, a snap-off detail was designed. Using this detail, the ends of the lamellae remain the same length during the lamination process (fig. 3). This allows the length of the element to remain constant and be easily snapped off after the lamination is completed.

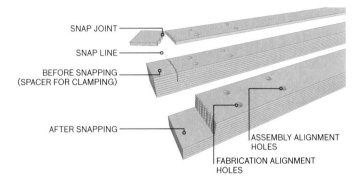

SNAP JOINT
SNAP LINE
BEFORE SNAPPING
(SPACER FOR CLAMPING)
AFTER SNAPPING
ASSEMBLY ALIGNMENT HOLES
FABRICATION ALIGNMENT HOLES

Fig. 3: Precut snap-off detail for finger joint: The top and bottom surfaces of the snapped part are covered to avoid adhesion.

Computational Design Workflow

A computational design workflow was developed to design a network of components and to simulate the bending and geometric formation of all curved elements, providing correct measurements and generating machine code for fabrication. Material properties including size, elasticity, and maximum bending and twisting radii helped define the design space of buildable elements (fig. 4). The workflow was implemented in Rhinoceros's Grasshopper environment, including the Kangaroo plug-in (Piker 2013).

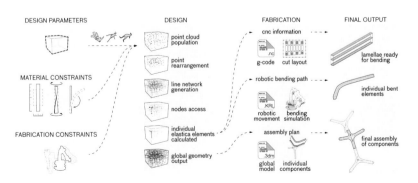

DESIGN PARAMETERS — DESIGN — FABRICATION — FINAL OUTPUT

MATERIAL CONSTRAINTS
FABRICATION CONSTRAINTS

point cloud population
point rearrangement
line network generation
nodes access
individual elastica elements calculated
global geometry output

cnc information
.nc
g-code   cut layout
robotic bending path
.KRL
robotic movement   bending simulation
assembly plan
.3dm
global model   individual components

lamellae ready for bending
individual bent elements
final assembly of components

Fig. 4: Overall project scope showing inputs and design stages, fabrication stages, and respective outputs

Fabrication

The lamellae are CNC-cut to their individual lengths, and in the same process holes are drilled into both ends of each lamella at the exact positions necessary to achieve the precalculated elastica curve. The holes are created in order to be able to hold the stack of lamellae using a pin that is part of the robotic effector.

For a fabrication prototype, lamellae of 3 × 100 × 1800 mm each were CNC-cut with accurate dimensions and hole positions in 10 minutes. Then, glue (Titebond III) was manually applied to the lamellae, which were then mounted onto the clamps in 15 minutes, and robotically bent into place in 2 minutes while dowels were inserted. The element was then left for 20 minutes to set (fig. 5), after which it was demounted. After 2 hours, the sides of the element were sanded in order to better reveal potential gaps in the lamination. The fabrication process is illustrated in figure 6.

Fig. 5: Fabrication setup consisting of a stationary clamp, a stack of lamellae, and a clamp that is attached to an industrial robot arm

The bending-active laminated elements could be fabricated with angles ranging from 10° to 120° measured between the two anchors where the lamellae are straight. The range of possible angles is dependent on the material dimensions and the number of strips grouped for bending.

Conclusion

This paper introduces a bending-active fabrication method for curved timber elements. Prototypical fabrication tests using a setup with an industrial robot shows that the method is viable (fig. 7), and measurements with pressure sensors confirmed that sufficient pressure is created between wood lamellae to realize a good glue bond with polymer glue.

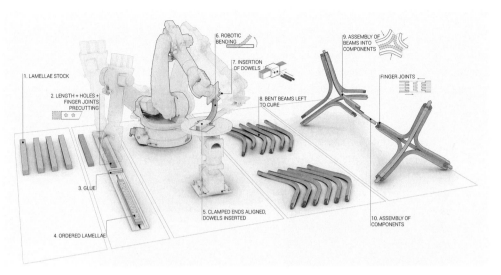

Fig. 6: Fabrication workflow showing the sequence from stock material to assembly

Fig. 7: Final prototypes of laminated elements

This method of forming bent laminated wood elements adds to the endeavors to utilize cross-disciplinarity between materiality, design, engineering, and fabrication in order to produce new forms and properties in ways that would have otherwise been difficult to achieve. This is due to the fact that the proposed method allows material properties to drive the process, necessitating computation for predictability, and robotic fabrication for precision and fabricability.

An architectural investigation demonstrates a potential component-based structural system for creating spatial arrangements with varying density (fig. 8). All elements in such a structure would be unique, but due to the proposed digital workflow encompassing both design and fabrication, geometric variety would not lead to increased fabrication complexity. The wood's fiber direction in this structure is largely aligned with the force flow.

This proof of concept opens a range of directions for further research, including a more detailed structural characterization of the proposed construction system and an investigation of increasing scale. However, even at its current state, this project demonstrates the high potential of combining computational design with material-informed fabrication methods.

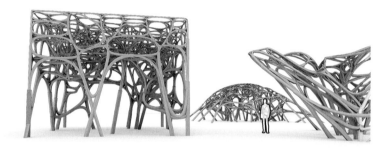

Fig. 8: Rendering of configurations that can be created using the proposed fabrication process

Acknowledgments

The work presented in this paper was part of a year-long individual master's thesis by Bahar Al Bahar under the supervision of Prof. Achim Menges, Oliver David Krieg, and Abel Groenewolt as part of the ITECH: Integrative Technologies and Architectural Design Research Master's Program at ICD/ITKE, University of Stuttgart, Germany.

References

Freas, Alan D'Yarmett, and Magnus Leonard Selbo. 1954. *Fabrication and Design of Glued Laminated Wood Structural Members.* Washington, DC: US Department of Agriculture.

Hoadley, R. Bruce. 2001. "Engineered Wood." In *Understanding Wood: A Craftsman's Guide to Wood Technology*, 242–43. Newtown, CT: Taunton.

Levien, Raph. 2008. *The Elastica: A Mathematical History.* EECS Department Technical Paper no. UCB/EECS-2008-103. Berkeley: University of California.

Liddell, Ian. 2015. "Frei Otto and the Development of Gridshells." *Case Studies in Structural Engineering* 4: 39–49. https://doi.org/10.1016/j.csse.2015.08.001.

Loucka, Martin, Oliver David Krieg, Oliver David, David Correa, and Achim Menges. 2014. "Robotically Fabricated Gluelam." Master's thesis (ITECH), ICD, University of Stuttgart.

McNeel, Robert. 2010. "Grasshopper Generative Modeling for Rhino." http://www.grasshopper3d.com.

Ong, C. B. 2015. "Glue-laminated Timber (Glulam)." In *Wood Composites*, ed. Martin Ansell, 123–40. Oxford: Woodhead Publishing.

Piker, Daniel. 2013. "Kangaroo: Form-Finding with Computational Physics." *Architectural Design* 83, no. 2: 136–37.

Ritter, Michael A. 1990. "Design of Beam Superstructures." In *Timber Bridges: Design, Construction, Inspection and Maintenance,* 4. Washington, DC: US Department of Agriculture, Forest Service, Engineering Staff.

Schwartz, Thibault, Joshua Bard, Madeline Ganon, Zack Jacobson-Weaver, Michael Jeffers, and Richard Tursky. 2016. "All Bent Out. …" In *Robotic Fabrication in Architecture, Art, and Design 2014*, edited by Wes McGee and Monica Ponce de Leon, 305–17. Cham: Springer.

Svilans, Tom, Paul Poinet, Martin Tamke, and Mette Ramsgaard Thomsen. 2018. "A Multi-scalar Approach for the Modelling and Fabrication of Free-Form Glue-Laminated Timber Structures." In *Humanizing Digital Reality: Design Modelling Symposium Paris 2017*, edited by Klaas De Rycke et al., 247–75. Singapore: Springer.

Thesiger, Wilfred. 1964. *The Marsh Arabs*. London: Longmans, Green & Co.

Wood, Dylan, Chiara Vailati, Achim Menges, and Markus Rüggeberg. 2018. "Hygroscopically Actuated Wood Elements for Weather Responsive and Self-forming Building Parts: Facilitating Upscaling and Complex Shape Changes." *Construction and Building Materials* 165: 782–91. https://doi.org/10.1016/j.conbuildmat.2017.12.134.

Yuan, Philip F., Hua Chai, Chao Yan, and Jin Jiang Zhou. 2016. "Robotic Fabrication of Structural Performance-based Timber Gridshell in Large-Scale Building Scenario." In *Acadia 2016: Posthuman Frontiers*, edited by Kathy Velikov, Sean Ahlquist, Matias del Campo, and Geoffrey Thün, 196–205. Dover, DE: Acadia Publishing Company.

Figure Credits

All images © by the authors

2 Timber Construction

Recycling of Cross-Laminated Timber Production Waste

Viktor Poteschkin[1], Jürgen Graf[1], Stefan Krötsch[2], and Wenchang Shi[1]

[1] FATUK, Technische Universität Kaiserslautern, Germany

[2] Architecture and Design Department, HTWG Konstanz – University of Applied Sciences, Germany

Abstract — The solid wood cross section of CLT in wall and ceiling has great advantages compared to light construction methods such as frame walls or beamed ceilings in terms of fire and sound protection and allows for high-quality visible wood surfaces. Because the calculated production waste, which can vary anywhere from 10 to 20 percent, increases production costs, the reuse of large amounts of production waste offers great potential to improve the efficiency, competitiveness, and environmental performance of the material. The usual thermal utilization with minimal added value simply cannot compensate for this.

The aim of this particular project is to develop a structural system of elements specifically tailored for their intended use only. At present, work is being done on two possible standardized ceiling constructions and a standardized wall construction.

Both concepts make use of the compressional strength of CLT combined with the tension strength of natural or glue-laminated timber. The basic module of the standardized components is interlocking CLT panels with loose tenons made of beech veneer plywood. The difference between ceiling and wall elements is the load transfer. Both ceiling constructions as components of high bending load use the CLT panels as pressure zone and glulam beams or board layers as tensile zone.

Introduction

Cross-laminated timber (CLT) is a high-performance building material for wall, ceiling, and roof elements. It is very dimensionally stable and reliably calculable. The solid wood cross section of CLT has great advantages compared to light construction methods such as frame walls or beamed ceilings in terms of fire protection and acoustic protection and allows high-quality visible wood surfaces. CLT has been approved by the building authorities in Germany since 1998. However, there is a lot of waste in the production of building components (wall/ceiling elements), as panels with production-related dimensions are cut to the required dimensions. In addition, the remainder material of window and door cutouts is noticeable on a large scale. Because the calculated production waste – which can vary anywhere from 10 percent (Züblin Timber) to 20 percent (Eugen Decker) up to 25 percent (smaller producers) – increases the production costs, the reuse of large amounts of production waste offers great potential to improve the efficiency, competitiveness, and environmental performance of the material. The usual thermal utilization with minimal added value simply cannot compensate for this. Not only is wood ideal for carbon capture and storage, but efficient and material saving usage of high-grade timber is to be striven as a substitute for mineral, metallic, and synthetic building materials, which contribute to the significant ecological impact of the building industry. Both structural and nonstructural (only spatial) wall or ceiling elements can be produced from residual pieces of CLT, such as composite ceiling elements with a compression zone of CLT cuttings and a layer of solid-sawn planks as a tension zone, bracing shear walls, or simple room dividers, all while simultaneously keeping the additional manufacturing costs at bay.

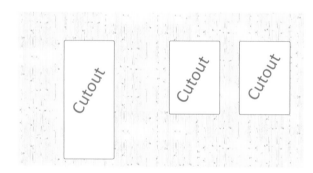

Fig. 1: Waste in production of CLT walls with openings

Research

The aim of this research project is to investigate how high-quality components can be obtained from production waste by engineering this expenseless material into efficient building elements. Window and door cutouts are the primary source of material for the research, since it is the only part of manufacturing waste that cannot be reduced or otherwise optimized. The most common are pieces of ca. 2 × 0.8 m (door cutout) and ca. 1.26 × 0.9 m (window cutout) of 106W-5 CLT panels (fig. 2). It is a 5-layer panel with top and middle layers with grain direction parallel to the longitudinal side of the panel (each 20 mm) and 2 transverse layers (each 23 mm). These two most common panel sizes were chosen as basic modules for the research. In order to fabricate these residual pieces in a simple and production-related manner into wall and ceiling elements, an interlocking joint for both structures is of major importance. One focus is to develop detachable connections for the transverse force and moment transfer, as well as form-fitting connections between the CLT pieces for bracing wall and ceilings. The resulting product is not used universally – that is primarily the domain of the original CLT. The aim of this particular project is to develop a structural system of elements specifically tailored for their intended use only. The resulting components are to be used in a standardized manner, which is why nesting patterns are developed for the production of the wall and ceiling elements.

Doors

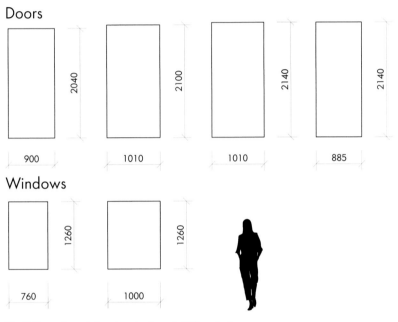

Fig. 2: Geometry and size of waste pieces in CLT production

The aim of this research project is not only to transform the production waste into new components as efficiently as possible, but to develop a new approach in dealing with wood as a resource. Instead of the common thermal use of conventional timber constructions after end of life, substantial reuse of the valuable material should be made possible. Recycling or reuse of conventional wooden components is often not profitable. In most cases reuse is impossible because the components are almost always a unique element tailored for a specific project. Therefore, the development of a standardized building system is needed, based on uniform elements that allows timber constructions to compete with steel and concrete. Although timber may not prevail in large engineering structures such as bridges and stadiums, the field of high-rise construction seems promising.

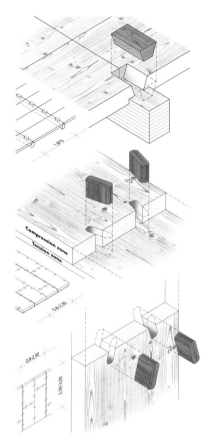

Compression zone
Tension zone

Fig. 3: Proposed wall and ceiling constructions

This research project makes a proposal for a reversible modular design. CLT waste serves as the basis for the research project, but the results are designed to enable a transfer of the developed solutions back into the industry of CLT production.

Standardization is required by the fact that CLT pieces have different dimensions; thus, optimal element dimensions must be found in order to use the most production waste. Planning and logistics are simplified if the components have the same size and connection details. Parts can be ordered on demand and reused in case of the demolition or modification of the building. Hence the requirement of reversibility – components must be removable with little effort so they can be reused at a new location. Profitability also is a major requirement, since disproportionate cost of reuse to the cost of production will lead to a loss of the idea of sustainability.

At present, work is being done on two possible standardized ceiling constructions and a standardized wall construction (fig. 3). There are two main approaches for ceiling elements: a puzzle-like structure of small CLT pieces laminated onto a layer of solid-sawn planks, manufactured into a large wall-to-wall-spanning ceiling plate; and a beam-plate structure, meant to be assembled on-site. Both concepts make use of the compressional strength of CLT combined with the tension strength of natural or glue-laminated timber. The basic module of the standardized components is interlocking CLT panels with loose tenons made of beech veneer plywood. The difference between ceiling and wall elements is the load transfer. Both ceiling constructions, as components of high bending load, use CLT panels in the pressure zone and glulam beams or board layers in the tensile zone. The compression-loaded and exposed-to-low-bending-load wall components are designed without additional tension zone. The ceiling and wall constructions are prefabricated in the factory as transport-ready panels from 80 cm to 2.50 m in width (depending on the project), which are assembled on the construction site into walls and ceilings. The interlocked arrangement of loose tenons creates a wedge effect, which form-fittingly closes the joints between the elements, which is of utmost importance for the pressure force transmission within the elements. Subsequently, the CLT is glued to a board layer in the hydraulic press. The number and length of the elements depends on the required spans and lengths of CLT panels. The span for ceilings with board layers in the tension zone is 4.5–6 m, the height of the wall elements 2.5–3.5 m.

For ceiling spans over 6 m, beam ceilings are examined (fig. 3, top). The CLT panels are inserted between and screwed onto the glulam beams with the help of wooden wedges made of beech veneer plywood. The load-bearing behavior can be adjusted by the beam height. The cutting of the CLT is carried out at the factory; the assembly with the beam layer takes place at the factory or on-site.

To fully benefit from available material, a parametric design script was written in Grasshopper that calculates the number and the required geometry of the individual elements for the desired ceiling and wall dimensions on the basis of available CLT waste panels. This script can be sent to a CNC-controlled processing unit, which manufactures the basic modules from the door and window cutouts during production of the actual wall elements. The script is constantly updated and developed with the progress in the research and development of the ceiling and wall constructions.

In order to process the waste efficiently, we suggest processing it directly during the production of the actual wall elements (fig. 4). In this case, the usable remainder piece is first equipped with all features, such as transverse force joints and pockets for the loose tenons, while it is still connected to the CLT panel in order to eliminate the need for clamping of the work piece. The remainder is then cut free – processing for further operations is thus completed. As a last step, the finishing of the actual door or window opening is performed.

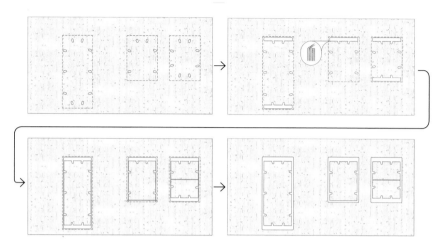

Fig. 4: Production sequence

If the delay in production due to the additional work steps is inadmissible, we suggest that the machining of work pieces be done with a robotic arm outside the processing unit. However, this will mean the extra effort of clamping and positioning.

The position of the joints of the wall and ceiling elements composed of individual panels influences the transverse force–carrying capacity and the bending resistance. The dimensioning of the composite slab structures can therefore not be the same as the load-bearing capacity of nonjointed standard cross-laminated timber constructions. The joints are to be arranged in relation to the transverse force and bending moment. For this purpose, the shear capacity is to be determined experimentally in the 4-point bending test as well as the bending resistance of the total cross section. The aim is to achieve at least the same mechanical properties as conventional CLT plates. This would greatly simplify the dimensioning of the composite panels, since the calculations for the manufacturer's standard CLT panels can be used for the composite panels as well.

Experimental Determination of the Transverse Force and Bending Load Capacities

For transverse force transmission, a staggered joint is added along the adjacent edges of the CLT panels. The experimental setup for determining the transverse force carrying capacity is shown in figure 5.

The test specimen consists of two parts. Part A is clamped horizontally; Part B is positioned between Part A and a vertical steel angle, so that Part B can only slide vertically along the steel angle under the force of the test machine. The contact surface is angled in such a way that the transverse force transfer is ensured via pressure diagonals through the contact surface (fig. 7). The steel angle prevents Part B from sliding off the contact surface.

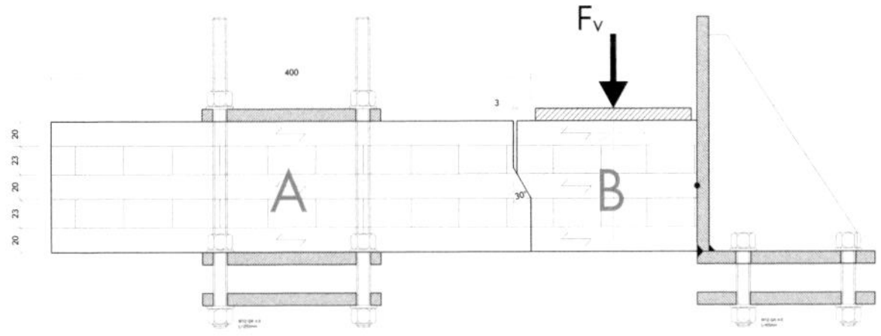

Fig. 5: Experimental setup for the determination of the lateral force carrying capacity – shear test

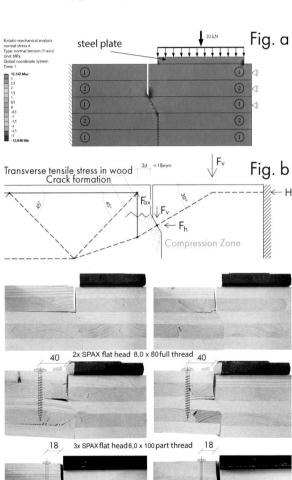

Fig. 6: Tension analysis (a) and truss model (b) of CLT

Fig. 7: Shear test – deformations and fracture patterns

Transverse tensile stresses in wood construction reduce the load capacity. As expected, high transverse tensile stress occurs in Part A in the upper region of the oblique notch. Truss models show that vertical tensile forces occur in Part A in the connection area between Parts A and B, which leads to transverse tensile stresses in the wood and thus to component failure (fig. 7, top). The implementation of tension patterns (fig. 6a) in framework models (fig. 6b) shows that reinforcement at the location of the vertical tensile stress allows an increase in tensile strength. Therefore, in a further step, screw reinforcements are introduced to increase the transverse force capacity. This results in the following experimental setups for vertical force transmission in transverse force joint, which are examined for their effectiveness:

1. Unreinforced CLT cross sections
2. CLT cross sections with transverse tensile reinforcement with flat head, full-thread screws, and larger edge distance
3. CLT cross sections with transverse tensile reinforcement with partial thread flat head screws and minimal edge distance

The unreinforced specimens reach a mean value of 104 kN (adjusted for 1 m wide CLT) before brittle transverse tensile failure occurs between the second and third board layers (fig. 7, top; fig. 8, green curve).

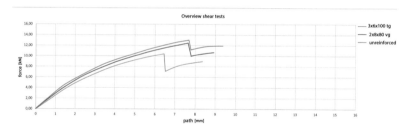

Fig. 8: Overview shear tests on 10 cm wide CLT specimens. Increase of carrying capacity in reinforced cross sections.

To counteract this, a series of tests with reinforced cross sections was carried out. The crack due to transverse tensile failure also occurred here, but with a less brittle behavior and at 10 percent higher force (fig. 7, middle; fig. 8, brown curve). In addition to transverse tensile failure, a combination of shear and transverse tensile failure in the fourth layer occurred, since the flat head screws with 80 mm length were too short – the screw must reach the lowest board layer – and the edge distance with 5d was too large. Since transverse tensile failure still significantly affects strength, an additional series of tests were performed on samples reinforced with partial thread screws spaced at 3d from the edge of the transverse force joint. Since the partial thread creates a pretension under the screw head and compresses the first, second and third layers, transverse tensile failure occurred only in a few specimens. Cracking can be avoided in this way, and a pronounced ductile behavior of the joint with 18 percent increased vertical load is achieved (fig. 7, bottom; fig. 8, blue curve). This concludes that the problem of low transverse tensile strength in cross-laminated timber can be solved by reinforcement with partial thread screws.

Experimental Determination of Bending Carrying Capacities

Three CLT waste panels equipped with a transverse force joint were assembled to form a panel element (fig. 9). The arrangement of additional board layers in the bending-tension zone produces panel elements suitable for uniaxial loads. The bending strength of the recycled CLT panels is therefore determined in 4-point bending tests on 200 mm wide CLT panels in accordance with DIN EN 408. To obtain a direct comparison of the load-bearing behavior, composite beams with the same test piece length, pressure points, and bearing distances are tested and compared with the original CLT panel 106W-5.

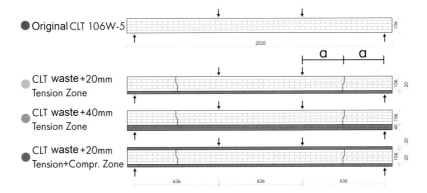

Fig. 9: Specimen types for 4-point bending tests

Bending Tests on Original CLT Panels

In bending tests on the original CLT panel strips, two types of failure occurred: shear and tensile failure. Tensile failure occurred only in the test specimens with finger joints in the form of brittle fiber tear in the lower tension-stressed lamellae. Since this behavior is not typical for cross-laminated timber – the test specimen width was decisive – the test results are only to be considered as a reference for the following tests.

Fig. 10: 4-Point bending test – deformations and fracture patterns.

Bending Tests on Composite CLT Panels

In the case of the bending beams composed of CLT waste panels, the transverse force joint of the individual CLT pieces is reinforced with Spax 6×100 mm partial thread flat head screws.

Fig. 11: 4-point bending test on CLT waste composite with additive tension zone. High residual carrying capacity due to screw reinforcement in the joint between the CLT plates.

The testing of specimens shows that the necessary full surface adhesion between the CLT and board layer was not achieved. The reason for this is the large tolerance in the thickness of the CLT panels. These have a nominal dimension of 106 mm, but the measured plates vary between 103 and 107 mm in thickness. CLT panels are milled from above with an identical profile for transverse force transmission joint; one of the panels is turned over, and then both are joined together. If the panels deviate from their nominal dimensions, a gap is created between the milled surfaces (fig. 12). This has the consequence that the required precision is not achieved during milling and gluing and the force transmission is compromised.

To counteract this, the CLT waste panels for the subsequent test specimens are planed to a uniform thickness prior to milling.

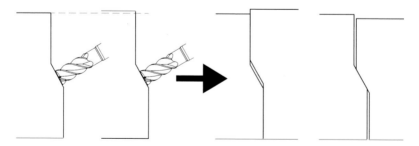

Fig. 12: Differences in CLT thickness cause manufacturing inaccuracies.

Conclusion

Composite panel elements made of cross-laminated timber provide a possibility of cascading use of production waste, possibly due to transverse force joints and additional board layers in the tension zone. The experimental determination of the bending resistance has shown that the composite panel elements made of cross-laminated timber and glued board layers can achieve a comparable or higher load capacity than the original CLT panel.

The best results, with 157 percent of the original CLT load, were achieved with two board layers (40 mm) as a tensile zone (fig. 13, orange curve).
In the course of the production and testing of the test specimens, thickness tolerances of the waste panels were discovered, which can lead to inaccuracies in the milling and bonding of the composite elements and, in the end, to the impairment of the load-bearing properties. The ceiling elements with transverse force joint are thus possible only with exact production.

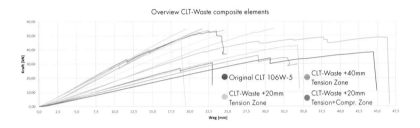

Overview CLT-Waste composite elements

Original CLT 106W-5
CLT-Waste +20mm Tension Zone
CLT-Waste +40mm Tension Zone
CLT-Waste +20mm Tension+Compr. Zone

Fig. 13: Overview diagram of the bending carrying capacity of the CLT waste composites

It requires additional research of the economic factors such as high production costs, storage and sorting of the CLT waste, and possible delay of the main production of cross-laminated timber; therefore the economics of CLT composites production are highly dependent on the production conditions of the respective manufacturers.
Innovation lies in material substitution through the replacement of energy-intensive construction products. However, the primary energy requirement and thus the production costs of the residual wood products from CLT are low, since pretreatment, dismantling, and mechanical and chemical treatment are not required in the recycling chain. The cost-effective, high-quality material use improves the competitiveness of the many German manufacturers of cross-laminated timber elements as well as those of its customers, the carpenters.

Fig. 14: CLT wall high-quality visible wood surfaces

References

DIN EN 408:2010+A1:2012.

Eugen Decker Holzindustrie KG. www.eugen-decker.de; ETA-12/0327
28.08.2017.

Schmidt, Tobias, and Hans Joachim Blaß. 2015. "Längsschubverbindungen
in den Schmalseiten von Brettsperrholzelementen." In *21. Internationales
Holzbau-Forum IHF 2015*, 11–12. Biel: Forum-Holzbau.

Figure Credits

All images and graphics © Viktor Poteschkin, Technische Universität
Kaiserslautern

Funding: Forschungsinitiative Zukunft Bau, SWD-10.08.18.7-17.13

Textile Architecture for Wood Construction

Steffi Silbermann[1], Jannis Heise[2], Daniel Kohl[2], Stefan Böhm[2], Zuardin Akbar[3], Philipp Eversmann[3], and Heike Klussmann[1]

[1] Bau Kunst Erfinden, University of Kassel, Germany

[2] Department for Cutting and Joining Manufacturing Processes, University of Kassel, Germany

[3] Department for Experimental and Digital Design and Construction, University of Kassel, Germany

Abstract — Our project is an investigation of the design, shaping, simulation, manufacture, and construction of lightweight load-bearing structural components made of wood-based continuous-fiber textiles. Our aim is to innovatively adapt established concepts in wood construction, such as panelized construction and wood framing, to textile construction. We are developing a continuous filament out of solid wood that can be made into wood-textile structures. Textiles have many advantages: excellent suitability for light construction, versatility of form and function, refined and tested manufacturing and processing technologies, and a characteristic, ever-changing, deeply familiar aesthetic of parallel and crossing threads. Our ultimate goal is to develop a material-efficient, functional, and aesthetically appealing architecture based on solid-wood textiles.

Introduction

Textile structures have been known for millennia. Over time, a variety of textile construction principles have been developed for building cohesive structures out of long, thin, flexible elements. For most of that time, textiles were made primarily by hand, but with the advent of industrial textile production, highly complex automated processes have become available, which are capable of joining different types of fibers to produce a range of textile structures (Cherif et al. 2011).

Such structures are of interest for construction, where they are used as semifinished products, primarily as the reinforcing element in fiber-reinforced plastics. In these materials, textiles (typically flat fabrics) are impregnated with plastic, providing stiffness once the plastic has hardened. Before it hardens completely, the composite can be formed into two- or three-dimensional shapes, taking advantage of the flexibility of textile structures. The reinforcing fabrics can be prepared for shaping (or even preshaped) during the manufacturing process. The combination of a rigid, pressure-resistant plastic matrix with the tensile strength of fiber creates composites with an excellent ratio of strength to weight.

Continuous-fiber textiles are especially interesting since they can be used to produce high-performance textile fabrics that can be designed for specific applications and formed into complex shapes (Cherif et al. 2011). Such fabrics are made from fine, flexible continuous fibers, typically made of plastic, glass, or carbon, as well as flax and sisal. Thanks to their lightweight design, such textile-based structural elements are seeing increasing use – for example, in vehicle manufacturing. By reducing weight, they produce greater fuel efficiency while still providing the strength required in such materials (Branchenbericht 2015).

Between 1956 and 1970, architects made a number of unsuccessful attempts to establish new construction methods using fiber-based materials (Knippers 2007). Now, more than forty years later, those attempts are being revived and adapted to robot-aided manufacturing by the Institute of Building Structures and Structural Design (ITKE) and the Institute for Computational Design and Construction (ICD), both in Stuttgart. Two experimental pavilions made of wound carbon and glass fibers impregnated with epoxy resin, built in 2014–15 and 2016–17, displayed the effectiveness of fiber-composite structures, as well as a textile aesthetic unusual in the building context (Knippers and Menges 2015, 2017).

Lightweight materials can help reduce energy consumption, and therefore CO_2 emissions, not only in use, but also during transport before or after use. The global reduction of CO_2 in all areas of human culture is an extremely high-priority goal in the twenty-first century (UNEP 2018). The energy consumed by a textile structure depends not only on its weight, but also on the environmental footprint of the fiber type used. Since the fibers currently used in light construction are predominantly mineral or petrochemical in origin and require a great deal of energy to produce, there is a strong interest in investigating the capabilities of textile structures made from previously unused fiber materials that are more environmentally sustainable.

Architecture – a field with little experience of textile-based structural components thus far – also presents an opportunity to discover and utilize other architecture-specific advantages of textile structures. Under the heading "Textile Architecture for Wood Construction," our project explores the possibilities of solid-wood-based textile construction, combining the outstanding environmental performance of wood with the exceptional structural potential of textile structures.

Research
SOLID WOOD MONOFILAMENT

Wood-weaving and the use of short wood fibers and drawn wood are recorded from the nineteenth and early twentieth centuries (Purfürst 1880; Klausegger et al. 2016). Willow withes have been used by basketmakers for centuries, providing durable strips for weaving. In the 1980s, the Forestry Institute of the East German Academy of Agronomic Sciences in Eberswalde attempted to produce continuous fibers from whole willow withes for use in looms (Gutwasser 1990), but German reunification put an end to those efforts. Today, continuous veneer ribbons are produced to conceal the edges of wood-composite panels, and can also be used in artisanal weaving (Janson 2001).

Building on the knowledge of basketmakers, we are using split willow withes as the raw material for a solid-wood monofilament that can be used in the large-scale automated manufacturing of high-performance structural elements. A monofilament is a continuous fiber consisting of a single filament, typically more than 0.1 mm in diameter and effectively unlimited in length. Split willow withes are thin strips about 1.5 m long that are irregular in cross section, measuring up to 8 mm wide and 1.5 mm thick. They are usually obtained from one-year-old withes using a cutting device that splits them off from the outer surface of the branch. Split willow withes are extremely flexible and tolerant of the bending required of continuous fibers (fig. 1).

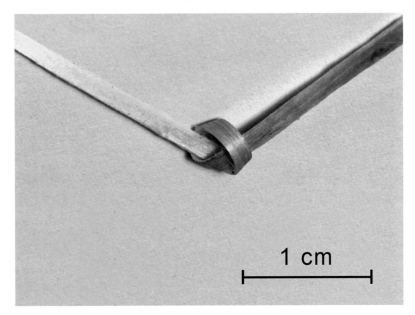

1 cm

Fig. 1: Split willow withe, knotted while wet (© Bau Kunst Erfinden / Silbermann)

The morphology of willow withes is naturally variable. Because growing withes are wider at the bottom than at the top, when they are sliced longitudinally the narrow ends of the resulting split withes are about 25 percent narrower than the wide ends. The straightness of the whole withes, which can vary dramatically in their curvature, carries over to the split withes (figs. 2 and 3). After splitting and stripping, the sides, top, and bottom remain wavy. Average thickness is about 1 mm, with a standard deviation of just under 19 percent.

All this means that the cross section varies over the entire length of the split withe, with tolerances of less than a millimeter. Standardizing the cross-sectional shape would be beneficial for all subsequent steps in the automated manufacturing process. Preliminary studies have also shown that standardization can increase the tensile strength of the withe's cross section in comparison to split-but-otherwise-unmodified withes. In addition, standardizing the thickness or width of the split withes has been observed to produce more uniform tensile strength and maximum tensile-force ratings. Furthermore, one of our aims is to produce different monofilaments in a range of standard cross-sectional shapes, which can then be manufactured into textiles with varying characteristics.

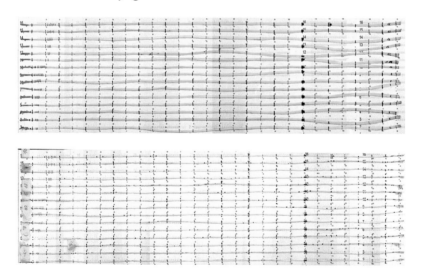

Fig. 2: Unmodified split willow withes, ca. 120 cm long (© Bau Kunst Erfinden)

Fig. 3: The withes from figure 2, reduced to 3.1 mm wide (length unchanged) (© Bau Kunst Erfinden)

Our first step has been to develop and compare several methods of standardizing the width and thickness of the split withes. Since these are quite small in cross section, generally measuring less than 8 × 1.5 mm, and tend to twist and bend during processing, familiar techniques for modifying the width and thickness of wood have been modified to account for these characteristics. This has primarily involved the development of semiautomated tools of our own construction.

To modify the width, we are experimenting with saws and shapers. Using a double-sided shaping tool on unstandardized withes measuring 120 cm long and 4–7.5 mm wide, we have succeeded in obtaining a uniform width of 3.1 mm, with variations of less than 0.1 mm, in over 80 percent of our test pieces. We are also conducting comparative analyses to assess the quality of the material removed. The object here is to prevent frayed edges and avoid defects that arise from common flaws in wood, such as knots. With careful handling of the workpiece, it is also possible to make maximum use of the material by following the curve of the withe with the shaper.

To combine individual withes into a continuous fiber, we have analyzed classic woodworking joints and adapted them to the characteristics and demands of willow withes to develop a suitable mechanical process for joining split withes end to end. The focus here is on developing the technology and geometry of the joint, taking into account influences such as residual moisture from the gluing process and aging caused by warmth, moisture, and other environmental factors. This process takes place in tandem with the sectional processing.

Split willow withes are available in Germany from a number of different countries. We have conducted a comparative analysis of material originating from Poland and Spain. Not only were the Spanish withes a lighter, more characteristic willow color, they had fewer flaws and broke much less frequently during initial manual processing tests. They were also about 1 mm wider on average (Silbermann n.d.). They have thus become our choice for further testing.

Besides disparities in width, the split withes also display varying textures and visual qualities that could potentially come into play when they are processed into monofilaments or textiles. These differences involve the integrity, straightness, width, flatness, and color of the material. We are developing a grading system for split willow withes based on these characteristics. By constantly shifting perspectives between classifying the raw material and modifying its width and thickness via the processes we are developing, outlined above, we can refine our grading criteria to better understand and exploit the relationships between raw material, processing, and monofilament performance.

Making Textiles out of Solid-Wood Monofilament

Our novel wood monofilament is next formed into textile fabrics (figs. 4 and 5). The most important types of fabrics for us are woven, laid, wound, and braided constructions. These possess the greatest strength, because the

fibers in them lie flat. Variations in the cross-sectional shape of the monofilament have a direct effect on the qualities of the textile. For example,
monofilament that is wider and thicker produces a textile that is coarser in
texture, stiffer, and faster to manufacture, whereas a fabric woven of thin
and narrow monofilament is much more delicate and laborious to produce
but much stronger in composites.

Using textiles as load-bearing elements requires a fundamental understanding of their structural connections and resulting properties. Each of the four
fabrication methods mentioned has its own unique parameters that affect the
textile's strength. These parameters (such as fiber spacing, weave pattern,
fiber direction, and fiber density) interact both with one another and with the
monofilament cross section, which can be adjusted as needed. To discover,
define, and consistently achieve promising combinations, we are investigating the basic characteristics of textile wood-monofilament constructions,
including both biaxial (anisotropic and orthotropic) and unidirectional structures. The parameters can be varied to obtain stiffness as well as pliability
in different component geometries. These technical-functional properties
can also be studied and specified in combination with the aesthetic qualities
of the wood-textile components to create structures that are both functional
and attractive.

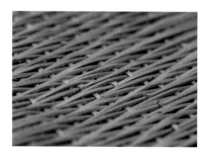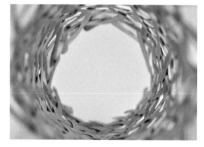

Fig. 4: Woven fabric made from solid-wood monofilament (© Bau Kunst Erfinden / Khorasani)

Fig. 5: Braided tube made from solid-wood monofilament (© Bau Kunst Erfinden / Rauch)

To make textile fabrics out of solid-wood monofilament, we plan to use established textile manufacturing processes and robots. The goal is an industrial,
fully automated process. Although willow monofilament is unusually flexible
in comparison to other solid-wood products, it is still relatively stiff compared
to more common fibers. Therefore, our processing methods must be adapted
to this new material. One of the first steps is to develop appropriate spools
on which the monofilament can be wound and transported (fig. 6). Other
adaptations will be necessary to feed the material into weaving machines or
robots.

A spool we have developed for weaving is 13 cm in diameter and 18 mm wide (fig. 7). It can hold approximately 15 m of 1 mm thick willow monofilament. To hold longer lengths, the diameter can be increased. This results in large spools, meaning that sufficient space must be provided on and around the machines used in processing. Normally, the warp beam of a loom holds all the fibers running lengthwise; the loom we are using has duplicate warp beams positioned at various heights. The fibers from these beams converge on one level to form the warp, into which the weft fibers are woven.

Fig. 6: Solid-wood monofilament wound on a spool for transport (© Bau Kunst Erfinden)

Fig. 7: Solid-wood monofilament on a spool adapted for weaving (© Bau Kunst Erfinden)

Simulation

A special challenge for digital simulations is to analyze and optimize the monofilament in terms not only of its material composition and joinery, but also of its conceptual applications and workability on the object or the architecture level. These discrete criteria place thoroughly different demands on the simulation technology. The goal here is to investigate the parameterizability of the joint geometry and implement an appropriate simulation method, using the finite element method and dynamic relaxation simulation, and ultimately developing a general material simulation model for strength-optimized textiles made from solid wood monofilament.

The weaving technique we have developed for this research is based on matrix multiplication and defines a fundamentally binary structure: When the weft interlaces with the warp, every warp thread is either up or down. We have developed an interface based on Grasshopper (fig. 8), a visual scripting plug-in for Rhinoceros 3D, to build a digital twin to help with modeling and organizing a material data space based on different matrix configurations. This data space will support the early design process by enabling us to develop different variations of patterns on a single surface or structure. A single pattern is developed using an interactive matrix editor as an instance of the object, with particular attributes related to pattern parameters such as matrix domain, pattern binary, and willow size, as well as parameters for later physics simulation, to be used in pattern form-finding. This model will work as a micro-scale material-system model that will then be calibrated with experimental test results. A multiscalar modeling approach will be investigated to develop a robust design tool with the flexibility to adjust the parameters of various details. The use of a GPU-accelerated application will also provide opportunities for further high-resolution modeling during the macro-scale design phase.

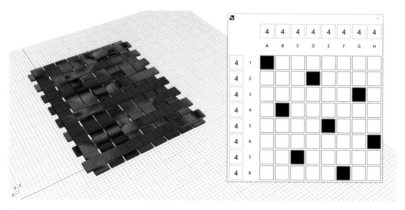

Fig. 8: Digital representation of a weaving binary pattern in Rhinoceros 3D and the interactive matrix editor (© Department for Experimental and Digital Design and Construction)

Conclusion

Our project is making possible the automated manufacturing of solid-wood textiles and harnessing the potential of their light weight, ability to be shaped, and aesthetic appeal. The key element is the continuous solid-wood fiber we are using: a novel monofilament made from willow withes, a rapidly renewable resource in Europe. By adapting existing textile manufacturing processes to the new material once development of the monofilament is complete, we can produce semifinished wood-based textile products for further processing into high-performance composites for construction. Because textile construction is a form of joinery, other fiber types can be added to the wood as well – for example, stabilizing or functional fibers – thus laying the foundation for a wide variety of possible wood-textile-based structural elements. These can be refined in an iterative process involving concepts from architecture, vehicle design, and product design, and connections between these areas can be developed as well. We are merging the aesthetics and structural advantages of textiles with those of wood, giving rise to a new formal language for wood construction – the language of textile tectonics.

References

Commerzbank. 2015. "Branchenbericht Technische Textilien." *Industrieverband Veredelung, Garne, Gewebe, Technische Textilien e.V.* Accessed December 10, 2018. http://www.ivgt.de/de/home/details/article/-0c83fa017a.html.

Cherif, Chokri. 2011. *Textile Werkstoffe für den Leichtbau*. Berlin-Heidelberg: Springer.

Gutwasser, Frank. 1990. "Chemische Vergütung und Verklebung von Weidenflechtmaterialien mit technologischen Konsequenzen für den Verarbeitungsprozess." Thesis, Akademie der Landwirtschaftswissenschaften der DDR, Institut für Forstwissenschaften.

Janson, Manfred. 2001. "Flechtmaterialstreifen zur Herstellung eines Flächenflechtwerkes oder eines Formflechtwerkes." Publication no. DE 201 20 158 U1.

Klausegger, Anton. n.d. "Holzdraht." *Atterwiki*. Accessed December 12, 2018. www.atterwiki.at/index.php?title=Holzdraht.

Knippers, Jan. 2007. "Faserverbundwerkstoffe in Architektur und Bauwesen." *Themenheft Forschung Leichtbau* 3: 58–68.

Knippers, Jan, and Achim Menges. 2015. "ICD/ITKE Forschungspavillon 2014-15." *itke*. Accessed December 12, 2018. www.itke.uni-stuttgart.de/de/archives/portfolio-type/icditke-research-pavilion-2014-15.

Knippers, Jan, and Achim Menges. 2017. "ICD/ITKE Forschungspavillon 2016-17." *itke*. Accessed December 12, 2018. www.itke.uni-stuttgart.de/de/archives/portfolio-type/icditke-research-pavilion-2016-17.

Purfürst, Otto. 1880. "Die Sparteriewaarenerzeugung." *Die Gartenlaube* 9: 148–51.

Silbermann, Steffi. n.d. "Gewebe aus Weidenholz-Monofil zum Einsatz in textilen Bauteilen." Unpublished thesis, University of Kassel.

UNEP. "Emissions Gap Report 2018." *United Nations Environment Programme.* Accessed February 10, 2019. www.unenvironment.org/resources/emissions-gap-report-2018.

Acetylated Beech in Structural Timber Constructions

Reiner Klopfer, Christian Weisgerber, and Jürgen Graf
FATUK, Technische Universität Kaiserslautern, Germany

Abstract — Beechwood is one of the strongest timbers there is, but its outdoor application in engineering structures is limited due to its distinct swelling and shrinking behavior as well as the low natural durability. Acetylation is a process that can drastically improve this behavior, but it also changes the mechanical properties of the wood. A variety of test series has been carried out to capture all positive and negative changes that come along with acetylation. One major aspect was to find suitable adhesives to produce glued laminated timber and laminated veneer lumber. Additionally, a tangible application of acetylated beech was examined by developing a wood concrete composite footbridge with minimal consumption of material. All relevant strengths and stiffnesses were determined to facilitate a complete FEM simulation of the structure. In that regard, a detachable connection to transmit shear forces between the timber and concrete cross sections was developed as well.

Introduction

Acetylation of wood progressed from an analytical technique to isolate cell wall polymers in the 1920s to commercial production of durable wood in Europe since 2007 (Accoya® by Accsys).

Acetylation is a chemical modification with acetic anhydride that replaces the accessible, hydrophilic hydroxyl groups in wood with the more hydrophobic acetyl groups. These acetyl groups embedded in the cell wall inhibit the uptake and release of water molecules.

Due to the inhibited ability to absorb water, dimensional stability is increased (~70 percent reduced shrinkage and swelling behavior) and at the same time a higher resistance against biological attack is achieved (durability class DK 1 according to DIN EN 350 2016, comparable to teak).

Due to its distinct shrinkage and swelling behavior and low natural durability, untreated beech is mostly used in dry indoor conditions for furniture and interior design. Glulam beech – with its high load capacity – is also limited to indoor use in the class NKL 1 (veneer lumber in the class NKL 2). Outdoor use for bridges and towers is currently not possible.

Acetylation as added value makes the finished product of beech more expensive. Since the product is in competition with other materials such as steel, it makes sense to use it therefore for high-strength lightweight constructions with slim dimensions.

High-quality beech can be used to produce high-strength glulam and veneer lumbers that require smaller dimensions and can contribute to the aesthetic improvement and thus to the acceptance of structures in an urban context. By using timber in structures like elegant footbridges, we are replacing steel and concrete, which means that we are working toward sustainable construction methods in multiple ways:

- The use of a renewable material saves limited resources
- Energy-intensive construction products are substituted with wood products
- CO_2 is stored in long-lasting timber structures

In addition, creating a structure with detachable joints allows for the separate disposal or recycling of the materials used.

Species	tangential [%]	radial [%]	axial [%]
spruce*	8.5	3.7	0.2...0.4
beech*	13.4	6.2	0.2...0.6
beech acetylated**	3.4	1.8	

Table 1: Swelling dimensions of spruce and beech, sources: * Niemz and Sonderegger 2017; ** Militz 1991, determined at RH 0–100%

Research

The aim of one research project was to analyze the changes in adhesiveness, strength, and stiffness to untreated beech as a result of the modification in order to use suitable adhesives for the production of, for example, glulam beech.

Based on these investigations we are able to describe properties and characteristics of the changed wood. For this purpose, tests were carried out, among other things, on the water permeability and the wetting behavior (bonding), as well as on the changed strength properties of native and finger-jointed beech boards.

It was found that acetylation inhibits water uptake compared to untreated beech. This changes the bonding properties for adhesives that interact with water, for example, 1K polyurethane adhesives (PUR), for which the bonding process needs to be adjusted. The rheological properties during the curing of the adhesives change due to acetylation. With one melamine-urea-formaldehyde adhesive (MUF), the reaction times increased significantly;

with a resorcinol-phenol-formaldehyde adhesive (PRF), they remained almost unchanged.

In order to use MUF and 1K-Pur adhesives and to achieve properties similar to the PRF adhesives, it is necessary to examine modifications to the wood or the adhesive formulations. Possible variations to consider are:

- Plasma treatment of the wood surface before bonding (increasing the polar properties)
- Addition of surfactants to the adhesive (increasing the wettability)
- Pretreating the wood with a surfactant (increasing the wettability)

Acetylation also changes the mechanical properties. It was found that bending strength and tensile strength in grain direction were reduced by acetylation, whereas compressive strength increased. Test series with at least 20 pieces each resulted in the following average strengths:

	untreated [N/mm²]	acetylated [N/mm²]	deviation [%]
bending strength	139.3	121.8	– 12.6
tensile strength	156.4	123.1	– 21.3
compressive strength	74.0	96.7	+ 30.8

Table 2: Changes of mechanical properties by acetylation

The lower tensile strength of the acetylated beech can be explained by the fact that, in consequence of the swollen state, less fiber material is available in the cross section. Another possible cause is the change in chemical bonds in the cell walls.

The reduction of tensile strength perpendicular to the grain direction was even more significant: The testing of untreated beech resulted in very steady strengths, averaging 8.4 N/mm² whereas the results for the acetylated beech ranged from 0.2 N/mm² to 6.8 N/mm². Despite the fact that timber is rarely loaded with tensile forces perpendicular to grain direction, the unpredictability of this mechanical property must be considered in any future construction. Ways to increase homogenization and predictability of tensile strength perpendicular to grain direction could be examined in future research.

Another factor that affects the various strengths is finger jointing. Finger joint geometry, bondability with various adhesives, and process parameters such as applied pressure and duration affect the resulting strengths and should be examined further to optimize the design of finger joints for acetylated beech and therefore to exploit the full potential of this high-strength material.

In order to reduce the large spreading of tensile and bending strength of acetylated solid wood boards, laminated veneer boards were produced from acetylated sawn veneers.

For first preliminary tests, 5 sawing veneers were glued with the PRF Adhesive Aerodux 185. Veneers were stacked on top of each other to annihilate the negative effect of slope of grain. From the glued raw boards, pieces were cut out and tested in the following directions:

- perpendicular to the veneer layers ("horizontal" veneer layers, Test Series A and B)
- direction of the veneer layers ("vertical" veneer layers, Test Series C).

Before the bonding and tests, the specimens were conditioned in standard atmosphere (20 °C, 65% RH) in a climate-controlled cabinet. The tests were carried out as 4-point bending tests until failure. With regard to the characteristic values, it can be stated that all veneer board values are above the values of solid wood boards; the spreads of the individual results are significantly lower than in the case of full boards.

Looking at the fracture patterns of the small test specimens, it is found that there are two different types of failure: a "splinter fracture" (in Test Series A = 30% and in Test Series B = 40% of the test specimens, in Test Series C = 100% of specimens) in the lower veneer layer or in all veneer layers (Test Series C) and a "slooping fracture," with transverse tensile failure of the lower veneer layer of (Test Series A and B). In the case of the specimens of Test Series A, the mean values of the bending strength with "splinter fracture" were 29% higher than those with "slooping fracture."

In addition to the test specimens of the preliminary tests, laminated veneer lumber boards with vertical veneer layers (b=96 mm, h=20 mm) were produced and tested in a four-point bending test.

Averages of bending strengths of 120.8 N/mm² and characteristic bending strengths of 115 N/mm² were achieved. Comparing the results of the laminated veneer boards with the solid wood boards, a significant increase in the characteristic bending strengths of 44% and a strong reduction of the spreading can be seen. This achieved a significant homogenization effect.

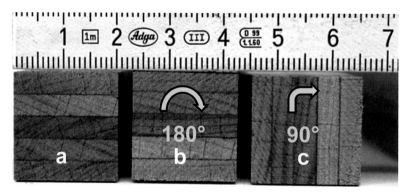

Fig. 1: Test specimens made from laminated veneer. Two specimens were rotated, one by 180°, the other by 90°

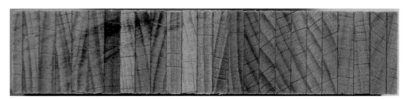

Fig. 2: Cross section of a laminated veneer lumber board with "vertical" veneer layers

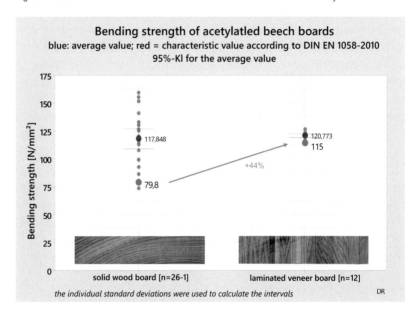

Fig. 3: Average and characteristic values of the bending strength of the acetylated laminated veneer boards compared to acetylated solid beech wood. The solid wood boards have a Young's Modulus > 15,000 N/mm². The Young's Modulus of the veneer is unknown.

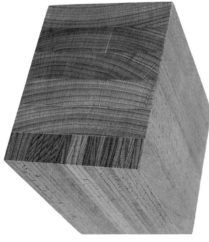

Fig. 4: "New" glulam beam made of acetylated beech. The lower board is made of vertical veneer layers and is arranged in the tension zone of the beam

As an application example, a wood-concrete composite bridge with a span of 30 meters was examined in another project. One of the main tasks was to develop a detachable connection that could transmit shear forces between the two materials efficiently. The high-tenacity wood and concrete should be used in slim cross sections to make use of their superior mechanical qualities. The 8 cm thick high-performance concrete serves several purposes: by absorbing some of the compression of the top chord, it helps accomplish the goal of a structure with maximal material exploitation. At the same time, it dispenses with the need for an added pavement for the wooden bridge, and its lateral cantilever arms provide extra protection from wetness for the underlying wood elements. Having concrete as the top layer enables planners to use well-known constructional details (for example, for handrails). The framework structure ensures that the timber beams are mainly loaded by axial forces as opposed to bending moments, which allows for a design with beams no taller than 14 cm.

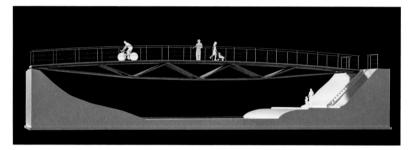

Fig. 5: Model of lightweight footbridge using high-performance concrete and acetylated beech

All mechanical qualities necessary were obtained in tests to examine if the reference wood-concrete bridge could be built with acetylated beech. The examination of the detachable connection was performed in a separate test series with one-to-one test pieces.

FEM simulation showed that the planned bridge would require a shear strength of at least 785 kN per 1 m width. The test specimens were 18 cm wide, so that the minimal intended strength was approximately 141 kN for each test. Another important aspect of the test series was to determine the slip modulus to further adjust the FEM simulation.

For that purpose, symmetrical test specimens with acetylated as well as untreated beech were produced. The high-performance concrete was tested in additional cube and cylinder compression tests, which showed that it could be classified as C100/115 according to DIN EN 2-1-1. Materials, geometries, and dimensions were chosen as expected in the actual bridge construction. Using minimal notch heights ensured that the wood cross section would be reduced as little as possible to provide a highly efficient design. Timber and concrete could easily be detached by removing the screws from the timber while the notches remain inside the concrete.

Fig. 6: Exploded view of test specimens with detachable notches

In addition, the loaded end distances were varied in order to review a guideline from DIN EN 1995 (2010). The guideline assumes that the tension is not equally distributed but instead has a maximum at the beginning of the loaded end and rapidly decreases. That is why the effective loaded end length is limited to 8 times the height of the notches. Since the actual loaded end length in the bridge construction is much longer, it should be reevaluated if the increased length has a positive effect on the capabilities of the examined connection. Tests were performed with loaded end lengths of 8, 12, and 16 times the height of the notches. The described variations resulted in a test program with 18 test pieces.

Fig. 7: Test setup including metrology

The pieces were tested under centric compression, with each of the two notches absorbing the same amount of stress. All notches had a height of 2 cm and an inclination of 5°, having regard to the oblique force application determined in a framework model. All relevant deformations on the wood and concrete were registered by displacement transducers. This way, not only the maximum stress, but also the slip modulus for each test could be determined. Force was applied with a speed of 1 mm/min, so that all tests reached the duration of 180 s to 420 s, as required in DIN EN 408 (2012).

The load-extension diagrams of each test showed linear-elastic material behavior for most of the progression of the tests, allowing for the determination of slip modules for each test. All tests ended in abrupt failure, with one or both loaded ends failing due to shear stress.

Test Series	Beech	Loaded End Length l_v [cm]	Maximum Force (average) $F_{max, m}$ [kN]	Deviation from 11.1.1 (=Reference) [%]	Test	Maximum Force F_{max} [kN]	Slip Modulus K_{ser} [$\frac{kN}{mm}$]
11.1.1	untreated	16	458.5	–	V1	402.0	1060
					V2	450.1	997
					V3	472.8	1036
					V4	509.0	1109
11.2.1	untreated	24	475.3	+3.5	V1	482.0	1434
					V2	479.0	1783
					V3	465.0	1221
11.1.2	acetylated	16	421.7	-8.7	V1	359.7	2467
					V2	441.4	2358
					V3	464.0	1045
11.2.2	acetylated	24	429.3	-6.8	V1	457.0	2660
					V2	394.5	2328
					V3	436.3	–
11.3.2	acetylated	32	451.0	-1.7	V1	503.4	1769
					V2	399.4	4060
					V3	450.2	5528

Table 3: Results of wood-concrete composite shear tests

The first test series – untreated beech, loaded end length according to DIN EN 408 (2012) – serves as a reference for all other series. Its average maximal force is defined as 100%. The evaluation of the measured results shows a small decrease in maximum strength of acetylated beech compared to untreated beech. This negative effect was partially compensated for by the use of increased loaded end lengths. It should be noted that both effects only lead to minor differences under 10%, so that all joints tested were suitable for their destined use. However, the deviation of results between the two timbers was much greater in regard to slip modulus. The stiffness in the tests using acetylated beech was much higher than with untreated beech. As assumed in DIN EN 408 (2012), the increased loaded end length did not result in a significant increase in shear strength. However, the required minimal shear strength of 141 kN was exceeded by far in every specification so that the examined detachable shear connection is appropriate for the planned bridge construction.

Conclusion

By the acetylation process, the shrinkage and swelling behavior of beech wood can be significantly improved and its resistance against wood-destroying fungi can be increased. With suitable adhesives, wood-based materials such as glulam and laminated veneer boards can be produced and applied outdoors without additional wood preservation measures.

The production of acetylated glulam beams with a laminated veneer board in the tension zone could be a convenient way to provide high-strength and durable wooden beams for outdoor use.

The bonding properties have not been fully investigated; the integration of suitable adhesives in the manufacturing process needs to be considered in more detail.

The test series showed that the examined wood-concrete composite joints are capable of transmitting large shear forces while keeping the weakening of the timber beams to a minimum, due to the very low height of the notches of only 2 cm. Highly loaded structures can be built and disassembled using this newly developed solution.

References

DIN EN 350. 2016. Dauerhaftigkeit von Holz und Holzprodukten: Prüfung und Klassifizierung der Dauerhaftigkeit von Holz und Holzprodukten gegen biologischen Angriff.

DIN EN 1992. 2011. Bemessung und Konstruktion von Stahlbeton- und Spannbetonwerken.

DIN EN 1995. 2010. Eurocode 5: Bemessung und Konstruktion von Holzbauten.

DIN EN 408. 2012. Holzbauwerke: Bauholz für tragende Zwecke und Brettschichtholz – Bestimmung einiger physikalischer und mechanischer Eigenschaften.

Graf, Jürgen. 2016. "Elegant gefügt: Holz-Beton-Verbundbrücken der Landesgartenschau in Schwäbisch Gmünd." In *Ingenieurbaukunst 2016*, edited by Bundesingenieurkammer, 8–15. Berlin: Ernst, Wilhelm & Sohn.

Graf, Jürgen. 2018. "Neue Potentiale im konstruktiven Holzbau durch acetylierte Buche; Abschlussbericht Forschungsinitiative Zukunft Bau." Gefördert vom Bundesamt für Bauwesen und Raumordnung.

Michelfelder, Birgit C. 2006. "Trag- und Verformungsverhalten von Kerven bei Brettstapel-Beton-Verbunddecken." Thesis, Universität Stuttgart.

Militz, H. 1991. "Die Verbesserung des Schwind und Quellverhaltens und der Dauerhaftigkeit von Holz mittels Behandlung mit unkatalysiertem Essigsäureanhydrid." *Holz- als Roh- und Werkstoff* 49: 147–52.

Militz, H. 2011. "Übersichtsbericht: Acetyliertes Holz (Naturwissenschaftliche und technologische Grundlagen, materialtechnische und ökonomische Möglichkeiten und Grenzen, aktueller Stand der Umsetzung)." SGD Süd-Forstliche Versuchsanstalt RLP.

Niemz, Peter, and Walter Ulrich Sonderegger. 2017. *Holzphysik: Physik des Holzes und der Holzwerkstoffe*. Munich: Fachbuchverlag Leipzig.

3 Architectural Practice
and Research

Developing Research Cultures in Architecture

Michael U. Hensel
Digital Architecture and Planning, Institute of Architectural Sciences, Vienna
University of Technology, Austria

Abstract — This chapter portrays an approach and particular case of developing research culture in architecture across practice, research organization, and education that commenced in the mid-1990s in the context of the OCEAN, an interdisciplinary network that pursues research-by-design activities across the creative sector, and more specifically architecture and urban design. These efforts were increasingly linked with teaching activities at numerous schools, including the Architectural Association in London and the Research Centre for Architecture and Tectonics at the Oslo School of Architecture and Design. In parallel OCEAN members began to research also the development of research in architectural practices and its own context in order to develop specifically targeted research strategy and development. This was linked with PhD and more specifically industrial PhD tracks in Oslo and examination of the lateral networks that emerged between practitioners with formal research capacity.

Introduction

What is the state of the discipline of architecture? Is it in transformation and, if yes, in which way? What are the characteristics and impact of current transformations? Answers to these questions can vary significantly depending on viewpoint and agenda. The variety in views is indicative of a pluralism that couples in the best case change with diversity. The past has shown that differences in views can result in vehement dispute. Change is affected by different drivers. Research is such a driver and at the same time a decidedly contested notion in architecture, especially concerning research by design. To come to terms with this unbiased inquiry is necessary. Given the pluralistic developments across the discipline it is necessary to examine particular strands of development and the underlying motivations.

This chapter portrays an approach and particular case of developing research culture in architecture across practice, research organization, and education that commenced in the mid-1990s in the context of the OCEAN, an interdisciplinary network that pursues research-by-design activities across the creative sector, and more specifically architecture and urban design. These efforts were increasingly linked with teaching activities at numerous schools, including the Architectural Association in London and the Research Centre for Architecture and Tectonics at the Oslo School of Architecture and Design. In parallel, OCEAN members began to research also the development of research in architectural practices and its own context in order to develop specifically targeted research strategy and development. This was linked with PhD and more specifically industrial PhD tracks in Oslo and examination of the lateral networks that emerged between practitioners with formal research capacity. This chapter focuses three related strands within this spectrum of undertakings. The first strand consists of the "Changing Shape of Practice" project, which was coinitiated by the author and the architect Prof. Dr. Fredrik Nilsson. The second strand focuses on a trajectory of development that commenced with the OCEAN network and continued in education contexts with a focus on research by design. The third strand focuses on current research-focused strategic developments in the Oslo region that have arisen out of the former two parts.

Research

The "Changing Shape of Practice" research project was initiated in 2010 by the author and Prof. Dr. Fredrik Nilsson. This was done with the aim to establish a research framework that analyses the growing element of research in architectural practice, to define objectives, modes, and modalities of practice-based and practice-oriented research, as well as developing new collaborative research platforms with practice. As architectural practices worldwide have to deal with increasingly complex design requirements, we asked: How do practices acquire the ability to do so? What kinds and forms of knowledge are needed and produced in different types of practices? How are results, new knowledge, and competences documented, shared, and disseminated internally as well as externally? Is research itself now used as a strategic tool by architectural offices? How do research and practice in architecture mutually shape one another? In the meantime, the research has led to a number of books (Hensel 2012b; Hensel and Nilsson 2016, 2019) (fig. 1), as well as five symposia in which numerous practices are portrayed in relation to their specific take on research in practice (fig. 2). The research indicates that an increasing number of practices is aware of the value of strategizing and conducting research, and to develop corresponding business models. The different ways in which practices undertake research is often a bespoke affair that reflects external and internal local circumstances, while relating to global drivers of change (that is, digitization, automation of production, new logistic requirements, etc.).

Fig. 1: The first two books in the Changing Shape of Practice series: The Changing Shape of Practice and The Changing Shape of Architecture

Fig. 2: (Left) Poster of the Changing Shape of Practice Symposium 2016 as part of the Oslo Architectural Triennial; (Right) Poster of the Changing Shape of Practice Conference 2017 at the Aarhus School of Architecture as part of the Aarhus Cultural Capital 2017 events

The OCEAN Design Research Association was portrayed as a special case. OCEAN started in 1994 as an international network for interdisciplinary experimental design that produced pioneering design research from the onset of the computational turn from the mid-1990s onward. Since 1994 OCEAN is involved in teaching and developing research by design approaches in experimental practice and education. Members of OCEAN were instrumental in the development of research by design in Diploma Unit 4 at the Architectural Association School of Architecture, as well as in the conception and delivery of the Emergent Technologies and Design master program (EmTech). The latter was initiated as an interdisciplinary program for architects, engineers, and industrial designers that was located at the intersection between architecture, engineering, computer science, and biomimetics with a pronounced research-by-design curriculum and focus on computational design, computer-aided analysis and digital fabrication (Hensel, Menges, and Weinstock 2010). The program became a blueprint for similar programs worldwide and former members of staff have since developed renowned versions or substantial further developments of this approach. One example was the Research Centre for Architecture and Tectonics (2011–18) together with its innovation hub the Advanced Computational Design Laboratory at the Oslo School of Architecture and Design. In this context interdisciplinary approaches to performance-oriented architecture (Hensel 2013), systems-thinking, and information-based design were focal areas for research by design, with focus on addressing complex design problems and alternative approaches to social, cultural, and environmental sustainability.

In order to handle complex design criteria related to architecture and environment interactions from a human and nonhuman perspective, OCEAN commonly deploy systems-thinking tools and mapping methods. In the design process this involves multimodal data collection, data structuring, computer-aided modeling, and analyses in conjunction with advanced visualization methods, including virtual, augmented, and mixed-reality visualizations. OCEAN termed this combination of computational methods information-based design. A parallel development was pursued in the context of the Research Centre for Architecture and Tectonics (RCAT) and the Advanced Computational Design Laboratory (ACDL) at the Oslo School of Architecture and Design (Hensel and Sørensen 2013, 2014). In collaboration with the practices Kieran Timberlake in Philadelphia and Snøhetta in Oslo, RCAT/ACDL examined the problem of designers' having limited access to environmental and more specifically ecological modeling and analysis methods and tools, leading to a succinct problem in the development of related sustainable science. This realization led to the formation of a collaborative research platform consisting of the two practices and RCAT/ACDL with the aim of establishing an approach and toolkit for identifying, measuring, and modeling biophysical factors on a site to inform design decision-making and elevate sustainability science by way of integrating methods for data gathering, processing, and interpretation to advance a multiscalar, multid-omain, and multistakeholder approach to the built environment. The dis-cussion and collaboration with the practices originated in the context of the aforementioned "Changing Shape of Practice" research project.

A second decisive factor was the collaboration with Snøhetta on indus-trial PhD research in the context of the Research Centre for Architecture and Tectonics. This track was implemented in 2011 at the Oslo School of Architecture and Design and led to the first industrial PhD in the humanities in Norway completed by Dr. Julia Schlegel, who is now research director at Snøhetta. The research and dissertation was supervised by the author in conjunction with Kjetil Thorsen and Eli Synnevag, and was completed in 2015. Industrial PhDs are cofinanced by practice and government via the Norwegian Research Council. Schlegel was supervised by a team from AHO and Snøhetta, and the investment from Snøhetta was strategic, with the aim of gaining a member of staff with formal research capacity as director of re-search. This strategic track has now become a blueprint for other practices in architecture in the Oslo region. As a broader development this has several consequences. Oslo has a relatively high proportion of interesting architec-ture and design practices that are beginning to profile themselves along a strong trajectory of research and research by design. These practices now acquire strategically staff with formal research capacity, that is, with a com-pleted doctoral study. During their PhD studies these individuals would have frequently met at universities and seminars, exchanged knowledge and skills, and codeveloped research in the context of formal academic research often within practice context and specific practice-related inquiries. It is in this context that the beginning of a network of practitioners with formal research capacity emerges outside of individual practices. In the case of Oslo, such lateral networks continue to exist after completion of the respective PhDs irrespective of practice competition and add a potentially significant element to a given context (Hensel 2012a). This can yield strong impact of practice and competitiveness through specific elements of exchange and collabora-tion, whether formal or informal. The question is, whether such trends are recognized and further strategically developed in order to enhance locally and regionally the accumulative positive impact beyond individual research activities and projects or practice portfolios. Such networks would add a significant element to research in a professional context, but it also enables the formation of longer-term practice and university collaboration above and beyond individual PhDs or research projects.

The identification of such trends and their impact are likely to shed detailed light on the current transformations of architecture and the related charac-teristics and impact. Moreover, this will help to develop ways of working impactfully in result of and throughout ongoing transformations of practice.

Some of this impact has been described, analyzed, and reflected as part of the "Quality for Impact" research self-assessment of the Oslo School of Architecture and Design (Morrison 2018).

Conclusion

It is of interest to examine developments such as the ones described above as correlated research development activities that emerge from or evolve toward higher-level strategic perspectives. Systemic studies show how research activities emerge and advance in architectural practices, research organizations, and universities and how these different contexts react to and steer these changes individually or jointly. This can inform a more versatile approach to research in each of these contexts individually or jointly. In particular, new joint ventures, emerging networks, and new platforms in research have the potential to go beyond current or projected requirements and goals by utilizing their accumulative resources. This entails that the systemic analysis of research in architecture can be of strategic and operational value and should continue, even though the resourcing of such activities is neither easy nor obvious. An overarching and comparative reflexive analysis of research activities is already pursued by research-oriented practices and university-based research environments and international symposia and conferences like the "Changing Shape of Practice" research project or the *RCA 2018 Research Culture in Architecture Conference* give evidence of the current recognition of this significant potential. New research efforts must then operate on multiple levels of reflection instead of letting insights be appropriated and constrained by the narrow view of silos, established domains of inquiry and knowledge production, or narrow strategic efforts. It is not a new insight that in this context inter- and transdisciplinary outlooks and approaches hold great potential to fuel projects and types of collaboration in research that would perhaps otherwise not take place. Such inquiries often hold great innovation potential above and beyond premeditated requirements and goals. For this reason, considerable effort needs to be invested in investigating and communicating what characterizes research in the creative disciplines and that design offers a momentous possibility for projecting ahead unlike in other disciplines. It is this projective aspect of research by design in the context of inter- and transdisciplinary design that might currently constitute one of the potent if still largely latent drivers in the transformation of the discipline.

References

Hensel, Michael. 2012a. "Evolving Contours in Rethinking, Reskilling, Retooling: Life-long Learning, Research Capacities and Lateral Networking." In Hensel 2012b, 43–58.

Hensel, Michael, ed. 2012b. *Design Innovation for the Built Environment: Research by Design and the Renovation of Practice*. London: Routledge.

Hensel, Michael. 2013. *Performance-oriented Architecture: Rethinking Architectural Design and the Built Environment*. London: AD Wiley.

Hensel, Michael, Achim Menges, and Michael Weinstock M. 2010. *Emergent Technologies and Design: A Biological Paradigm for Architecture*. London: Routledge.

Hensel, Michael, and Fredrik Nilsson, eds. 2016. *The Changing Shape of Practice: Integrating Research and Design in Architecture*. London: Routledge.

Hensel, Michael, and Fredrik Nilsson, eds. 2019. *The Changing Shape of Architecture: Further Cases of Integrating Research and Design in Practice*. London: Routledge.

Hensel, Michael, and Defne Sunguroğlu Hensel. 2016. "The Future Practices of OCEAN." In Hensel and Nilsson 2016, 168–80.

Hensel, Michael, and Søren Sørensen. 2013. "En Route to Performance-oriented Architecture: The Research Centre for Architecture and Tectonics: Integrating Architectural Education with Research by Design along a Practice-Oriented Perspective." *SAJ Serbian Architecture Journal* 5, no. 2: 106–31.

Hensel, Michael, and Søren Sørensen. 2014. "Intersecting Knowledge Fields and Integrating Data-Driven Computational Design en Route to Performance-oriented and Intensely Local Architectures." *Dynamics of Data-driven Design Footprint* 15: 59–74.

Morrison, Andrew, ed. 2018. "Quality for Impact: AHO Research Review." The Oslo School of Architecture and Design.

Public Debate, Public Interior, Circular Economy – Forms of Exchange: Approaching the Reconversion of an Iconic 1966 Office Tower in Brussels

Tomas Ooms
Studio Tuin en Wereld, and Faculty of Architecture, KU Leuven, Belgium

Abstract — In a late Modernist gesture, the Dutch Philips Company constructed in 1966 its headquarters in the historical center of Brussels. Two entire and densely populated city blocks were demolished. A dissociation and discontinuity of the urban tissue was the consequence. The project, a rationally designed tower on a three-story-tall plinth, was to be the inner-city "touchdown" of an oversized real estate development.

Currently the Brouckère Tower (or Philips Tower) is being converted from a monofunctional, single-tenant, and stand-alone urban object into a multi-tenant office environment with an emphasis on conviviality, publicness, and "spatial engagement."

The project is a conversion in three different ways:

- From a late Modernist mutilation of the historical urban tissue to an updated Brutalist modernism reinserted in the ideal of the organically evolving European City.
- Second, from a dissociated edifice to an engaging urban space exchanger between the central boulevards and the area of the Saint-Cathérine Church. And between the plinth levels, the urban platforms and the newly created winter garden on the eighteenth floor.
- And eventually, from a closed and hermetic strange body (Fremdkörper) to a contributor of publicness through interlacing the interior with the public realm, transforming it into a public interior and a civic edifice.

The article will share some conclusions relating to design processes in the context of circularity and BIM and regarding the public-private dichotomy in private real estate.

A Case of Severe Bruxellization Between Two Urban Conditions

To approach the reconversion of this iconic 1966 office tower, an in-depth understanding of the original intentions and how they were realized, or failed, is paramount.

The article will give the account on how the three main project ambitions have been addressed. These ambitions are to envision the project:

- as a public debate;
- as a public interior;
- within a circular economy.

Because of speculative real estate developments in the 1960s, the Philips Tower is the exponent of "Bruxellization": the drastic modernization of the urban fabric.

In its current state, the Brouckère Tower is a dissociation and discontinuity of the urban tissue. The tower could be experienced as being out of proportion in relation to its surroundings. Because of its robustness, the mainly opaque facades in precious bluestone, the prominence of the parking entrances in the public space, combined with a bus underpass, the edifice is not contributing to the quality of the public space and is now considered an urban accident.

The Brouckère Tower forms a duo with the Munt building; both were designed by Groupes Structures. They use the same volumetric vocabulary: a three-level plinth with a platform, an intermediate level, and a tower seemingly floating above the plinth, clearly inspired by the Lever House (SOM, NY).

The Brouckère Tower is situated between two types of city fabric: On the south side, it flanks the boulevards Anspach and Adolf Max. This zone is one of the most important shopping areas in Brussels (fig. 1). To the north side the Brouckère Tower faces the small-grained district of Saint-Catherine, a lively area with small restaurants, cafés, and the remnants of the old port (fig. 2).

Fig. 1: The existing situation of the plinth facing the Boulevard Anspach (© Jasper Van der Linden)

Fig. 2: The existing situation of the plinth facing the Saint-Catherine Church (© Jasper Van der Linden)

Toward the boulevards, where the Philips flagship store and the HQ-lobby were originally accommodated, the building is open and contains the entrances and retail space. Here, the project celebrates the open, modern urban condition. Toward the picturesque neighborhood of Saint-Catherine, the facade is closed, dark, and uncommunicative. The parking entrances eat into the public space on the ground floor, creating a discontinuity of the city. A bus route passes under the plinth and forms a barrier, obstructing pedestrians.

The building has an H-shaped tower of sixteen levels on top of the three-story plinth. There is a four-level underground parking. The edifice has a low floor-to-floor height, making the integration of contemporary techniques extremely difficult. The facades need an update to address issues of daylight and energy efficiency. At the same time the extraordinary views on the city can be improved.

Public Debate and Public Interior as a Condition for Exchange and the Project as Civic Edifice

The decision to work with the existing building, instead of demolishing it, was induced through the realization that we could save time: not having to demolish first, then construct again. Secondly, the demolition would bring with it a lot of mobility issues and waste production. But above all, there are some great qualities in this 1966 Brutalist/Modernist construction. The proposal is not one of pure conservation but is based on an integration of existing valuable elements and qualitative materials. And above all, it starts from an understanding of and work within the framework of the original intentions of the project.

When dealing with an emblematic, iconic "urban accident," every intervention demands a thoughtful approach. The goal is to conjoin the project within the urban condition. Working with the existing building was the first step. A second is to bring the design process within the public realm and create a public debate based on transparency. The idea of exchange is central to our understanding of the urban condition. Exchange in the form of knowledge, money, goods, diseases, ideas; but more important, exchange of space: interior and exterior, open spaces, private and collective spaces, interspaces. If we want exchange to happen, there needs to be an interface, an overlap. This reconversion facilitates and enhances this idea of urban exchange with an emphasis on the public interior, striving to make it a "civic" edifice.

Since the project is situated between two distinct urban neighborhoods of different morphology and scale, it has the potential of acting as a go-between, as a facilitator. The design tries to realize that potential and reconvert the currently closed and dissociated project into "an urban space exchanger" and an urban platform. To overcome the risk of becoming a self-effacing go-between, the project's interior is developed as a continuation of the public space (fig. 3).

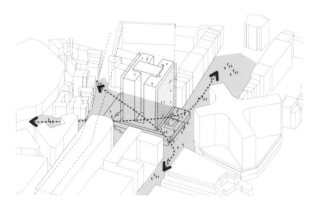

Fig. 3: The Brouckère Tower as an urban space exchanger between two different urban conditions. Design drawing

To conduct this dialectic design process in public, in open communication, only physical architectural artifacts were presented on a large table during meetings and stakeholder interactions. This enabled everybody to bring their concerns and suggestions "to the table." Someone could even change things and sort of, say, "turn the table." But above all it meant that all the stakeholders are "together at the table" (fig. 4).

Fig. 4: The working model of the reconversion project mounted on a large table in an exhibition setup to support the open dialogue. The exhibition was organized on the thirteenth floor of the Brouckère Tower. As a miniature version of itself, the model is inserted in the real thing. (© Jasper Van der Linden)

A Series of Collective Spaces within a Strange Body

To overhaul the Brouckère Tower and convert it into a civic edifice, the following gestures drive the design: First, a stitching of the lower levels (plinth) to the surrounding public space and the street life. Second, the creation of a certain porosity and permeability through the introduction of a series of collective spaces, topped with a winter garden on the eighteenth floor. Third, by integrating the parking access into the footprint of the plinth, the sidewalk is extended and new public spaces are created. Forth, an offset of the tower volume combined with the realization of a high-performative facade reduces energy consumption and increases the possible uses of the floor plan. The proposal works with the building's rationality and in the process, becomes a celebration of its somewhat brutal materiality and form (fig. 5).

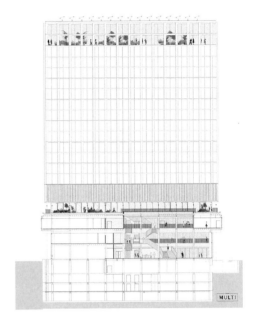

Fig. 5: A sequence of collectivities is proposed throughout the building: the atria in the plinth, the urban platforms on the third floor, and the winter garden on top. Project design section

Two public atria are created within the plinth. The vestibule, a larger-scale atrium, faces the boulevards and the pedestrian zone and will remain publicly accessible, leading to the urban platform on the third floor, thus bringing daylight deep into the currently dark plinth. The second atrium is a space with a series of lanterns (skylights), and will relate to the smaller scale of Saint-Catherine (fig. 6). On the eighteenth floor, a double-height winter garden is provided as a civic meeting center.

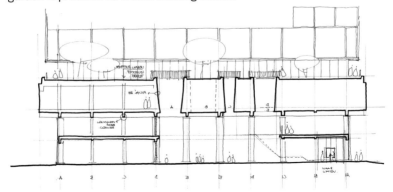

Fig. 6: A series of lanterns is proposed to increase the porosity of the closed plinth. The lanterns refer to the scale of the neighboring Saint-Catherine area. Project design sketch

The free height typical of these tertiary constructions for the 1960s and 1970s is rather low (315 cm floor-to-floor but with a T-floor construction 34 cm thick). Which means that the integration of current techniques of HVAC, insulation, and energy-use reduction is difficult when combined with an optimal use of space. To address these issues, a high-performative tower facade is proposed at an offset of 250 cm from the existing structure. This combines the integration of new special techniques with an increase in rentable surface. To keep the proportions of the tower in balance, an extra double-height floor on top is realized. Because of this, new types of functions become possible, such as the winter garden and the auditorium.

With regards to the materiality of the proposal, the new facade will be, contrary to the existing black volume, white with a nonglossy texture. The base for the design is the rationality that is characteristic of the existing building and will be based on the square. The basic frame facade elements will be prefabricated. They are designed to reduce the amount of material needed and the same time to generate a shadow. This will contribute to the more anthropometric appearance.

The plinth volume is restored in its original Brutalist detailing and materiality but with a more open and engaging attitude toward the public space that surrounds it. This way the current disconnected interior will be stitched and conjoined with the exterior.

The integration of the parking access within the footprint of the plinth is an important feature of the proposal. The entrance and exit are combined into one, reducing their impact. The decision means less retail area, but increases the amount of public space. Consequently, the sidewalks will be enlarged and the continuation of the public space will be restored.

The second measure is to remove the bus underpass and deroute the buses over the surrounding streets. The sum of these action allows for a new public square facing Saint-Catherine to be created. This new public space refers both in scale and atmosphere to the Saint-Catherine neighborhood, attracting sunlight in the afternoon, while being linked and related to the public interiors in the plinth and leading to the series of collective spaces. As an urban space-exchanger, the project supports the new pedestrian zone that is realized in form of the building. The reconversion of the Brouckère Tower maximizes accessibility for the public. The existing building has large platforms on the third floor originally intended to be connected to the North District. The reconversion proposes to actualize these platforms on the third floor on either side of the tower by linking them (for the first time) to the public space. They become urban civic platforms overlooking the urban spaces around. The platforms will be refurbished as urban terraces and urban gardens.

Throughout the design process, the project discusses, explores, and aims to contribute, as a private project, to the quality of the public space. The reconversion project will create a public sphere and become part of the public realm. In the design discourse, the question of how a private project could contribute to the quality of the public space was always at the foreground. Too often, this idea of seeing a private real estate development as a positive engaging agent in the public sphere is overlooked or not addressed. It is however the real intent of the reconversion of the Brouckère Tower by converting it from a corporate headquarters into a civic continuation of the public realm, but on private property.

Circularity as a Matter of "Harvesting" in Three Ways

Each year a substantial amount of reusable materials available from construction sites in Brussels becomes available. But because the demand for these reusable materials is very low, almost nothing is reused; most is destroyed and treated as waste. The demand is low partially because projects of a certain size are not seen and hence not organized as potential receivers and clients for these materials.

This reconversion project aims at addressing this by becoming a precedent and pioneer when it comes to reusing materials from a large-scale tertiary building. To this aim, a clear and concrete ambition is stated: that at least 2 percent of all materials in the project are a form of reuse. This is on top of the reusing of the existing volume and structure. This may not seem that much, but on a project of this scale, it is unprecedented.

To become a pioneer project of reusing materials, three modes are applied: First, the building is considered as a source for harvesting materials for reuse in situ. For example, some of the bluestone is recuperated to clad the newly created columns. Another is the repurposing of the aluminium H-shaped elements that form the facade of the existing emergency exits and technical floor. These elements are up-cycled as interior balustrade in the atrium. The second mode is for the recuperating of materials and making them available for reuse in other projects on other locations (fig. 7). This is done with some of the bluestone, some technical equipment, doors, ceilings, appliances, etc. A third mode is to see the project as a receiver of materials that have been harvested from other projects. Predominantly they would come from other tertiary buildings in Brussels. One example is the natural stone floor from the Belgian designer Jules Wabbes. But the project will also repurpose a natural stone form the Zand Square in Brugge. About 50 doors from one of the WTC towers of the Brussels North District will find a place in the newly reconverted Brouckère Tower.

Fig. 7: The bluestone and the aluminum facade elements are being repurposed on-site. (© Jasper Van der Linden)

Emerging Research Lines: Prototype, BIM and the Civic

When giving the account of a practice-based project in the context of research cultures in architecture it is evident and crucial to have a reflective part. This article has been written from the double perspective of a practicing architect who is at the same time doing a PhD in practice-based research. He is also the lead architect for the discussed project. The perspective here is that of sharing a personal practice and through communicating about it, it becomes professional knowledge through making it criticizable. What follows are some research lines or lines of inquiry that emerged out of working on, working with and working in the Brouckère Tower.

The first such research line deals with the insight in the importance of designing with flows and the role of "progressional" insights and knowledge. More and more assignments and design briefs are less clearly defined and they are more open-ended. Projects are less stand-alone and need to be inscribed into a rather complex reality. The design is then identifying currents (the flows) and trying to tie them and create closed circuits: circularity.

A second line of inquiry is that during the design process, it became clear that working with the concept of circularity has some particularities. One of those is the need to prototype. Several prototypes are being made to test the repurposing of harvested materials. You do not always know up front what is available and how this will behave in a new situation. Without going into the technicalities, this created legal voids when it comes to, for example, certification. This will be one of the many challenges for the field of circularity.

Another observation is that within a circularity mindset, a lot of agility is required of a designer and maybe even more so as a client. Because it is never clear what materials will be available, when they will be available, in what shade of color they will be, what are the specifications of that material, what are the dimensions and so on. It will pose a new paradigm for the designer. Although currently a hot topic in architecture (and the economy at large), circularity probably will only really take on or get some grip the moment reusing materials is cheaper than resourcing new materials, as in the nineteenth century when steel was expensive but labor was cheap. This led to very refined steel constructions: the cheap manpower was used to calculate until the limit of material use.

A third line links circularity with BIM (Building Information Modeling). Throughout the design process and during the construction phase, an atlas of sites of harvesting and reusing is kept. This document shows where materials come from and where they are going to be used in what form. This atlas is amended with flow charts that show the track of the used materials. It is a kind of graphical material passport.

Currently the project team is exploring the potential of BIM in relation to the theme of circularity, starting with the question how BIM can support the knowledge of circularity? Material passports are already established as a possibility. But less obvious lines of inquiry, such as ways of calculating the impact of the circularity. Or whether it is possible to express circularity in terms of performance? Another is to make sure that the procedure for demounting parts of the building is integrated in the BIM.

The next step is the integration of this information in a usable way in BIM and the integrated practice. The questions that popped up in the application of BIM to the project is a question of representation. It is a question about the role of the drawing in (architectural) practice and how BIM can become a design method early in the design process. Recently this has led to the creation of the academic design office REVAMP: BIM and Mediality at the faculty of architecture at the KU Leuven.

And a fourth line of inquiry is more philosophical in nature and is related to the intent of the reconversion of the Brouckère Tower: the agency of the impact of private space on the public realm and the idea of the civic. How can you ensure that the proposed publicness of these large-scale real estate projects is continued over time, maintained and supported by its owners and tenants? And what can we as designers contribute further to this debate? For my practice, this means exploring the concept of the urban space exchanger and the idea of the urban platform in a condition of distinction and overlap, toward the edifice as a civic gesture (fig. 8).

Fig. 8: Axonometric view of the final proposal. At the time of writing, the demounting of the reusable materials is in full swing and the removal of the asbestos is ongoing.

Acknowledgments

The reconversion of the Brouckère Tower into the Multi Tower is the joint effort of: Whitewood Capital, CONIX RDBM architects, ROTOR DC, 3E, CES, SGI, ECOWORKS, BOPRO, and STUDIO TUIN EN WERELD. I would like to express my gratitude to the organizers of the RCA conference for being so patient and supportive toward the production of this paper. All photographs are by Jasper Van der Linden. Thanks to architect Annebel Courtens for proofreading.

References

Ghyoot, Michaël, et al. 2017. *Déconstruction et Réemploi*. Lausanne: Presses polytechniques et universitaires romandes.

Pimlott, Mark. 2017. *The Public Interior as Idea and Project*. Heijningen: Jap Sam Books.

Scheer, David Ross. 2014. *The Death of Drawing*. New York: Routledge.

Schön, Donald. 1991. *The Reflective Practitioner: How Professionals Think in Action*. Abingdon, Oxon: Taylor & Francis.

Making Architecture Public: The Architecture Exhibition – An Environment for a Radical Redesign of the Discipline?

Charlott Greub
North Dakota State University, USA

Abstract — This article reviews innovations in creative practices in architecture and design as reflected through both the medium of architecture exhibitions and the deliberate strategy of off-site reuse of building materials. To illustrate these innovative techniques, two architecture exhibitions by Rotor will be examined as illustrative case studies. The first is Rotor's exhibitions presented in 2010 at the Venice Biennale, and the second one was staged at the 2014 Bomel Cultural Center in Namur, Belgium. These exhibitions will be reviewed in order to explore the innovative and sustainable architectural reuse of building materials.

Exhibiting Architecture

Architecture exhibitions have continued to play a major role in architecture. It is difficult bringing architecture into the space of galleries, museums, or multinational biennials because once built it is always on display. Architecture exhibitions are almost always representations of architecture works or products. There are few exceptions that include the construction of actual buildings for exhibition such as *Home Delivery*, curated by Barry Bergdoll and Peter Christensen for MoMA in 2008 and the *Die Wohnung* exhibition organized by Mies van der Rohe in Stuttgart Weißenhof in 1927. The 2008 exhibition included five built-to-scale prefabricated houses, and the one in Stuttgart Weißenhof comprised of fifteen full freestanding scale buildings. Bergdoll (2015) notes that "nearly every lecture on the architectural exhibition begins by rehearsing the truism that architecture can only be exhibited through simulacra, substitute objects, or representations – which means original drawings, models, mock-ups, prints, illustrated books, photos or other images – created after the building's completion or original projection." He adds that "Architecture exhibitions, in the most diverse formats, have been a vital instrument for advancing some of the greatest features of modern architecture since the Enlightenment, and facilitated the emergence of a critical discourse on the public character and the responsibilities of architecture."

The architecture exhibition since the twentieth century has allowed architects to take speculative positions and use exhibitions as laboratories for architectural ideas. This ethos was particularly captured by a number of exhibitions in the 1960s and 1970s, such as the group shows the Trigon Biennales of 1967 (*Ambience/Environment*) and 1969 (*Architecture/Freedom*) in Graz. These kinds of experimental, installation-based environments demonstrate that architectural exhibitions have not only played a role in canonizing architects and buildings but also can affect architecture's social role.

In Italy, architects' collaboratives such as Superstudio (one of the participants of the Trigon 67); Archizoom; Global Tools; Gruppo 9999; and U.F.O. expanded their role in society to shape the contemporary political and cultural agenda through radical architecture without the intervention of a building. Radical architects rejected the various mediums of architecture in favor of other, nontectonic modes, such as montages; models; films and exhibitions; installations and magazines; and various other modern forms of mass communication. In 1972 these groups participated in an important exhibition at the New York Museum of Modern Art, curated by Emilio Ambasz and titled *Italy: The New Domestic Landscape* (Celant 1972). The "Casa Orto – Vegetable Garden House" was one of the exhibition's feature items and later became an important example in the early ecology movement.

Lettuces and cabbages were presented against the backdrop of the museum and used as the raw material for a collage of the Home Garden. Environmentally conscious and communally oriented design approaches like Casa Orto promoted a globalist perspective predicated on the belief in a common culture for human survival and evolution and for serving a "global commons" imagined as "open work" rather than as "owned" resources.

The radical movement presaged some of the urgent social and development concerns that the world is now contending with, including globalization, technology, social justice, and environmental protection. The world of radical architects is now being represented and projected by younger contemporaries. These younger advocates include: Rotor ("Usus/Usures," Venice Biennale, 2010; "Behind the Green Door," the Oslo Architecture Triennale, 2014) and Raumlabor Berlin ("Kitchenmonument," Berlinische Galerie, 2014; and "Urban Matrass," Kunstverein Wolfburg, 2011).

Curating the Architect's Role and Responsibility for the Built Environment

Through their work as curators and producers of several exhibitions, Rotor raises many important questions. For example: how can the design profession reinvent the discourse on the issue of social responsibility? Rotor's work explores the notion of wear as it relates to the use of materials, objects, and building structures. Use is not to be conflated with program or function but rather the social aspect of occupation and inhabitation of architecture during the life-span of a building. Rotor focuses on modernist and contemporary buildings slated for demolition in order to reuse their material components for radical redesign. This preoccupation with off-site reuse is intended to question the standard use of demolition as a way to create a tabula rasa for new projects. Rotor seeks to save condemned materials while introducing a conservational social perspective. Material reuse encourages one to consider buildings as cultural repositories, not just of the materials but also of the knowledge and past practices of crafting buildings. These past practices are also given as raw material – in this case, of knowledge and skill – that might find new applications and contribute to new value systems.

Reusability, Sustainability of the Built Environment as Part of a Political Project

Rotor's design approach addresses reusability and sustainability as part of a sociopolitical project. It critiques the modern throwaway consumer culture and highlights how product outsourcing to global supply chains conceals poor labor conditions that result in the depoliticization of working conditions and environmental costs. To counter this wastefulness, Rotor has developed guidelines, protocols, and regulatory frameworks for the reclamation of reusable materials and the integration of "waste" into the current building processes. In 2015 Rotor developed a handbook for off-site reuse in Belgium, a model of legal and practical guidelines for the reclamation of reusable materials from public buildings. They are also advocating for regulatory policies within the European market that will reintroduce salvaged building material into the building construction process. Rotor hopes to contribute to the reevaluation, redesign, and reusability of the building-materials economy.

Case Study 1: Usus/Usures: The Architecture Exhibition as an Environment for Reuse Strategies

The work of Rotor represents a new kind of emerging multidisciplinary practice in architecture: from research and exhibition-making to material studies and reuse strategies. Rotor is interested in material flows in industry and construction, particularly in relation to resources (waste, use, and reuse) that challenge historical conceptualization of building culture, heritage, and social value. They deconstruct buildings into elements (construction, materials) and reassemble them in new ways. This is an approach about material and knowledge of past practices of crafting buildings and interiors. They aim for both new applications and new value systems around materials and their assembling. Rotor undermines the conventional professional divisions of responsibilities between clients, contractors, workers, designers, users, and other stakeholders.

Rotor's distinct interdisciplinary approach could be described as deconstruction, relocation, and assemblage. This distinct interdisciplinary approach of Rotor was at the center of their exhibition *Usus/Usures* for the Belgian Pavilion at the Venice Biennale in 2010. At the international architecture exhibition, they displayed mundane materials and products salvaged from Belgian social housing projects as abstract art. The selection and framing of used materials and architectural elements of a social housing complex is not a purely aesthetic or neutral act but points to the growing problem of unavailable low-income housing in Belgium and other Western countries. *Usus/Usures* (figs. 1–5) was entirely made from salvaged building components that are usually overlooked and treated as waste (deconstruction), such as carpet, stairs, railings, etc. These were then exhibited in a reassembled manner (assemblage) in the Belgian Pavilion at the Venice Biennale (relocation).

Fig. 1: Rotor: Usus/Usures, Acrylic fiber carpet, staircase, railing, Belgium Pavilion, Venice Biennale 2010 (Photo: Eric Mairiaux)

Fig. 2: Rotor: Usus/Usures, Acrylic fiber carpet, railing, Belgium Pavilion, Venice Biennale 2010 (Photo: Eric Mairiaux)

Fig. 3: Rotor: Usus/Usures, Acrylic fiber carpet in a living room adjacent to an entryway, a hallway, a bedroom, and a kitchen, Belgium Pavilion, Venice Biennale 2010 (Photo: Eric Mairiaux)

Unlike common architectural practice, where thinking about material and making means the design of new objects, description through specifications, and ordering through product catalogs, with *Usus/Usures* there is an entirely different process in place: thinking of materials as something physical and tangible to be identified, transported from one place to another, and then reframed or reused.

A red carpet, for example, was taken from an apartment in a social housing block (relocation) and mounted on the wall of the exhibition as the apartment's floor plan (assemblage). The caption for this piece merely noted: "Acrylic fiber carpet in a living room adjacent to an entryway, a hallway, a bedroom, and a kitchen." The red industrial carpet is represented as a diagram of the wear and tear created by the occupants through the processes of habit and inhabitation. Thus, this carpet, already condemned as waste, becomes a kind of manual for reuse and instead of being a deficiency, the traces of wear and tear lead to critical reflections on use, users, and construction practices through the new context of the art exhibition. In a similar fashion, an extracted banal industrial staircase shown in the Belgian Pavilion could be read as a map of human movements walking up and down this stair. These works create an understanding of the human body as a formative tool that leaves distinct material traces of everyday human activity. The building components were exhibited in an isolated manner so as to draw closer attention to their own intrinsic qualities – despite or perhaps because of their anonymous and ordinary appearance. Though minimalist in appearance, the *Usus/Usures* exhibition resulted from Rotor's extended research on material wear and tear as well as the reusability of buildings and building materials.

Rotor underscores the fact that sustainability cannot be defined in a scientific way; rather, it is also a sociopolitical matter because it emerges from a multifaceted process with many contributors. The stakes for architecture are aesthetic, socioeconomic, and environmental. Rotor's intention for *Usus/Usures* "was to bring the subject of materiality into the arena of the Venice Biennale opposing the glorification of 'the New' that is implicit in this kind of exhibition format." They intended the subject of wear and tear to draw attention to the reaction of buildings to longtime use while challenging architects to critically anticipate this depreciating process. Thus, looking at buildings through the wear-and-tear lens leads to reflections on use, users, and construction practices. Rotor encourages the public to change their attitude toward building materials, and more broadly toward all objects around us. The discussion of wear and tear is largely taboo in architectural circles partly because it contrasts fundamentally with the value of purgation as well as with construction cycles that have become shorter and shorter. As Rotor notes, "In the twentieth century, under the combined influence of increased real estate pressure, an obsession for speed in demolition, the availability of power machines and explosives and fiscal constructions had encouraged accelerated building obsolescence" (Rotor 2017).

Fig. 4: Rotor: Usus/Usures, railing, Belgium Pavilion, Venice Biennale 2010 (Photo: Eric Mairiaux)

Fig. 5: Rotor: Usus/Usures, staircase, Belgium Pavilion, Venice Biennale 2010 (Photo: Eric Mairiaux)

Case Study 2: Bomel Cultural Center: Exhibition of a Building Assemblage

Rotor's 2014 Bomel Cultural Center in Namur, Belgium (fig. 6), provides another example of how to integrate this reframing and reuse of material practice productive within the framework of architecture. Here, they identify building parts and materials for reuse, relocation, and assemblage and reintegrate reused objects and worn-out materials into their design strategy. Their work with reused materials and building elements is more than just recycling or a mere economic and ecological "functional" assemblage. In this work, Rotor employs a strategy where building parts and interior objects are interpreted through partial integration into several sometimes-conflicting layers of narratives. The Bomel Cultural Center is an adaptive reuse of a former slaughterhouse built in the 1940s in an underprivileged neighborhood of Namur; it was renovated and transformed into a cultural center by BAEB architects in 2014. Rotor was asked to provide equipment and interior design, but also to reflect upon how this place could be utilized. The former interior of the slaughterhouse had been lost in the newly finished renovation, leaving little historical context as reference.

Given the white box situation of a generic, abstract "designed" space, Rotor decided to add a number of new narratives to the building in the form of a building assemblage. For example, they reused decommissioned interiors acquired from financial institutions as a new functional interior for the Bomel Cultural Center and as part of a permanent exhibition that would have guided tours by the curators. They translocated and reused a cappuccino bar from the CEO's headquarters office of the BNP/Paribas Bank in Paris. Of course, this was not simply a neutral or opportunistic move of acquiring parts of a

random interior to serve a cultural center. Rather the former state bank BNP/
Paribas-Fortis had been transformed into a private institution in 1987, but was
saved in the global financial crisis of 2008/09 by public funds. Rotor wanted
to indicate that European taxpayers had helped to save this private financial institution and that, in using the Bomel Cultural Center in Namur, the people had
already (or at least indirectly) "paid" for the former bank CEO's cappuccino bar.
Rotor's strategy is a critical voice against the trend of public support for
lopsided private financial institutions, which leads to austerity measures
against public social support for education, culture, and public housing. In
addition, Rotor's creative intervention has to be read as a critical commentary
on the disparities between the built environment and conventional practices of
heritage preservation. Rather than pure conservation and renovation, Rotor's
engagement with heritage and public interest moves in an entirely different
direction. As Rotor notes: "Looking at a building as an assemblage of elements that can be dismantled and reassembled again, possibly into totally
new configurations forces us to reassess our understanding of architectural
heritage" (Rotor 2017).

*Fig. 6: Rotor: Bomel Cultural Center, Namur, Belgium, 2014, permanent exhibition of reused cap-
puccino bar (Photo: Jean Francois Flamery)*

Conclusion
The Rotor exhibitions deploy the techniques, materials, processes, and spaces
of the art world (museum, galleries, Biennale) as realms for political commentary that are critical of the current global political-economic system. Their distinct analytical approaches entail urgent questions of sustainability, reuse, and

appropriation and suggest a different perspective on the established modes of historical production. They recharge the critical aspect of curating architecture (as already present in the 1960s and 1970s with architect collectives like Superstudio, Archizoom, UFO and Gruppo 9999, Global Tools) and expand it to the problem of reuse: the reuse of materials and of building elements, but also the reuse of ideas, knowledge, archives, and memory. They deconstruct existing value systems in art and architecture and seek to create opportunities for architecture exhibitions as environments that can initiate or foster a radical redesign of the built environment. Rotor continued its critical investigations in sustainability issues in architecture by curating and designing various exhibitions, including the Oslo Triennale 2013 "Behind the Green Door" and the 2016 exhibition *Constellations* in Bordeaux.

References

Bergdoll, Barry. 2015. "Out of site/In plain View: on the Origins and Actuality of the Architecture Exhibition." In *Exhibiting Architecture a Paradox?*, edited by Eeva-Liisa Pelkonen, 13–21. New Haven: Yale University Press.

Borgonuovo, Valerio, and Silvia Franceschini. 2015. *Global Tools*, 1973–1975. Istanbul: SALT/Garanti Kültür AS.

Celant, Germano. 1972. "Radical Architecture." In *Italy: The New Domestic Landscape*, edited by Emilio Ambasz, 380–87. New York: Museum of Modern Art.

Eco, Umberto. 1989. *The Open Work*. Cambridge, MA: Harvard University Press.

Gielen, Maarten. 2016a. "Rotor: Current Preoccupations." Lecture given at AA School of Architecture, London. Accessed February 20, 2019. https://www.youtube.com/watch?v=o4-5uXW7dWo.

Gielen, Maarten. 2016b. "Rotor Deconstruction." Lecture given at CCA. Accessed February 20, 2019. https://www.youtube.com/watch?v=YL-HlxEh_oRk.

Greub, Charlott. 2018. "Craft as a Process and Performance of Resistance: Rotor, Wim Delvoye and Deconstructing Architecture." In *Dialectic: Craft VI*, edited by Ole W. Fischer and Shundana Yusaf, 46–53. Salt Lake City: University of Utah/Novato: ORO Editions.

Rotor. 2015. "Comment extraire les matériaux réutilisables de bâtiments publics?" Accessed February 23, 2019. http://www.vademecum-reuse.org/Vademecum_extraire_les_materiaux_reutilisables-Rotor.pdf.

Rotor. 2017. "Urban Mining, Salvaging Materials: Conference Statement." In *Deconstruction: An International Symposium on Off-Site Reuse in Architecture*, edited by Dirk van den Heuvel, Maarten Gielen, and Lionel Devlieger. 7–12. Accessed February 20, 2019. http://deconstructionconference.nl/booklet.pdf.

Grounding Associative Geometry: From Universal Style toward Specific Form

Corneel Cannaerts[1] and Holger Hoffmann[2]
[1] KU Leuven, Belgium
[2] University of Wuppertal (BUW), Germany

Abstract — This paper describes the application of associative geometry to specific issues of local architectural practice and building culture. It is a deliberate deviation from a mere technological fascination with computation-based form toward a refined understanding of place-form that is explored and specified with the help of parametric design. Two houses, designed and built with recent digital design and construction techniques at very specific places, illustrate the argument. Since their designs have profited from the ramifications and contingencies of architectural and building practice, they help to address questions on context, typology, tectonics, material articulation, craftsmanship, and place-form. Thus, the reciprocal reflection on building practice and architectural research helps to enrich both: the development of digital technologies in relation to disciplinary topics, such as a refined approach toward context.

Introduction

Today, some twenty years after Greg Lynn's book *Animate Form*, digital technologies have deeply steeped in contemporary architectural practice and culture. Since the 1990s the digital has, formulated, questioned, reformulated, and varied its methodological and aesthetic agendas and has reached a stage in which – indeed – "being digital will be noticed only by its absence, not its presence" (Negroponte 1998).

Contemporary methods and formal strategies, such as calculus-based curvature or the geometrical differentiation of building parts, widely rely on what is called *parametric design* that again primarily depends on associative geometry. Other than traditional ways of drawing architecture that happen in a linear fashion, associative geometry introduces a comparably broad design space; its geometric elasticity and continuous reversibility allows it to simultaneously assess a great number of possible results. Certain parameters of an architectural project, such as the distribution of its program, its climatic relations, or structural logic, are quantified, parametrized, and translated into geometrical relations.

Apparently, other important influences, such as the cultural demands of a specific place, are hard to quantify and to address, as such information might oppose a predefined formal vocabulary. This can be understood as being problematic, as it interferes with the cause-and-effect logic of parametric design. However, if one accepts this confrontation as a main influence to the project, a sort of parametric semiology (Yuan 2016) can help to build a strong relationship between contemporary architecture and the demands of its actual place. Then architectural form is neither alienated because of the overwhelming power of digital tools nor unnecessarily unresponsive to the novelties the digital turn has introduced into our discipline.

Parametricism and Beyond

Architects initially approached digital technologies to merely reproduce their analog tools of drafting, modeling, and rendering in a digital medium (Gänshirt 2007). In order to pursue their conceptual and formal agenda the digital avant-garde of the 1990s borrowed software from digital animations and the aviation industry (Allen 2009, 84). These comparably mighty tools helped to gain back a great deal of formal, spatial, and structural complexity in architecture that, with the preeminence of modernism, seemed to have widely diminished during the second half of the twentieth century. Rising from the sound theoretical and methodological groundwork of Deconstructivism, the ostensibly new and obviously complex forms allowed architects to formulate another paradigm shift for their discipline. Patrik Schumacher's (2008) formulation of parametricism as an epochal style might be the most vehement demand in that sense. His claim built on the emergence of parametric design tools specifically developed for architecture and coincided with the arrival of digital fabrication machines in academia and practice.

Today architectural design tools have matured into a discipline-specific digital toolbox. Through building information modeling (BIM), lighting and energy simulations, modeling material specifications, and structural performance, digital models have become more than digital versions of representation: they increasingly include information for the construction and performance of architecture. Accordingly, parametric architecture often justifies its complex geometry by a so-called indexical relationship of heteronomic parameters (performative aspects, such as climatic influences or structural optimization) and form. In this sense, we have shifted from a regime of representation to one of simulation (Sheer 2014).

The maturing of digital architectural design tools has also led to standardization: the majority of architects use the same handful of software tools. BIM is increasingly becoming a shared model that incorporates different aspects and stakeholders active within architectural design. We see an increased democratization of the development of software, through add-ons and plug-ins, often addressing requirements arising from practice. A prime example of this is Grasshopper, an associative geometry add-on for Rhinoceros3D, which has given rise to a whole ecosystem of extensions, expanding its functionality into simulation, fabrication, electronics, and robotics. Architects nowadays have access to a design environment that is highly customizable to the needs of their practice (Davis and Brady 2013).

Generic Solutions and Specific Form

Designing with associative geometry instead of explicit geometry shifts the attention of the architect from modeling a singular design solution to modeling a parametric definition that encodes associations between numeric inputs and geometry. Working with associative geometry changes how variations in design solutions are explored. The parametric model defines a solution space and provides a tool for exploring it (Woodbury 2010). While considerable effort is spent on developing a parametric model, it allows for design parameters to be changed later in the design process, which would be unfeasible when explicitly modeling geometry.

Architects known for using computational design, through either parametric modeling or scripting, identify avoiding repetitive work as a major reason for introducing these techniques to their design practice (Burry 2011, 28). While repetition has been called the computer's unique talent (Reas and McWilliams 2010, 53), equally important is the idea of differentiation, or variable. Associative geometry decouples the logic of the algorithm as a precise set of instructions from the specific numeric and geometric instances it operates on. Although algorithms are inherently repeatable, each iteration can be different, based on variables (ibid., 95). This idea of iterative differentiation has been crucial in the development of digital architecture, based on Deleuze's concept of difference and repetition, and introduced into architecture by Greg Lynn (1999, 33).

Using associative geometry within practice there are some limitations to both arguments presented above. The additional interface allows for a different kind of feedback: as there is no clear difference between making the parametric model and using it to explore variations, often the parametric model is built up while designing, requiring the alteration of the associations during the design process. Furthermore, while associative geometry allows for iterative differentiation, where each repetition is different, each element in this iterative series follows the same parametric layout or graph of associations.

In architectural practice, often more radical differences are needed to adapt to local circumstances, breaking the underlying associations (Davis et al. 2011).

Those processual imponderables confront an idealized and comprehensive digital chain. Place-specific possibilities and mentalities of, for instance, local craftsmanship are not understood as an obstacle, but as an important cultural impact that helps to inform computation-based design and construction. By deliberately incorporating the logics and needs of local context and culture, computer-based design processes are opened toward information that questions and confronts hierarchies often embedded in digital form-making. Such a project-specific parametric definition, while solving a particular design problem on a generic level, can be used to generate highly specific forms.

Autonomy and Contexts

With today's broad understanding of not only the possibilities, but also the obstacles of digital processes, architects have started to look at comparably resilient conceptual frameworks to steer parametric relations. This interest has shifted the focus toward preceding solutions that are derived from architecture as such. Thus, it is not just quantifiable information that informs a design. Instead, tectonic, typological, or figurative themes process and carefully contextualize architectural form. This contextualization establishes relationships between the formal logic of parametric design and relevant architectural themes, such as concrete patterns or figures that are derived from a specific place. Parametricism's claim for a universality of style is answered with the specificity of an architectural solution, whereby the elasticity of associative geometry allows for iterative adaptation, specification, and thus contextualization. Such an architectural object is neither alienated nor entirely embedded. However, it estranges the nature of a specific place due to the transformative nature of its underlying digital tools.

Two Houses

Two houses built within specific contexts in Germany (Haus H) and in Flanders (House EC) shall elucidate the above-described methods. While the Flemish architectural culture is known for its inventiveness in working within heterogeneous and diverse textured contexts, the east Westphalian landscape shows rather homogeneous formal and typological patterns. Thus, the comparison of the two houses and their specific responses to local conditions will illustrate how parametric techniques were employed in the design process in order to support the contextualization of architectural form.

Haus H

Haus H is based on a morphological transformation of vernacular farmhouse typologies (a so-called Vierständerhaus, see fig. 1) that are very common in the northern part of Germany. In order to further develop and adapt those typologies, their geometric relations were analyzed and migrated into an associative digital model that connects the transformative logic of digital hybridization with explicitly formulated regional figures, such as the tripartite plan (fig. 2) and multidirectional gabled roofs (fig. 3).

The use of current algorithmic transformation tools has thus resulted in a sort of gestalt-amalgam that is both a truly digital and a deeply contextual project. It is a version of "place form" that is bound to and yet clearly estranged from its context. Thus, the elasticity that is key to associative geometry helps to balance required functions, building legislation – but first and foremost it transforms local gestalt-patterns, such as the now multidirectional gabled roof. While the well-known shapes of the four gables remain undisturbed, the "tweening" of the gables results in a row of distorted surfaces that together obscure the familiar image of a traditional gabled roof (fig. 4).

Fig. 1: Diagram showing the transformation of a Vierständerhaus typology, One Fine Fay Architects

Fig. 2: Ground-floor plan that shows the transformed tripartite plan, One Fine Day Architects

Fig. 3: Top view of interconnected roof surfaces (Photo: courtesy One Fine Day Architects)

Fig. 4: Estranged gabled roofs (Photo: courtesy One Fine Day Architects)

This combination of digital techniques and local, place-specific, content has helped to gain twofold information: on the one hand, the house illustrates a method to estrange place-form. On the other hand, it generally contributes to the design of connected, distorted hyperbolic-surfaces and their construction logic in architecture.

House EC

House EC is a renovation project of a single-family house on the banks of a river developed by Perneel Osten Architecten in collaboration with Corneel Cannaerts (De Caigny 2016). The central element of the project consists of a timber roof structure that refers to the typology of barns typical of the respective region. The roof structure covers the existing part of the house, is folded over the new extension, and comes down to demarcate the entrance and exterior functions. For the largest part of the project the timber roof structure is visible, both on the inside and on the outside. It is supported by new and existing brick walls and three concrete volumes. The roof structure unites different spaces, providing a similar architectural articulation throughout the project while adapting to various local requirements and the new and existing support structures.

Three parametric models were made during the design of the roof structure and its support structures, encoding geometric and material constraints, allowing for exploring design variations and form specification. A first model (fig. 5) shows the design of the overall shape of the roof and the material articulations and specification of the primary and secondary beams, structures, incorporating constraints related to construction fabrication, planarity, roof pitches and adapting to the support structures.

A second model (fig. 6) shows the design of the concrete volumes and the formwork for casting and connections to the timber structure.

A third model (figs. 7 and 8) shows the resolution of complex timber joints where varying numbers of the main beams meet, allowing for the specification of different sizes and angles of beams. While these three models use associative geometry, incorporating technical parameters of construction and fabrication, they are not integrated in one large parametric scheme. The models only parametrize the geometries where associative geometry is beneficial for exploring algorithmic design variation, while keeping the possibility for architects to intervene and manipulate local geometries manually. The digital models were also complemented with physical models at various stages of the design process to verify geometries coming out of the modeling process.

Both houses show a range of applications of associative geometries that are set in relation to specific contexts. We have focused on two aspects to foster the argument: Haus H shows the estrangement of place-specific formal gestures through digital transformation. House EC shows the integration of as-found building parts with a contemporary formal approach and a response to constraints that result from the necessities of structural design and local manufacturing possibilities.

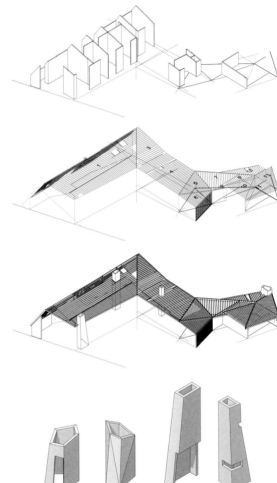

Fig. 5: Model 1: Folding roof structure over existing structure and extension, negotiating support structure and material articulation (Diagram: Corneel Cannaerts)

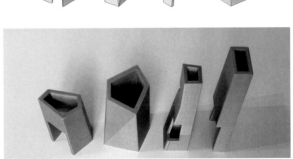

Fig. 6: Model 2: Concrete supporting volumes and 1:50 scale models (Models: Corneel Cannaerts)

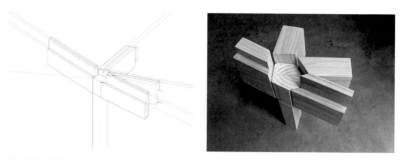

Fig. 7: Model 3: Timber joint detailing (Model: Corneel Cannaerts)
Fig. 8: Model 3: Timber joint mock-up scale 1:2 (Photo: courtesy Perneel Osten Architecten)

Fig. 9: Roof structure model (Photo: courtesy Perneel Osten Architecten)

Fig. 10: Exterior view toward extension (Photo: courtesy Arnout Fonck)

Fig. 11: Interior view of extension (Photo: courtesy Arnout Fonck)

Conclusion

This paper demonstrates how a contemporary approach toward associative geometry addresses aspects of architectural design that extend the intentions and application of digital architecture. The explicit incorporation of, for instance, aspects of typology, tectonics, material articulation, craftsmanship, or place-form on a computer-generated form hints at a possible path of grounding contemporary formal language and methods. As the examples of two houses show, vernacular form and typologies as well as local craft and tectonics can blend the messiness of handed-down building culture with the idealist approach that often is embedded in research projects within the field of digital design and construction. And, while the discussed houses differ in context and in the way associative geometries are operationalized, both projects point at an approach toward associative geometry that is specifically related to context, craft, and grounded within architectural practice.

References

Allen, Stan. 2009. "Post-Script, the Digital Complex Ten Years Later," In *Practice: Architecture, Technique + Representation*, edited by Stan Allen, 84–93. London: Routledge.

Burry, Mark. 2011. *Scripting Cultures: Architectural Design and Programming*. New York: Wiley.

Centre Georges Pompidou, ed. 2003. *Architectures Non Standard: Exposition Présentée Au Centre Pompidou*. Paris: Centre Pompidou.

Davis, Daniel, and Brady Peters. 2013. "Design Ecosystems: Customising the Architectural Design Enviroment with Software Plug-ins." In *Computation Works: The Building of Algorithmic Thought*, edited by Brady Peters and Xavier De Kestelier, 124–31. Chichester: Wiley.

Davis, Daniel, Jane Burry, and Mark Burry. 2011. "Untangling Parametric Schemata: Enhancing Collaboration through Modular Programming." In *CAAD Futures 2011: Designing Together*, edited by Pierre Leclercq, Ann Heylighen, and Genevieve Martin, 55–68. Liège: Les Editions de l'Université de Liège.

De Caigny, Sophie, ed. 2016. *Maatwerk/Made to Measure: Concept and Craft in Architecture from Flanders and the Netherlands*. Antwerp: Flanders Architecture Institute.

Gänshirt, Christian. 2007. *Tools for Ideas*. Zurich: Birkhäuser.

Lynn, Greg. 1999. *Animate Form*. New York: Princeton Architectural Press.

Negroponte, Nicholas. 1998. "Beyond Digital." *WIRED* 6, no. 12. Accessed February 24, 2019. https://web.media.mit.edu/~nicholas/Wired/WIRED6-12.html. 1998.

Reas, Casey, and Chandler McWilliams. 2010. *Form+Code in Design, Art, and Architecture*. New York: Princeton Architectural Press.

Scheer, David R. 2014. *The Death of Drawing: Architecture in the Age of Simulation*. London: Routledge.

Schumacher, Patrik. 2008. "Parametricism as Style: Parametricist Manifesto," https://www.patrikschumacher.com/Texts/Parametricism%20as%20Style.htm#_edn1.

Woodbury, Robert. 2010. *Elements of Parametric Design*. London: Routledge.

Yuan, Philipp. 2016. "Parametric Regionalism." In *Parametricism 2.0.*, edited by Patrik Schumacher, 92–99. London: Wiley.

4 Design Methods

Why Evidence-Based Methods Are Useful for Architectural and Urban Design

Beatrix Emo
ETH Zurich, Switzerland

Abstract — Several methods exist for analyzing how people experience and behave in the built environment. Many of such methods can also be used to predict how people might behave in an as-yet-unbuilt space, thus providing the opportunity to inform design decisions. One term that has been used to describe such methods is *evidence-based design*. The aim of this paper is to elucidate the term itself and to discuss whether such methods are useful for architectural design. The paper gives an overview of the current state of this toolkit and describes several of the methods currently being adopted, including space syntax, spatial cognition, behavioral observation, and virtual and mixed reality. Interdisciplinary research between architects and psychologists have brought useful advances in developing such methods; examples are given from such work at the crossroads of architectural design and applied spatial cognition. The paper argues that such methods are useful for architectural design.

Introduction

Evidence-based methods have become popular over the last few decades in a number of fields (Hamilton 2003). The use of the term in architectural and urban design, however, is not yet fully established. The term has been used when discussing hospital design and there is a consensus as to what the term means in that context: to redesign hospitals so that the needs of the users (doctors, patients, hospital staff, visitors, etc.) are met. Case studies have shown the effectiveness of evidence-based design methods to reach these goals. For example, the pioneering study by Roger Ulrich (1984) showed the health benefits for surgery patients who could see natural landscapes from their rooms compared to those who looked onto a brick wall. Evidence-based design methods have also been discussed in the context of office design, and have been used to show how spatial relationships can affect workplace performance and staff satisfaction (Sailer et al. 2008). Furthermore, there seems to be an interest in discussing how such methods might be useful for the field of architecture, as the newly established journal entitled *Evidence-Based Design* suggests. This paper discusses why evidence-based methods are useful for architectural design.

For the fields of architectural and urban design, evidence-based design methods refer to the use of some form of data that informs the design process. Architecture and urban design have different design processes; broadly speaking, it can be said that architecture refers to building-scale projects, whereas urban design refers to projects that span several buildings, and so includes how individual elements fit into a larger context. The way these two disciplines use evidence-based design methods is, however, not too distinct; therefore, this paper covers both the building and urban scale. The use of evidence-based design methods as a design tool, and therefore the use of data during the design process, does not necessarily limit the creativity of the designer. It depends on how the methods are used. For centuries the classification of architecture as either an art or a science, or the discipline's place in an art-science spectrum has been debated. This paper does not seek to enter into such a debate, but argues that evidence-based design methods can be useful for architectural and urban design.

Evidence-based design methods are one possible input into the design process, to be used alongside the creative genius of the designer. They often refer to a simulation or analytic tool that can provide information on a specific aspect of the design that could not otherwise be reflected in the design proposal. Architects and urban planners usually develop a proposal over time, and the process is defined by a series of intermediate milestones. Evidence-based design methods fit in seamlessly with such a workflow as they are most effective when used iteratively. The feedback loop between the findings from a simulation or analysis ("evidence-based design method") and the design process is one exciting aspect behind using evidence-based design methods in architectural and urban design.

This paper focuses on evidence-based design methods in architectural and urban design that help to understand the needs of the eventual end user.[1] Such methods differ from other commonly used tools such as BIM (Building Information Modeling) which provides static information related to a building, and transport models or Geographical Information Systems (GIS) modeling, which are used in urban planning to account for certain properties of a project, but not the users' experience.[2] Architects seldomly ignore the needs of the eventual end user. Quite on the contrary, a competition brief, and the ensuing design program, often places the needs of the user at the forefront. It is quite common for the design team to hold workshops with people who will end up using the building and for lessons drawn from such workshops to be brought into the design project in varying levels of detail. The question arises therefore, in projects where this is the case, why are users' needs not met? Put another way, why do people get lost in buildings that were designed to be easy to navigate? There is no simple answer to this question, as it is bound to the context and circumstances of each project. This paper argues that an elaborate set of methods could be helpful in addressing this point. Such a toolkit should be able to explain why spaces don't work (once built) and to be able to flag such spaces during the design process.

Evidence-Based Design Methods

Evidence-based design methods for architectural and urban design use data to inform the design process. Typically, this data takes the form of a simulation or analytic tool. The methods can be used iteratively in the various design stages of a proposal. This paper discusses only a selection of possible methods that elucidate the needs of the eventual end user. This draws on a relatively new body of research that analyses the complexity behind how a designer anticipates the eventual end user of a certain building or urban space (fig. 1). The strength of such research is that it lies at the interface of architecture and spatial cognition, allowing designers to gain a greater understanding of how people will end up using and inhabiting the space that they design (Emo, Al Sayed, and Varoudis 2016).

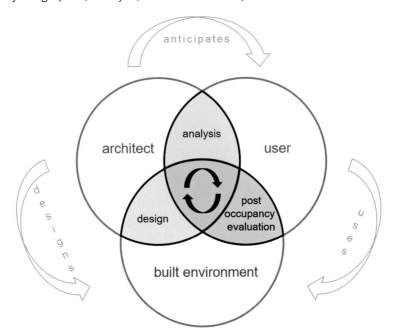

Fig. 1: The design-analysis feedback loop, indicated at the center of this diagram, is at the heart of the evidence-based design toolkit (image after Dalton and Hölscher, 2017)

The field of spatial cognition is concerned with how humans and animals "perceive, interpret, mentally represent, and interact with the spatial characteristics of their environment" (Waller and Nadel 2013, 3). It is a branch of cognitive science that spans a vast number of topics and applies methods from different disciplines. Collaborative research between cognitive scientists and architects have highlighted an exciting area of overlap between the disciplines that is of mutual interest between the two groups (Dalton, Hölscher, and Turner 2012). One aim of this interdisciplinary research field is to develop cognitively-relevant design heuristics that can be applied during the design process: the subsequent section describes current research in this direction.

The paper gives a brief overview of some of the methods that are currently being adopted to address user-oriented architectural and urban design. The focus is on space syntax and spatial cognition, and the given examples reflect such a focus. Many of the examples come from research, only a few from actually implemented projects. One way to address the gap between the application of evidence-based design methods in research and in practice is to include such methods as part of the architectural curriculum so that students are familiar with such methods when they embark on their professional careers. There is a strong tradition of specialised master-level courses aimed at qualified architects, prevalent also in the space syntax community. It has been notoriously difficult to embed such knowledge within the architectural curriculum; one such attempt is documented in figure 2 (Emo and Hölscher 2017). The following section gives a brief overview of different types of methods that form part of the toolkit.

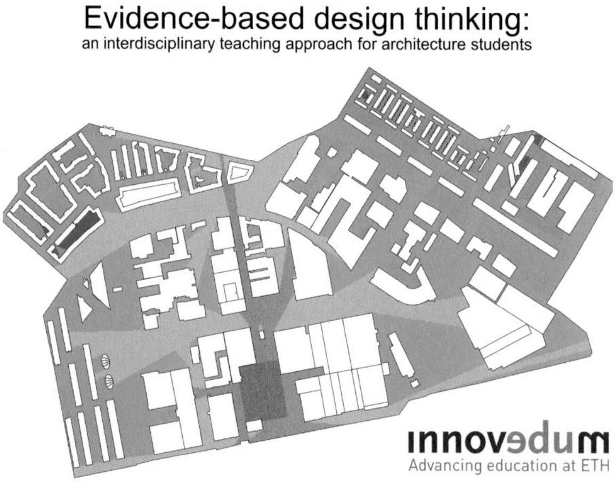

Evidence-based design thinking:
an interdisciplinary teaching approach for architecture students

innovꙅdum
Advancing education at ETH

Fig. 2: An example of an interdisciplinary teaching initiative embedding evidence-based design methods within the architectural curriculum

BEHAVIORAL OBSERVATIONS

Behavioral observations involve collecting empirical data on how users behave in space. Several methods exist (for a review of the most common ones that are used in architecture, see Al Sayed 2014). Often these are conducted in such a way that the observer does not interfere with the users' activity. Gate counts are used to estimate the average density of people and/or cars moving in a certain space. They are helpful for places where people and cars are moving. Route traces allow the observer to form an idea of what direction people tend to take by recording the actual path taken. Static snapshots allow the observer to gain a good idea of what activities people undertake in a space in a short amount of time. The observer takes a mental snapshot of what people are doing at a given moment and documents these on a floor plan/map of the space.

QUESTIONNAIRE AND INTERVIEW DATA

Another set of methods for collecting data on how people behave in space involve asking respondents directly. This is quite different from the aforementioned set of methods, which instead rely on observed behavior, because of the subjectivity of the response. One method, common in the social sciences, is to collect questionnaire or survey data. This type of data is useful because it can be collected easily for large numbers, and can be analyzed statistically to make inferences about the sampled population. Questionnaire data is often used alongside interview data. Interview data is useful in built environment studies because there is no standard way to describe the built environment, and people often use different words when referring to the same thing. The type of data collected varies according to how the interview is set up (for example, structured, semistructured, open-ended, etc.), but is generally used for a smaller sample population than with questionnaire data. Another key difference between questionnaire and interview data is that the former is mainly quantitative, whereas the latter is mainly qualitative.

VISIBILITY ANALYSES AND SPACE SYNTAX

Users' behavior in space can be linked to what one can see from any particular standpoint. This is a central tenet of the set of theories and methods collectively known as space syntax. Broadly speaking, space syntax methods link people's use of a space to its layout; visibility is one of the key characteristics of spatial layout that has been examined. Space syntax connects spatial layout at the building and urban scale to users' behavior in terms of pedestrian movement, vehicular movement, people's behavior, and even socioeconomic activity (for example, the distribution of land use). Applying this type of knowledge in the design process is an effective way of accounting for the eventual end users' behavior in space.

Paying attention to the visibility properties of a space during the design process is not new. Architects have always worked with visibility and lines of sight. What space syntax adds is the ability to predict how the space will end up being used based on an in-depth analysis of a design's visibility characteristics. The tools that have been, and are being, developed to achieve this goal are useful, but there are some limitations. For a designer to gain maximum benefit of such tools, they should be computationally fast and imbedded within a designers' software of choice. This would allow the designer to truly use visibility as a design tool by developing design variations based on feedback from the visibility-based analysis. Current space syntax tools, which require design files to be imported before (and exported after) they are processed, hinder practitioners from using them, as they cannot be used seamlessly during the design process. Another limitation is that visibility and the link with user behavior is just one part of a successful design proposal, and practitioners need to choose where to allocate resources given the numerous possible inputs available. Nevertheless, several examples exist of spaces where the modeling of the visibility properties of a space was influential in the redesign of an eventually built space.

A classic example of the use of visibility as a design tool for a project that went on to be built is the analysis done by Space Syntax Ltd for Foster and Partners as part of the competition to redesign Trafalgar Square, London, in the 1990s (Hillier 1998). Advanced spatial modeling of the street network and behavioral observations of pedestrian activity patterns showed that locals usually avoided passing through the center of the square and that tourists had difficulty connecting with Parliament Square nearby. This analysis was embedded into the winning master plan proposal; behavioral observations of the completed redesign show a much better use of the space by locals and tourists alike. Countless other examples exist in which advanced spatial modeling of the visibility properties of a space have led to informed design proposals that have been implemented in the completed redesigned space, both at the building and urban scale (see www.spacesyntax.com). As the above example shows, visibility is often used together with other tools to be able to reach an in-depth understanding of how a space is used.

SIMULATION AND AGENT-BASED MODELING

Of the numerous types of simulation tools available, agent-based modeling (ABM), or agent-based modeling and simulation (ABMS), is the most adept at providing information relating to how people use spaces in order to inform the design process. This section provides only a very brief overview of current work using ABM to inform user-oriented architectural design (for more general reviews of ABM see Chen 2012; for AMBS, see Macal 2016). Given the literature mentioned above, ABM that centers on visibility is particularly relevant. An early such model is quite rudimentary, in that agents are pro-grammed to choose the longest line of sight based on a defined field of view, and they reassess their path after three steps (Turner and Penn 2002). Cur-rent work is seeking to develop a more cognitive agent which would include many more parameters than simply visibility (see Raubal 2001; Becker-Asano et al. 2014; Schaumann et al. 2016; and Mavros et al. 2019).

BEHAVIORAL EXPERIMENTS

Behavioral experiments collect empirical data on user behavior in a system-atic way and are a common data collection method in the cognitive sciences (Eysenck and Keane 2013). They can be conducted in outdoor settings or in the lab.[3] Combining such methods to gain insights on how individuals use the built environment is part of the aim of many groups across the globe, includ-ing my current group at the Chair of Cognitive Science at ETH Zurich (for an overview of projects see www.cog.ethz.ch/research). The limitation of such an approach for architectural and urban design is that the results are dependent on the responses of a small sample, given a specific context and experimental design. Architectural design is also context-specific; however, it is difficult to translate the findings of a behavioral experiment into a design recommen-dation. Furthermore, much more work is needed to be able to elaborate some-thing close to a set of heuristics that could be used during the design process as a checklist for good navigability in buildings and urban spaces.

Limitations of Evidence-Based Design Methods

One limitation of evidence-based design methods is that it is difficult for practitioners to implement them in their daily work. Of the several types of evidence-based design methods described above, only some are common-ly used by practitioners. The most commonly used tool is simulation, and those tools that integrate seamlessly with the designer's CAD software are the most successful. Although many architectural offices develop their own tools, several software tools or plug-ins exist (some are also open source) that allow for evidence-based design concepts to be tested, evaluated, and integrated. Another commonly used tool, usually integrated by default into larger projects, is to collect data directly from the eventual end user through specific workshops. The type of data collected is not dissimilar to that collected during questionnaires and/or interviews; the main difference is that the data collection procedure, as described above, is systematic, whereas data collected during stakeholder workshops might not be.

Another limitation is that evidence-based design work is often seen to evalu-ate what makes a design good or bad. This is problematic because it impinges on the creativity of the design process. Evidence-based design methods are intended to allow the designer to use the eventual end users as input during the design process. Much research to date has focused on the case of spaces where people get lost (for example, Carlson et al. 2010). The logic behind this is that spaces are designed for the people who use them, and people dislike getting lost; it has therefore been suggested that spaces where people get lost are worthy of further analysis, to see how the space's navigability can be improved. An example of such research comes from a collaboration between architects and psychologists on the Seattle Public Library, designed by OMA and opened in 2004 (Dalton and Hölscher 2017). Through a number of empirical studies, the book shows how people actually use the building today and, in instances where users relate dissatisfaction with the building, discusses what the original design intentions were. Critics of such research take issue with the assumption that a building should be navigable. The next generation of evidence-based design methods should work closely with designers to make sure that developments in the toolkit match the input that designers strive for. Only in this way can spaces be designed and built that truly accommodate how people use them.

Conclusions

This paper discusses the methods developed as part of architectural research that focuses on the user of built spaces. It discusses the term *evidence-based design* in terms of designing with a focus on the needs of the eventual end user. Although the term does not occur frequently in the field, the paper argues that it is the appropriate term for a set of methods developed for the purpose of analyzing and predicting users' experience of the built environment. A more detailed analysis is needed to see how the methods described in this paper link to methods used in other fields, such as sociology (Stanek, Schmid and Moravánsky 2015) and ethnography (Kaijima, Stalder and Iseki 2018). The paper outlines the current state of an evidence-based design toolkit, with a focus on space syntax and spatial cognition methods, and gives examples of how such methods are currently being used in practice, research, and teaching.

References

Becker-Asano, Christian, Felix Ruzzoli, Christoph Hölscher, and Bernhard Nebel. 2014. "A Multi-Agent System Based on Unity 4 for Virtual Perception and Wayfinding." *Transportation Research Procedia* 2: 452–55.

Brown, Robert D., and Robert C. Corry. 2011. "Evidence-Based Landscape Architecture: The Maturing of a Profession." *Landscape and Urban Planning* 100, no. 4: 327–29.

Carlson, Laura A., Christoph Hölscher, Thomas F. Shipley, and Ruth Conroy Dalton. 2010. "Getting Lost in Buildings." *Current Directions in Psychological Science* 19, no. 5: 284–89.

Chen, Liang. 2012. "Agent-Based Modeling in Urban and Architectural Research: A Brief Literature Review." *Frontiers of Architectural Research* 1, no. 2: 166–77.

Dalton, Ruth Conroy, and Christoph Hölscher. 2017. *Take One Building: Interdisciplinary Research Perspectives of the Seattle Central Library*. London: Routledge.

Dalton, Ruth Conroy, Christoph Hölscher, and Alasdair Turner. 2012. "Understanding Space: The Nascent Synthesis of Cognition and the Syntax of Spatial Morphologies." *Environment and Planning B: Planning and Design* 39, no. 1: 7–11.

Emo, Beatrix, and Christoph Hölscher. 2017. "Evidence-Based Design Thinking." ETH Zurich, Innoview Project. Accessed February 28, 2019. https://www.innoview.ethz.ch/projekt/evidence-based-design-thinking.

Emo, Beatrix, Kinda Al-Sayed, and Tasos Varoudis. 2016. "Design, Cognition and Behaviour: Usability in the Built Environment." *International Journal of Design Creativity and Innovation* 4, no. 2: 63–66.

Evidence-Based Design. Accessed February 28, 2019. http://ebdjournal.com/.

Eysenck, Michael W., and Mark T. Keane. 2013. *Cognitive Psychology: A Student's Handbook*. Psychology Press, 2013.

Hamilton, D. Kirk. 2003. "The Four Levels of Evidence-Based Practice." *Healthcare Design* 3, no. 4: 18–26.

Hillier, Bill. 1998. "From Research to Design: Re-engineering the Space of Trafalgar Square." *Urban Design Quarterly*, 68, October, pp 35-37.

Kaijima, Momoyo, Laurent Stalder, and Yu Iseki. 2018. *Architectural Ethnography: Japanese Pavilion Venice Biennale 2018*. Tokyo: Toto.

Karimi, Kayvan. 2012. "Evidence-Informed and Analytical Methods in Urban Design." *Urban Design International* 17, no. 4: 253–56.

Krukar, Jakub, Ruth Conroy Dalton, and Christoph Hölscher. 2016. "Applying HCI Methods and Concepts to Architectural Design (Or Why Architects Could Use HCI Even if They Don't Know It)." In *Architecture and Interaction*, 17–35. Cham: Springer.

Kuliga, Saskia F., Tyler Thrash, Ruth Conroy Dalton, and Christoph Hölscher. 2015. "Virtual Reality as an Empirical Research Tool: Exploring User Experience in a Real Building and a Corresponding Virtual Model." *Computers, Environment and Urban Systems* 54: 363–75.

Macal, Charles M. 2016. "Everything You Need to Know about Agent-Based Modelling and Simulation." *Journal of Simulation* 10, no. 2: 144–56.

Mavros, Panos, Rohit Dubey, Kristina Jazuk, Hengshan Li, and Christoph Hölscher. 2019. "Architectural Psychology for Mixed-Use Cities." In *Future Cities Lab: Indicia 02*, 128–36. Zurich: Lars Müller Publisher.

Raubal, Martin. 2001. "Ontology and Epistemology for Agent-Based Way-finding Simulation." *International Journal of Geographical Information Science* 15, no. 7 (2001): 653–65.

"Research." n.d. *ETH Zürich Department of Humanities, Social and Political Sciences*. Accessed April 24, 2019. www.cog.ethz.ch/research.

Sailer, Kerstin, Andrew Budgen, Nathan Lonsdale, Alasdair Turner, and Alan Penn. 2008. "Evidence-Based Design: Theoretical and Practical Reflections of an Emerging Approach in Office Architecture." In *Undisciplined! Design Research Society Conference 2008*, Sheffield: Hallam University, 2009.

Schaumann, Davide, Michal Gath Morad, Einat Zinger, Nirit Putievsky Pilosof, Hadas Sopher, Michal Brodeschi, Kartikeya Date, and Yehuda E. Kalay. 2016. "A Computational Framework to Simulate Human Spatial Behavior in Built Environments." In *SimAUD 2016: Proceedings of the Symposium on Simulation for Architecture and Urban Design*, edited by Ramtin Attar, Angelos Chronis, Sean Hanna, and Michela Turrin, 121–28. San Diego, CA: SCS.

Stanek, Lukasz, Christian Schmid, and Ákos Moravánszky, eds. 2015. *Urban Revolution Now: Henri Lefebvre in Social Research and Architecture*. Burlington: Ashgate Publishing.

Turner, Alasdair, and Alan Penn. 2002. "Encoding Natural Movement as an Agent-Based System: An Investigation into Human Pedestrian Behaviour in the Built Environment." *Environment and Planning B: Planning and Design* 29, no. 4: 473–90.

Ulrich, Roger S. 1984. "View through a Window May Influence Recovery from Surgery." *Science* 224, no. 4647: 420–21.

Waller, David, and Lynn Nadel. 2013. "Introduction: Frameworks for Understanding Spatial Thought (or Wrapping Our Heads around Space)." In *Handbook of Spatial Cognition*. Washington, DC: American Psychological Association.

----

[1] For a review of evidence-based methods focusing on other facets within built environment studies, see Brown and Corry 2011 for landscape architecture; and Karimi 2012 on urban design.

[2] For a discussion on the use of Human Computer Interaction (HCI) techniques in architecture see Krukar et al. 2016.

[3] Very few examples that directly compare the use of virtual reality versus the real world have been done; see, for example, Kuliga et al. 2015.

Architecture as Science of Structures

Toni Kotnik
Aalto University, Finland

Abstract — Digital design techniques are not only an extension of design methods but are also changing the way of thinking. The digital enforces a precision in design methods and techniques with the operative as an index of this shift in thinking. This paper argues that the digital unleashes architecture as a discipline with a close relationship to mathematics and aims at sketching digital design thinking as a phenomenological computation, a space-oriented exploration of organizational patterns and a new form of structuralism understood as an active act of construction relationships. This opens up a way of linking scientific and artistic ways of thinking by means of computation and helps to view the design process as research activity and systematic locus of production of knowledge within architecture.

Introduction

Over the past decades, digital technologies have been adapted almost universally as the predominant means of production in architectural practice. These technologies have enabled new methods of design and enlarged the possibilities of architectural expression. But up to the present, the discourse on the digital in architecture as a discipline is dominated by this focus on architectural form, its rule-based generation as well as its fabrication (Kolarevic 2003; Picon 2010; Oxman and Oxman 2013). This focus on making is overshadowing the transformative potential of the digital for architectural thinking. With the digital, architecture is taking part in an "intellectual revolution [that] is happening all around us, but few people are remarking on it. Computational thinking is influencing research in nearly all disciplines, both in the sciences and the humanities. [...] It is changing the way we think" (Bundy 2007, 67).

A change of thinking is apparent already in early writings on digital architectural design, like for example in the publications of Greg Lynn. His *Folding in Architecture* (1993) was a catalyst for a wave of change that marked the turn of the millennium, when the avant-garde that evolved out of it was regarded as "the quintessential architectural embodiment of the new digital technologies that were booming at that time" (Carpo 2004, 14). This embodiment of the digital into design thinking is made explicit in Lynn's subsequent publication *Animate Form* (1999) in which he argues that form in architecture is not static anymore but rather a dynamic entity in constant interaction with its contextual conditions. What is new in Lynn's argumentation is not that architecture is reacting to its immediate environment but that this interaction is made explicit by means of formalization – that is, the interaction of the architectural form with its surroundings is made operative.

Operative Structures

Traditionally, teaching in design thinking is based on providing conceptual tools and embodied processes foundational to architectural design with the design process itself as a sequence of steps taken to arrive at a conclusion. Within this sequence of steps, design methods are used as generative tools but the exact nature of the methods or of overall process is often obscure (Rowe 1987, 2; Plowright 2014, 2). The use of computers as an active agent in the design process fosters an operative approach to design grounded in the formalization of design concepts and methods as computable function, that is, as transformation of data through a finite sequence of calculable rules (Kotnik 2010). Consequently, in an operative design approach, attention shifts away from the architectural form itself toward the logic of the underlying computational function, that is, to the organizational pattern that governs the interaction of the form with the context.
The digital enforces a precision in the design methods and techniques with the operative as an index of this shift in thinking. The need for precision results in the expression of design ideas within a formalized notation of data handling which, as a more than welcome side effect, offers the opportunity of communicating design methods and techniques in a transparent and replicable way. Based on this, the inclusion of the digital into the design process has the potential to change our perspective on architecture as an academic endeavor and its relation to other disciplines (Lorenzo-Eiroa and Sprecher 2013).
This is especially apparent in the interaction of architecture with various engineering disciplines. Over the past decade, the availability of formalized descriptions of phenomena like stress distribution in spatial configurations or energy transmission in materials has resulted in the development of numerous design tools that support the integration of engineering knowledge into the design process. Comparable utilization of operative descriptions into architecture from disciplines with traditions of formalized notation in knowledge generation can be observed in the design on a large

scale like urban design and planning or landscape architecture (Walliss and Rahmann 2016). With the increasing digitalization of all levels of human life and the availability of large amounts of data as well as new methods of pattern recognition in data at a progressive rate, knowledge from humanities and sociology is becoming available for operative design approaches (Kelleher and Tierney 2018).

Such interaction between disciplines has not only resulted in new concepts within the architectural discourse but also established new realms of interdisciplinary inquiry such as architectural geometry, an active field of research at the intersection of architecture, engineering, mathematics, and computer graphics. What unites these developments in science, engineering, humanities, and sociology caused by the digital and their application in architecture over all scales, from nanometers in the development of material properties (Schodek et al. 2009) to kilometers in regional planning (M'Closky and VanDerSys 2017), is the observation that the control of properties of the system under observation is not depending primarily on the specificity of the entities but rather on the organizational pattern between these entities, on the structure of the system.

In other words: the structure is the carrier of information!

Mathesis

With the integration of the digital into the design process and the shift toward the operative in design thinking, architecture is joining the structural perspective. Up to now, however, contemporary use of the digital has mostly been driven by an understanding of computation, as an ability to handle an ever-increasing complexity of data and relationships. This has fostered a perspective of the digital that is comparable to the traditional role of the engineer as consultant in the design process: specialists disjoint from the process as provider of geometry-based tools and problem-solver. But digital design should be used to support the fundamental human ability of design thinking. Digital design is about the granting of an operative medium for a structural diagramatology, it is an epistemological schema that enables an inquiry into how we learn and know about things (Kotnik 2013).

This request is the starting point of an ongoing design research into the notion of structures and its impact on architectural design thinking. As a design approach, digital-driven operative design is about the detection of patterns as "the 'how' or the means by which we come to know, understand, or express these relationships" (M'Closky and VanDerSys 2017). This means a structure can be understood as a pattern which results from the network of formal relationships between elements of a set of examined objects. Such thinking in patterns places operative design in conceptual proximity to mathematics: A contemporary mathematical understanding is reflected in the concept of structure, for "a structure is any set of objects (also called elements) along with certain relations among those objects" (Rickart 1995, 7). This contextual proximity to mathematics is not the result of chance; mathematics is the science of patterns, whereby the fundamental patterns result from the formalization of human perception (Devlin 1994, 14).

The world is a construct whose main reference point is the here and now of the body. It is from the body that surrounding reality is perceived, structured, and accessed. Mathematics takes part in this act of orientation in the world through an active and constructive act of appropriating the environment by setting boundaries by means of structured differentiation (Kotnik 2014). According to Heidegger, this human capability of recognizing order is the "truly mathematical," which stems from the original meaning of the Greek *ta mathēmata*. "The *mathēmata* are the things insofar as we take cognizance of them as what we already know them to be in advance. [...] Therefore, we do not first get it out of things, but, in a certain way, we bring it already with us" (Heidegger 1993, 271). In this way, the process of structuring is not such an abstract, logical construct of order, but rather describes humans' internal capacity to perceive various relationships in sets of entities.

This fundamental understanding of structures as perceived order in sets is governing modern mathematics in a more formalized manner, too. Under the pseudonym Nicolas Bourbaki, a group of mainly French mathematicians worked on the systematic organization of mathematics since 1934. Bourbaki, building on the concept of set, attempted to generalize mathematical ideas that were already recognized, and were aiming at systematizing mathematical knowledge in such a way that the inherent dependencies between different branches of mathematics would be clear. The Bourbaki project, running over several decades, made evident that three types of organizational patterns form the fundamental and reoccurring structures in mathematics: organizational structures, algebraic structures, and topological structures.

The three types of mathematical structures thus formalize elemental perspectives of sets. At the same time, these three types of structures can be viewed as fundamental patterns of human perception: ta *mathēmata*. As patterns of perception, these structures are not bound to the mathematical context. Rather, mathematics as a scientific discipline only forms a specific context within which these figures of thought become visible (fig. 1).

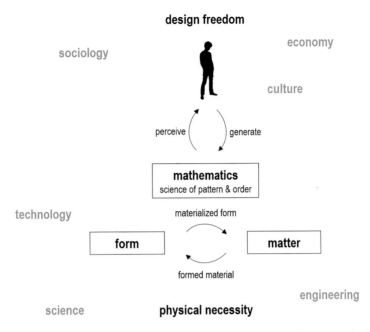

Fig. 1: Organizational patterns, described as mathematical structures, as mediator between disciplines and driver of design development

Spatial Dynamics

Organizational structures, algebraic structures, and topological structures can be understood as exemplary descriptions of patterns of human involvement with the environment, as typological representations of a modus of thinking in structures internal to humans. Due to this understanding of mathematical structures as *mathēsis*, as structuring grounded in human perception, the three fundamental structures can provide a framework for a systematic exploration of design strategies and help link elements of visual grammar to operative design approaches (Kotnik 2016).

Such linking between the computational and the perceptible provides the basis of a meaningful design process in architecture with the operation as diagrammatic description of spatial conceptions. As Rudolf Arnheim has already observed in his famous *Dynamics of Architectural Form*, "space is created as a relation between objects. These relations persist in perceptual experience. [...] There are many aspects of experience of which we are not explicitly conscious that nonetheless tinge our awareness in important ways. The visual relations between objects are of this kind. Space between things turns out not to look simply empty" (Arnheim 1977, 17). The resulting operation thus can be seen as the condensed description of the underlying field condition given by the parametric variation of the "form between things," as Stan Allen has defined it.

It is the dynamic of space captured in the operational description, its rhythmic change, its speed of flow, its directionality that defines its architectural potential, its usability for specific functions and organizational schemes. In other words, within an operational design approach, it is not a given architectural program that drives the creation of a specific architectural form but rather the architectural form that defines the appropriate program. It is the spatial dynamics of the operation that informs the architecture and defines its functionality. In the case of the intervention into an urban void, the operation describes the interaction of two pairs of walls onto each other (fig. 2). Applied onto a closed configuration of walls, this results in sequences of spatial transformations of varying degree of openness and spatial dynamics that is used in the design of a linear urban park defined by a flow of spatial conditions of changing intimacy.

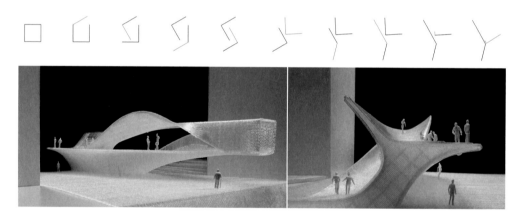

Fig. 2: Variational exploration of a diagram as operational logic for the design of an urban park (Formal Design Studio, Aalto University, 2015: student Hanna Jahkonen)

The generative force of the operation, however, is not rigid. Rather it is a topological description of a set of relationships that has not solidified into a fixed architectural expression yet. The sequence of transforming walls is a diagrammatic description of a spatial idea reflected in the operation as a kind of communication between the pairs of walls. This immanent flexibility enables an adaptation of the internal structure of the diagram to a given context by means of translation of the external conditions into formative sets of geometric rules that help to actualize the operation based on the inherent dynamic of space.

Structuralism

As a consequence, operative design should not be perceived as technical calculation, despite the seemingly abstract notation, but rather as phenomenological exploration. An understanding of formal structures as *mathēsis* provides a perspective onto computational design not only as common ground for an interdisciplinary exchange among the natural and technical sciences, well established for centuries, but also opens up a way of linking scientific and artistic ways of thinking by means of computation. With this, operative design thinking is grounded in structuralism. Not in the sense of an anthropological structuralism based on the linguistic studies of Ferdinand de Saussure, but rather a structuralism of the natural and technical sciences that has its grounding in Norbert Wiener's studies on cybernetics and the work of Ludwig von Bertalanffy on general systems theory (Schäffner 2016; Kotnik 2011).

The design-oriented exploration of relationships results in a bottom-up process that enables a linking of environmental phenomena with architectural intentions in a seamless way, thereby establishing a sustainable design thinking that dissolves the dichotomy of the man-made versus the natural. In the investigation of the interplay between the city Concepción, Chile, and the Andalién River (fig. 3) this allows for the formulation of a design speculation grounded in a site-specific dialogue between natural systems characterized by seasonal changes, sedimentation, water dynamics, and annual flooding and the interest in urban growth and economic development. Data on the amount of rain, soil conditions, and related maximum level of drenching, and geometric information on degrees of sloping and its influence on possible landslides is combined into local relationships between neighboring plots and informs the identification of potential areas for urban development along the surrounding hillsides and the integration of drainage systems for the controlled collection of water for new economic opportunities like fish farming. This means the flow of rainwater is not perceived anymore as a force that needs to be controlled but rather as a field condition, as a topological relation that can be adapted to local needs. The structuring of data and knowledge into a set of relationships thus opens up new options for urban development and a symbiotic use of natural resources.

Conclusion

The architectural exploration of an operative design approach is at the same time an investigation into the changing role of mathematics in architecture. For centuries, mathematics was understood within the design process as the rational foundation of architectural thinking. This stabilizing effect of mathematics was achieved, according to Robin Evans (1995, xxvii), above all by the application of "dead geometry," that is, geometric knowledge which undergoes no further development. This is no longer true; in digital design thinking, mathematics is an active agent of the design development. With the ongoing digitalization, formalization based in mathematics is available in almost all disciplines. This opens up the chance to utilize mathematics as a mediator between the disciplines and as a central element in the integration of external knowledge into the architectural design process.

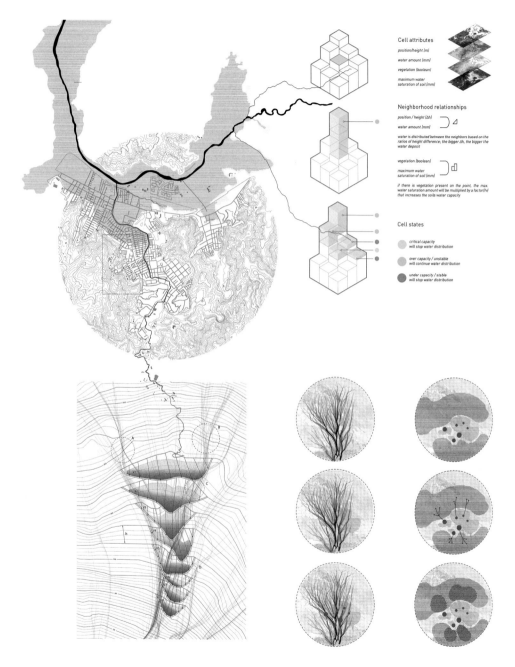

Cell attributes

position/height [m]

water amount [mm]

vegetation (boolean)

maximum water saturation of soil [mm]

Neighborhood relationships

position / height [Δh]

water amount [mm]

water is distributed between the neighbors based on the ratios of height difference; the bigger Δh, the bigger the water deposit

vegetation (boolean)

maximum water saturation of soil [mm]

if there is vegetation present on the point, the max. water saturation amount will be multiplied by a factor [v] that increases the soils water capacity

Cell states

critical capacity will stop water distribution

over capacity / unstable will continue water distribution

under capacity / stable will stop water distribution

Fig. 3: Construction of a performative landscape based on local relationships (Design of Structures Studio, Aalto University, 2018: students Jenna Ahonen, Tina Cerpnjak, and Feng Ye)

With this, architecture can be viewed as truly synthetic thinking and knowledge production that complements the sciences and humanities and merges the necessity of physics with the freedom of design. This view, however, requires not only an epistemological shift away from the architectural object itself toward the intellectual, corporal, and technical process behind the object but also the development of techniques and investigation methods of these processes. The structuralistic perspective as an active construction of relationships allows design to be viewed as a proper research activity and aims at the demystification of the design process as a spontaneous and ingenious act of creation and its systematization as a locus of knowledge production within architecture.

References

Arnheim, Rudolf. 1977. *The Dynamics of Architectural Form*. Berkeley: University of California Press.

Bundy, Alan. 2007. "Computational Thinking Is Pervasive." *Journal of Scientific and Practical Computing* 1, no. 2: 67–69.

Carpo, Mario. 2004. "Ten Years of Folding." In *Folding in Architecture*, rev. ed., edited by Greg Lynn, 14–19. London: Academy Press, 2004.

Devlin, Keith. 1994. *Mathematics: The Science of Patterns*. New York: Henry Holt.

Evans, Robin. 1995. *The Projective Cast: Architecture and Its Three Geometries*, Cambridge, MA: MIT Press.

Heidegger, Martin. 1993. "Modern Science, Metaphysics, and Mathematics." In *Martin Heidegger: Basic Writings*, edited by David Farrell Krell, 267–305. New York: HarperCollins.

Kelleher, John, and Brendan Tierney. 2018. *Data Science*. Cambridge, MA: MIT Press.

Kolarevic, Branko, ed. 2003. *Architecture in the Digital Age: Design and Manufacturing*. New York: Spon Press.

Kotnik, Toni. 2010. "Digital Architectural Design as Exploration of Computable Functions." *International Journal of Architectural Computing* 8, no. 1: 1–16.

Kotnik, Toni. 2014. "… there is geometry in architecture." In *Form–Rule | Rule–Form 2013*, edited by Günther Filz, Rupert Maleczek, and Christian Scheiber, 35–43. Innsbruck: University Press.

Kotnik, Toni. 2016. "Algorithmic Design: Structuralism Reloaded?" In *Structuralism Reloaded: Rule-based Design in Architecture and Urbanism*, edited by Tomas Valena, Tom Avermaete, and Georg Vrachliotis, 327–35. Stuttgart: Edition Axel Menges.

Kotnik, Toni. 2016. "Formal Diagrams." In *Perspectives in Metropolitan Research: Passion for the Built Environment*, edited by Annette Bögle and Christiane Sörensen, 88–97. Berlin: Jovis Verlag.

Kotnik, Toni, and Pierluigi D'Acunto. 2013. "Operative Diagramatology: Structural Folding for Architectural Design." In *Rethinking Prototyping: Proceedings of the Design Modeling Symposium 2013*, edited by Christoph Gengnagel, Axel Kilian, Norbert Palz, and Fabian Scheurer, 193–203. Berlin: Springer.

Lorenzo-Eiroa, Pablo, and Aaron Sprecher. 2013. *Architecture in Formation*. New York: Routledge.

Lynn, Greg, ed. 1993. *Folding in Architecture*. London: Academy Editions.

Lynn, Greg. 1999. *Animate Form.* New York: Princeton Architectural Press.

M'Closky, Karen, and Keith VanDerSys. 2017. *Dynamic Pattern: Visualizing Landscapes in a Digital Age*. New York: Routledge.

Oxman, Rivka, and Robert Oxman. 2013. *Theories of the Digital in Architecture*. New York: Routledge.

Picon, Antoine. 2010. *Digital Culture in Architecture: An Introduction for the Design Professions*. Basel: Birkhäuser.

Plowright, Philip D. 2014. *Revealing Architectural Design: Methods, Frameworks, and Tools*. Abingdon: Routledge.

Rickart, Charles E. 1995. *Structuralism and Structures*. Singapore: World Scientific Publishing.

Rowe, Peter G. 1987. *Design Thinking*. Cambridge, MA: MIT Press.

Schäffner, Wolfgang. 2016. "New Structuralism: A Field of Human and Material Science." *Grazer Architektur Magazin GAM* 12 (2016): 10–30.

Schodek, Daniel L., Paulo Ferreira, and Michael F Ashby. 2009. *Nanomaterials, Nanotechnologies and Design: An Introduction for Engineers and Architects*. Oxford: Elsevier.

Walliss, Jillian, and Heike Rahmann. 2016. *Landscape Architecture and Digital Technologies: Re-Conceptualising Design and Making*. New York: Routledge.

Dexterity-Controlled Design Procedures

Joost Meyer[1] *and Federico Garrido*[2]
[1] *RWTH Aachen University, Germany*
[2] *Technische Universität Kaiserslautern, Germany*

Abstract — This paper explores the development of design procedures in relationship to their digital proceedings, in order to interface human movement and parametric design procedures. The research studied the use of Leap Motion controller, a gesture-recognition device using infrared sensors combined with time-based generative tools in Rhinoceros Grasshopper. A physical, artistic procedure was used as a reference to model a digital design procedure, including a series of parametric definitions combined with them in an attempt to produce complex three-dimensional designs in real time. In a later stage of this research, a modular, open-source digitizing arm was developed to capture hand movement and interact with an autonomous parametric definition, augmenting even more the range of applications of dexterity-based digital design. The challenge of this experimental investigation lies in the balance between the designer's needs for a complex yet open design process and the possibilities of defined soft- and hardware solutions.

Introduction

The establishment of gesture-based control is embedded on digital architecture's history since Sutherland's first explorations in CAD technologies using a light pen. The invention of the computer mouse and the quest for precision eventually drove away these experimental devices in architecture, while other artistic disciplines made use of them intensively, like illustrators or digital sculptors. For the last two decades and perhaps more, architectural research in the field of digital design tools has focused on algorithmic tools and their derivatives: NURBS, scripting, parametric design, genetic algorithms, and so on. Fueled first by the popularization of personal computing and then by the advancements in digital fabrication, the center of attention was set on geometry: how to control it, how to represent it, how to manufacture it.

Scripting and parametric tools serve their purpose efficiently and elegantly; complex geometrical compositions are generated and controlled by a series of intertwined values, variables, and parameters. Control is the keyword: every geometrical aspect of the design is governed by a numeric value, a slider, or a mathematical formula.

A common critique to this approach arises in regard to authorship and the role of the designer: there is a frequent sensation that the more (geometric) control we exercise, the more freedom we gain, yet the authorial oversight seems to diminish. This leads to a general rule regarding computational tools: what cannot be parameterized cannot be part of the digital project.

An analog design process is, in most cases, a creative act, which is accompanied by an immediate, often implicit reaction to the material and its properties. Throughout the digital design procedure most of the time, there is a lack of material and time-based response, a spontaneous feedback through the soft or hardware. With this research, we aim to contribute to fill this gap between the needs of the designer for a creative process and opportunities which arise through the digital possibilities where parameters can be fixed to improve the results of an idea becoming form.

In this regard, this paper explores how to generate complex geometries by using motion-sensor devices in order to capture hand movement and incorporate it into a parametric definition. The purpose is to capture human movements, acceleration, and dexterity and translate them into algorithmic values in order to generate and control geometry.

The questions that this research proposes are: Which hidden design possibilities arise from capturing human movement in a design process? What is gained and what is lost in this translation procedure? And finally, is it possible to code these movements, to automate and optimize such processes in order to reuse them?

State of the Art

The interest of this research is to capture human movement, either with optical or mechanical sensors, enhance it with algorithmic procedures, and incorporate it into a design process. To achieve this, we use a parametric design environment (Rhinoceros with Grasshopper) and sensors like the Leap Motion infrared sensor and a self-developed device similar to a digitizing arm.

There were several attempts to capture and digitize human movement in a tridimensional environment with a considerable amount of precision. Sketch Furniture (Benda 2006) is an interesting example of a design process based on body movement. In this project, an operator would freely sketch a three-dimensional line in space by moving his or her arms in the air, while a series of sensors captured the movement and a design software converted the drawn lines into 3-D "pipes" that would later be manufactured. In this way, the user can design tables, chairs, and tube lamps with hand movements by drawing in the air. The Swedish studio uses an array of infrared cameras in order to produce the motion capture, similarly to the Leap Motion tracker. In the same way, the *L'Artisan Électronique* installation by Unfold (2010) uses laser sensors to capture the hand's position in order to generate vases by a rotational movement, similar to the ceramic ones created on a potter's wheel. In both cases, the sensor information is translated into a closed design system; the first one is a sketch-based 3-D pipe, and the second one is based on a revolving solid. Both projects lack any sort of material constraints, and since the movement is unrestrained, there is no haptic feedback that can influence or limit the design.

Several research teams have developed a series of gesture-based applications using various sensors like the Kinect, Leap Motion, and the Wiimote tracker. The use of complex sensory devices such as Microsoft Kinect and Leap Motion (Marin 2014) is also relevant to this research, but the aim is to include it into a wider, more open design framework, such as the case with Rhinoceros with Grasshopper. In addition to this application, we have designed various custom scripts or small programs that act as design procedures, performing a series of geometric operations using hand and finger movement as input data. The idea of this study is to bring together the advantages of both approaches, manual and digital. It begins with a mimicry of manual procedures with digital tools, which aims at a better understanding of what qualities a digital design procedure can have and where its limitations and opportunities lie. Instead of using the hand movement to draw lines freely like Front's Sketch Furniture project, our research tracks the hand and fingers and mounts a set of geometrical tools on top of them. So, it is not just the hand movement but also stabilization algorithms, drawing presets, and self-generating geometry.

Devices like Leap Motion have proved an interesting exploration tool but also showed a limited functionality in terms of precision and feedback, since they use an array of infrared cameras to detect fingers and articulations. The user experiences no physical feedback as to the position of the hands or fingers in three-dimensional space, nor a precise idea of what he or she is drawing in space. Unfold's project (Unfold 2010) solves this issue partially by allowing the user to draw only a flat line in space, which will in turn be used as a revolving profile, limiting the drawing to a two-dimensional task. The combination of new tools, which respond to manual dexterity (Grunwald 2016) and software instrumentalization aims to improve a digital workflow. We operate under the definition of dexterity as a degree of ease, speed, and accuracy of human actions (Fröhlich and Drever 1983, 134); this also includes a better awareness and understanding of spatial conditions and the precise use of those tools throughout the design process.

For this reason, at the Faculty of Architecture, RWTH Aachen University, Joost Meyer and Federico Garrido have developed extensive experiments on these algorithms using sensors, the initial results of which were presented and discussed at the RCA Conference 2018 for the first time; then they designed and developed a 5-axis digitizing arm to improve precision and add more design features to the drawing procedure.

The use of digitizing arms to control a robotic arm was developed for Grasshopper some time ago (Payne 2011) as a scaled copy of the segments and articulations of a robot arm. In this way, the control is directed by the user and mimicked by the robot in real time using an FTDI chip as interface. In this case, we designed a modular arm using an Arduino microcontroller and angle sensors with the intention of creating a modular, upgradable design.

Research Procedure

The research consisted in translating dexterity-based procedures into a digital design environment gradually using sensory devices, microcontrollers, and parametric design software (fig. 1). We first analyzed the manual method, tried on a transformation of the procedure to digital tools, and then worked on the interaction of artistic approach and parametric design solution. This benefits from the designer's skills and abilities, which then can be brought directly into a digital design process.

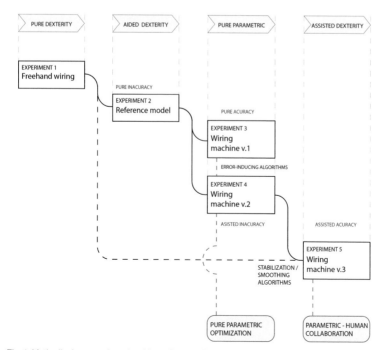

Fig. 1: Methodical approach to the object of research

The first assignment of this research consisted of studying and analyzing a procedure, based on a material-related task. With this intention, we studied the artist Joost Meyer and his *Shark* series. This group of sculptures was made by winding wire around a base structure. These works are procedure-based; they cannot be projected with precision, since their final form depends on the execution of a task, influenced by materials and a shaping process. First Meyer creates a wooden structure according to the shape and proportions of each particular fish and then proceeds to wind metal wire (of different diameters) around the structure. The steel wire takes the form of the fish by adjusting itself more or less precisely to the shape of the wooden parts. Finally, the wooden structure is burned, exposing the wire and some of the burnt remains. The process is time-consuming, not only because of the size (some sharks are on a 1:1 scale) but also because of the winding procedure using a continuous wire; the weight of the material, its resistance to bending, and elasticity make its manipulation difficult (fig. 2).

Fig. 2: Burning shark (Joost Meyer, 2017)

The purpose was to study Meyer's movements and manipulation of the steel wire, particularly in relation to the complex shark geometry. Sharks have a longitudinal shape which determines the main direction of the winding movement. The presence of fins (dorsal, pectoral, and caudal) forces Meyer to change the "rolling" direction in order to precisely mimic each shape. Material properties like stiffness and ductility need to be considered, since rolling thick wire with sharp curvatures becomes difficult. The whole procedure is based on dexterity, experience, craftmanship, and material knowledge.

A second task involved the study of Leap Motion, an input device originally designed for virtual and augmented reality applications. The device uses stereoscopic infrared cameras in order to track the movement of both hands; it can recognize fingers, palm orientation, and some gestures such as pinching or grabbing. The integration between the Leap Motion controller and Grass-hopper is made with two plug-ins, one is Primate (specifically designed for the controller) and Firefly (also used to integrate with other microcontrollers like Arduino). Thanks to this integration, Grasshopper can interpret the hand as three-dimensional geometry; the fingertips and finger joints as points, the hand palm as planes, and bones as lines.

The third phase consisted in the design of a parametric definition that iden-tifies the index fingertip and uses it to draw in a three-dimensional environ-ment. Leap Motion can capture all five fingers from each hand, but for the purposes of this research, the use of more than one finger proved to be un-necessary. The definition is fairly straightforward, as it captures the position of the index finger two hundred times per second, stamps a point on each location, and then draws a line connecting them; this was also inspired by a picture of raindrops reflecting light off one of the physical objects similar to a digital point cloud, typical in 3-D scanning processes (fig. 3).

Fig. 3: Wired shark with raindrops reflecting light conditions (Joost Meyer, 2013)

This phase was useful to test the controller and its capabilities, as the result is a doodle-like curve drawn in three-dimensional space. This result is also simi-lar to the abovementioned Sketch Furniture project, but on a smaller scale. Several iterations of this definition were tested, changing the sample rate and averaging algorithms in order to stabilize the finger's position into a more fluid movement. There are several ways in which these smoothing algorithms work, by reducing the amount of readings per second or the number of "stamps" on space; or by averaging the continuous stream of data.

By altering these parameters, the shaky lines began to smooth into more NURBS-like curves. This is yet another procedure with which we managed to make the result of the drawing smoother. By generating a 0-degree NURBS curve, the connection between each point is direct, similar to a polyline. If we increase this degree parameter, the component uses the points as weights, which pull the curve, resulting in a smoother line. The higher the degree, the smoother the result, but also, the less precise. A digital design process involves the translation of material properties into digital parameters. We used curve types and sample rates to emulate material behavior. To complete this material understanding, it would be necessary to consider and include manufacturing information into the process as well.

Similar to the *L'Artisan Électronique* installation by the Unfold collective (2010) and the "Digital Hammer" project by Kathryn Hinton, the intention was to convert precise human movement into an artistic digital operation, so several combinations of these algorithms were tested in order to strike a balance between smoothness and precision. Several 3-D sketches were made with this procedure; however, lacking any sort of haptic feedback, spatial reference or any other sort of guide apart from the visual, the result relied more on the user's dexterity than a robust, controlled drawing framework.

For this matter, we decided to imitate Meyer's procedure and work with a substrate. An organic mesh was inserted in the work environment, much like the shark's wooden structure in order to guide the user and his movements on the three-dimensional environment. A base mesh was scanned from a previous Meyer sculpture and imported into the Rhinoceros environment (fig. 4).

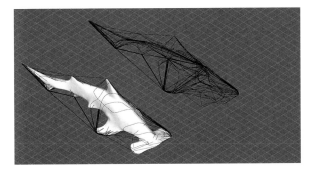

Fig. 4: Working in Rhinoceros environment with mesh structures and wiring machine (Federico Garrido and Joost Meyer, 2018)

The final definition would use this base mesh as a support structure, projecting the hand-drawn wire to it, adjusting the drawing lines to its shape, much like Meyer's wire. The precision of this projection can be altered along with the resistance of the wire, allowing the exploration of even more aesthetical effects. The degree with which the hand-drawn lines attach or detach from the base mesh can be calibrated in order to obtain figures more or less resembling the original sculpture (fig. 5).

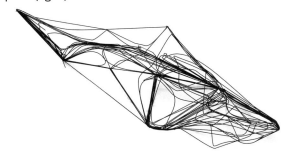

Fig. 5: Dexterity-based form generation
(Federico Garrido and Joost Meyer, 2018)

The next step consisted in the creation of a definition that performs Meyer's procedure autonomously. The basic procedure is similar to the one previously described: a wire-rolling machine that translates from one end of the fish structure to the other, creating a wire-cage structure mimicking its substrate. A time-based definition with movement controls such as speed, precision, and direction was designed, operating either linearly (along an axis) or following a predetermined path. Similarly, the degree of precision with which the wire sticks to the substrate can be altered, along with several other factors like the speed of the machine or the maximum bending radius. Finally, a combination of the last two definitions was developed: on the one hand, the creative possibilities of freehand modeling, and on the other hand, the precision of computer-generated form. This definition uses hand location to move the wire-bending apparatus while the winding movement is active. Due to this, the user can position the wire three-dimensionally and decide in which direction the wiring is performed while the base mesh remains in place (fig. 6).

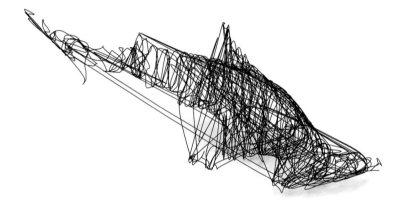

Fig. 6: Human parametric design collaboration for form generation (Federico Garrido and Joost Meyer, 2018)

This definition provides even more detail and creative possibilities, since it allows the user to reorient the wiring direction in order to adjust it to the form he or she wants to cover, which becomes particularly useful in areas like fins and other parts (fig. 7). Similar to other previous definitions, the lack of feedback and location makes the wiring process occasionally difficult. A similar definition was also developed, but this time, the user's hand moves the support mesh while the wiring machine stays in a fixed position.

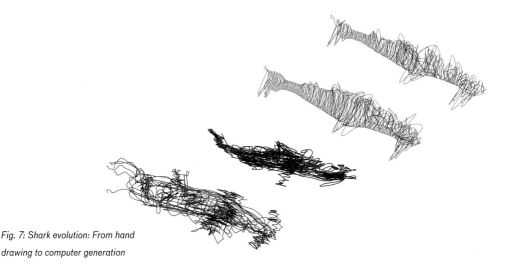

Fig. 7: Shark evolution: From hand
drawing to computer generation

Conclusions and Future Steps

This study is linked to other attempts to improve communication between digital tools and designers. Throughout the digital design process while creating the wired silhouettes of a shark, new perspectives on creating form emerged. The negotiation between designer and scripter lead to an inspirational cooperation in the use of tools and design ambition. Still the problem of haptic feedback and spatial referencing remains. Therefore, this research started to develop a 5-axis digitizing arm to capture hand movement in real time, providing a physical interface (unlike a purely optical sensor like the Leap Motion) that can also provide spatial feedback. The idea is to build this arm using modular components and open source sensors in order to exercise even more control not only on the design process but also on a hardware level, adjusting the measuring device to specific design tasks, such as Meyer's wiring process (fig. 8).

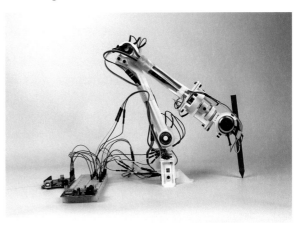

Fig. 8: 5-axis digitizing arm by F. Garrido, 2019

The popularization of alternative input devices and microcontrollers has enabled this type of research to reach a broader public, creating interesting projects such as the aforementioned investigations. Despite the latest advancements, there is still room for improvement and new applications, in our opinion, regarding the collaboration between digital processes and hand-controlled procedures. These procedures demand a new consciousness about fabrication process, combining traditional technique and digital ones in new hybrid ways of designing. The expressive and aesthetic possibilities are in the combination of machine procedures and precise hand movement, which can create detailed, intricate geometries, impossible to create with either method on its own. In conclusion, on the one hand, the multifaceted possibilities of digital methods need to be further explored. On the other hand, these developments, especially concerning usability, material properties, and aspects of spatial awareness and haptic resonance to designers, are still in their infancy. We would like to contribute with this research to a better understanding of the interrelationship of designers and digital design methods.

References

Benda, Friedman. 2006. "Sketch Furniture." *FrontProjects*2006. Accessed August 5, 2018. http://www.designfront.org/category.php?id=81&product =93.

Fröhlich, Werner D., and James Drever. 1983. *dtv-Wörterbuch zur Psychologie*. 14th rev. ed. Munich: Deutscher Taschenbuch-Verlag.

Grunwald, Martin. 2016. "Haptik: Der handgreiflich–körperliche Zugang des Menschen zur Welt und zu sich selbst." In *Manifestationen im Entwurf: Design, Architektur, Ingenieurwesen*, edited by Thomas H. Schmitz et al., 95–125. Bielefeld: transcript.

Hinton, Kathryn. 2010. *The Craft of Digital Tooling*. London: Royal College of Art.

Marin, Giulio, Fabio Dominio, and Pietro Zanuttigh. 2014. "Hand Gesture Recognition with Leap Motion and Kinect Devices." *IEEE International Conference on Image Processing (ICIP)*, 1565–69. Paris: IEEE. https://doi.org/10.1109/ICIP.2014.7025313.

Payne, Andrew. 2011. "A Five-Axis Robotic Motion Controller for Designers." In *Acadia 2011: Integration through Computation*, edited by Joshua Taron, Vera Parlac, Branko Kolarevic, and S. Jason, 162–69. Banff: University of Calgary.

Unfold and Tim Knapen. 2010. *L'Artisan Électronique: Installation*. Accessed August 5, 2018. http://unfold.be/pages/l-artisan-electronique.

Warnier, Claire, Dries Verbruggen, Sven Ehmann, and Robert Klanten, eds. 2014. *Printing Things: Visions and Essentials for 3-D Printing*. Berlin: Gestalten Verlag.

Willis, Karl D.D., Juncong Lin, Jun Mitani, and Takeo Igarashi. 2010. "Spatial Sketch: Bridging between Movement and Fabrication." In *Proceedings of the Fourth International Conference on Tangible, Embedded, and Embodied Interaction*, 5–12. New York: Association for Computing Machinery.

Werkstücke – Making Objects into Houses: Understanding by the Way of the Hands in Design Teaching

Bettina Kraus[1], Nandini Oehlmann[1], and Mathias Peppler[2]
[1] Technische Universität Berlin, Germany
[2] Brandenburg University of Technology Cottbus-Senftenberg, Germany

Abstract — Presented in this publication are the results and the process of a two-year studio course between 2014 to 2016 with architecture debutantes at BTU Cottbus-Senftenberg, Germany, whose lack of specialist knowledge and vibrant naïveté were channeled to form the basis for a reflective design process. The aim was to encourage the participants to discover their personal fetishes and develop a distinguishable signature while searching for a method where not only does one's head not impede the hand, but also where ideas are not simply blindly followed and materialized. Our reflections on teaching design reveal something about the nature of architecture. For an experienced architect, an empty sheet of paper presents an exciting moment full of prospects. For an inexperienced architect, it often provides too many possible outcomes and a sense of paralysis. The gap between the suggestive sketch and the material model is a vast one. In order to narrow the transition between the second and third dimensions, our teaching begins with the production of an individual, handmade Werkstück (workpiece) intended to record each personal signature (fig. 1).

Introduction

The practice of teaching architecture takes place at the intersection of knowledge and ability. In architectural education, design is classically taught in studio courses with a focus on semester-long projects. It is here that methods and skills are imparted directly to the participants. However, a significant portion of the knowledge conveyed does not consist of formalized abilities, but is passed on in the form of metaphors, sketches, or similar means. It's worth mentioning that even many experts are often unable to

Fig. 1: Werkstück and floor plan by Henrik Lück

expound upon the competencies they possess, or how they apply such skills or knowledge. Therefore, the production of knowledge in architecture has little to do with the practice, where one operates mostly with implied knowledge. In line with Polyani's idea of tacit knowledge, the knower and the knowledge form a single entity (Polanyi 1966, 17ff.). A useful comparison here is the process of learning a language, which is similarly one of learning by doing. Our ability to use language is comprised of the interplay between cognitive knowledge and intuition. When speaking or writing, complex grammatical rules are intuitively applied to form correct sentences without the need to actively recall the applicable rules. This is in fact how a native language is implicitly acquired.

By comparison, in architectural education this process is often replaced with the search for a concept to illustrate a thought. During the design process, and analogous to the language, it is possible to develop a feeling for how the parts can be best combined to form a whole. One could even view (physical) experiences and our dealings with gravity, space, and the built environment as a kind of experiential, a priori knowledge incidentally accrued during the activities of everyday life. And this knowledge can be called upon when designing spaces and structures. Or, through repetition, a rule can be internalized until it can be applied with ease:

"All skills, even the most abstract, begin with physical experience. Knowledge is collected through contact with and movement of the hand" (Sennett 2008, 10). In other words, understanding is by way of the hands.

The process of creating these works began with the choice to work with one material – wood, felt, stone, or metal, as well as the parameter of a limited number of work processes. The choice of material, its fabrication and handling have a defining influence on the expression of each object. Through a simple series of dividing and manipulating, different raw materials are transformed into a group of remarkable figures with a sculptural presence that make us aware of the possibilities and limitations of the respective materials. In the process of dividing, re-building and deforming the different materials, which are largely industrially produced, the connections between form, structure, and the material-specific properties are discovered.

Within the experiment of dealing with isolated aspects of situatedness, scale, function, circulation, and points of intersection, the objects become associative resources for the house. Different from the traditional Werkstück, for which the treatment of materials is not in itself of interest, the process of working brings forth questions and conflicts that lead to ideas for architecture, space, and the situations taking place within.

In trade and industry, a Werkstück, or workpiece, is a distinct object made of solid material and worked on in some form or another – its production method is of little significance. It is the link between the finished *Werk*, or the desired outcome, and the *Stück* used to achieve the final result. With regard to the design process in our studio – and in contrast to a classic workpiece – the way such an object is formed is of great significance. During the confrontation with (or handling of) isolated architectural parameters such as the reconciliation of the interior space with the exterior appearance, functional causalities, or the selection of a suitable construction, the workpiece is gradually transformed into a building.

An essential prerequisite for spatializing a notion of life is the ability to recall internalized images based on past situational experiences. Accordingly, it is necessary to practice, thereby actively enhancing the perceptive senses on various levels and allowing the eye to travel. This entails simultaneously looking back at personal experiences and looking forward to the form and narrative that the architectural task should begin to take on. The design emanates from the superimposition of recalled and fictive images and the material-specific formulation and processing of a workpiece. The particular and limiting characteristics of each material are revealed during the process of cutting and reassembling, taking on a clarifying role in answering narrative, spatial, and structural questions. Instead of an ill-fitting copy of a formal, preexisting, and already ingrained architectural concept, associative thinking and making are paramount. But beyond just developing an individual sense of expression and character, the spatial impact also needs to be verified in the end (fig. 2).

Together, we have evolved a creative framework, the intermediate and final results of which are presented in our book *Werkstücke* (Kraus et al. 2017).

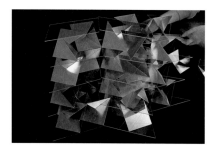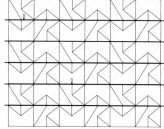

Fig. 2: Werkstück and elevation by Edda Meinertz, Paula Bruns

Werkstücke: On Objects

The exercises from which the objects emerged are essentially rudimentary prompts to do something, and above all specify boundary conditions with the intention of precluding certain decisions and making it easier to act. Their scope spans the actual question asked and the constraints inherent to each material – felt, wood, metal, stone, bamboo, hemp, turf – which subsequently become an integral part of the exercise and outcome. The result is a speculative space that can only be truly understood in hindsight when the object is analyzed and the question posed: What, in fact, is it? The established boundary conditions and material limitations, however, are not inhibitors, but rather catalysts for making intuitive decisions that help one move beyond preconceived notions or mental barriers. The boundary conditions preclude certain choices, narrow down the possibilities, and focus one's view. One could describe this with the term *metamorphosis* in the search for a form: The final state of the object is potentially already recorded in the material as part of its DNA.

Surprisingly, it is not only the evident choice within the objects that are comprehensible, but also their faults, which cannot be immediately deduced from the rest of the construct or their style. Although it is almost impossible to find overriding explanations for these faults, they do not seem out of key. Instead, they are a self-explanatory part of the entire piece, remnants of the path followed apart from a systematic decision-making process – be they spontaneous inspirations, technical mishaps, or irregularities already present in the raw material that leave their mark on the finished object. Thus, the objects are entities in which the systematic and happenstance overlap and can seem plausible within its own microcosm. This may be due to the plain fact that it was possible, nothing prevented it from occurring, or that it was already present from the beginning (fig. 3). In a sense it is a naïve method, but also one that elicits a desire to act.

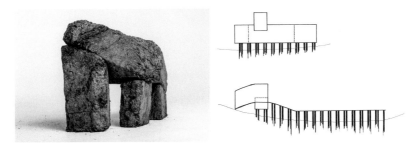

Fig. 3: Werkstück and section by Constantin Beiküfer, Adrian Ebert

Werkstücke: On Making

Once started, our design process is starkly fragmented into smaller subtasks. Each excerpt focuses on only part of the final design and is dealt with individually, an approach that aims to generate moments of varying complexity and to improve one's capability to act. However, it goes without saying that when these excerpts are combined, a succession of collisions between the existing and new arises. The unintentional and the happenstance that necessarily result from these collisions are of particular importance here. By removing parts of the whole, complexity is reduced, and an operating space is generated where one can pursue a more focused working method. Similar to looking through a microscope, the focus shifts from the macro- to the microcosm. Control over the situation in its entirety is set aside for a moment, so that something new and free from outside influence can emerge. When the existing collides with the new, one has to zoom out and again regain control.

This constant back and forth, zooming in and out, is an enriching process, and one that demands losing sight of the whole picture, and thus relinquishing control. Learning to design in this way is like learning to observe more precisely in order to detect and identify fortuitous coincidences. A language with the ability to best anticipate and guide these actions is necessarily simple and precise. Accordingly, the assignments are formatted and divided into individual sections and procedural steps. With each additional step, a new design parameter is introduced, increasing the intricacy of the task in a way that takes into account the complexity of dealing with architecture. During this cycle of action, appropriation, and understanding, the object becomes a house.

It is difficult to theoretically anticipate the final results and their impact when working by hand, and an unintentional and unpredictable surplus almost inevitably arises somewhere between what we already know and what materializes in the end. There exists a difference between the intended outcome and actual result. And the extent of this indeterminate surplus is dependent on a number of factors, including the manner in which the object was produced, manual and other personal skills, the material, and the complexity of the idea. The initial exercises, which led to the development of the objects, are rudimentary in their explanations of what is expected and seemingly useless in establishing a possible overarching set of goals. In a minimally simplistic way, a maximally complex form is created – and in a much shorter period of time than would be necessary for a more theoretical working process.

After the initial step, the prompts call much less for an additive method of working and much more for an understanding of what this difference between intention and reality actually is. The term *serendipity* can be described as the surprise discovery of something originally not sought but arrived at after careful and in-depth observation, and can be applied quite accurately to describe a portion of the work with the objects. The reflective work that follows is therefore a design-based reappraisal, which at its core generates a constant contextual analysis. It is a design process, which above all else is directed at refining the skills of observation (fig. 4).

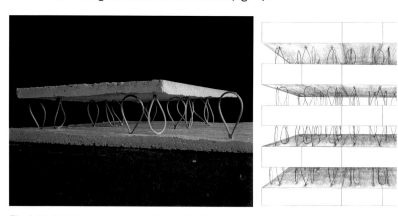

Fig. 4: Werkstück and perspective by Hanna Strahl

Werkstücke: On Houses

Traditionally, a space allocation plan or project brief taken together with other parameters like site, personal preferences, etc., form the starting point in the search for an architecture and the space it is intended to contain. In contrast, by critically engaging the objects, the relationship between content and form is reversed. Instead of spatially formulating the function, the preexisting space within the object is asked what it can potentially accommodate. The starting point for this dialogue is not the desire to produce a specific shape or an interest in a particular style, but rather the handmade form itself.

As the design process continues and the form is charged with the parameters of function, scale, context, etc., the house is inevitably emancipated from the original object. Or in other words, the object automatically begins to transition from its original state of embryonic implicitness as it is observed with increased complexity. From that moment on, working with the house resembles the search for a lost ideal condition, which is simply not transferrable to reality and has to be completely redefined. As references, the objects are simultaneously extreme in their expression and in the ways they can be interpreted with respect to their material and spatial potential. Unlike using a preexisting building as a reference, the images of what can transpire within the object when it is transformed into a house still have to be generated. Questions that would otherwise arise during the design stage are already encapsulated in and radically formatted and compressed into the object so that one can focus more clearly. Material, density, circulation, etc., are already so tightly interwoven and extreme in their formulation that the design process can focus on more essential spatial questions. Spaces and houses emerge more from a process of omission than one of addition.

And at the same time, the objects debunk any preconceived or clichéd notions and images while their consistency in character allows for a detached working method that finds its footing solely in the piece itself. For the most part, the structures are spatially complete and just need to be understood. In this way, an eclectic working method is avoided. It becomes less a cognitive task of piecing things together and more about meaningful understanding and, as such, about the house itself.

The houses thereby are handmade and arise from an authentic understanding of what was there before and what could be. They demonstrate that the relationship between space and function is hardly contingent on a general formatting, but that this can be redefined time and again. The process of inner referencing does not necessarily generate useful houses in our classic understanding of city (in the meaning of negotiating collective space and individual interests) but leads to an architecture that is the opposite of generic space, with which we are more and more confronted in the cities where we live.

In teaching young students, as in our own work as architects with clients and more broadly during the developmental stages of our career, we are repeatedly confronted with a similar experience in varying contexts: The blatant obviousness of a design is readily understood while an understanding of the inherent subtleties has to be won over time. In other words, what is said loud and clear is heard by everyone, but what remains quiet and subtle is more often than not drowned out. Both instances can be found in the objects, which serve as the starting point for the design process.

Working with the house – or rather striking a balance between the object and the house – demonstrates quite plainly that, in both the production and our perception of space and forms, there exists a sense of what is right and wrong. It is a process of seeking out and tracking down the different conditions of a form within a given context, whereby only through the ongoing process of refining one's observational abilities can subtlety, and with it also ambivalence, become a natural and more steadfast part of the design process (fig. 5).

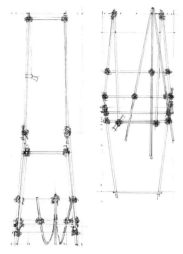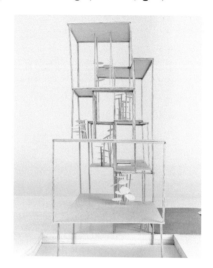

Fig. 5: Sketch and model by Xinyao Peng

Conclusion

The particular and limiting characteristics of each material are revealed during the process of cutting and reassembling into a Werkstück, taking on a clarifying role in answering narrative, spatial, and structural questions. Instead of an ill-fitting copy of a formal, preexisting, and already ingrained architectural concept, associative thinking and making are paramount. But beyond just developing an individual sense of expression and character, the spatial impact also needs to be verified in the end.

The houses developed from working with the objects show that there is no right or wrong in regard to style and how living space is created, and that repetitive comparisons between the ideal state and reality can, in a best-case scenario, little by little, impart an understanding for the subtleties in the appearance of the form as a house. Architecture is not only created in the mind: The design process is maybe better understood as a language which at once provides a sense of what and how something should be said, and in which context this should occur.

References

Polanyi, Michael. 1966. *The Tacit Dimension*. London: Routledge.

Sennett, Richard. 2008. *The Craftsman*. New Haven. CT: Yale University Press.

Kraus, Bettina, Nandini Oehlmann, and Mathias Peppler. 2017. *Werkstücke: Making Objects into Houses*. Berlin: Jovis.

Biorealism in the Settlement Architecture of Richard Neutra

Isabell Schütz
Technische Universität Darmstadt, Germany

Abstract — The Austrian-American architect Richard Neutra dedicated his work to the ideal of a human-adapted architecture that aims to serve and activate its inhabitants' vitality and capability. Neutra chose the term *biorealism* to describe his claims and published them in his book *Survival through Design* (1954). His German settlements near Frankfurt and Hamburg allow a unique analysis of the biorealistic planning approach in a homogeneous context. Professor Michael Ostwald itemized Neutra's theories of biorealism into three core issues. He developed an analytical process based on space syntax analysis to investigate whether Neutra's strategies are measurably present in his designs. A comparative analysis between Neutra's settlement buildings and adjacent buildings which were modeled on his characteristic style, is the foundation for the discussions on whether biorealism is constructible, and whether it can have any meaning for today's planning.

Biorealism in Neutra's Oeuvre

"... a practical designer is, evidently, engaged to manipulate almost directly the entire and manifold sense equipment with which his client, the consumer, the human species is endowed. Schools that train the student will be obliged to familiarize him with this physiological keyboard on which he must try to play with understanding and harmony." (Neutra 1969, 201)

Richard Neutra's life and aspirations as an architect can be clearly outlined with the quote above taken from his book Survival through Design from 1954 (1969). Born in 1892 in Vienna of the fin-de-siècle, Richard Neutra grew up during the thriving Viennese Modern Age. His technical and medical interests arose from his familial environment and were sharpened in the culture-critical discussions of social upheaval (Wandel-Hoefer 1989, 5–7). For his professional self-conception, Neutra found his role models in Otto Wagner and Adolf Loos during his studies. Inspired by the reading of Frank Lloyd Wright's *Wasmuth Portfolio* in the prewar years, Neutra escaped his traumatic war experiences and the following years of privation in Europe by emigrating to the United States in 1923.

During a brief collaboration with Wright in Taliesin, Neutra drew inspiration from the old master such as the tight integration of interior and exterior space, flowing floor plans, and the dissolution of wall as well as roof into articulated planes by translating them into his own conceptual considerations. He is similar to Wagner and Wright in their positive attitude toward the technical possibilities of mass production, which he expressed in his first publication, *Wie baut Amerika* in 1927 (Neutra 1980, 1-2). In his manifesto in 1912, Rudolph Schindler, Neutra's fellow student at Loos and also his office partner from 1925 to 1931 in Los Angeles, formulated the prospect of domestication of the world through mankind's increasing mastery of tools. He predicted that the comfort of a home would be completely dependent on the control of space, climate, light, and mood (Colomina and Wigley 2016, 128) at some point. Schindler thus anticipated Neutra's orchestration of the senses formulated in his book *Survival through Design*.

By building the Lovell Health House for the therapist and journalist Philipp Lovell, Neutra combined his "physiological inclinations" (Neutra 1962, 297) with the most innovative construction methods of his time. In 1932 Henry Russell Hitchcock wrote in the exhibition catalog of the Museum of Modern Art: "It is without question stylistically the most advanced house built in America since the war" (MoMA 1932, 158). Whereas the Lovell Health House established Neutra as a technical wizard (McCoy 1962, 18), he himself formulated a more comprehensive claim on the architect's profession in one of his lectures at the Academy of Modern Art in Los Angeles: "The architect [...] has to balance in his conception the influences from the process of building production or manufacture, with the influences based on the psychology of consumption" (Goldhagen 2000, 99). Neutra planned numerous well-known residential buildings in the following years that deal with the different poles of technical optimization and the well-being of inhabitants, such as the Sternberg house (1935) and the Kaufmann Desert house (1957).

His office partnership with Robert Alexander from 1950 to 1960 brought larger and more public commissions in America as well as abroad. While Arthur Drexler marks the work of this period as "hasty, perfunctory, lacking any fundamental rethinking of possibilities" (Drexler 1982, 20), the collaboration allowed Neutra to substantiate his theoretical position in lectures and publications. Based on the writings of Wilhelm Wundt, a physician from Leipzig, Germany, and the founder of experimental psychology, Neutra developed the theory of a holistic spatial experience that consistently demands psychological compatibility in addition to physical compatibility of the built environment. In his autobiography *Life and Shape*, Neutra explained that, "instead of grafting an arbitrary selection of technical novelties on to a design so that it does not lag behind the fashionable, architects should apply these technical inventions with a deep understanding of mankind's biologically long-established nature and lovingly adapted to its organic needs – then the house will not only outlive the current trends in the real estate market but, far more importantly is – it will have a lasting effect on the lives of its inhabitants and visitors" (Neutra 1962, 311).

Therefore, the architect should "pledge himself to serve wholesomeness honestly. If physicians take such a humane oath [Hippocratic oath], the designer must too" (Neutra 1969, 325). Through the foundation of the Neutra Institute for Survival through Design in 1962, Richard Neutra wanted to facilitate his required communication between design professionals and scientists. Despite the emphasized scientific claim, Neutra's writings offer no concrete approaches to the methodological implementation of his theoretical claims, which he first named *biorealism* in his publication *Life and Human Habitat* in 1954 (Neutra 1957, 30). The Australian professor of architecture, Dr. Michael J. Ostwald, focused on the optical stimuli in Neutra's architecture in his research. He developed a test method based on Space Syntax Analysis to check the feasibility of biorealism. In the following, this approach is to be tested on Richard Neutra's German housing developments of 1960.

Neutra's German Settlements

Richard Neutra was commissioned in 1960 by the housing cooperative BEWOBAU, a subsidiary of the housing construction company Neue Heimat Hamburg, to plan a housing estate in Walldorf. It was meant to comprise around 360 single and double houses. His urban concept and the development of nine housing types, eight of them one-, and one two-storied, are used in the same year for another settlement in Quickborn near Hamburg. Both projects were then built at the same time. Through long visual axes from the living spaces to the private outdoor spaces, the outdoor facilities – planned by the garden architect Gustav Lüttge – are interwoven with the interiors into a sense-perceptible unit. Neutra's inclusion of kindergartens and schools as well as local amenities in the settlement context (Neutra 1957, 31) were discarded by the developer in both plans, whereas the BEWOBAU believed a basement and wind screen to be indispensable for the German market (Neutra 1962, 382). Despite the adjustments, the 67 houses built in the first phase of construction in Quickborn sold just as slowly as the 42 houses in Walldorf. "The circle of people who buy such houses is very small," the BEWOBAU director was cited in the German magazine *Spiegel* (*Spiegel* 1964, 26). The following construction phases were realized without Neutra, even though they were based on his plans. A planned cooperation for a settlement construction in Hohenbuchau near Wiesbaden was therefore never realized, despite the advanced planning stage. Neutra deeply regretted the termination of the project cooperation in Hohenbuchau, which he considered to be the culmination of his cooperation with BEWOBAU (Leuschel 2010, 185).

Analytical Methods and Results

The German settlement buildings enable the exploration of Neutra's conception of biorealism with individual buildings in the context of a neighborhood, and not just as single buildings. Due to the anonymity of the future residents, a personalization of the planning concept can be excluded. Considering the known interventions by the BEWOBAU, the implementation of Neutra's planning principles can be assumed in their pure form. In addition, the adjoining construction sections of BEWOBAU, which were created only on Neutra's characteristic style, can be used as objects for comparison and will be called BEWOBAU houses in the following. The designation of the settlement in Walldorf as a listed ensemble in 1991 with additionally listed single buildings was the determining factor in the choice against the settlement of Quickborn where the declaration followed fourteen years later.

In his book *The Mathematics of the Modernist Villa*, Michael J. Ostwald presents the method to examine five exemplary single-family homes in Neutra's oeuvre, including the Kaufmann Desert House of 1947. Ostwald sums up that "[u]ltimately, the success of Neutra's theory of Biorealism rests on his capacity to achieve three properties in a design. First, the creation of long, distinct vistas, to draw the eye and the body through space. Second, the creation of plans with improved connectivity to support cognitive clarity. Third, to ensure that the exterior environment is part of the experience of the house. Through the application of these strategies, his architecture was intended to promote heightened sensory appeal, reduce distractions, and increase awareness of nature. [...]" (Ostwald 2018, 184)

Table 1 shows the previously named characteristics of Neutra's spatial strategies, the hypothesis and analytical method developed from it, as well as the indicators for a positive result.

	PROPERTY	HYPOTHESIS	METHOD	INDICATOR OF A POSITIVE RESULT
1	Vision leads to movement	Long sight lines will dominate the network of vistas and paths in each plan	Axial line analysis	The most integrated line(s) should encompass a large proportion of each plan's functional zones and participate in their major circulation loops
2	Movement leads to understanding	Plans will possess a high level of cognitive clarity	Intelligibility comparison	R2 > 0.75
3	Experience of the exterior is integral	(1) The most private spaces will be topologically close to the exterior (2) The structure of the plan will require exterior connections	Step distance and structural comparison	(1) Step distance will be less than two in 80% of the cases (2) Exterior spaces will be integral to the social structure of at least 80% of the cases

Fig. 1: Spatial properties mapped to scientific hypotheses, analytical methods and result indicators

Table 1: Spatial properties mapped to scientific hypotheses, analytical methods, and result indicators (based on Ostwald 2018, 185, adaptations by Isabell Schütz)

The success indicators in the first and third approaches are met in Ostwald's study objects, but the result in the second approach remains below the set indicator size. Nevertheless, Ostwald considers the study a success, having uncovered some important features of Richard Neutra's architecture (Ostwald 2018, 205). Subsequently, the analysis methods developed by Ostwald are applied to three houses of the Neutra settlement and three buildings planned by the BEWOBAU in consecutive construction phases. Within the realms of possibility, floor plans and room sizes were chosen with the highest mutual equivalence.

In a first step the following research will investigate whether Neutra's settlements fulfill Ostwald's hypotheses. Afterward, the values of the BEWOBAU houses will be determined and compared with the former to assess if the original Neutra planning shows different values than the houses that were designed according to his principles but not by himself.

Ostwald's first hypothesis assumes that long sight lines dominate the network of perspectives and paths in Neutra's floor plans, thereby creating a high degree of understanding of the overall building: "To assess the first hypothesis, Total Depth (TD) and Mean Depth (MD) are employed to classify and differentiate those spaces that are shallow or deep relative to the entire building, and integration (i) is calculated to investigate how accessible a line is to every other line in the system. Integration was calculated from Real Relative Asymmetry (RRA), which means that the results are relativized for direct comparison between the differently sized houses." (Ostwald 2018, 185)

For this purpose, all six floor plans are subjected to an axial line analysis, which in the first step depicts all possible linear paths through the floor plan (figs. 1 and 2). By applying an elimination algorithm which uses subset reductions, these lines are reduced to the minimum of necessary lines needed to reliably describe the system (Turner 2004, 24).

Although the location of the axial lines with the highest integration values is similar, large deviations in the determined values can be detected. While the BEWOBAU houses have a small margin between the highest and lowest integration values, the range is more pronounced in the Neutra houses. In particular, the range between average and maximum values is distinct and reflects the results of Ostwald's analysis. Neutra's designs show a small number of highly integrated axial lines that run through the geometric cores of the respective floor plans. The combined analysis of the qualitative and quantitative data validates the hypothesis of long sight lines in all of the examined houses. The generally high integration values in the Neutra houses and the elevated measured values of single lines compared to the average could therefore acknowledge Neutra's focus on this aspect of his designs, in comparison to the BEWOBAU floor plans.

NEUTRA HOUSES

TYPE ‚D'

FLOORPLAN   TYPE ‚D'

AXIAL MAP TYPE ‚D'

RESUL TT YPE ‚D'

	highest i-values		min	mean	max
	1a	1b			
MD	1,2307	1,4615	1,2307	1,6593	2
RA	0,0385	0,0769	0,0384	0,1098	0,1667
RRA	0,1442	0,2883	0,6247	0,3508	0,1442
i	6,9368	3,4684	1,6008	2,8508	6,9368
length	15,346	13,917	6,9417	12,189	16,865
connectivity	10	8	3	5,4286	10

step distance	3
total lines in ma p	14
intelligibility	0,8556

TYPE ‚H'

FLOORPLAN   TYPE ‚H'

AXIAL MAP TYPE ‚H'

RESUL TT YPE ‚H'

	highest i-values		min	mean	max
	1a	1b			
MD	1,1852	1,1852	1,1852	1,5582	2,4444
RA	0,0142	0,0142	0,0142	0,0429	0,1111
RRA	0,0757	0,0757	0,5908	0,1813	0,0757
i	13,203	13,203	1,6927	5,5165	13,203
length	21,393	21,449	2,3677	11,987	23,478
connectivity	22	22	3	13,5	22

step distance	2
total lines in ma p	28
intelligibility	0,771 1

TYPE ‚N'

FLOORPLAN   TYPE ‚N'

AXIAL MAP TYPE ‚N'

RESUL TT YPE ‚N'

	highest i-values		min	mean	max
	1a	1b			
MD	1,3103	1,3448	1,3103	1,6207	2,2069
RA	0,0222	0,0246	0,0222	0,0443	0,0862
RRA	0,1225	0,1361	0,4765	0,2190	0,1225
i	8,1612	7,3451	2,0986	4,5664	8,1612
length	16,29	16,19	1,96	10,86	28,36
connectivity	20	19	4	12,8	20

step distance	2
total lines in ma p	30
intelligibility	0,9092

Key to result annotations: MD = mean depth; RA= relative assymmetry; RRA= real relative assymmetry; i= integration-value; lengt   h= line length;

Fig. 1: Neutra Houses: floor plans, axial maps, and results

TYPE ,ELB   11′

FLOORPLAN   TYPE ,ELB   11′

AXIAL MAP TYPE ,ELB   11′

RESUL T T YPE ,ELB   11′

	highest i-values		min	mean	max
	1a	1b			
MD	1,2857	1,4285	1,2857	1,8285	2,1428
RA	0,0439	0,0659	0,0439	0,1274	0,1758
RRA	0,1699	0,2549	0,6798	0,4207	0,1699
i	5,8843	3,9229	1,4711	2,3769	5,8843
length	17,974	14,074	4,6619	9,5512	17,974
connectivity	10	8	2	5,6	10

step distance	3
total lines in ma p	15
intelligibility	0,7136

TYPE ,ELN 12′

FLOORPLAN   TYPE ,ELN 12′

AXIAL MAP T YPE ,ELN 12′

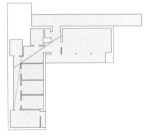

RESUL T T YPE ,ELN 12′

	highest i-values		min	mean	max
	1a	1b			
MD	1,3076	1,3846	1,3076	1,8131	2,1538
RA	0,0512	0,0641	0,0512	0,1355	0,1923
RRA	0,1922	0,2403	0,7208	0,4269	0,1922
i	5,2026	4,1621	1,3873	2,3426	5,2026
length	10,020	9,1246	4,6619	8,3913	14,652
connectivity	9	8	2	5,2026	9

step distance	3
total lines in ma p	14
intelligibility	0,7195

TYPE ,ELK 9′

FLOORPLAN   TYPE ,ELK 9′

AXIAL MAP T YPE ,ELK 9′

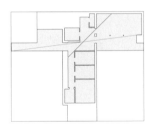

RESUL T T YPE ,ELK 9′

	highest i-values		min	mean	max
	1a	1b			
MD	1,3636	1,4545	1,3636	1,8333	2,6363
RA	0,0727	0,0909	0,0727	0,1666	0,3272
RRA	0,2553	0,3191	1,1488	0,4849	0,2553
i	3,9171	3,1337	0,8704	2,0622	3,9171
length	11,746	25,426	4,8072	10,781	25,426
connectivity	7	6	2	4,8333	7

step distance	2
total lines in ma p	12
intelligibility	0,8059

Key to result annotations: MD = mean depth; RA= relative assymmetry; RRA= real relative assymmetry; i= integration-value; lengt   h= line length;

Fig. 2: BEWOBAU Houses: floor plans, axial maps, and results

Ostwald's second hypothesis is based on the determination of the spatial intelligibility as a mathematical comparative figure and its evaluation based on known measured values. Although Ostwald's measurements fall short of his set limits, he does not doubt the method (Ostwald 2018, 205), so that it is also used in the comparative analysis of the Walldorf housing developments. "Axial intelligibility indexes the degree to which the number of immediate connections a line has is a reliable guide to the importance of that line in the system as a whole (namely, it is a correlation between axial connectivity and axial global integration). A strong correlation, or 'high intelligibility,' implies that the whole can be read from the parts." (UCL Space Syntax Glossary n.d.) The retrieved parameter by Ostwald is derived from known measurements in the urban environment where the threshold for above-average intelligibility at $R^2 > 0.68$ was determined. The lower complexity of a domestic environment leads to an increase of the limit to $R^2 > 0.75$. While all Neutra houses comply with this threshold, two out of three houses of the BEWOBAU remain below the limit value, so that a better intelligibility of Neutra's designed floor plans can be determined in comparison to the developers' houses.

The third hypothesis consists of two parts. First, the most private parts of the floor plan should be close to the outside. The key parameters here are the necessary changes of direction from the front door to the master bedroom, which in Ostwald's analysis should be less than two, in four out of five cases (Ostwald 2018, 185). The lowest value of all Walldorf houses, however, is with two changes of direction – two out of three Neutra houses need two changes of direction from the front door to the master bedroom and only house type D needs three. In the case of the BEWOBAU houses, only the house type ELK9 requires two changes in direction; the other two require three. Although all buildings are below the threshold set by Ostwald, the lower values of the Neutra houses compared to the BEWOBAU houses point to an increased focus on this aspect in the design process by Richard Neutra. The second part of the analysis shows that the developments in the BEWOBAU houses have a linear strategy, while the Neutra houses have a circular loop through the kitchen and the living room supplemented by a linear corridor leading to the bedrooms. French windows in the master bedroom allow for a circular access through the sliding doors of the living room of all examined Neutra houses. An additional French door in the kitchen of housing types D and N as well as the French door close to the kitchen in housing type H allow for further circular movements. The floor plans of the types ELN12 and ELB11 also allow for a circular access through the French windows of the master bedroom with the living room. Type ELK9 has only a circular movement between the storeroom, house entrance, and hall, which is also characteristic for the other two examined BEWOBAU houses. This serving loop is not available in the Neutra houses, where storerooms are located in the basement, upon request from BEWOBAU. These serving access loops cannot be understood as an integral part of the social structures of the buildings. Hence, the criteria for the second subhypothesis for an integral outdoor perception were not met by the building type ELK9. While the analysis of the floor plans ELN12 and ELB11 basically meet the conditions but could be improved by strengthening the outdoor route between the terraces, only the Neutra houses generally comply with the requirements.

Conclusion

While Ostwald notes the lack of a mathematical basis for comparability with other designs and therefore wants to understand his methodological approach as a basis for discussion, I believe that the desired adaptation of the Neutra expression to the BEWOBAU houses provides a sufficient basis for comparison. The quantitative and qualitative studies of the selected Neutra houses show a significantly higher comprehensibility in terms of Ostwald's evaluation parameters than the examined BEWOBAU houses, which are modeled on Neutra's ductus. A successful implementation of Neutra's spatial strategies in his housing developments can therefore be derived from it, but, according to Ostwald, not the general effectiveness of biorealism as such (Ostwald 2018, 182).

The focus of the analysis on optical stimuli is in contradiction to Neutra's holistically formulated approach which anticipated this delimitation: "We should therefore be interested in all the nonvisual aspects of architecture environment and design even if they are not customarily in the foreground of our awareness" (Neutra 1969, 138). This makes it clear that a thorough analysis of the visual axes can only reflect a partial aspect of the implementation of the multilayered biorealism. While the realization of further aspects – such as the wide spatial separation of pavements and driveways required by Neutra (1969, 360) – can generally be observed within a local inspection of the Walldorf settlement, the basic proof of its effectiveness on the human organism lies in the field of modern neurology. In her book *Welcome to Your World*, Sarah Williams Goldhagen exemplifies the scientific proof of the mental simulation of the production process when looking at surfaces with traces of craftsmanship – a reaction that Neutra anticipated without being able to prove it (Goldhagen 2017, 160). The comparison with current research findings should not only serve as a retrospective proof, but in the sense of Neutra's approach find application in our current planning tasks: "when carefully correlated with organized policies of design, [systematic biological investigation] will redound to the benefit of a broader human consumership" (Neutra 1969, 383). While Neutra sees the survival of humankind endangered by the lack of consideration of human nature in all aspects of design (Neutra 1969, 21), the continuation of his studies can be a key element in the current debate on sustainability and the future of housing.

References

Colomina, Beatriz, and Mark Wigley. 2016. *Are We Human? Notes on an Archaeology of Design*. Zürich: Lars Müller Publishers.

Drexler, Arthur, and Thomas S. Hines. 1989. *The Architecture of Richard Neutra: From International Style to California Modern*. 2nd ed. New York: Museum of Modern Art.

Goldhagen, Sarah Williams. 2017. *Welcome to Your World: How the Built Environment Shapes Our Lives*. New York: Harper.

Goldhagen, Sarah Williams, and Réjean Legault. 2000. *Anxious Modernisms: Experimentation in Postwar Architectural Culture*. Cambridge, MA: MIT Press.

Leuschel, Klaus, and Marta Herford. 2010. *Richard Neutra in Europa: Bauten und Projekte 1960–1970*. Cologne: DuMont.

McCoy, Esther. 1962. *Richard Neutra*. Große Meister der Architektur 9. Ravensburg: Otto Maier Verlag.

Museum of Modern Art. 1932. *Modern Architecture: International Exhibition*. New York: The Museum of Modern Art. Accessed February 11, 2019. https://www.moma.org/documents/moma_catalogue_2044_300061 855.pdf.

Neutra, Richard. 1957. *Mensch und Wohnen: Life and Human Habitat*. 2nd ed. Stuttgart: Verlagsanstalt Alexander Koch.

Neutra, Richard. 1962. *Auftrag für morgen*. Hamburg: Claassen Verlag.

Neutra, Richard. 1969 [1954]. *Survival through Design*. New York: Oxford University Press.

Neutra, Richard. 1980 [1927]. *Wie baut Amerika*. Munich: Kraus-Reprint.

Ostwald, Michael J., and Michael J. Dawes. 2018. *The Mathematics of the Modernist Villa*. Cham: Birkhäuser.

Spiegel. 1964. "Neutra Häuser: Schlecht geträumt." Spiegel 35: 26. Accessed March 7, 2019. http://magazin.spiegel.de/EpubDelivery/spiegel/pdf/46175088.

Turner, Alasdair. 2004. *Depthmap 4: A Researcher's Handbook*. London: Bartlett.

School of Graduate Studies, UCL. n.d. Accessed March 1, 2019. http://www.vr.ucl.ac.uk/depthmap/depthmap4.pdf.

UCL Space Syntax Glossary. n.d. "Axial Intelligibility." Accessed March 1, 2019. http://otp.spacesyntax.net/term/axial-intelligibility/.

Wandel-Hoefer, Rena. 1989. *Zur Architektur Richard Neutras: Eine Analyse seines theoretischen Werkes und der Umsetzung in seinen Bauten*. Darmstadt: Technische Hochschule Darmstadt.

Exploring Chinese Scholar Gardens as a Paradigm of Lifestyle Landscape Architecture

Luyi Liu and Luigi Cocchiarella
Politecnico di Milano, Italy

Abstract — This research is based on two clues: one is the chronological development of the concept of space in Western architectural theory, which leads to nowadays global-wide universal spatial design; the other is retroactive research of the Chinese scholar gardens, which put Chinese scholar gardens in the perspective of a particular spatial notion that is rooted in Chinese original culture and philosophy. Taking inspiration from phenomenological narrative analysis, Chinese scholar gardens are investigated from the Western academic point of view as well as in their own cultural context. Such research methods, putting the research object in contrasting (however relevant) perspective, respond to the expectation that this matter originating from ancient China could really contribute to the academic discourse in today's international and interdisciplinary community. This research points out ways to synergize Western and Eastern historical culture and have an impact on the present architectural spatial design.

Looking at the History of the Concept of Space in Western Architecture

SPACE AS A PRIMARY QUALITY OF ARCHITECTURAL COMPOSITION: SPACE-CONCERNED

After the modern revolution, no one will doubt that space is an essential aspect of architecture. The practical works by Frank Lloyd Wright and Mies van der Rohe, as well as other numerous critical works always remind us of the great influence of August Schmarsow, Nikolaus Pevsner, Bruno Zevi, and other theoreticians.

As Peter Collins (1965) wrote, "[U]ntil the eighteenth century, no architectural treatise ever used the word [space], whilst the idea of space as a primary quality of architectural composition was not fully developed until the last few years," which implies that the conscious use of the notion of space appeared quite late in Western architectural history. In this paper, the way of composing an architecture by considering space as a primary quality, as Collins put it, is named as the *space-primarily-concerned* or *space-concerned* method, for short.

Although there are layers of criticism by criticism in theory, in the practical architecture realm the development of space-concerned methods has rarely been carried out in the built environment, and sometimes with controversy. However, there are two typical architectural schools that are often considered to be spawned by the notion of space: organic architecture and phenomenological architecture. By the way, the former one was also criticized for finally falling into formalism, and later on it was questioned as "Minimal Moralia" (Frampton 1996) that serves fairly limited well-educated persons. After holding the awareness about the notion of space as the primary quality of architecture, the question arose how the conception of space could be translated into architectural design approaches and methodologies in order to serve contemporary society in a context of cultural diversity.

SPACE AND HUMAN PERCEPTION, LANDSCAPE ARCHITECTURE AND EVENTS

In urban realm – that is, at a bigger spatial scale – in 1957, Situationist International (SI) points out the relevance of "moments of life concretely and deliberately constructed by the collective organization of a unitary ambiance and a game of events" (Debord 1958).[1] The *Derive* was one of the most famous urban space experiments following this manifesto. It was an exploration of the relationship between human perception and urban space from the perspective of architects and urban planners, which resulted from a continuing and progressing discussion triggered by the artistic experiments of Dadaism and Surrealism in the 1920s. *The Naked City*, one of the representations of *Derive*, as a psychogeographic map, discusses the linkage between human collective consciousness and urban space.

Inspired by SI, a group of architects also proposed some advancements in translating the concept of space into the smaller-scale space realm: landscape architecture and buildings. Bernard Tschumi, for example, set red pavilions in his famous project Parc de la Villette as a series of events montage, which was a system defined in terms of defamiliarization. By doing so, Tschumi strove to break the preset relationship between "space use" and "behavior mode." Another example would be the work of Rem Koolhaas. In *Delirious New York*, he presented the idea of deconstructing the inherent relationship between space and activity; furthermore, he deconstructs activities. Koolhaas applied this idea in his later projects to reach the multiple uncertainty experience in space.

This series of efforts reveals the essential relationship between space and human action and perception. Either basing on the collective consciousness, or standing on the opposite side of daily life, they have shown the possible ways that the concept of space could be recognized and developed after the modern revolution. This is because the SI mainly considers the real urban realm in combination with the social/political scenario, in the meantime holding the criticism of advanced capitalism.

Therefore, the question raised above may be better asked as if the individual consciousness, in daily life, can also have some links with space, and what are those links. With this question in mind, we turn our focus of study to ancient China.

Ancient Chinese Scholar Gardens and Its Roots in Philosophy
THE BIRTH OF CHINESE SCHOLAR GARDENS

Scholar gardens can be categorized as a specific kind of Chinese landscape. It is generally believed that ancient Chinese landscape architecture originated from the mountain worship 3,000 years ago, and the Tai (High Platform) was built for the emperor to pray to heaven. In early ancient time, only the emperor had such authority to build this type of landscape in the name of etiquette restrictions, also because of the human and financial resources limitations. In the Qin dynasty (221–206 BC), the first dynasty of Imperial China, Tai had been developed into a symbol of the states' unification and a representation of highest power.

After another unified dynasty (the Han dynasty), in Northern and Southern dynasties (220–589 AD), it suffered from a long period of turbulence and wars, and unification could not be further maintained. The division of states also led to the collapse of rituals. The building of Tai, which was the symbol of the high power of the emperor, could then be emulated by kings of the separatist countries. The looseness of the ritual laid the foundation of the emergence of the scholar, or literati, garden. Meanwhile, due to political changes and social development, a new social class arose: the scholars, who are also known as Literati. Though they lost their wealth, which used to be the patronage from the emperor, they acquired a relatively independent social status that allowed them to present their ideas more freely. Similar to those kings, they also began to build landscapes of their own, which are gardens in countryside. These gardens were partly used to present that they were educated well and they held high taste of the art and life. Comparing with the empire style landscape, which represented political status, they turned their gardens to represent personal insights and set it in their daily lives. Thereafter, Chinese scholar gardens started to develop.

THE FIRST IMAGE PROOF: THE BRICKS PAINTING OF SEVEN SCHOLARS OF BAMBOO GROVE AND RONG QIQI

The bricks painting of seven scholars of Bamboo Grove and Rong Qiqi, unearthed in the 1960s in Nanjing, is the earliest image proof of scholar gardens. It shows one of the normal events among scholars in that era. Under different types of trees, some characters appear playing instruments, some others tasting beverages (usually tea and wine); one is smoking, another looks like he is working at the identification of some items (usually antiques), one is just sitting, probably writing a poem.

Fig. 1: Seven Scholars of Bamboo Grove and Rong Qiqi, the picture printed from bricks from the Southern dynasty (220–598 AD). Unearthed in 1960 in Nanjing, China.
(Source: Nanjing Museum, China)

The combination of trees and people from this print represents the notion that humans live in harmony with nature. Furthermore, the different kinds of trees have one-to-one correspondence to each of these Literati, that is, according to their personalities and what they were doing at that moment. It is the scholar, his activity, and the special kind of tree, that together compose this meaningful event. Therefore, we can come to the following inference:

- First of all, the event is space-concerned. There are persons and trees in the print with no heavyweight building components, such as masonry curing the visual composition. This matches "the idea of space as a primary quality of architectural composition" (Collins 1965).
- Secondly, in Chinese scholar gardens, obviously plants are seen as physical elements that make up space, defining and creating space. It

should further be emphasized that different from stone walls or some other tough self-enclosed materials located in the garden, the plant is a living and accessible spatial element. In other words, one can sit beside trees in the shade to enjoy the space, with smelling of the new leaves and listening to birds singing.

- Additionally, it is important that different trees hold different meanings. Each one should be set in a special position to match the corresponding spatial event. This means that there are complex interactions between human consciousness and the material world. This is also similar to the idea of ambiance construction that "the construction of situations, moments of life deliberately constructed for the purpose of reawakening and pursuing authentic desires, experiencing the feeling of life and adventure, and the liberation of everyday life" (Debord 1958).

THE NOTION OF SPACE IN CHINA

To find the root of this spatial phenomenon, we should look back into history. Indeed, the notion of space has a long history in ancient China.

It is well known that the *Tao Te Ching* is one of the most important Chinese classical texts, which was credited to the sixth century BC. It is also the fundamental text for both philosophical and religious Taoism. It also strongly influenced the whole ancient China culture; Chinese scholars including poets, painters, calligraphers, and gardeners took it as a source of inspiration. In Chapter 11, it is written: "Mold clay into a vessel; From its not-being [in the vessel's hollow] arises the utility of the vessel. Cut out doors and windows in the house [-walls], from their not-being [empty space] arises the utility of the house. Therefore, by the existence of things we profit. And by the non-existence of things we are served." [埏埴以为器, 当其无, 有器之用。凿户牖以为室, 当其无, 有室之用。故有之以为利, 无之以为用.]

In the traditional Chinese text's writing, usually the last part of the sentence is the highlighted part, which shows the core idea of the whole sentence, while the other parts generally work as the supporting points. In this phrase, here are three times of appearance of the character 无 (pinyin: WU). The first two WU were tagged separately, to explain the hollow of the vessels and the empty space of a room, that is, the physical space in the real world. But they both allude and allegorize the last philosophical WU in this sentence, that is, the not-being. In other words, space here not only means the physical void as part of architecture. It somehow means the space/gap between human perceptual/cognition/memories/experiences and the material world, in other words, the space between realities and minds. It is rather similar to the idea of a perception field in phenomenology, when the interaction of perception and memory is happening. This old and plain perceptive interactivity concept can be found in almost all art fields of ancient China, like paintings, poem composition, and appreciation, as well as some folk games. Therefore, it deeply influenced and shaped the entire ancient China culture system, that is, its whole cultural system. In the spatial design realm, scholar gardens, as one kind of the ancient China's landscape architectures, also reflect such notion. Coming back to the brick painting mentioned above, it is typically space-concerned, and pertains some kind of perception field where it is letting some events to happen.

Chinese Scholar Gardens as Lifestyle Landscape Architecture
ANCIENT CHINESE SCHOLARS IN GARDEN LIFESTYLE
Lifestyle is defined as any thing in life that is related to the interests, opinions, behaviors, and behavioral orientations of an individual, group, or culture. It was first introduced by psychologists to describe the motivations of an individual's behavior. This concept is also applied here in this study because it is consistent with the characteristics of scholar gardens. And it is also a critical reflection on the alienation of SI described above, that is, breaking the daily life and creating a perception atmosphere.

Figure 2, showing *YaJi in Garden*, is an official documentary painting of the Ming dynasty (1437 AD). It shows the further development of the scholar garden in later ancient China; and more importantly, it reveals one of the life scenes of scholars in the garden at that time. The name YaJi (in Chinese: 雅集) is made up of two characters in Chinese: *Ya* (雅) means "refined" or "elegant" and *Ji* (集) means "to gather, to collect." In term of the event happening in the garden, as shown in the painting, it is a traditional gathering with a group of distinguished assembly, usually literati or scholars, who play and discuss arts in the event.

Specifically, in the painting there are scholars in the garden playing, listening to, and discussing music; they are also painting or making calligraphy works; tasting good wine and tea; playing Go (Chinese traditional chess), and so on.

Fig. 2: YaJi in Garden, Xie Huan, 1437, Ming dynasty. (Source: Zhenjiang Museum, China)

It is instructive to say that those events are not linked with collective conscious-ness, but rather are related to a group of persons and their own perceptions of the environment. In other words, Chinese scholar gardens represent a kind of "lifestyle architecture" based on the linkage between human perception and space. Compared with the explorations proposed by SI, which were more about considering society and setting the defamiliarization as a strategy tool, the Chinese way is more linked with personal experience in their daily life. In the following a case study will be explained in detail.

A CASE STUDY: QU SHUI LIU SHANG

Qu Shui Liu Shang is a kind of landscape installation that originally emerged in the famous scholars' assembly – *Lantingji*. In the spring of 353 AD, as recorded in the literature, the assembly was held on a beautiful day. At the event, some literati gathered along the banks of an artificial coursing stream and were engaged in a drinking contest. Cups of wine were drifting down from upstream, and whenever a cup stopped in front of one guest, he had to compose a poem, otherwise, he had to drink this cup of wine. At the end of the day, twenty-six literati composed thirty-seven poems in total. The widely accepted best calligraphy works, *Lantingji Xu*, is one of the results of this assembly. It served as a preface of the collection of those poems written by Wang Xizhi on spot, who was the host of the assembly.

Fig. 3: Lantingji Xu, copy attributed to Feng Chengsu (617–672 AD), Tang dynasty
(Source: Palace Museum in Beijing, China)

From this story, we first discover that the scholars also played as creators during the time spent in the space and in the events, thanks to the interactions. And this beautiful improvised calligraphy, *Lantingji Xu*, is the visible cultural icon inherited until now.

Unlimited in terms of spatial design, the artificial coursing stream, the landscape installation dug to create the ambiance for the events during the mentioned assembly, namely *Qu Shui Liu Shang*, also became a visible cultural iconic landscape installation and it is still copied and used nowadays.

The three pictures in figure 4 are examples of *Qu Shui Liu Shang* realized in different scales. In figure 4(a), the *Qu Shui Liu Shang* is set as a grand table, represented in a super-furniture scale, or, if we prefer, in a mini-landscape scale. In figure 4(b), it is located in a pavilion, showing the landscape at an architectural scale, namely, at the typical scale of interior space. In figure 4(c) the stream is dug in a garden courtyard; it is shown at the landscape scale, or at a mini-urban scale.

Fig. 4: The Qu Shui Liu Shang landscape installation in various scales: (a) in super-furniture / mini-landscape scale; (b) in architectural / interior scale; (c) in landscape / mini-urban scale
Source: (a) Archaeological News pictures and the restoration diagram, by People's Daily (November 11, 2011); (b) National Architecture Institute of China, http://www.naic.org.cn/html/2017/gjzg_1112/32242.html; (c) Yizai Pavilion, Langya Hill, International picture, http://www.nipic.com/show/4888365.html

These various scales of Qu Shui Liu Shang landscape installations reveal an important aspect of Chinese concept of space: crossing scales. And it works both for culture and entertainment, according to the ancient Chinese lifestyle. From a philosophical point of view, it can be understood that meaningful spatial elements won't be limited by physical size. It is not the exact size of elements, but rather the elements themselves that could recall people's perception and memory. Here, again, there would be some kind of interaction between the person and space. And the different sizes of representations make this spatial culture icon more flexible, allowing it to be more easily inherited. As it can be seen in the above three cases, since the interaction of human perceptual cognition/memories/experiences is more emphasized, the physical size limitation is dissolved. Then, originally used for the courtyard only, the *Qu Shui Liu Shang* is now inherited on a wider spatial scale.

The abovementioned three scales of *Qu Shui Liu Shang* can be graphically summarized in the diagrams shown in figure 5.

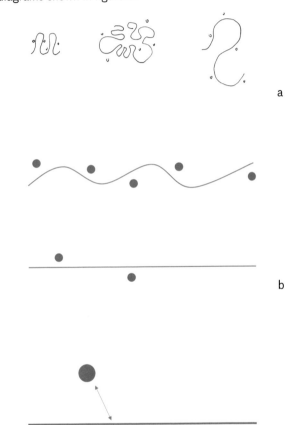

a

b

Fig. 5: Abstract diagrams about the three different scales of Qu Shui Liu Shang landscape installations: (a) using lines to refer to the stream, and the points refer to the persons; (b) the essential relations of line and points; (c) the interaction between line and the point represents an event happening in the space.

c

Graphicalization further abstracts the interaction described in the previous section, emphasized by the red line with arrows. The abstract pictograms strip away the unique cultural traits of *Qu Shui Liu Shang*, focusing on its essence only – the interaction of human perception and space. This offers a possible way to heritage for a contemporary general use.

On the other hand, it also reveals that in this kind of interaction, both human and space are the subjectivity, that is, it goes beyond the traditional dominant subject-object relationship to let the monads play an equally important role in this interaction (and it is usually immediate). This puts forward a phenomenological intersubjective premise requirement for this interaction. It is easy to imagine that for a person without the knowledge/cognition about the story of *LanTing* assembly, the interaction would neither be understood nor work well; it could even lead to a misreading.

As Kevin Lynch mentioned in the final paragraph of *The Image of the City*, which discussed the urban space visual perception, "education in seeing will be quite as important as the reshaping of what is seen" (Lynch 1960). In the development of lifestyle architecture (also including gardens and urban space, etc.), some education in lifestyle (awareness) is as important as creating the perception field where the lifestyle takes place.

Conclusion: Lifestyle Architecture Nowadays

Looking at both the progress of the notion of space in Western architecture and the history of Chinese gardens, present research defines that Chinese scholar gardens are one kind of lifestyle landscape architecture, that is, space-concerned, and lets daily life activities happen inside them, as human-space-interaction in the perceptual field. Then taking into account the phenomenological point of view, the research tried to discuss the abstract model of this perceptual interaction. It may be possible to make this space-creating method, which is interpreted from the ancient Chinese space phenomenon, serving contemporary society as well. At the same time, the limitations of this interaction and the vision of possible solutions are also discussed. Further working on this topic from the disciplinary field of an architect should be an interesting research activity. Human life is a dynamic action, is changed by time, changes day by day, season by season, year by year... At the standpoint of human beings, be s/he naïve as kids or mature or old, s/he will have different lifestyles in different situations. It means certain sort of essential everlasting dynamism. Research on this point, referring to the various geographic situations, and supported by history and philosophy, would be therefore encouraged. With specific reference to our field, they could be beneficial for the architects, including academics, in order to figure out future scenarios as well as to better focus on the humanized space in relation to the social contexts in the present globalized era. We have many pieces of evidence of the dynamism connected with the increasing cultural diversity, including not at least the effects of some particular events, like immigration. They are characterizing today's architectural contexts of life. However, it seems, we are not yet adequately prepared to face this issue. The contemporary interpretation of Chinese scholar gardens in this research, which explains it as lifestyle architecture, may provide some inspirations in relation to some of the open questions of the present time.

Acknowledgments

The paper was supported by grant from China Scholarship Council. Thanks to Dr. Zilong Wang for his kind and constructive language support and suggestions.

References

Cocchiarella, Luigi. 2009. *La forma oltre il codice: ambiente architettonico, teoria, rappresentazione*. Florence: Academia Universa Press.

Collins, Peter. 1998. *Changing Ideals in Modern Architecture: 1750–1950*. 2nd ed. Montreal: McGill-Queen's University Press.

Crary, Jonathan. 1990. *Techniques of the Observer: On Vision and Modernity in the Nineteenth Century*. Cambridge, MA: MIT Press.

Debord, Guy. 1958. "Definitions." Translated by Ken Knabb. *Internationale Situationniste*, no. 1 (June).

Frampton, Kenneth. 1996. "Minimal Moralia: Reflections on Recent Swiss German Production." *Scroope Cambridge Architecture Journal*, no. 9: 19–25.

Fung, Stanislaus. 2015. "Non-perspectival Effects in the Liu Yuan." *Proceedings of The International Conference on East Asian Architectural Culture, Gwangju, Korea, November 10–14*.

Knabb, Ken. 1981. *Situationist International Anthology*. Berkeley: Bureau of Public Secrets.

Koolhaas, Rem. 1978. *Delirious New York: A Retroactive Manifesto for Manhattan*. New York: Oxford University Press.

Lao, Zi. 1948 [ca. 300 BCE]. *Tao Te Ching* (道德经). Translated by Lin Yutang. New York: Random House. Retrieved from: https://terebess.hu/english/tao/yutang.html.

Lynch, Kevin. 1960. *The Image of the City*. Cambridge, MA: MIT Press.

Tschumi, Bernard. 1994. *Event-cities*. Cambridge, MA: MIT Press.

Tschumi, Bernard. 2014. *Tschumi Parc de la Villette*. London: Artefice Books.

Wang, Yi. 2004 中国园林文化史. Shanghai: Shanghai People's Publishing House.

---

[1] The Situationist International (SI) was an organization of social revolutionaries made up of avant-garde artists, intellectuals, and political theorists, prominent in Europe from its formation in 1957 to its dissolution in 1972. See also Sadie Plant, *The Most Radical Gesture* (New York: Routledge, 1992).

5 Sustainability

Designing Natural Buildings

Eike Roswag-Klinge
Natural Building Lab, Technische Universität Berlin and ZRS Architekten
Ingenieure, Berlin, Germany

Abstract — Architecture offices in Germany are generally of such a size that it is difficult for them to integrate research activities economically and organizationally into their everyday practice. Nevertheless, architecture firms have a large potential to generate important topics and knowledge as partners in research consortia. ZRS Architekten Ingenieure have developed over a number of years expertise in the field of natural building materials such as earth, wood, and bamboo and deploy this in the development of low-tech building systems for various global climatic contexts. The research activities undertaken by the office have given ZRS a specific knowledge that has proved valuable as a sound scientific basis upon which to develop and justify healthy and circular building using natural building materials.

The Natural Building Lab at the Technische Universität Berlin applies and further develops this knowledge in a university context. It serves as a basis for the development of innovative design projects and for a design-build pedagogy, where students work in transdisciplinary teams in a real context.

Introduction

Our society is increasingly built on the consumption and commodification of resources, goods, and knowledge to the detriment of our planet and well-being. Despite ongoing sustainability efforts and increasingly earners public discourse, the building sector remains responsible for around 40 percent of European energy consumption (Directive 2010/31/EU) and 50 percent of the overall use of material resources. In addition, around 60 percent of the waste in Europe (approx. 750 Mio. tons) is classified as construction and demolition waste generated by the building sector (Deloitte 2017). To meet the Paris climate goals will require us to radically reconsider the way we live, work, and interact with each other and our environment on all scales. The common approach still pretends to solve our problems through an increased level of building technology, that is, mechanical ventilation or air-conditioning systems. On the other hand, a trend toward reduction

of building technology is noticeable and showcased in, for example, the
"20/26 Project" by Baumschlager Eberle (Eberle and Aicher 2015).
Globally, around half of the world population lives in buildings that do not
rely on any building services and which are fully or partly constructed out
of reusable or recyclable materials. Natural materials like earth, timber, and
natural fiber offer numerous potentials. They are vapor-active and can in
combination with vapor-permeable constructions hydrothermally condition
spaces and reduce the need for building technology throughout the year.
ZRS Architekten Ingenieure (ZRS) researches, designs, and builds globally
architecture out of natural materials like the big three: earth, timber, and
bamboo. Based on a traditional knowledge regarding resources and climate
adaptation, ZRS designs new typologies for a future-oriented, post-fossil,
post-consume society. ZRS's practical work is supported by research to
prove historical knowledge on a scientific level and aid in the development
of innovative typologies and cultural adapted architecture based on their
scientific results.
The Natural Building Lab (NBL) at the Technische Universität Berlin is active
in the fields of teaching, research, and practice focusing on the use of natural
building materials and low-tech, climate-adapted building systems. The lab
links research and learning (teaching) through transdisciplinary design-build
projects in a close dialogue with a rapidly changing society, aiming to develop visionary ideas for post fossil, post-consume built environment.

**ZRS EU Research Project [H]house: Healthier Life with Eco-
Innovative Components for Housing Constructions (2013–2017)**
Innovative building systems for external and internal application in residential buildings were developed for new construction as well as refurbishment.
[H]house solutions cover aspects of hygrothermal "activity" of the developed
building materials, their embodied energy, suitability for different applications and environments, durability, cost-efficiency, and long-term improvement of energy efficiency of buildings. Special emphasis was placed on the
improvement of the indoor environmental quality of spaces through the use
of natural building materials that help to control relative humidity levels but
also adsorb airborne pollutants.
ZRS was responsible for the architectural and detailed design for all developed elements as well as to prove their integration into buildings up to
the demonstration level. Its specific scope consisted in the development of
climate-active, vapor-permeable systems for internal partition walls as well
as internal insulation for external walls out of natural materials.
A large number of different materials has been tested and evaluated. Based
on these results a variety of wall systems have been developed and tested
again at the component level regarding vapor activity, adsorption of airborne

pollutants, but also structural behavior and noise protection. The entire test campaign was supported by an in-depth Life Cycle Assessment (LCA) and Life Cycle Costing (LCC) assessment.

The results of the [H]house project form the basis of a ZRS low-tech building system made out of natural building materials. Due to the vapor-active and permeable building envelope, the system can be highly insulated and airtight without causing common problems regarding increased relative humidity levels or mold growth. As conventional energy-efficient buildings require mechanical ventilation to avoid damp problems, they dry out buildings in wintertime and cause discomfort and health problems for building occupants. The vapor-active ZRS system instead ensures stable relative humidity levels between 40 percent and 60 percent and increases occupant comfort and health. Through the research the traditional knowledge for natural building materials like earth, straw, and timber used for example for traditional half-timber workhouses is scientifically proved and transformed into a new building system for the future.

ZRS EU Research Project RE4: REuse and REcycling of CDW Materials and Structures in Energy Efficient pREfabricated Elements for Building REfurbishment and Construction (2016–2020)

Construction and demolition waste (CDW) is one of the priority targets of the European Commission, because of the large volume of generated waste and its high potential for reuse and recycling. The European waste generation should be reduced by 70 percent until 2020 (BIO Intelligence Service 2011). In contrast, a negligible percentage of waste is destined to reuse mainly because the majority of existing buildings was not designed for disassembly and reuse.

The main purpose of the project is to develop a RE4 prefabricated energy-efficient building concept that can be easily assembled and disassembled for future reuse, containing up to 65 percent in weight of recycled materials from CDW (ranging from 50 percent for the medium replacement of the mineral fraction, up to 65 percent). The reusable structures will range from 15–20 percent for existing buildings, to 80–90 percent for the RE4 prefabricated building concept (fig. 1).

The RE4 project aims to promote new technological solutions and strategies for the development of prefabricated elements with a high degree of recycled materials and reused structures from dismantled buildings. The main aim of the project is to develop energy-efficient buildings produced from CDW, thus minimizing environmental impacts in the construction industry. The building component will be suitable for both new construction and building refurbishment.

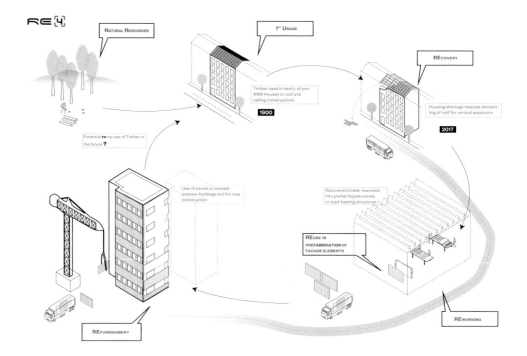

Fig. 1: RE4 European Research Project, circular construction built out of recycled timber elements
(© ZRS Architekten Ingenieure)

ZRS is responsible within the project for the architectural and detailed design for all elements, to develop and to prove their integration into the buildings up to the demonstration objects. The main ZRS focus is to evaluate the
life cycle and reuse of timber and earthen products. Architectural design and
reversible constructions for circular buildings are going to be developed.

NBL BMU Research Project BiMoka: Development of Educational Modules on Climate-Resilient Architecture, NBL 2019/21

BiMoKa is a research project supported by the German Ministry for Environment aiming to develop innovative educational modules on climate-resilient
architecture for digital delivery (BiMoKa n.d.). The rise in global temperatures coupled with increasing urbanization and the resulting urban heat
island effect require the development of adaptation strategies at the building
level. In professional practice as well as over the course of architectural
studies, the specific realities of the effects of climate change on architectural concepts and infrastructural projects still receive insufficient attention.
This applies to strategies for energy-efficient building cooling based on
renewable energies and environmental strategies, decentralized rainwater

management as well as water supply and sanitation. In professional practice, this currently leads to considerable problems in planning processes and the delegation of these tasks to contractors and isolated specialized planning offices. This project serves to introduce the basics to a wide range of users in professional and academic practice. New forms of knowledge transfer enable an efficient and widely distributed information pool.

Fig. 2: RE4 European Research Project, models and samples of new circular timber elements
(© ZRS Architekten Ingenieure)

Fig. 3: Infozentrale auf dem Rollberg, Berlin, result of a Natural Building Lab DesignBuild Studio
(© Natural Building Lab, Technische Universität Berlin, Leon Klaßen)

NBL DesignBuild Project Building Cycle: Transdisciplinary DesignBuild Project, NBL 2017/18

The "Infozentrale auf dem Vollgut" was designed and realized by a group of 36 students as part of the BUILDinG CYCLE design studio from the Natural Building Lab at the Technische Universität Berlin during the winter semester 2017/18. In cooperation with the research project RE4, a building embodying circular construction was realized from waste materials as a design-build project, offering an answer to questions relating to resource-positive construction in an urban context and embodying a new method of architectural production for a post-consumer society. In the opening weeks of the project the student groups undertook a material research, where innovative low-tech constructive elements were created using a wide range of waste materials Through this research the groups established a network, through which they were able to source larger amounts of the waste materials used for the building – recovered timber and cardboard. The load-bearing structure of the building is formed from timber recovered from local demolition sites and a dismantled architectural installation from the International Garden Festival 2017, thus providing a second usage cycle for this valuable resource. The 5.5 × 7.0 m roof structure is formed by a prestressed grid of layered and interlocking reused timber beams with reversible connections designed for disassembly. For the wall elements, an experimental system was developed utilizing stacked upcycled cardboard fruit boxes filled with shredded paper as insulation and covered with large-format posters and plotted drawings – common waste materials within architectural faculties. The project embodies circular construction principles and serves as a prototype for a low-tech post-fossil architecture based on the realities of resource scarcity and climate change. During the design and construction phase, students networked with around 200 participants on and around the site in order to get a deep understanding of the situation, to anchor the project locally, and to resource materials for building (fig. 4).

Outputs of Practice Integrated Research

Through H-House and RE4 research projects the ZRS low-tech building system could be scientifically validated. Based on the scientific knowledge the system was further developed and implemented in a number of projects, ranging between housing, production, and public buildings. The building system offers healthy, comfortable spaces throughout the year, if the architectural design is appropriate, glazing levels are balanced, and nighttime cooling is possible. As adaptive skeleton structures combined with reversible interior fit-outs and facade constructions, they offer a long-lasting circular future.

Through this unique knowledge ZRS is scaling its projects and has a unique position on the market. In addition there is a new trend toward healthy, low-tech buildings, which ZRS is giving a solid foundation and showcases of build projects.

Fig. 4: Infozentrale auf dem Rollberg, Berlin, network of the Building Cycle Collective during concept, design and building (© Building Cycle Collective, Maria Nesterova)

Results of Transdiciplinary Design-Build Projects

Within the NBL projects, research and teaching are closely interwoven (fig. 5). Thus, teaching research projects are looking for specific solutions, for example, on sustainable housing in rural areas of Bangladesh. A first research project on adaptation to climate change has begun with the BiMoKa project and further applications are pending.

Through their design-build projects, the students have created their own networks and architecture collectives with which they continue to work community-oriented in the projects in the most varied ways. They critically reflect their projects and develop their own position to the activity of the architect. The practical examination of building as part of the design-build projects gives them new insights into the design of building structures and the sustainable use of resources.

Thus a new group of self-determined architects is growing up, reflecting in cooperation with residents, working on future-oriented questions, and realizing small projects by taking social responsibility.

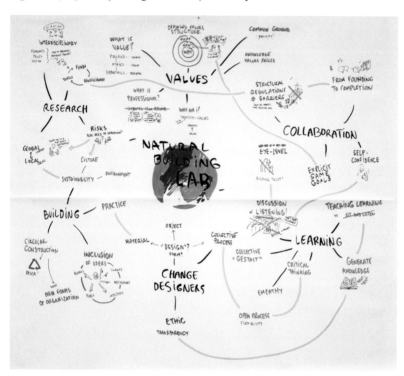

Fig. 5: Natural Building Lab, Technische Universität Berlin, documentation kickoff meeting, April 2017 (© Natural Building Lab, Flore Vigneron)

Conclusion

In order to face the challenges of the architectural profession in the times of climate change, there is a huge potential for architects to use their specific skills to help today's society combating the challenges posed to the built environment. Architects tend to delude themselves that they undertake research and break new ground on every new project.

Yet in truth, current practice and education still relies largely on fossil materials that came to prominence during the modernist era – concrete, glass and steel – and these are the materials that still receive the most attention in university studies. Compounding this problem is the legacy of the high-tech neoliberal architecture of the 1990s, where poor interior room climates were created by the use of nonbreathable materials or inappropriate climatic design strategies. This was mitigated is through the increased use of building technology in the form of mechanical ventilation or air-conditioning.

We continue to blindly trust in technology, in the form of "smart" buildings or even cities, as a way to mitigate our effect on the climate, allowing us to continue practice as if resources were unlimited. The entire construction sector will require a radical restructuring and increased deployment of resources for research in order to be able to react to the new Anthropocene context where resource scarcity is an unavoidable reality. In this context renewable natural building materials such as earth, timber, and bamboo have a huge potential for a post-fossil-built environment.

There is still a huge requirement for further research in the field of natural building materials in the global north over the coming years, if they are to become a serious rival to the politically established fossil industry lobby across the construction sector. Yet the global south also offers enormous potential for the appropriation and future of proofing of vernacular natural building materials and techniques, which can be improved with simple means.

Research activities can offer an excellent potential for development for smaller architectural offices, while additionally producing valuable knowledge for architects. While the economic challenges can be great, further measures could be taken to promote the integration of research in architecture offices. In universities, potential research resources must be better utilized and integrated with teaching and practice activities if the resulting knowledge is to be applicable to a wider context. Students can be integrated into these processes and co-own and produce the resulting knowledge, as well as rooting it further in a wider societal context.

Design-build projects can form a bridge between research and society; by working in transdisciplinary teams in a realization context, students are able to take ownership of change processes and new knowledge. The Building Cycle project is an excellent example, where knowledge from the RE4 research project was used as an input, further developed, and explored in 1:1 by the students and other actors, and then implemented in a 1:1 prototype in the form of the Infozentrale building. The project was awarded a special prize in the German Holzbau+ competition.

In order to combat the climate change challenges, our society will have to reevaluate the values, knowledge, and rules accepted in the fields of construction and architecture. Achieving this goal will require an increased focus on the productivity of research both in practice and universities, with an emphasis on transparency and collaboration instead of competition. Design-build projects are an excellent vehicle to foster transdisciplinary collaborations between society and research institutions, instigating change and coproducing new shared knowledge.

References

BiMoKa. n.d. Entwicklung von Bildungsmodulen zu klimaresilienter Architektur. Accessed July 3, 2019. www.bimoka.de.

BIO Intelligence Service. 2011. "Implementing EU Waste Legislation for Green Growth," Final Report prepared for European Commission DG ENV. http://ec.europa.eu/environment/waste/studies/pdf/study%20 12%20FINAL%20REPORT.pdf.

Building Cycle. n.d. *Natural Building Lab*. Accessed July 3, 2019. www.nbl. berlin/BUILDinG-CYCLE.

Deloitte. 2017. Study on Resource Efficient Use of Mixed Wastes, Improving management of construction and demolition waste, Final Report prepared for the European Commission DV ENV. http://ec.europa.eu/ environment/waste/studies/mixed_waste.htm.

Directive 2010/31/EU of the European Parliament and of the Council of 19 May 2010 on the energy performance of buildings.

Eberle, Dietmar, and Florian Aicher. 2015. *be 2226: Die Temperatur der Architektur*. Basel: Birkhäuser.

Dye-Sensitized Solar Concrete

Samira Jama Aden[1,3], Rebecca A. Milhuisen[2,3], Muhammad Kalim Kashif[2,3], Udo Bach[2,3], Heike Klussmann[1,3]

[1] *Bau Kunst Erfinden, University of Kassel, Germany*
[2] *Monash University, Melbourne, Australia*
[3] *ARC Center of Excellence in Exciton Science, Melbourne, Australia*

Abstract — Dye-Sensitized Solar Concrete is a transdisciplinary, transnational research project dedicated to the development of a novel photoactive building material for use in architecture, infrastructure, and design. Based on the technology of a dye-sensitized solar cell (O'Regan and Grätzel 1991), this material uses organic dyes on concrete to absorb light and produce electricity through electrochemical reactions. One great advantage of this type of cell is its ability to utilize diffuse light. As a result, its potential applications are almost unlimited with regard to shape, design, and location. The ultimate goal is to develop a fully structurally integrated photovoltaic material.

Introduction

The Nobel Prize winner Richard Smalley stated that "energy is the single most important problem humanity is facing today" (Smalley 2003). The world's leading economies are burning fossil fuels at more than a million times the rate at which they can be replenished. Current estimates indicate that there are less than 100 years of supply left, depending on the rates at which the emerging E7 economies develop. The G7 countries (representing more than 64 percent of net global wealth) have pledged to phase out fossil fuels and decarbonize the global economy during this century (US Department of Energy 2005). To transition the entire planet to long-term sustainability, there is an urgent need for better energy solutions. Human activity on earth is only as sustainable as the amount of energy we can harvest renewably from the environment. With a doubling of global energy demand expected in the next thirty years, we need advanced materials and structurally integrated energy solutions that can better harvest sunlight (Smalley 2003).

To accomplish this, laboratory experiments must be directed toward developing industrial technologies. In particular, to achieve success in architecture and building design, renewable energy-generating materials must be integrated into building materials. This paper presents the unique concept of a concrete-based dye-sensitized solar cell (DSSC). It describes how the energy challenge has brought together specialists from different disciplines, who are working together in inspiring ways to come up with new solutions for aesthetic, sustainable design. We believe that the aesthetic requirements of future buildings can be met by the principles of renewable energy, architecture, and materials design. Activating the energy-generating potential of a building's materials can be part of the aesthetic activation of the building's surface.

Research

The Dye-Sensitized Solar Concrete project aims to develop a novel structurally integrated photovoltaic (SIPV) as a comprehensive, reliable, minimally complex technological system for generating solar energy. The dye-sensitized solar cell is one of the most innovative solar-cell technologies, but most researchers have focused on the potential of glass-based translucent modules (Klooster and Klussmann 2015, 2017). Until now, the possibility of combining DSSCs with construction materials such as concrete has been overlooked. We have proven that cement can serve as the basis for a targeted synthesis of photoactive dyes and building materials. The purpose of our research project is to design, develop, test, and evaluate the generation of energy from Dye-Sensitized Solar Concrete in architecture and infrastructure as a step toward sustainable cities.

Through transnational, transdisciplinary collaboration, we have developed a way of using organic dyes on concrete surfaces to absorb light and produce electricity through electrochemical reactions. Our analysis of this novel process has revealed a high degree of compatibility between dye-sensitized solar technology and the chemistry and physics of concrete, including its materials logic and production methods. The functional principle of DSSCs is based on the natural process of photosynthesis. Much like chlorophyll-bearing plants, DSSCs absorb light with organic dyes. In this sense, the technology is an adaptation of the photosynthetic process.

The Dye-Sensitized Solar Concrete cell is a structure of functional layers. These combine to form a redox reaction coating that generates energy through an electrochemical process when exposed to light. Such coatings can be applied on concrete surfaces by systematically modifying their physical and chemical structures. The electricity-generating material is refined through a process of synthesis and layering, a combination of sintering and spray deposition or screen printing. By adjusting components, the layer system can be tuned to specific wavebands of light, including the very edges of the visible spectrum.

Dye-Sensitized Solar Concrete: A Novel Photovoltaic Technology

In fact, all DSSCs use a functional layer system to generate electricity directly from sunlight. In traditional DSSCs, the substances involved are processed in liquid form, usually by coating two glass substrates, which are then fastened together with a spacer to create a fully functional solar cell (fig. 1). The coated glass substrates act as electrodes: a photoelectrode covered with a light-converting photoactive dye to absorb photons and generate free electric charge carriers, and a counterelectrode coated with carbon-based materials to allow current to flow within the cell when connected to a load.

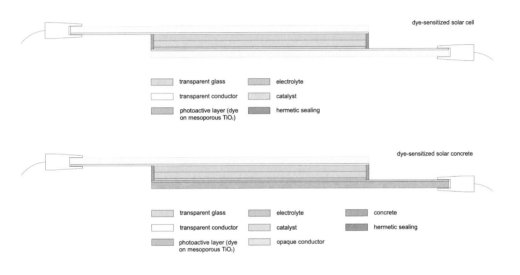

Fig. 1: Dye-Sensitized Solar Cell: concrete-based dye-sensitized solar cell
(© 2019 Bau Kunst Erfinden)

Dye-Sensitized Solar Concrete replaces the glass-based counterelectrode with concrete. Since the concrete substrate is chemically, electrotechnically, mechanically, and geometrically in contact and indirect interaction with all other cell components, the cell architecture is a central component of this innovative concept. The cell architecture defines the position and layout of each functional layer and substrate within the cell. It is thus critical to the functionality, durability, and performance of the Dye-Sensitized Solar Concrete cell, and also forms the basis for integrating present-day and next-generation photoactive layer systems into concrete and other opaque substrate materials.

Processes from thin-film technology, such as screen printing, slot printing, and spraying, have been adapted and further developed with the aim of consistently depositing layers of a specific thickness on the concrete surface with a high adhesive bond, functionality, and freedom of choice with regard to the shape of the cell and the concrete. This freedom allows the cells to be integrated into manufacturing processes for building materials.

The design of the formwork and the materials used in it constitute another decisive factor for the functionality of concrete as a substrate, counterelectrode, and structural material. As a result, the wiring architecture is fully integrated as a multifunctional textile reinforcement with mechanical properties in addition to its function as an energy conduit. The wiring architecture defines the position and layout of the energy transport system within the concrete panel. Simply put, the electrical contacts are placed on the concrete surface and form the connection to the energy-generating surface (fig. 2). The interconnection and physical separation of photoelectrode and counterelectrode are based on a surface treatment implemented in the architecture of the formwork. This architecture permits modifications in the form of series, parallel, or combination interconnections. Due to the textile reinforcement, the concrete panels are only 15–20 mm thick and can be installed as lightweight facade-cladding units. With their multifunctional reinforcement and photoactive surface, these panels could form the structural and functional interface of an energy-generating facade (fig. 2). In principle, the system can be adapted to all third-generation photovoltaic systems, including solid-state dye-sensitized solar cells, organic photovoltaics, tandem solar cells, and perovskite solar cells.

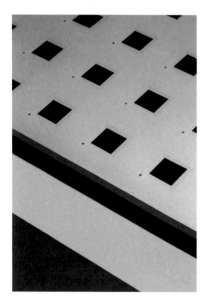

Fig. 2: Close-up of Dye-Sensitized Solar Concrete
(© 2019 Bau Kunst Erfinden; photo: Haw-lin)

Materials Research for an Emerging Photovoltaic Technology
Dye-Sensitized Solar Concrete is a structurally integrated photovoltaic material that incorporates a multifunctional materials technology. The potential

of this material lies in the integrated development of technological, physical, chemical, and aesthetic functions on the nano, micro, and macro scales that match the materials in use. For example, Figure 3 presents a concept for a facade panel that combines a photoactive concrete surface with sound-absorbing qualities and a structural shaping system. This type of advanced materials research seeks to shape new technologies at an early stage so that these can be simultaneously incorporated into planning. However, this challenge can only be met through cross-disciplinary research and collaboration.

Fig. 3: Prototype of a Dye-Sensitized Solar Concrete facade element (100 × 100 cm)
(© 2019 Bau Kunst Erfinden; photo: Haw-lin)

Conclusion

Dye-Sensitized Solar Concrete has been proven to be highly compatible with both the functional principle of DSSCs and the logic of prefabricated concrete materials. For the first time, sensitization of concrete using an organic dye has been shown to efficiently convert simulated sunlight into electricity, with lab-based devices reaching efficiencies as high as 5 percent under simulated sunlight (AM 1.5, 1000 W/m²). The basis of the system is concrete, with all its qualities as a structural product, including fire resistance, high strength and durability, and a variety of construction methods. It generates energy using readily available components, with no toxic emissions. A major advantage of Dye-Sensitized Solar Concrete is its relatively low production cost, giving the system great potential as a low-cost energy source. Silicon-based building-integrated photovoltaics are widely perceived as a structural add-on with no aesthetic value. Dye-Sensitized Solar

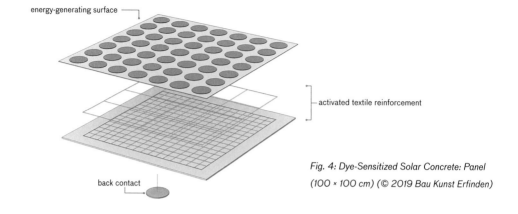

energy-generating surface

activated textile reinforcement

back contact

Fig. 4: Dye-Sensitized Solar Concrete: Panel
(100 × 100 cm) (© 2019 Bau Kunst Erfinden)

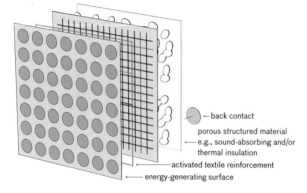

back contact

porous structured material
e.g., sound-absorbing and/or
thermal insulation

activated textile reinforcement

energy-generating surface

Fig. 5: Dye-Sensitized Solar Concrete Concept:
Multifunctional facade panel
(© 2019 Bau Kunst Erfinden)

Fig. 6: Dye-Sensitized Solar Concrete,
cell 5 × 5 cm (© 2019 Bau Kunst Erfinden)

Fig. 7: Dye-Sensitized Solar Concrete,
test setup: Sun simulator (© 2019 Bau Kunst
Erfinden)

Concrete overcomes these issues and can be incorporated into the architectural planning process at an early stage, imposing no design constraints and offering a wide variety of photoactive dyes as an additional design tool. The innovative materials system is renewable, largely recyclable, and environmentally friendly. Because it can make use of the energy in diffuse light, its structural applications are virtually unlimited compared to conventional photovoltaic systems, opening up a world of immense possibilities in the field of SIPVs. Dye-Sensitized Solar Concrete is ideally suited for manufacturing prefabricated concrete panels for building construction, for new types of building facades, and indoor and outdoor wall and floor systems. Furthermore, it offers the opportunity to significantly increase the proportion of space available for solar energy harvesting.

References

Klooster, Thorsten, and Heike Klussmann. 2015. "Sonnenstrom aus Beton: DysCrete/Dye-Sensitized Solar Active Concrete." In *Beton Bauteile 2015*, 154–61. Gütersloh: Bauverlag.

Klooster, Thorsten, and Heike Klussmann. 2017. "Research and Development of Innovative Materials at the Convergence of Art, Architecture and New Technologies." In *PowerSkin Conference Proceedings*, 135–46. Delft: TU Delft Open.

O'Regan, Brian, and Michael Grätzel. 1991. "A Low-Cost, High-Efficiency Solar Cell Based on Dye-Sensitized Colloidal TiO_2 Films." *Nature* 353: 737–40.

Smalley, Richard E. 2003. "Our Energy Challenge." Lecture, MIT Forum, River Oaks, Texas, January 22.

US Department of Energy. 2005. Basic Research Needs for Solar Energy Utilization. Washington, DC: US Department of Energy.

Form-Finding of the ParaKnot3D's Gridshell with Equal Line Length Rods

Cristoph Dijoux, Martin Dembski, and Alexander Stahr
Leipzig University of Applied Sciences (HTWK Leipzig), Germany

Abstract — A concept to efficiently realize doubly curved shell structures has been developed and presented in the context of the ParaKnot3D-Pavilion project: low variance of elements by solely using similar-length rods, concentrating the structural complexity into 3-D-printable nodes and planning them with a certain rigidity to guarantee an easy erection process. Besides the full parametrization of the resulting individual nodes, defining a grid with equal line lengths, that shows membrane load-bearing was necessary. The usual one-step approaches of deforming a flat grid or generation of a grid on a shell surface could not satisfy these constraints.

The difficulties in satisfying the constraints and a way to overcome them are presented. A multistep approach has been successfully used in the construction of a pavilion and allows defining grids of equal-length rods, while preserving the optimization goals of structural form-finding.

Introduction

The construction industry plays a major role in the current situation of rising environmental problems. As Becker (2013) notes, it is one of the most re-source-intensive industries and therefore contains a large potential for generally saving energy. That is, it is a duty for architects and engineers to strive for ways to build material-efficiently. Therefore new efficient technologies should be devoloped and the usage of efficient principles that are already known should be maximized. A principle, considered as being extremely material efficient for roofing structures, are gridshells. Their performant in-plane load-bearing behavior, combined with the possibility of utilizing environment-friendly materials, yields to favorable systems. As mentioned below, there are different examples known, but they remain rarely being built due to different reasons, hence any step toward a broader application of these systems is important.

Already at the beginning of the twentieth century a system to build shell-like constructions out of small building elements had been developed by Friedrich Zollinger. A broad collection of the topic has been done by Zimmermann (2003). The well-known system has had its flaws, but was able to prove that building curved geometries with sustainable and cost-effective materials is possible, mostly because of its low complexity due to the low variance of elements. About a contemporary application of said system at HanseMesse Rostock, Schlaich, Stavenhagen, and Krüger (2003) noted that while retaining the big number of similar lamellae, only the need of complex steel-connections inhibited the possible economic advantages of the system.

The MERO-System has been very successful by following an inverse approach. It relays on using efficiently fabricable, similar nodes and a fixed set of various rod-lengths (Mengeringhausen 1966). In the context of traditional manufacturing methods, that approach has been extremely efficient. The underlying problem was that the local concentration of geometric complexity could only be faced with the means of production of its time, for example, welding of the node's components. That has not changed much, and the production of varying nodes is still relatively complex. That fixation has limited its use cases, but its success suggests that the reduction of constructional complexity to specific constructional elements might be the key to the efficient construction of complex rod-based systems (fig. 1).

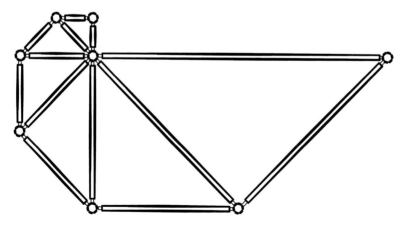

Fig. 1: Elements of the MERO-System: similar nodes, varying rod lengths (based on Chilton 2000)

Two other branches in the world of gridshells, avoiding nodal complexities, are the elastic gridshells (or lattice shells) and ribbed shells. A world-famous example for the former is Multihalle Mannheim by Otto (1974). Some examples were built recently, for example, the Savill Garden gridshell by Harris and Roynon (2008). While holding extremely simple joint constructions, they incorporate their specific difficulties, mostly in the erection phase, with expensive formworks, as described by Quinn and Gengnagel (2014). Ribbed shells are well researched by Natterer et al. (2001), Weinand (2017), Pirazzi (2005), and others. They are based on bending boards on geodesic lines of a surface and getting screwed or glued together, causing high labor costs. Summarizing, formworks and/or big amounts of manual work are significantly raising the costs of gridshells. The ParaKnot3D concept targets the use of additive manufactures nodes – at the moment at a model scale. It follows a nonelastic approach, but the described correlations remain the same. Thus, it is assumed that a reduction of complexity is helping to make gridshells applicable in a bigger field.

As a consequence, ParaKnot3D allows building of shape-optimized gridshells out of similar, straight rods, via a concentration of the structural complexity into the connecting nodes. The complexity is efficiently handled with state-of-the-art algorithmic planning and automatic, additive manufacturing. Furthermore, the erection should be fast and easy, and the need of formworks minimized.

Methods

Form-finding of gridshells can be done via the Dynamic Relaxation method. The method is used as described by Senatore and Piker (2015). If a fixed rod length and specific constraints are used at the same time, this approach frequently delivers "wrong" solutions – most obvious at triangular networks. The effect can be compared with experiments on real nets, most prominently described by Otto (1974). For many nets, respectively grids, it is impossible to deform into a funicular shape and preserve the distance between the nodes. As a result, net experiments show sagging chain elements and the Dynamic Relaxation returns unwanted solutions like creasing or crumpling grids. Another option is first finding a continuous shell surface and generating an equal line-length grid onto it. One grid type with four equal-length sided cells is known as Chebyshev Net. It is often set equal with grids generated by the Compass Method, for example, by Li and Knippers (2011). It is a geometric technique after Otto (1974), using only a compass to find the right points on a surface. A geometric and computational approach to the generation of Chebyshev Nets on NURBS surface-representations has been presented by Popov (2002).

Grids, generated with said method, are often showing a variable density on surfaces with varying curvature. But during form finding, surfaces are usually considered with a constant density and stiffness. Therefore, the structurally optimal shape of a surface is often different to the optimal shape of an equal line-length grid on that given surface. Eventually, the form-finding of a surface does not deliver a solution for the desired grid.

Form-Finding via a Proxy Surface

To overcome these problems, the process can be split into multiple steps by introducing a so-called proxy surface. If it is generated with certain properties first, the Compass Method can be applied successfully. The proxy surface needs to approximate the final shape of the gridshell to fulfill its purpose. Therefore, the proxy surface is found via Dynamic Relaxation itself. It also needs to get prepared for the grid generator, which is run afterward. As a last step the grid gets reevaluated via Dynamic Relaxation and carefully chosen constraints. An illustration of these steps can be found in figure 2.

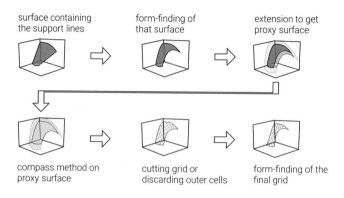

surface containing the support lines ⇒ form-finding of that surface ⇒ extension to get proxy surface

compass method on proxy surface ⇒ cutting grid or discarding outer cells ⇒ form-finding of the final grid

Fig. 2: Sequential steps to ensure a valid form-finding solution for gridshells with equal length rods

IMPLEMENTATION OF THE COMPASS METHOD

The Compass Method is implemented by splitting two guide curves that are on the surface and dividing them into segments with the desired length. The four resulting quadrants on the surface are handled sequentially, row by row. Instead of circles, spheres are being intersected. Each resulting circle is then intersected with the given surface to find the next point. If intersecting surface and circle return two points, the right one has to be chosen and the algorithm can continue from there. If only one point is returned, the surface edge is reached, and the iteration has to stop. Hence, the algorithm cannot fill a surface edge to edge (fig. 3).

Fig. 3: Demonstration of the grid generation algorithm on an arbitrary surface. The guides are indicated by blue and green dashed lines. The failure of the algorithm at the surface edges and its propagation is indicated by the red arrows

FINDING THE PROXY SURFACE

These characteristics have to be taken into account when generating the intermediate proxy surface. It needs to be sufficiently close to the final geometry of the gridshell and allow generating a Chebyshev Net with the algorithm explained above, covering the supports and planned width. To obtain these goals, a regular form-finding process based on a flat surface is done. To prepare the application of the grid generator, the deformed surface has to be enlarged. The result is the needed proxy surface.

CHOOSING A GRID

The grid can be created with the Compass Method on the proxy surface. A too-big grid will be returned, which avoids inconsistent results at the surface boundaries, illustrated in figure 3. To reduce its size, it can be either cut by projection of the base surface's edges or the outer cells can be discarded. The later results in a reduction of the grid size with very clean outer edges, without the need of shorter rods.

FINAL FORM-FINDING

With these preparations, the final form-finding is relatively unproblematic. The Dynamic Relaxation method can be used with a strong constraint on preserving the rod length. As the Compass Method produces quadrangular nets, a deformation is possible without stretching or compressing them. It is best to allow a certain change, smaller than building accuracy, for better convergence and to avoid problems caused by the triangulations at the supports and edges. Also, the length of shorter rods does not need to be preserved. A color-coded visualization of the resulting rod lengths in case of the pavilion can be found in figure 4. The blue rods at the border lines hint to overly long rods, which are twice as long as the others and can therefore each be seen as two single rods with an identical length (fig. 4).

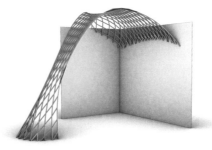

Fig. 4: The application of the presented method on the pavilion project delivered a clean grid, with almost exclusively identical rods

Application at the ParaKnot3D-Pavilion

A pavilion project has been initiated as a platform to directly apply the approach on a smaller scale and to test an additive manufacturing approach for the individual shaped constructive knots. The harmonization of rod lengths to almost exclusively a single one, reduces the complexity of the construction to the nodes. To vividly illustrate the positive effects of being able to use identical elements only, drinking straws made out of paper have been used in the pavilion. They are exceptionally cheap, identical, produced by industrial means, and environmentally friendly. Compared to the rods, the nodes make up only a small part of the construction. Therefore, it was possible to fabricate them in a comparably slow additive 3-D printing process. As individual geometries do not raise printing times, that combination of fabrication methods proved to be very efficient and applicable. The principle is visualized in figure 5.

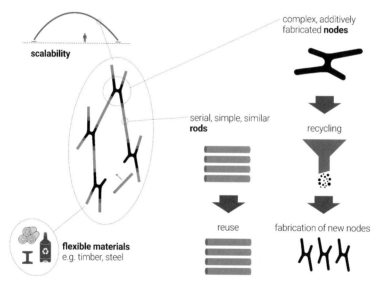

Fig. 5: The ParaKnot3D concept

A simple plug-connection as shown in figure 6 has been developed to facilitate the on-site assembly of the pavilion. Its bending stiffness allows abandoning the need for bracing, but it only allows small tension forces. Due to the lack of wind inside a fair hall and to prove the functionality of the approach, the shell was designed to act theoretically as a funicular shell and no tension forces appear in the connections (fig. 6).

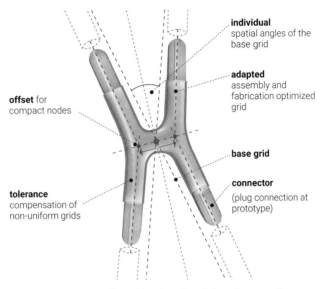

individual spatial angles of the base grid

adapted assembly and fabrication optimized grid

offset for compact nodes

base grid

connector (plug connection at prototype)

tolerance compensation of non-uniform grids

Fig. 6: The nodes are based on an offset grid, to keep the printing volumes small

Reflection

Following the proposed sequence, it is possible to maintain the rod length of grids while respecting form-finding goals with relatively little effort. Grid generation with the Compass Method delivers good and controllable results, but it usually causes boundary problems. The introduced proxy surface overcomes these problems as well as it facilitates the final form-finding process. Creases due to the fixed rod length are completely avoided.

The approach showed its functionality and applicability in the pavilion. The structure consists almost completely of uncut, identical drinking straws made of paper. Out of the 554 straws only 40 had to be cut. The geometry of the 334 Nodes is parametrically defined, and they could be 3-D-printed with very little manual work. As a result, the rods did not have to be sorted and the whole erection could be done quickly. The shape optimization allowed the pavilion to weigh only 2.5 kg with a surface area of ca. 8 m². The students involved in the project earned an insight into the possibilities of lightweight construction, form-finding, and parametric design. Problems arouse, as the dominant load case was not the self-weight. It never is for lightweight constructions, but of course wind and snow could be foreclosed inside the exhibition hall. In fact, the dominant load case were visitors testing the pavilion's stability in unobserved moments, one actually succeeding in letting the structure collapse – completely not dangerous due to the low weight. As unpleasant as such an incident is, it revealed one major advantage of the low part variance: Crippled straws could be simply exchanged, and it was put up again within a few minutes (fig. 7).

Fig. 7: The ParaKnot3D Pavilion at the Designers Open 2017 in Leipzig

Outlook

In the construction of larger-scale gridshells, the greater amount of manual work is a major price point. As Schlaich (2003) notes, labor is more expensive than material. That is, it needs to be minimized, and the rods should not need to be manually cut. A grid with equal line lengths, to use similar rods is preferable. As a proof of concept, manual work could be mainly reduced to the erection of the ParaKnot3D pavilion, and using drinking straws has been extremely cost-efficient. The well-manageable approach can be used in an architectural scale and can deliver a contribution to a broader use of material-efficient gridshell structures.

References

Becker, Nicole. 2013. "Kurzanalyse Nr. 2: Ressourceneffizienz der Trag-
    werke." VDI Zentrum Ressourceneffizienz (VDI ZRE) GmbH.
Chilton, John. 2000. *Space Grid Structures*. Oxford: Architectural Press.
Harris, Richard, and Jonathan Roynon. 2008. "The Savill Garden Gridshell
    Design and Construction." In *10th World Conference of Timber Engineer-
    ing*, 2174–81. Bath: University of Bath.
Li, Jian-Min, and Jan Knippers. 2011. "Form-Finding of Grid Shells with
    Continuous Elastic Rods." In *Proceedings of the IABSE-IASS Symposi-
    um 2011*, 1–7. London: International Association for Shell and Spatial
    Structures (IASS).

Mengeringhausen, Max. 1966. "Kompositionslehre räumlicher Stab-Fachwerke." In *Proceedings of the International Conference on Space Structures*, edited by R. M. Davies, 99: 1109–20. Surrey: Blackwell Scientific Publications.

Natterer, Julius, Norbert Burger, and A. Müller. 2001. "Das EXPO-Dach in Hannover als Pilotprojekt für die Holzbau-Entwicklung und Einsatz nicht geregelter Bauweisen." *Bautechnik* 78, no. 10 (October): 693–705.

Otto, Frei. 1974. *IL10: Gitterschalen = Grid Shells*. Mitteilungen des Instituts für leichte Flächentragwerke (IL) 10. Stuttgart: Institut für leichte Flächentragwerke, Universität Stuttgart.

Pirazzi, Claudio. 2005. "Zur Berechnung von Holzschalen in Brettrippenbauweise mit elastischem Verbundquerschnitt." Dissertation, École Polytechnique Fédérale de Lausanne (EPFL).

Popov, Eugene Vladimirovich. 2002. "Geometric Approach to Chebyshev Net Generation Along an Arbitrary Surface Represented by NURBS." In *GraphiCon'2002*, 4. Nizhny Novgorod.

Quinn, G., and C. Gengnagel. 2014. "A Review of Elastic Grid Shells, Their Erection Methods and the Potential Use of Pneumatic Formwork." In *Mobile and Rapidly Assembled Structures* 4: 129–43.

Schlaich, Mike, Lothar Stavenhagen, and G. Krüger. 2003. "Die Hanse-Messe in Rostock: Zollinger mit moderner Technik." *Bautechnik* 80, no. 5: 279–84.

Senatore, Gennaro, and Daniel Piker. 2015. "Interactive Real-Time Physics." *Computer-Aided Design* 61 (April): 32–41.

Weinand, Yves. 2017. *Neue Holztragwerke, Architektonische Entwürfe und digitale Bemessung*. Basel: Birkhäuser.

Zimmermann, Florian, ed. 2003. *Das Dach der Zukunft: Zollinger Lamellendächer der 20er Jahre; Konstruktion, Statik, Ästhetik, Verbreitung, Nachfolge, Beispiele in Bayern*. Munich: FH München.

Figure Credits

FLEX@HTWK-Leipzig

Botanical Concrete: Novel Composites for Urban Greening

Roman Polster[1], Lucas Büscher[2], Wigbert Riehl[2], and Heike Klussmann[1]
[1] *Bau Kunst Erfinden, University of Kassel, Germany*
[2] *Landscape Architecture | Technology, University of Kassel, Germany*

Abstract — The aim of Botanical Concrete, an interdisciplinary research project at the University of Kassel, is to develop a structurally viable cement-based material that will support the systematic, long-term, nondamaging cultivation of vascular and nonvascular plants. This combination of vegetation and innovative material seeks to find air-purifying, climate-optimized uses for vertical surfaces while also presenting new applications and design possibilities. The qualities required of a substrate for plant cultivation, such as optimal pH value, water retention, and a structured surface, are to be integratively combined with the material, structural, and aesthetic qualities of concrete to form the basis of this new material. Botanical Concrete is the first material to combine the characteristics of structural stability and durability with the positive qualities of a substrate for the establishment and sustainable cultivation of plant life.

Introduction

City dwellers are increasingly impacted by emissions of carbon dioxide, nitrogen dioxide, and particulates, which significantly exceed the levels recommended by the World Health Organization (Umweltbundesamt 2016). At the same time, the demand for urban space is constantly growing, with a concomitant increase in the amount of impermeable surface area, which has significant negative effects on the urban climate (Statistisches Bundesamt 2015) and availability of open space.

Consequently, researchers have been working for some time on vertical greening systems to improve the climate in specific urban areas (microclimates) and to achieve climatic optimization of the building envelope through the greening of facades and roofs. Plants – both vascular and nonvascular – are capable of absorbing nitrogen, capturing carbon, emitting oxygen, storing and releasing water, and reducing noise levels (Frahm 2008). The greening of buildings also allows qualified open space to be established in high-density areas and on disturbed soils around buildings. Open space and vegetation are essential components of sustainable urban development, with well-documented positive effects on the well-being of residents.

Current research centers on the search for an appropriate substrate to enable vertical cultivation of plants, with most projects involving non-load-bearing substrates and growing mediums anchored to the load-bearing wall in various configurations of individual components. A joint project conducted by the ITKE at the University of Stuttgart and the IFK at the Stuttgart State Museum of Natural History is investigating the potential of mosses for active particulate reduction. Using a wall of mosses grown on synthetic mesh, installed in central Stuttgart in 2017, this outdoor experiment seeks to gather further information about the impact of moss on air quality (ITKE 2017). Bio-receptivity Optimization of Concrete, a research project at the Polytechnic University of Catalonia, centered on lowering the pH value of the concrete mix in order to enhance the random growth of cryptogams on concrete surfaces (Manso Blanco 2014). And the City Tree project is examining the possibilities and benefits of biotech filters for air purification (Sänger 2019). However, the design potential of vertical greening as an aesthetically ambitious enrichment of urban space and architecture is far from exhausted. A permanently installable, structurally viable, resource-efficient concrete-based building material suitable for the establishment and long-term cultivation of plants in targeted vertical locations does not yet exist. This was the starting point for our interdisciplinary research project.

Research

We are conducting basic research on the systematic establishment of vegetation on concrete, and preliminary studies have confirmed the feasibility of developing a composite material for targeted vertical greening based on high-performance and ultra-high-performance concrete incorporating mineral substrates (fig. 1). Given the high density and strength required of the structural layer, we are testing recipes for concrete in various strength classes. Parameters under investigation include aggregate type, grain-size distribution, cement type, use of plasticizers, water-cement ratio, and curing techniques. The concrete-substrate composite we aim to produce will combine the material qualities of a load-bearing structural material with those of a planting substrate. It is thus fundamentally different from the additive vertical-greening systems described above, which are characterized by a modular approach involving separate components, the current state-of-the-art in accordance with the FLL 2018.

In choosing building materials well-suited to vegetation-supporting applications, we have been particularly interested in nonorganic substances such as pumice, expanded clay, and expanded slate. Such materials must be dimensionally stable, rot-resistant, and weatherproof while also possessing moisture-retaining qualities. In addition, some of these materials, such as pumice, are already used in concrete production as insulating or weight-reducing ingredients.

These parameters constitute the basic requirements for the development of the desired concrete substrate matrix, as well as for substrate inlays and their stable and long-lasting implementation in and/or on the concrete matrix. Our project will run a series of tests to systematically investigate these technical parameters in relation to the biocompatibility of highly alkaline binding agents in combination with substrates to promote plant growth. We plan to pursue two strategies.

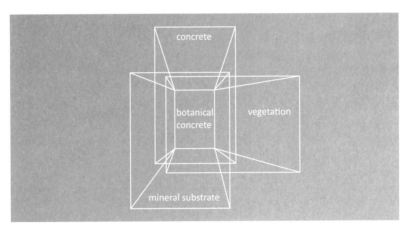

Fig. 1: Schematical layout of botanical concrete

(© Bau Kunst Erfinden, Landschaftsarchitektur | Technik)

Strategy A: 3-D Microstructuring and Development of a Monolayer Substrate for the Cultivation of Lower Plants

Concrete is alkaline, whereas mosses require a neutral or acid environment for sustained growth. In Strategy A, we begin by inserting starter cultures of moss into pH-optimized substrate inlays, which are then integrated into the surface of the concrete matrix. Not only is this beneficial to the establishment of mosses, it also promotes and ensures their rapid, sustained, and uniform growth.

The novel moss-concrete composite we are developing consists of three components (fig. 2):

1. a concrete base layer with a three-dimensionally structured surface to provide shade
2. pH-optimized substrate inlays containing moss starter cultures
3. a supply infrastructure to continuously provide water and nutrients.

For the base layer, we are investigating different types of concrete in various quality grades. Dense formulations with relatively few capillary pores are of particular interest, as a way of preventing water infiltration and increasing the durability of the composite.

substrate inlays / moss cultures   supply infrastructure   concrete base layer / 3-D microstructured surface

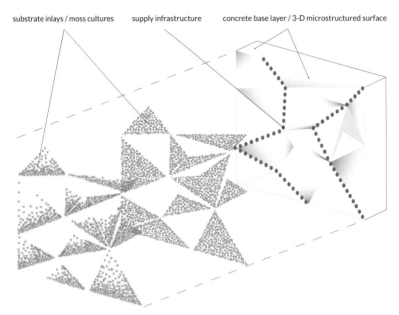

Fig. 2: Components of the moss-concrete composite (© Bau Kunst Erfinden, Polster)

Figure 3 shows a test unit with substrate inlays integrated into the surface of the concrete matrix. This approach has two distinct advantages over incorporating the substrate into the wet concrete matrix. The material is not intermixed with the substrate, so there are no negative effects on the strength and other mechanical characteristics of the bearing layer. Furthermore, the amount of substrate material required is substantially less, since it is only included where it is needed to support the growth of the moss.

Fig. 3: Test unit with substrate monolayer
(© Bau Kunst Erfinden, Polster)

Using a special templating process, substrate inlays in various shapes and consistencies are positioned and secured within a concrete form. Once the concrete matrix has cured, the inlays will be integrated into the surface in their proper positions, forming a permanent bond with the matrix. This creates two- and/or three-dimensional growth zones on the surface of the concrete (fig. 4). The bond between the concrete surface and the integrated substrate inlays is a particular area of focus for our project, since this is where weathering places the greatest demands on the material in terms of bonding strength and surface impermeability.

A three-dimensionally structured surface provides shade for the growing moss. We are investigating ways of producing this structuring in the process of forming the base layer. We are also developing various shapes for use on inclined and vertical surfaces, and under various angles of solar radiation. To ensure optimum growth conditions, the moss cultures must be provided with a continuous supply of nutrients and water. To this end, we are developing a supply infrastructure that will provide efficient mist or drip irrigation to the vegetation zones (Polster n.d.).

Fig. 4: 3-D microstructured test unit with substrate inlays (© Bau Kunst Erfinden, Polster)

Strategy B: 3-D Macrostructuring and Development of a Concrete-Substrate Matrix for the Cultivation of Vascular Plants

Thanks to their greater diversity of size, shape, and color, vascular plants offer more options for design than the two-dimensional greening provided by moss. The ability of some vascular plants to survive for relatively long periods without an external water supply suggests a high potential for extensive vertical greening. Plants that naturally grow on masonry are especially capable of surviving and thriving over long periods of time in marginal, highly alkaline environments in urban settings without human intervention or irrigation. It is thus important to catalog and analyze suitable sites for plants and to translate this information into structural characteristics.

Accordingly, we have developed criteria based on the study of naturally occurring vertical greening. As figure 5 shows, four overarching parameters define the technical concept, which is based on the 3-D macrostructuring of the concrete. While algae and mosses can provide initial greening by establishing themselves on the microrelief offered by vertical surfaces, higher plants require cavities, such as cracks, that are capable of retaining a substrate. The macrostructuring process deliberately creates cavities for the germination and long-term establishment of vegetation. At the same time, it also aids irrigation by channeling and storing surface water. Cavity size and shape, suitable forming techniques, and the response of cavity shapes to freezing conditions are all under investigation and development.

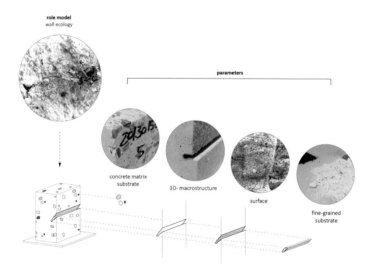

Fig. 5: Overarching technical parameters
(© Landschaftsarchitektur | Technik, Büscher)

The macrostructuring process allows for variation in the extent of plant coverage. It is not necessary to maximize coverage to hide wall structures or purely functional substrates. The concrete and its structure are the growing medium, and they are designed to form part of the visible surface of the wall. The interplay of vegetation and relief offers a wide array of design possibilities (fig. 6).
The concrete is conceptualized as a C horizon. Consequently, its macrostructure is not simply a container for plants. Important site-specific qualities relating to plant cultivation, such as pH value and availability of water, are built into the concrete matrix through variations in cement type

Fig. 6: Comparative water absorption after 10 minutes [M%]
(© Landschaftsarchitektur | Technik, Büscher)

(pH reduction via carbonation), water-cement ratio (pores, carbonation), and aggregate type. To optimize our use of resources, we are experimenting with materials with vegetation-promoting qualities that are already in use in green-roof systems, as well as recycled building materials possessing similar characteristics (fig. 7).

Fig. 7: Design study of higher plants and relief
(© Landschaftsarchitektur | Technik, Büscher)

Texturing the inner surfaces of the cavities helps plant roots anchor themselves. In our tests, we are exploring ways of incorporating root-promoting surfaces via form design and post-casting treatments. At the same time, we are also studying ways of preventing damage from root growth. Specially developed fine-grained substrates are built into the finished concrete structure. Optimal integration and cultivation methods (direct sowing vs. seedlings) are being investigated and evaluated. In the final stage, all parameters will be combined in concrete models, and construction methods will be tested with indicator plants (Büscher n.d.).

In subsequent phases, the formwork will be adapted to the demands of positioning structural components in specific orientations (that is, in relation to the sun) and of specific applications (roof, wall, horizontal, vertical). Plant cultivation methods will be investigated and analyzed, and an extensified, efficient irrigation system (via 3-D micro-/macrostructuring, the concrete matrix, and/or a microarchitecture integrated into the concrete-substrate composite) will be developed.

The behavior and bond quality of the material samples produced for testing will be subjected to ongoing physical performance tests (compressive and flexural strength) throughout the project. Plant development will be analyzed and assessed on a laboratory scale in plant growth chambers and/or greenhouses, and also under real-life conditions in outdoor trials with test plantings in selected locations.

The design potential of our interdisciplinary project lies in the variety of site-specific solutions for component geometry, surface treatment, and shaping of growth zones. Construction methods (for example, solid masonry, facade element), irrigation, and vegetation are all customizable parameters. The goal is to develop a concrete-substrate composite suitable for the long-term sustainable cultivation of plants on concrete for a wide range of uses in architecture and structural engineering.

Conclusion

A novel combination of concrete and incorporated mineral substrates, either as a monolayer or in a concrete-substrate matrix, provides an innovative, resource-efficient, low-maintenance composite material for the establishment of vegetation in targeted vertical locations. It combines the positive qualities of concrete (durability, noncombustibility, serial production) with those of the substrate (adsorptivity and ability to supply air, nutrients, and water).

The 3-D micro-/macrostructuring of the surface and an optional custom-designed irrigation infrastructure promote and ensure consistent plant growth and the long-term establishment of vegetation. Growing site-optimized plants directly on the substrate minimizes failure rates while simultaneously lessening the need for watering and other supplementary measures. By reducing costly infrastructure and developing intelligent, material-based solutions to support plant growth, we increase flexibility and the range of potential applications.

At the same time, our approach allows a reinterpretation of the architectural and sociocultural significance of vertical greening, and reinvigorates theoretical discourse on the symbiosis of building and plant. Using low-growing mosses and more voluminous higher plants in combination with an understructure made of concrete, a highly malleable material, opens up new design possibilities for architecture and built space, worlds apart from the prevailing distinction between roof and facade greening.

Possible applications for the composite as a load-bearing structural material include innovative climate-optimized systems in building construction, especially facades and wall systems. Because of its physical characteristics, the material also lends itself to the optimization of energy efficiency, acoustics, and indoor climate in buildings. The feasibility of resource-efficient, low-maintenance solutions makes for a smaller economic footprint, while improved irrigation efficiency contributes to water quality. And in addition to the aesthetic, acoustic, and energy-efficiency benefits, microclimate improvements in high particulate urban areas can be expected as well.

The true potential of the Botanical Concrete project lies in its adaptability. The structural versatility represented by Strategies A and B offers the promise of both site- and building-specific solutions, enabling designers and builders to respond appropriately to the varied demands of urban environments.

References

Büscher, Lucas. n.d. "Concrete Habitat: Beton als Basis einer vertikalen Begrünung" (working title). Unpublished diss., Universität Kassel.

Frahm, Jan-Peter. 2008. "Feinstaubreduktion an Straßenrändern durch Moosmatten." Lecture, Bundesanstalt für Straßenwesen (BASt), Fachtagung Luftqualität an Straßen, Bergisch Gladbach, March 5.

ITKE. 2017. "Moos versus Feinstaub: Stuttgarter Mooswand." Accessed July 20, 2018. https://www.itke.unistuttgart. de/de/archives/8557.

Manso Blanco, Sandra. 2014. "Bioreceptivity Optimisation of Concrete Substratum to Stimulate Biological Colonisation." Universitat Politècnica de Catalunya.

Polster, Roman. n.d. "BryoCrete: Entwicklung eines betonbasierten Materialkomposits mit pH-Wert optimierten Substratinlays zur gezielten Kultivierung von Moos" (working title). Unpublished diss., Universität Kassel.

Sänger, Peter. 2019. "Der CityTree: Der weltweit erste Bio-Tech-Filter zur nachweisbaren Verbesserung der Luftqualität." Accessed January 7, 2019. https://greencitysolutions.de/losungen/section2.

Statistisches Bundesamt. 2016. "Land- und Forstwirtschaft, Fischerei: Bodenfläche nach Art der tatsächlichen Nutzung." Fachserie 3 Reihe 5.1. November 18, 2016.

Umweltbundesamt. 2016. "Luftqualität 2016: Vorläufige Auswertung." umweltbundesamt.de. Accessed November 13, 2017. http://www. umweltbundesamt.de/sites/default/files/medien/2546/publikationen/ hgp_luftqualitaet_2016.pdf.

6 Architectural Space

6.1 Perception and Visualization

The Role of Expertise in the Perception of Architectural Space

Holger Mertins[1], Renate Delucchi Danhier[2], Barbara Mertins[2], Ansgar Schulz[3], and Benedikt Schulz[3]

[1] Faculty of Architecture and Civil Engineering, TU Dortmund University, Germany

[2] Faculty of Culture Studies, psycholinguistics laboratories, TU Dortmund University, Germany

[3] Faculty of Architecture, Technische Universität Dresden, Germany

Abstract — Spatial perception is a fundamental cognitive skill developed lifelong. In architecture, this skill is taken for granted. However, evidence from decades of psycholinguistic research shows that spatial cognition is not universal but depends on factors like native language, gender, or expertise. This interdisciplinary study aims to identify patterns of visual attention characteristic for architects. Results of an eye-tracking experiment provide evidence that architectural expertise influences the distribution of visuospatial attention: In outdoor contexts architects pay more attention to upper parts of buildings; in indoor contexts they pay less attention to people. In both contexts, architects allocate more attention to the spatial layout itself compared with a non-architect control group. We interpret these differences as arising from architects using the grammar of space to decode spatial information. It is desirable for architects to implement the insights from research on spatial cognition when designing spaces, since their own spatial perception differs from that of the users they are designing for.

Introduction

People in Western societies spend about 90 percent of their lifetime in built environments, which implies a constant conscious or unconscious exposure to architecture. The ability to understand spatial configurations is mostly taken for granted by architects as a given constant. Empirical research shows that spatial cognition is not universal but shaped by factors such as language, gender, or expertise (Levinson 2003; Levinson and Wilkins

2006). In general, expertise arises from any human activity that implies a long-lasting occupation resulting in excellent command.

We are interested in understanding how specific expertise guides visual attention, and how the mind manages different, potentially concurring types of expertise. We use eye-tracking (ET) to investigate the visuospatial perception of architectural experts (critical group) compared with nonexperts (control group).

State-of-the-Art

In this section, the most important results from psychological, neurological, and psycholinguistic research on language, gender, and expertise affecting spatial cognition are presented. Speakers tend to rely on the abstract concepts of their mother tongue even when performing tasks that do not require speech (nonlinguistic tasks), showing that linguistic categories are always active and influencing the underlying cognitive processes.

LANGUAGE

All speakers are experts in the language(s) they have grown up with. Monolingual speakers often tend to assume that the conceptual categories of their own language are universal. But languages vary considerably in respect to the spatial categories available in their grammar (fig. 1).

Languages vary in the spatial meanings that their prepositions and verbs encode (Bowerman and Choi 2001). In Korean, the spatial verb *kkita* means "fit together tightly." In English, the preferred expressions are *put + in* or *put + on*. When asked to classify actions such as the ones shown in figure 1a, speakers of Korean will form two groups corresponding to the spatial verbs *kkita* (put into tight containment) and *nehta* (put loosely in or around), while speakers of English will form two different groups, corresponding to the prepositions *in* and *on*. This means that Korean and English native speakers will cognitively process different categories, whenever involved in judgments on shapes and their relation, which is another central concept in architecture.

The grammars of some languages (for example, Korean, Chinese, Japanese, indigenous American languages) contain classifiers, count-words that follow a noun and denote to which category the referent belongs. While English or German lack classifiers, a similar meaning can be found in expressions such as "ten *stem* of roses," or "five *head* of cattle." In languages with classifiers, their use is grammatically encoded, obligatory, such as with numerals. These languages may have several hundred different classifiers. Native speakers classify different nouns that go along with the same classifiers as belonging to the same category.

In an experiment, participants were presented a target object with a specific shape and materiality, and two other objects (one with same shape but altered materiality, the other with persisting materiality but altered shape) and asked to choose the one corresponding more closely to the target. Speakers of Japanese, for example, showed a strong preference for material over shape, since the material is encoded in the classifier (Lucy 1992). Speakers of languages with no classifiers preferred shape over material (fig. 1b). Such preferences affect speakers' visuospatial perception whenever categorizing relations of shape and materiality, which is a fundamental principle in architecture.

Languages also differ in the frame of reference they employ to localize objects in space. Indo-European languages prefer a relative frame of reference, in which entities are located with respect to the position of the observer: "I left the keys in the right drawer." Even though an absolute frame of reference is also available in these languages, it is not preferred. Other languages by contrast – for example Australian Aboriginal or Mayan languages – are completely lacking the relative frame of reference (and thus do not have words for right or left) but rather locate other entities using the absolute frame of reference: "I left the keys in the northwest drawer." Frames of reference influence subjects even in nonlinguistic tasks: In the "turning tables" experiment (see Levinson et al. 2002) subjects were positioned in front of a table and asked to replicate the specific arrangement of objects seen on the table on another table located behind them. Speakers of languages with a preference for a relative frame of reference place the objects so that orientation was kept unaltered seen from their own point of view. The subject served as point of reference during displacement, although the subject itself was changing orientation, which resulted in an altered order of objects when seen from an absolute point of reference (such as a bird's-eye view). Speakers of languages with a preference for the absolute frame of reference typically placed the objects using exactly the same orientation as seen from the bird's-eye view, even if it meant resorting the objects after having turned around to the target table (fig. 1c).

The reference system is so central to spatial orientation and navigation that it is extremely difficult to just imagine how one's visuospatial perception and speech would need to change if a foreign reference system would need to be applied.

When asked to verbalize a locomotion event (such as a person moving through space), speakers of different languages show specific preferences for mentioning the inferred goal of the movement. The preference depends on whether their language has a grammaticalized aspectual system, such as the option to express ongoingness (English: somebody is walk*ing* right now). Observers of languages with a grammaticalized aspectual system are less likely to mention the endpoint of a locomotion event. They can readily express without further examination what is happening at the very moment of their observation, which results in faster speech onset times (Mertins 2018). Speakers of languages without a grammaticalized aspect (such as German) mention the goal far more often. Due to their grammar lacking a progressive form, German native speakers tend to provide information about a possible goal of the locomotion, interpreting the event as a closed one with a logical end. This results in more delayed speech onset times and more endpoints mentioned (Mertins 2018). ET studies demonstrated that this affects also the allocation of visual perception and increases memory performance for inferred goals (fig. 1d).

Architecture can be seen as the experience of locations connected in space through paths, which implies movement. Locomotion is yet another central element in architecture.

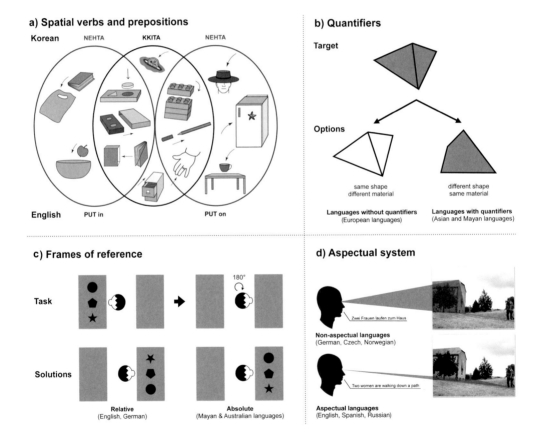

Fig. 1: Examples of experimental tasks for investigating differences in spatial performance

GENDER

In mental rotation tasks participants imagine to rotate a figure and picture how it would look from their perspective after rotation. This is one of the few tasks in which male participants consistently outperform female participants (Richardson 1994; Quaiser-Pohl et al. 2006). Newer research shows that this gap in performance can be closed by training (Jaušovec and Jaušovec 2012) or disappears when the task has to be performed in a less abstract way, such as by using virtual reality (Parsons et al. 2004). This may indicate that the problem lies with abstraction or training.

In the architectural design process, mental rotation is a fundamental ability and implies change of scale (drawing on paper, imagining in real size). It is adequately important in navigational tasks (such as rotating a topography to foresee situations in wayfinding) and can obviously be altered by training (expertise).

EXPERTISE

Comparing MRIs of taxi-drivers (right-handed males, N = 16) with those of nondrivers, a neuroimaging study (Maguire et al. 2000) showed that profound navigational expertise results in an altered structure of the posterior hippocampus, an area of the brain which stores a spatial representation of the environment. Thus, this area can expand regionally in people with a high dependence on navigational skills.

This study is yet another link into spatial perception in architecture and effects of acquired expertise through training.

Methods

Given the findings presented above, visuospatial perception of architectural space should almost expectedly be affected by expertise. To test the role of architectural expertise in the perception of space, a large-scale ET study was carried out. The method was chosen as the access point since the visual sense plays a key role in architectural perception and eye movements are highly automatized, so that they cannot easily be consciously influenced by participants. The goal was to investigate the visual attention patterns of architects while looking at a scene with architectural content but with no architectural task in focus. Architectural experts (critical group) and a control group (nonexperts) were compared in terms of their visual patterns. Two consecutive sub-experiments were conducted: Experiment A, focusing on outdoor scenes; and Experiment B, investigating indoor scenes.

For the outdoor scenes real-world photos were used, since they are usually characterized by disturbances that are difficult to reproduce in renderings generated via virtual models (signage, dirt, leaves, traffic, etc.). We controlled for the number of such disturbances but did not eliminate them completely, so that the stimuli still appeared realistic. Interior scenes are more readily accepted as realistic even if they show little or no disturbances. We took advantage of this fact to render highly controlled interior stimuli for Experiment B.

Stimuli were presented as still images on a monitor in randomized order (fig. 2). After six seconds a question appeared as text in the lower portion of the image for five seconds. The participants responded orally. Questions were related to the image but not directly connected to the research interest and responses were not analyzed. The question was there to give participants an explicit task and keep their attention high. Fillers were used, doubling the critical stimuli in number and showing nonarchitectural content.

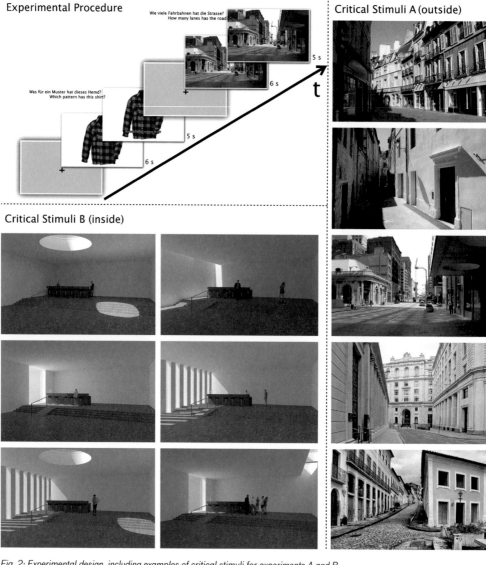

Fig. 2: Experimental design, including examples of critical stimuli for experiments A and B

The participants' gaze positions were recorded for the first six seconds before the appearance of the question, using an SMI RED500 eye-tracker under laboratory conditions and then analyzed. All participants were native speakers of German, and the experiment was conducted in German. The experts were architects or graduate students of architecture. The control group consisted of age-matched graduate students of humanities with no expertise in architecture or related spatial skills such as arts, photography, modeling, gaming, or sports (controlled by questionnaire).

EXPERIMENT A: EXTERIOR (N = 96)
The critical stimuli were five photographs depicting built environments (urban scenes). The critical group comprised 48 experts and 48 nonexperts, both balanced for gender.

EXPERIMENT B: INTERIOR (N = 64)
The interior stimuli were six daylight pictures rendered from digital models using natural lighting parameters and raytracing. They were derived from a common spatial geometry (box shape) shown from an identical camera position. Natural light was let in either via openings in the walls, through the ceiling, or a combination of both with two geometries per condition. The scenes included presenting different numbers of humans in alternating positions around a bar counter. The critical group consisted of 19 experts and 45 controls with mixed gender.

Results
The ET data was analyzed using the SMI software BeGaze, and the amount of visual attention both groups dedicated to the predefined areas of interest then compared (dwell times in ms). The statistical data analysis and examples for the areas of interest for both experiments are presented in figure 3.
The statistical analysis showed that for the outside scenes, architects dedicated more attention to the upper area of the stimuli, while nonarchitects looked longer at the lower portion of the scene (pedestrian level). The results of the inside scenes showed that nonarchitects looked significantly longer at people and furniture than architects. Additionally, for the outside contexts, there was a gender effect within the expert group. This difference was not confirmed for the inside scenes.

Discussion
The results demonstrate that experts allocate their attention differently from nonexperts when looking at outdoor and indoor spaces. Even though the mixed-gender architects performed differently to the group of laypersons, gender differences inside the expert group were also giving hints to a possible sublevel of expertise.

OUTSIDE Stimuli (N = 5)		Dwell time (ms)		Statistical test			Effect size	
Comparison	Group	average	SD	t-value	p-value	DF	Cohen's d	Size
experts vs. non-experts	architects	2487	1193	359.27	0.00017	478	0.60	medium
	control	1778	1155					
male experts vs. female experts	male	2685	1194	198.99	0.024	233	0.54	medium
	female	2065	1103					

INSIDE Stimuli (N = 6)		Dwell time (ms)		Statistical test			Effect size	
Comparison	Group	average	SD	t-value	p-value	DF	Cohen's d	Size
experts vs. non-experts	architects	1352	875	2.05	0.0203	190	0.51	medium
	control	1881	1191					
male experts vs. female experts	male	1033	744	0.16	0.87	86	not significant	
	female	1080	722					

Fig 3: Results of the statistical analysis based on dwell times on areas of interest
Interior people: Male 13, Female 75

While looking at the interior spaces, nonexperts were mostly interested in the human occupation or potential use of the space (exterior: pedestrian level, interior: people) while architects spent less time paying attention to these elements. This enables experts to dedicate more attention to the architectural space housing the human scene. These patterns mirror the architects' professional occupation with connecting spatial layouts to possible uses. We interpret these findings as evidence that architects are structuring the architectural space following the grammar of space (Mertins et al. 2017), which is in this case developed through professional expertise, specifically concerning elements such as the geometrical layout of the urban space, information about the cubature of a structure, zoning and articulation of facades, building style, and architectural detailing, but also the lighting situation and conditions. The latter two are especially important when structuring interior spaces. Cognitive and visual attention has limits: focusing on one element necessarily implies not paying attention to others. Individuals manage this distribution of attention unconsciously in line with their expertise. Attention seems to be in interaction with and driven by expertise. The different variables affecting the allocation of attention (native language, expertise, gender) have to be somehow balanced and managed by the brain in order to decide to which elements in the visual field how much attention in real time is spent to, which explains the different strengths of the effects found between various groups. Until now, not much is known about how exactly these different factors are weighed against each other. More research is needed to clarify this process.

Conclusions and Consequences for Architects

In line with previous research we argue that general spatial cognition is not universal and expertise in architecture based on the grammar of space is one of the most relevant factors guiding the perception of architectural space. These findings are of great importance for applied architecture: For exterior and interior spaces the perspective of experts differs profoundly from the perspective of nonexperts. This has immediate consequences for the way architectural design should be thought through and executed: not as a top-down process implemented from the viewpoint of the experts (planners) but far more as a bottom-up process executed by experts through the eyes of the target group – the nonexperts (users).

Stated this: How can architects evaluate the architectural means deployed in their designs if they lack knowledge about how these actually perform with nonexpert users? Empirical research has the potential to advance these questions beyond personal taste and fashions into a more scientifically based understanding of spatial design. This is not to imply losing creativity in the design process but would make the process less arbitrary, more justified, and more targeted. Empirical research on architectural design has as yet been underused as a tool by architects. It has the potential, if empirical testing of architectural designs can be integrated into the field, to bring about more objective and user-friendly results.

References

Bowerman, Melissa, and Soonja Choi. 2001. "Shaping Meanings for Language: Universal and Language-Specific in the Acquisition of Spatial Semantic Categories." In *Language Acquisition and Conceptual Development,* edited by Melissa Bowerman and Stephen C. Levinson, 475–511. Language, Culture, and Cognition 3. Cambridge: Cambridge University Press.

Jaušovec, Norbert, and Ksenija Jaušovec. 2012. "Sex Differences in Mental Rotation and Cortical Activation Patterns: Can Training Change Them?" *Intelligence* 40, no. 2: 151–62.

Levinson, Stephen C. 2003. *Space in Language and Cognition: Explorations in Cognitive Diversity*. Cambridge: Cambridge University Press.

Levinson, Stephen C., and David P. Wilkins. 2006. *Grammars of Space: Explorations in Cognitive Diversity*. Cambridge: Cambridge University Press.

Levinson, Stephen C., Sotaro Kita, Daniel B. M. Haun, and Björn H. Rasch. 2002. "Returning the Tables: Language Affects Spatial Reasoning." *Cognition* 84, no. 2: 155–88.

Lucy, John. 1992. *Grammatical Categories and Cognition: A Case Study of the Linguistic Relativity Hypothesis*. Cambridge: Cambridge University Press.

Maguire, Eleanor A., David G. Gadian, Ingrid S. Johnsrude, Catriona D. Good, John Ashburner, Richard S. J. Frackowiak and Christoper D. Frith. 2000. "Navigation-Related Structural Change in the Hippocampi of Taxi Drivers." *Proceedings of the National Academy of Sciences of the United States of America* 97, no. 8: 4398–403.

Mertins, Barbara. 2018. *Sprache und Kognition: Ereigniskonzeptualisierung im Deutschen und Tschechischen*. Berlin: De Gruyter.

Mertins, Holger, Barbara Mertins, Renate Delucchi Danhier, Ansgar Schulz, and Benedikt Schulz. 2017. "Architekten haben eine andere Raumwahrnehmung." *Detail* 9: 80–81.

Parsons, Thomas D., Peter Larson, Kris Kartz, Marcus Thiebaux, Brendon Bluestein, J. Galen Buckwalter, and Albert A. Rizzo. 2004. "Sex Differences in Mental Rotation and Spatial Rotation in a Virtual Environment." *Neuropsychologia* 42: 555–62.

Quaiser-Pohl, Claudia, Christian Geiser, and Wolfgang Lehmann. 2006. "The Relationship between Computer-Game Preference, Gender, and Mental-Rotation Ability." *Personality and Individual Differences* 40: 609–19.

Richardson, John T. E. 1994. "Gender Differences in Mental Rotation." *Perceptual and Motor Skills* 78: 435–48.

Does Space Matter?
A Cross-Disciplinary
Investigation upon Spatial
Abilities of Architects

Andri Gerber[1], Michal Berkowitz[2], Beatrix Emo[2], Stefan Kurath[1], Christoph Hölscher[2], and Elsbeth Stern[2]
[1] *ZHAW Zurich University of Applied Sciences, Switzerland*
[2] *ETH Zurich, Switzerland*

"It is hard to talk about the importance of space with those who have no sense for it."
Albert Erich Brinckmann, 1926

Abstract — Spatial ability is considered a key ability for STEM disciplines and has been correspondingly studied extensively, not least by the development of a vast number of psychometric tests. Based on the assumption that spatial ability is also central for architecture, the present paper presents an ongoing research on the development of a new test, specifically made to capture the spatial ability of architects. The test is based on aspects of the architectural process of design that have been broken down into single test items. The output of the research project will be both a finalized version of the test and a book for training purposes, based on this test. As spatial ability is malleable, it can be improved by exercise. This appears particularly relevant in relation to the gender gap emerging from this and former studies on spatial ability. The project is intended as a contribution to a better understanding of the nature of spatial ability in architecture in relation to the better-known visual ability as developed by art historians, among others.

Visual Ability vs. Spatial Ability

If there is one thing architects can be envious of with respect to art historians, it is their long tradition of training and theorizing visual skills that they have developed to analyze works of art. While in antiquity there was already the established tradition of *Ekphrasis* – the practice of describing a work of art – it was the rediscovery 1506 of the sculpture group *Laocoön and His Sons* that triggered a new discussion. Since then, art historians have fostered this visual ability up to the so-called iconic turn that emphasized the role of images in our society and the need to be able to read them. One comparison is often made: the same way as a radiologist learns to read radiographies and other imagining techniques and to infer information from these – which a layman would never be able to do – art historians learn to read images (or sculptures) and to extract information from them.

The most impressive contribution in this sense probably comes from art historian Ernst H. Gombrich (1909–2001) who, influenced by the psychology of perception and Gestalttheorie, used these references to approach works of arts (Gombrich 1960, 1982). Unfortunately, it cannot be said that a comparable process has ever occurred in architecture, in the sense of the development of a spatial ability, that is, the capacity of reading architectural spaces the same way one reads images. Even though the iconic turn was anticipated by a spatial turn, initiated among others by geographer Edward Soja (1940–2015), its outcome, in particular for architecture, was meager: it only resulted in a series of readers with collection of texts (for example, Hensel and Hight 2009). There we would find a set of the usual suspects, such as Gaston Bachelard's (1884–1962) *Poetics of Space* (1957) or Georges Perec's (1936–1982) *Species of Spaces* (1974) and a few new entries, such as the work of German Philosopher Gernot Böhme (*1937) on atmosphere. All these references are very suggestive but not really helpful in relation to the question of spatial ability and spatial knowledge in architecture, in particular when it comes not only to the analysis of built or unbuilt spaces, but also to designing space. This ability implies in particular the capacity to anticipate the effect of the spaces one builds on the beholder. This is obviously a very complex issue, and it is not surprising that beyond these references from literature or philosophy, inside the more specific architecture literature, we only find hints from architects casually referring to such a spatial ability or knowledge. If one looks for a more conspicuous body of theory, one will find it at the end of the nineteenth and the beginning of the twentieth centuries, where physiologists, psychologists, art historians, and architects in Germany and Austria started an extremely fruitful investigation on the nature of space and of spatial perception. One of the most eminent agents of this early spatial turn of the nineteenth and twentieth centuries was art historian Albert Erich Brinckmann (1881–1958), who not only transferred the space discussion from architecture to urban design, extending the groundwork of Camillo Sitte (1843–1903) or Hermann Maertens, but also included considerations both about perception and production of space. In his contribution to the *Handbuch der Kunstwissenschaft*, he would, for example, explicitly foster the spatial imagination of particular architects or cultures, such as the "Hochbarocke italienische Raumvorstellungskraft" or "komplizierte Raumvorstellungen" (Brinckmann 1927). Space was therefore not only something to be found in the eye of the beholder, which had to be trained in order to be able to read it, but also as a specific spatial imagination, something architects would have to possess in order to design spaces and architecture, according to their intentions. In an article of 1926 Brinckmann discusses the training of this spatial sense (Raumsinn), comparing it to the sense for colors (Farbensinn), which is a characteristic of painters (Brinckmann 1926, 51). While in his understanding only few individuals are gifted with a high spatial sense – notably architects – this can be trained and improved, the same way as it is possible for the sense of colors. Brinckmann – and he was not the only one from that period of time – thus anticipated later findings from cognitive science! He named three ways to improve it: through training in descriptive geometry, through "good examples" of architecture and urban situations one encounters in daily life – "good" buildings – and by comparison and analysis of examples that would have to be represented in plans, sections, and diagrams. In this context he not only speaks of the Raumsinn, but again also of a "räumliches Vorstellungsvermögen" of students.

Measuring Spatial Ability

Building upon these references, a research project was launched in 2016 between the Institute of Urban Landscape at the ZHAW in Winterthur and the Chairs of Cognitive Sciences and for Research on Learning and Instruction at ETH Zurich, which is funded by the Swiss National Science Foundation. The primary question in this project was how one could come closer to a definition of the specific type of spatial ability that characterizes the architect. Among the many possible approaches, we have decided to take on the development of a specific psychometric test for architects. In fact, there is a long tradition of measuring spatial ability in STEM disciplines with psychometric tests, as spatial ability has been recognized as a key ability for success in these disciplines. Longitudinal studies conducted in the United States over several decades show that high spatial abilities at an early age predicted later success in school, choice in scientific studies, and obtainment of advanced academic degrees in STEM (Newcombe 2010; Uttal and Cohen 2012).
In the psychological literature, spatial ability in fact refers to several distinct abilities that involve mental processing of spatial information. For example, one classification finds five different types of spatial ability: spatial relation (SR), spatial perception (SP), spatial visualization (SV), mental rotation (MR), and spatial orientation (SO) (Williams, Sutton, and Allen 2008). Other classifications have been made, and there is no single definition of each of these factors (Carroll 1993; Uttal et al. 2012). Based on this prior work, our research project aimed at developing a new spatial ability test

specifically adapted for architects. Previous research in other disciplines has shown that such domain-specific spatial ability is possible to capture. For example, works by Thomas Shipley characterized spatial mental processes that are unique to problems in geology and assessed these with a new test developed specifically for geology students and experts (Shipley et al. 2013). Berkowitz and Stern (2018) confirmed the domain-specificity of spatial abilities in a study with students from mechanical engineering. Incremental explanatory power of tests on spatial abilities was only found for achievement measures presented in classes on technical drawing and machine elements.

Developing test items for the architecture context was the most challenging part of the project, not only because the nature of space is elusive, but also since the process of architectural design is not clearly defined. The design process is a mixture of experience and tacit and explicit knowledge that cannot be readily put into words. The architect implicitly knows how to perform the process of design. She/he has certain technical and functional constraints to fulfill and relies on available methods and instruments such as plans, sections, diagrams, and physical or computer models, as well as on her/his own mental visualization ability. We assumed that several of the known spatial abilities will play a role also in the architect's tasks, although some processes may not be readily captured by existing tests. The architect is presumed to be particularly good at visualizing the 2-D spaces inside 3-D models, as well as in translating from 2-D to 3-D and vice versa. This movement back and forth plays a fundamental role in the overall design process, not only between 2-D and 3-D, but also between different types of media and scales. Other critical aspects in the architect's work is the constant switching between perspectives (that is, egocentric vs. allocentric) and between scales (that is, zooming in and out of objects and scenes); as well as the composition and decomposition of objects and spaces. Based on these premises, we have developed a set of test items that aim to tap these abilities: Street Views, Indoor Perspective, Packing Test, and Proportions Test (figs. 1, 2, 3, and 4).[1]

In the Street Views Test, the observer has to identify the correct perspectives corresponding to two marked standpoints in a given array of objects, which is represented either in a plan or in an axonometric view. In the Indoor Perspective Test, the observer has to imagine himself inside a shape shown from two axonometric views, and identify the correct perspective corresponding to a particular point of view. In the Packing Test, the observer has to determine which set of components can be "packed" together in a target shape. In the Proportions Test, the observer has to mentally perform a set of transformations to a given shape and decide which target corresponds to these transformations.

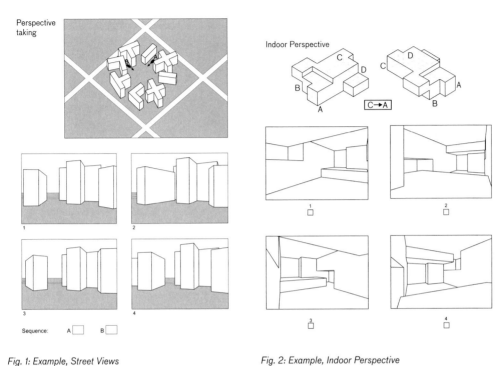

Fig. 1: Example, Street Views

Fig. 2: Example, Indoor Perspective

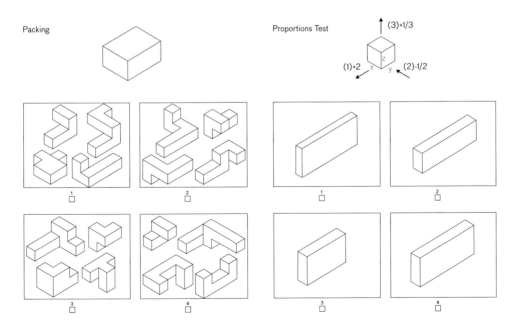

Fig. 3: Example, Packing Test

Fig. 4: Example, Proportions Test

With these tests, we aimed to capture specific spatial abilities of the architect: the capacity to imagine oneself in external or internal spaces (allocentric and egocentric perspective), the capacity to mentally modify volumes and combine them together, the capacity to read specific proportional measures in 3-D objects, and the capacity to scale spaces. All tests were developed by defining and manipulating a set of parameters such as positions, angles, number of objects, complexity of objects, etc. Additionally, wrong answers were constructed to reflect specific types of mistakes we expected, such as inverting left/right positions, or failing to identify that objects collide when put together. In order to capture specific spatial abilities that are distinct from those measured in standard spatial tests, the new test was hypothesized to:

- be distinguished from other measures of spatial abilities
- differentiate expert/advanced architects from beginners
- differentiate architects from experts in other spatial disciplines

The stimuli used in the new tests are generic and not specifically designed in the language of architecture, in order to be able to compare architects with nonarchitects. Thus, no architectural code such as floor plans or sections, which would give architects an advantage, were used here. At the same time, the stimuli are close to typical architectonic objects, and thus intend to simulate tasks with real architectural content. It should be mentioned that while in reality, the abilities and skills of architects involve relating and coordinating several mental processes at the same time, psychometric tests are often designed to restrain the mental operations to a single or only few elements, so that these can be studied separately. This is a limitation to be taken into account when administering such tests to architects.

Administering the Test

The research project started in fall 2016. In a first phase, architecture students from five architectural schools in Switzerland were recruited. Students were either in their first semester of bachelor studies or first semester of master studies. An additional group of beginner biology students was recruited as a comparison group. We selected biology students because of the similar gender distribution (around 50 percent) and also because it is expected to be spatially demanding, though in a different way from architecture. In this phase, only existing spatial ability tests were administered, along with general reasoning tests. The aim here was to establish a baseline of student's spatial abilities as assessed by standard measures. The following spatial tests were included: Mental Rotations Test (Peters et al. 1995), PVST Rotations (Guay 1977), The Paper Folding Test (Ekstrom et al. 1976), The Mental Cutting Test (CEEB 1939), and Visualization of Views, and Perspective Taking (Kozhevnikov and Hegarty 2001). Two subtests – Figural Matrices and

Number Series from the IST – were included as general ability measures. The results of this first testing session revealed no significant differences between beginner architecture and biology students. Among architecture students, advanced students outperformed beginners only on The Mental Cutting Test. This test requires the visualization of cross sections – cutting a 3-D shape with a plane – which is a common activity in architecture design. Thus, of all general spatial ability tests, The Mental Cutting Test seemed the most relevant to architecture. It should be noted that some of the tests turned out to be too easy for our sample and were close to ceiling effects. In particular, the Perspective Taking Test yielded high scores, and thus might have not been sensitive enough for detecting group differences. Since perspective taking is a key ability for architecture, these results further motivated our effort to develop more difficult tests that involve perspective taking.

In the next phase, the research team started developing the new spatial ability tests, and these were implemented for the first time in fall 2017. In this phase, students were recruited from only three architectural schools: ETH Zurich, EPF Lausanne, and ZHAW. It was not possible to test biology students at this point. In this new sample, we included two existing spatial ability tests – Mental Rotation Test and Mental Cutting Test; one general reasoning test, namely Figural Matrices; and three newly developed tests: Street Views, Indoor Test, and Packing Test. A total of 593 students participated in this round, of them 502 beginners (first semester bachelor) and 91 advanced (master students). The results revealed that advanced students outperformed beginners on the Packing Test, Indoor Perspective, and the Mental Cutting Test. The new tests correlated significantly with both Mental Rotation and Mental Cutting, confirming their construct validity as measures of spatial ability. At the same time, the correlations between the new tests were not higher than with the existing tests (all in the range of .30–.43), thus it could not yet be clearly shown that the new tests capture domain-specific spatial ability as hypothesized. It should nonetheless be noted that the new tests had lower reliability estimates (that is, internal consistency) than the conventional tests, indicating they were less unitary than the conventional tests, which may have in turn contributed to their lower intercorrelations. Based on item analyses on data from this phase, the research team further modified and adjusted some of the test items, as well as added new ones to the existing format.

In the current and last phase of the study, we have been recruiting again students who took part in fall 2017 for a follow-up study, where we administer again the same set of tests. In fall 2018 we have reached a subsample of N=93 students, most of them (N=74) bachelor students and only 19 master students. Since this sample is substantially smaller than the initial sample, we continue follow-up testing during the current spring semester, as well as recruiting advanced biology students for a comparison with a nonarchitecture group. The data so far from this last phase indicates that advanced students had slightly higher scores on the Street Views Test as well as on the Mental Cutting Test, but since the advanced group is very small, no strong inferences about these results can be currently made. Additionally, examining change in performance among students who participated in both testing sessions (2017 and 2018), preliminary results reveal significant improvements on the two existing tests (MCT and MRT), as well as on the Packing Test, but no significant differences on Street Views and Indoor Perspective tests.

One aspect we examined in our data, although not the focus of the study, was gender differences in performance. Since gender differences on spatial ability tests have been documented before, particularly on those involving mental rotations, we assumed some gender differences may emerge in our sample. In line with previous findings, our tests indeed revealed gender differences, with men outperforming women on both new and existing spatial ability tests (fig. 5).

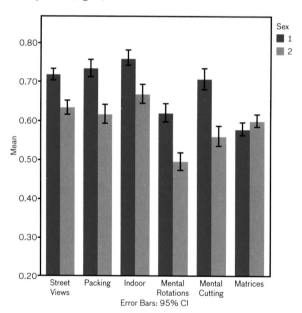

Fig. 5: Gender Differences

These differences could not have resulted from differences in general cognitive ability, since men and women did not differ in their performance on the general reasoning measure (figural matrices). Various factors might have contributed to the differences on spatial tests. Some might be situational factors such as the setting of group testing and a strict time limit on some of the tests. Other factors might be differences in prior experiences with spatial tasks. It has been shown that from childhood, boys often engage more than girls in activities and play that foster spatial thinking, which may later result in women's poorer performance on spatial ability tests. Possibly, male and female students selecting architecture may differ already at the starting point in their prior experiences with spatial tasks. In either case, the differences cannot be dismissed in light of the existing and very problematic gender gap in architecture. While many women leave the profession because of factors such as incompatibility with part-time work or a highly competitive atmosphere, a gap in spatial ability performance might add difficulties for women during their studies and work. Notably, our data shows that the gender gap in spatial ability is reduced among advanced students, indicating that the long training period throughout architecture studies improves initial spatial abilities. One implication of these results is that a more intensive training of specific spatial abilities earlier in architecture studies might be particularly beneficial for women.

A question that currently remains unanswered in our data is whether performance on specific spatial ability tests is predictive of success in architecture. The main challenge in this respect is to find a good criterion variable for success. We have collected grades on design courses for a part of our sample, and examined whether performance on our tests predicted these grades. All correlations of test results and grades were weak, thus not allowing much inference on this relation. Since design grades in architecture are highly subjective and rest upon the personal judgment of a professor, they might not be the optimal criterion for assessing success or degree of spatial skills. It is well known that many famous architects have a high spatial ability – this is said to be the case for example with Jacques Herzog – but this has never been measured so far.

Conclusions

The research project is ongoing and is to be finalized in fall 2019. Further modifications and refining of the tests may still be needed in order to improve their reliability and construct validity. The tests are not intended to be used as a measure for entrance examination, but rather as a tool for students' self-assessment or for teachers in the course of design courses. Since spatial ability has been shown to be malleable via training, we conceive of the tests presented here as potentially suitable as a training tool. Future research could show whether training architecture students on test items as the ones presented here will result in improved spatial abilities that are relevant for architecture. Related to this possibility, the first author is developing tasks similar to those presented here, though closer in content to the type of objects architects work with, which could potentially serve as training tools. These will be collected into a book in a form of exercises students could try out (figs. 6 and 7).

The present research project is an attempt to bridge cognitive sciences and design theory and to produce a corpus of knowledge that has a real impact on the discipline and is formulated in an understandable way. While there exists a quite large corpus of investigations on architecture based on the analysis of language and of sketches, these often remain constrained in a scientific language and have no real application and are not understandable for architects. Last but not least, the project was intended as an extension to the abovementioned theory of space of the end of the nineteenth/beginning of the twentieth centuries and to the cultivation of a specific spatial ability of architects.

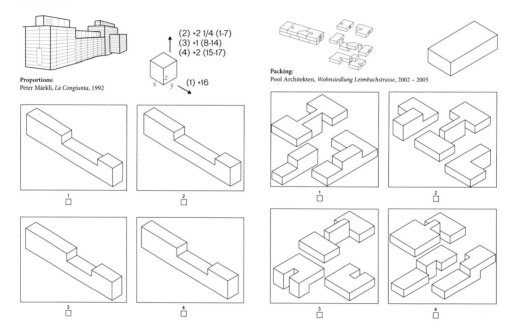

Fig. 6: Architectural example of Proportions Test   Fig. 7: Architectural example of Packing Test

Acknowledgments

The project has been accompanied by a series of experts that we would like to thank: Ruth Conroy Dalton, Dafna Fischer Gewirtzman, Peter Holgate, Thomas Shipley, Margaret Tarampi, and David Uttal.

Furthermore, we would like to thank the design professors who granted us access to their students: François Charbonnet, Andrea Deplazes, Dieter Dietz, Harry Gugger, Patrick Heiz, Cornelie Leopold, Marco Merz, Urs Primas, Wolfgang Rossbauer, Lando Rossmaier, Detlef Schulz, Christina Schumacher, Peter Staub, and Toni Wirth.

Finally, we would like to thank Nuno De Matos Ferreira for his valuable assistance in carrying out various phases of this project.

References

Berkowitz, Michal, and Elsbeth Stern. 2018. "Which Cognitive Abilities Make the Difference? Predicting Academic Achievements in Advanced STEM Studies." *Journal of Intelligence*, 6, no. 4: 48. https://doi.org/10.3390/jintelligence6040048.

Berkowitz, Michal, Beatrix Emo, Andri Gerber, Christoph Hölscher, Stefan Kurath, and Elsbeth Stern. 2018. "Development of a Novel Test to Measure Spatial Abilities of Architecture Students: Preliminary Findings." *Cognitive Processing* 19, suppl. 1: 34.

Brinckmann, Albert Erich. 1926. "Erziehung zum Raumsinn." *Zeitschrift für Deutschkunde*, no. 1: 51.

Brinckmann, Albert Erich. 1927. *Baukunst des 17. und 18. Jahrhunderts in den romanischen Ländern*. Wildpark Potsdam: Akademische Verlagsgesellschaft Athenaion.

Carroll, John Bissell. 1993. *Human Cognitive Abilities: A Survey of Factor-Analytic Studies*. Cambridge: Cambridge University Press.

CEEB. 1939. *Special Aptitude Test in Spatial Relations*. New York: College Entrance Examination Board.

Ekstrom, Ruth B., John W. French, Harry H. Harman, and Diran Dermen. 1976. *Manual for Kit of Factor-Referenced Cognitive Tests*. Princeton, NJ: Educational Testing Service.

Gombrich, Ernst. 1960. *Art and Illusion: A Study in the Psychology of Pictorial Representation*. London: Phaidon.

Gombrich, Ernst. 1982. *The Image and the Eye*. Oxford: Phaidon.

Guay, Roland. 1977. *Purdue Spatial Visualization Test: Visualization of Views*. West Lafayette, IN: Purdue Research Foundation.

Hensel, Michael, and Christopher Hight, eds. 2009. *Space Reader: Heterogeneous Space in Architecture*. Chichester: Wiley.

Kahn, Louis. 1967. "Space and the Inspirations." In *Louis Kahn, Essential Texts*, edited by Robert Twombly, 223. New York: W. W. Norton & Company Inc.

Kozhevnikov, Maria, and Mary Hegarty. 2001. "A Dissociation between Object Manipulation Spatial Ability and Spatial Orientation Ability." *Memory & Cognition* 29, no. 5: 745–56.

Mallgrave, Harry. 1994. *Empathy, Form and Space: Problems in German Aesthetics, 1873–1893*. Santa Monica: Getty Center for the History of Art and the Humanities.

Newcombe, Nora S. 2010. "Picture This: Increasing Math and Science Learning by Improving Spatial Thinking." *American Educator*: 29–34.

Opel, Adolf, ed. 2010. *Adolf Loos, gesammelte Schriften*. Vienna: Lesethek.

Peters, Michael, Bruno Laeng, Kerry Latham, Marla Jackson, Raghad Zaiyouna, and Chris Richardson. 1995. "A Redrawn Vandenberg & Kuse Mental Rotations Test: Different Versions and Factors That Affect Performance." *Brain and Cognition* 28: 39–58.

Shipley, Thomas F., Basil Tikoff, Carol Ormand, and Cathy Manduca. 2013. "Structural Geology Practice and Learning, from the Perspective of Cognitive Science." *Journal of Structural Geology* 54: 72–84.

Uttal, David H., and Cheryl Ann Cohen. 2012. "Spatial Thinking and STEM Education: When, Why and How." *Psychology of Learning and Motivation* 57: 147–81.

Uttal, David H., Nathaniel G. Meadow, Elizabeth Tipton, Linda L. Hand, Alison R. Alden, Christopher Warren, and Nora S. Newcombe. 2012. "The Malleability of Spatial Skills: A Meta-Analysis of Training Studies." *Psychological Bulletin*. Advance online publication, June 4: 352–402.

Williams, Anthony, Ken Sutton, and Rebecca Allen. 2008. "Spatial Ability: Issues Associated with Engineering and Gender." *Proceedings of the 2008 AaeE Conference*, Yeppoon, 1–6.

----

[1] Proportions Test has not been tested in our study.

Augmented Reality and Virtual Reality: New Tools for Architectural Visualization and Design

Shilong Tan, Yuxin Yang, and Luigi Cocchiarella
Politecnico di Milano, Italy

Abstract — This paper focuses on the use of augmented reality (AR) and virtual reality (VR) technologies aiming at innovating architectural design and architectural visualization through some reference projects and two pilot researches. The reference projects focus on the feasibilities in using AR and VR techniques in the architecture field, that generate the pilot researches based on testing them in both architecture design and architectural visualization. The first research presents the use of augmented reality in a three-dimensional model and illustrates how the technique works in the design process. To figure out a viable system in using VR technique, the second research experiments the VR technique in a properly said testing project.

Thereby, after analyzing the potential of some existing applications of AR and VR technologies, and the use of these techniques in the experimental research, this paper aims to provide some guidelines and suggestions for their use in architectural design, architectural education, and other related fields.

Introduction

In recent years, augmented reality (AR) and virtual reality (VR) technologies became more and more recognizable by the public, especially as the leading technology giants, such as Apple (WWDC2018) and Google (Google I/O 2018), turned their marketing strategy to these technologies and made the related techniques more fluent in their practical use. Based on this context, AR and VR applications seem feasible and reasonable to support architecture design and architectural visualization.

In terms of architectural design, indeed, architects can be supported by AR and VR technologies in order to have an entirely new design experience and process. In traditional design methods, there are more or less various deficiencies: for example, the paper drawings have the lack of a full understanding of the third dimension; computer modeling is mostly based on God's perspective, without showing the design logic on which the user's view is based; in the physical model the proportions cannot fully express the details and the materials characterizing the real scale. VR technology instead, thanks to the virtual environment, can help architects avoid these design deficiencies. Based on this virtual technology, the architect can be fully immersed in the true scale of the design, while the space experience will be converted into the most intuitive visual sense, coupled with real-time rendering technology to assist the control of material, light, and other details, which can also be synchronized into the design environment.

From the architectural visualization point of view, VR technology can offer a high degree of immersion experience. This is a new type of interactive experience that ordinary architectural drawings, renderings, and even videos cannot bring to the user. Thanks to VR technology, the user can complete a free view in a virtual building model. Both architects and clients can have a more accurate judgment on the design and the estimation of the possibility of the building's final construction at the same time. AR technology, on the other hand, can add a new layer to the real world, even by using a portable smart device (such as a phone or tablet), which means more elements can be easily displayed, not only to the architect, but also to clients or non-professionals, who can see directly from 2-D drawings the generation of predesigned interactive 3-D models.

Architectural Representation Trends in the Digital Era

As we already know from the digital era, indeed, architectural representation is an indispensable operational means during the architecture design process stages, not only for architects, but also for clients and construction workers. Traditional architectural representations such as sketches and solid models are the most widely recognized and accepted forms. Today, designers and architects have more efficient ways to depict their ideas thanks to the explosion of digital technology which brings us computer-aided drafting and photo-realistic rendering, as well as augmented reality and virtual reality to support architectural design and architectural visualization. Decades ago, realistic images with accurate perspective, lights and shadows, and materials simulations were the height of aspirational innovation. Nowadays, in the digital age, we can make a beautifully rendered picture effortlessly with software. Sketches and 2-D drawings as the most basic architectural representations, allow grandiose building volumes to be presented in a two-dimensional platform. In order to meet the needs of modern production, the development of computer technology such as BIM systems can assure that the accuracy of the two-dimensional drawings, directly generated from the 3-D models, better serve the entire building design procedure.

On the other hand, the progress of digital image processing brings another advantage to the architectural representation. Based on the simulation of rendering technology, designers can better control the design and refine the materials, lights, and shadows, through timely feedback of computer images to test the possible final perceptual impact of the building, even though these three-dimensional images are still presented in a two-dimensional plane, that is, a screen or a paper. In this context, thanks to the popularity of smart devices making augmented reality and virtual reality of more practical use, a new opportunity has emerged for architectural representation: the immersive experience. Due to the real-time feedback on user behavior and interaction, it combines virtual space with real space, providing a new experience for architectural representation and design.

Augmented Reality for Architectural Representation

As it has been defined in *The Concise Fintech Compendium*, "Augmented reality is an enhanced version of the physical, real-world reality of which elements are superimposed by computer-generated or extracted real-world sensory input such as sound, video, graphics or haptics" (Schueffel 2017, 2). With the help of AR technology (for example, adding computer vision and object recognition), the information about the surrounding real world of the user becomes interactive and digitally tractable. Information about the environment and its objects is overlaid on the real world (an example is described below in figure 1). Like the figure explains, when you use a specific program to open the phone camera and capture the target picture, the screen simultaneously presents a new 3-D model on the picture, which is prepared and recorded in advance into the application of the smartphone. This newly generated model is just like the real one in this picture. When you move and rotate the position of the picture, the model changes accordingly, based on the new position of the camera.

Fig. 1: Smartphone AR schematic (made by the authors)

The augmented experience can be easily understood as a tool of layers overlaying, where the extra layering information is applied over the real physical space. "Augmented space research gives us new terms with which to think about previous spatial practices. Before we would think of an architect, a fresco painter, or a display designer working to combine architecture and images, or architecture and text, or to incorporate different symbolic systems in one spatial construction, we can now say that all of them were working on the problem of augmented space. The problem, that is, of how to overlay physical space with layers of data. Therefore, to imagine what can be done culturally with augmented spaces, we may begin by combing cultural history for useful precedents" (Manovich 2002, 13).

AR DEMO: THE 3-D SAMPLE ROOM THROUGH 2-D IMAGE
From an architectural point of view, generating this building model based on a floor plan can not only satisfy the correlation between picture and three-dimensional model, but it also achieves a new user experience. Thus, the first demo we made is to test the above visualization result by AR progress.

During the preparation stage, we need to preset the target image and to prepare the 3-D model of the virtual object. The purpose of the target picture is to generate a three-dimensional model that the user can recall when the phone camera captures the bidimensional picture. Because the phone camera analyzes all the elements in its viewfinder range, there are enough feature points for the target picture, which cannot be too simple to elaborate. When you upload the target image, the system will determine if the image has enough feature points to support the camera recognition. As shown in the figure below (fig. 2), the yellow dots indicate the feature points that can be recognized. The more feature points there are, the easier it is for the camera to make the correct identification of the related image.

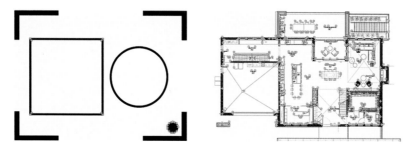

Fig. 2: Feature points in two images with different levels of complexity

Then we prepare the corresponding 3-D model and export it to the FBX[1] format, which is imported into the Unity3D[2] software along with the previous target picture. In this demo, we need to set up the architectural model material and place the model on the related floor plan (target image). At the same time, we need to add an optical environment to ensure that the model can display the correct light and shade information.

Once these basic preparations are ready, we can start packing them into apps available on your mobile phone system. Referring to our case, Unity3D has simplified the mainstream for smartphone, so that we could install the app on the phone with just few simple steps.

Finally, we could test the demo with our smartphone. As you can see from the final effect (fig. 3), a 3-D model "grows" on paper through the screen. Once this floor plan appears on the phone screen, the previously designed three-dimensional model will be generated in its corresponding position, thus achieving a three-dimensional (model feature) and two-dimensional (screen show) interactive experience. Of course, the model can be visualized from any point of view in the semispace above the printed paper, from a certain given range of distances from it.

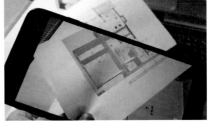

Fig. 3: AR Demo

In summary, the workflow of AR combined with architecture can be summed up as: 1. Identifying target pictures; 2. Making three-dimensional models; 3. Importing them into Unity engine production apps; 4. Debugging materials in unities and lighting; and eventually 5. Generating apps available on your phone (fig. 4).

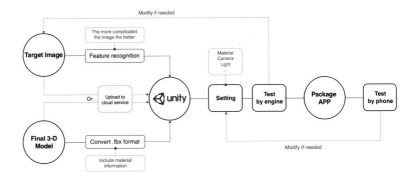

Fig. 4: A viable AR workflow (Diagram: authors)

The AR in the process of combining with architectural perceptual experience embodies some advantages that traditional expression methods cannot have: real-time interaction with two-dimensional images and generation of three-dimensional models, and some basic ways of dynamic real-time interactions. However, AR technology may be constrained by hardware devices, as both tablets and phones have border limitations, for example, the size of the screen limits the digital object representation (even though a head-mounted device similar to HoloLens eliminates borders, the actual experience is not ideal); and achieving this AR experience requires the preparation of a corresponding three-dimensional model for different two-dimensional graphics in advance, and this upfront preparation workload is still enormous.

Virtual Reality for Architectural Representation

Unlike AR, virtual reality (VR) is a computer technology that uses devices like glasses, headsets, or helmets, sometimes in combination with physical spaces or multiprojected environments, to generate realistic 3-D stereoscopic images, sounds, and other sensations that simulate a user's physical presence in a real-like or imaginary environment. A person using virtual reality equipment is able to look around the artificial world and, thanks to high-quality VR, to move inside it and to thereby manipulate virtual features or items. The spatial simulation brought by VR technology can restore the original appearance of three-dimensional space to the greatest extent, and can even accurately express the change of material and lights and shadows based on a realistic rendering technology. Using VR technology to represent buildings can fully immerse users in their own designs.

VR DEMO: THE TESTING ROOM

VR technology is a panoramic experience in which the user not only sees the graphic information inside the frame, but is immersed in a complete, 360-degree digital environment, surrounded by a panoramic three-dimensional model. Compared with the traditional perspective image, the VR image uses the spherical coordinate system. Then, a panoramic picture in this system normally works as shown in the following images (fig. 5).

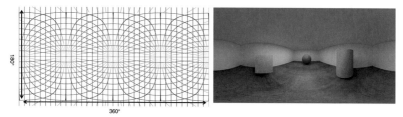

Fig. 5: 360-degree panoramic model of our testing room (Images: authors)

In traditional rendering and avatar, we usually only need to render objects that can be seen in the range of view chosen. Compared with the traditional rendering method, making a VR panoramic picture rendering requires the establishment of a complete 3-D model, rather than just the portion of a model that the lens can see under a specific visual angle. During the rendering process, a spherical camera has to be used and the aspect ratio of 2:1 has to be set, in order to ensure that the horizontal view is a 360-degree view and the vertical view is a 180-degree one. In order to have a more immersive experience for the user, it is recommended that the height of the camera be set to an altitude similar to that of the human eye (normally about 1.6 m from the floor level).

Again, to achieve this type of visual simulation, it is necessary to prepare the three-dimensional whole model of the space in advance, supplemented by certain rendering techniques to enhance its realism. In this research, we have chosen to use static VR, that is, a purely visual type of VR, where the user is not free to move within the given space. We selected some relevant viewing points in this model and rendered 360-degree panoramic images based on those camera points. Once we got the mentioned images, we could import them into VR equipment (VR glasses through phone in this case). With VR equipment, users can then enter and experience the 3-D dynamic visual perception of the space we simulated at any time. In a dynamic virtual reality experience, users can walk freely in a virtual space created by the designer. Equivalent to each move, the system will render spherical images in real time.

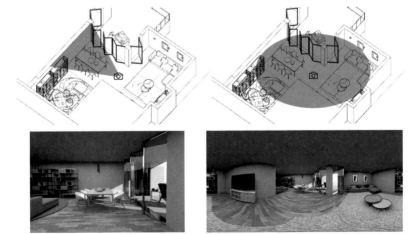

Fig. 6: Diagram and render: traditional and spherical camera in the testing room (Images: authors)

In terms of workflow, as long as the designer completes a complete model and sets the position of the camera, s/he can complete a VR picture with the help of a renderer (fig. 7). If further developments are required, interactive designs can also be carried out through other software programs to complete the movement, to transform the scene, and even to simply interact with the objects placed in the scene.

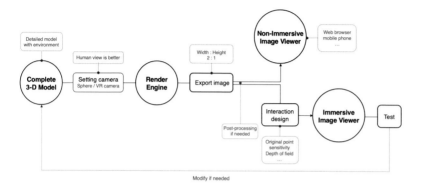

Fig. 7: The VR workflow (Diagram: authors)

AR and VR Applications Opportunities

In addition to the architectural performance and assistance in the design process and in the immersive visual experience of 3-D models, people can also use VR and AR applications in architecture education, including descriptive geometry education and three-dimensional composition education. Concerning descriptive geometry, as we know it allows representation of three-dimensional objects in two graphic dimensions, by using a specific set of projective procedures. One scope of traditional descriptive geometry was and still is, indeed, supporting the understanding of spatial properties and relations, which for a student in architecture is one of the most relevant educational goals, that is, in order to make students able to figure out and control the architectural space starting from planar images set as graphic projections of spatial configurations. Last but not least, the attraction of spatial simulations is also a key point for the prospective innovative educational programs in our field.

Conclusions

Due to the development of technology, techniques such as AR and VR technologies as well as computer-aided modeling, parameterization, and computer rendering are promoting an emerging impact on architectural design and architectural visualization. However, in real practices, there are a few key issues and challenges that need to be identified for prospective future researches.

1. Relying on the traditional computer-aided drawing to carry out the basic model output, VR and AR can only make simple independent modifications. More complex structural modifications still need the assistance of traditional computer modeling.

2. Since the interactive methods are currently not uniform, there are many limitations in using these two techniques. For example, installation and software support for VR devices is relatively cumbersome and requires high operating space, while AR handheld devices are also limited by the standard display ranges, which affects the experience.
3. Compared to AR technique, VR devices need to have some preparation time before starting a fully immersive experience – for example, for installing devices and learning how to use them – and this currently makes it difficult to achieve high-precision operations through interactive devices.

References

Bayer, Herbert. 1939. "Fundamentals of Exhibition Design." *PM* 6, no. 2: 17–25.

Diodato, Roberto. 2005. *Estetica del virtuale*. Milan: Pearson Italia Spa.

Dünser, Andreas, Karin Steinbügl, Hannes Kaufmann, and Judith Glück. 2006. "Virtual and Augmented Reality as Spatial Ability Training Tools." In *Proceedings of the 7th ACM SIGCHI New Zealand Chapter's International Conference on Computer-Human Interaction: Design-Centered HCI*, 125–32.

Hsu, Pei-Hsien. 2015. "Architectural Visualization and Communication through Mobile Augmented Reality." In *Proceedings of the 20th International Conference on Computer-Aided Architectural Design Research in Asia (CAADRIA 2015): Emerging Experiences in the Past, Present and Future of Digital Architecture*, 283–92.

Lévy, Pierre. 1995. *Qu'est-ce que le virtuel?* Paris: La Découverte.

Manovich, Lev. 2002. "The Poetics of Augmented Space: Learning from Prada." *manovich.net*. Accessed March 21, 2019. http://manovich.net/content/04-projects/034-the-poetics-of-augmented-space/31_article_2002.pdf.

Manovich, Lev, and Roger F. Malina. 2001. *The Language of New Media*. Cambridge, MA: MIT Press.

Schueffel, Patrick. 2017. *The Concise Fintech Compendium*. Fribourg: School of Management.

---

[1] FBX (Filmbox) is a proprietary file format (.fbx) developed by Kaydara and owned by Autodesk since 2006. It is used to provide interoperability between digital content creation and applications.

[2] Unity is a cross-platform game engine developed by Unity Technologies.

6.2 Human Body

Embodied Emotions: A Methodology for Experiments in Architecture and Corporeality

Maria da Piedade Ferreira[1], José Pinto Duarte[2], and Andreas Kretzer[3]
[1] Fatuk, Technische Universität Kaiserslautern, Germany
[2] Stuckeman Center for Design Computing, Penn State University, USA
[3] Faculty of Architecture and Design, University of Applied Sciences Stuttgart, Germany

Abstract — This paper describes a set of experiments focused on the study of the relationship between architecture and the body. These experiments were part of a larger study on the topic and followed an analysis of historical architectural texts from Vitruvius to current theories of embodiment. The experiments addressed the problem of how it is possible to influence user's emotions through architectural space and design objects. Our hypothesis was that this can be achieved through a process of empathy between the user's body and the surrounding space. The methodology employed combined the use of biometric technology, a Presence Questionnaire, and a pictorial assessment technique, the Self-Assessment Manikin chart (SAM) to analyze psychophysiological changes in the body's sensory perception during performances with designed objects and architectural spaces at different scales. Results show that this methodology can be useful in the design process and in architectural teaching to evaluate design outcomes and users' emotional responses.

Introduction

The experiments described in this paper were undertaken in the context of a larger research work (Ferreira 2016). The larger research encompassed two phases, the first aimed at a revision of the literature which dealt with the topic of the body and architecture (Eberhard 2009, Mallgrave 2010; Vesalius, Garrison, and Hast 2003, Zeizel 2006) from Vitruvius to the theories of embodiment (Damásio 1999, Gallagher 2005). The principal conclusion of the historical revision on the topic was that, with few exceptions, there

EMBODIED EMOTIONS

313

still isn't an established methodology that permits us to understand how buildings and design objects directly affect how users feel. As such, the second phase was concerned with the development and testing of such a methodology, which proposes the incorporation of the somatic practices of performance art (Goldberg 1988) in the teaching of architecture and combines these with the use of emotion measurement tools in order to evaluate during the design process the experience of architectural space and design objects. Our aim was to understand how it is possible to influence users' emotions through architectural space and design objects, as we argued that this can be achieved through a process of empathy between the user's body and the surrounding space. To demonstrate this claim, a set of experiments were undertaken in the context of architectural teaching and the results of such experiments were evaluated through the analysis of quantitative data collected by emotion measurement tools and qualitative data gathered using questionnaires.

The experiments were designed to evaluate the subject's emotional experience while performing with an object that extended the body's usual range of action, therefore, conditioning the performer's emotional reaction by changing hers/his usual sensory perception (fig. 1).

Fig. 1: Corporeal architecture: performer with body extension

The methodology used in the experiments was a multicomponential response approach consisting of a variety of components that can provide a comprehensive way of measuring emotions. The results collected with these experiments evaluate the subject's recall of their experience and the believability of the simulation, systematized according to specific parameters.

This data gave us information on the subject's physiological response and emotional activation during the experiments. We concluded that experiments designed with the goal of evaluating the emotional experience of a user in an architectural space can take place in existing environments and virtual simulations, and it is possible to analyze changes in sensory reaction and emotional activation with quantifiable means. Based on our conclusions, we propose that it would be possible and advantageous to integrate such a methodology in the design process.

Methodology

As referred to above, the methodology used in the experiments was a multi-componential response approach, consisting of a variety of components that can provide a comprehensive way of measuring emotions. According to Kim, Cho, and Kim (2015), "three main components of emotional response are currently accepted in Human-Computer-Interaction: experiential response, physiological response, and behavioral response." In the experiments under-taken to test the thesis hypothesis, the methodology combined the assess-ment of the experiential response (SAM charts), the measurement of the physiology response using the e-Health Platform (fig. 2), and the evaluation of the behavioral response (Presence Questionnaire). A description of each of the measurement components, respectively, SAM charts, Presence Ques-tionnaires, and e-Health Platform follows.

Fig. 2: Installing e-Health Platform on performer's body

The Self-Assessment Manikin, SAM (Bradley and Lang 1994) is an image-based instrument and consists in a graphical representation of different emotional states, organized into three categories of major affective dimensions (valence, activation, and control) and is intended to directly assess the response of a subject to an object or event.

SAM has been widely accepted by the scientific community as an easy, nonverbal and reliable method for quickly assessing people's reports of affective experiences (Lang, Bradley, and Cuthbert 1998). Initially SAM was implemented as an interactive computer program but since this version was not flexible enough and required both knowledge of the technology, at least on a basic level, it was adapted to a paper-and-pencil version that illustrates in a graphic way various points along each of the three categories. A Presence Questionnaire (PQ) was created for military purposes (Witmer and Singer 1998) to evaluate how immersed and present a person can feel in a virtual simulation. The PQ used in the first two experiments – Experiment #1: Raum-metaphern and Experiment #2: Feel your Design – was based on the original one by Witmer and Singer. For the other two experiments – Experiment #3: Corporeal Architecture (fig. 1) and Experiment #4: De Humani Corporis Fabrica (figs. 3 and 4) – a shorter, more optimized version was developed. Finally, the machinery used in the experiments to measure the participants' physiological response was the e-Health Sensor Shield V2.0 (fig. 2). The e-Health Sensor allows Arduino and Raspberry Pi users to perform biometric and medical applications where body monitoring is needed, by using 10 different sensors: pulse, oxygen in blood (SPO2), airflow (breathing), body temperature, electrocardiogram (ECG), glucometer, galvanic skin response (GSR – sweating), blood pressure (sphygmomanometer), subjects' position (accelerometer), and muscle/electromyography (EMG) sensors. This information was used to monitor the emotional and physiological state of each subject in real time and obtain data on such states to be subsequently analyzed.

Fig. 3: De Humani Corporis Fabrica: performer in setting "eating dinner"

Fig. 4: De Humani Corporis Fabrica: performer in setting "office space"

The goal of the experiment is related directly to the main hypothesis of the study that it is possible to consciously influence a user's emotional reaction through a design object that conditions hers/his movements. The goal was to explore through a performance the interaction between body, movement, and space. Namely, the idea was to evaluate the subject's emotional experience while performing with an object that extended the body's usual range of action, therefore conditioning the performer's emotional reaction by changing hers/his usual sensory perception. For the experiment, each student was instructed to prepare a performance that explored the relationship between the body, space, and the object conceived. These were respectively: for Experiment #1: Raummetaphern, spatial metaphors; for Experiment #3: Corporeal Architecture, body extensions, restrictions, and the body as an architecture element (fig. 1); and for Experiment #4: De Humani Corporis Fabrica, architecture settings or interior spaces (figs. 3 and 4). Students were advised to wear comfortable black clothing for the performances, since they would be moving rather freely in space. In addition to the original, required performance, they also were expected to improvise further uses and meanings for/with the objects created. Each student performed with her/his own design, which was important to understand through the performance the emotional connection to the object that each student developed during the design process. The experimental settings were conceived having in mind Muybridge's studies on human locomotion. The neutral mask, a standard fabric mask used for cosmetic purposes, was chosen following the pedagogy of theater director Jacques Lecoq (Lecoq 2006; Lecoq and Carasso 2001). Lecoq developed ideas on the use of the neutral mask as a liberating tool that allowed the performer to transmit through hers/his body the spatial idea s/he had in mind, without the constraints of the everyday persona, which usually is expressed mainly through the face.

Discussion

The initial research plan foresaw simulations in virtual environments to verify the study's hypothesis. However, the literature review led to the conclusion that for assessing the emotional experience of architecture, especially involving movement in space, it was necessary to work in real space. Also, it seemed more appropriate to work with objects and settings that had real properties of weight, scale, scent, and texture, as these aspects cannot be simulated very accurately in a virtual environment. For these reasons, in the experiments it was sought to evaluate the effectiveness of computer-simulated virtual environments to influence the subjects' emotional experience, although this is still a possibility for future work. Instead, they were designed to evaluate the ability of "real" environments and objects to create specific changes in the sensorial and emotional landscape of the subjects. Therefore, the situations explored in the experiments were simulated through architecture models, through objects that functioned as body extensions or restrictions – "props" as one would call in performance, and through 1:1 scale models of architectural settings. It was also important to understand how such material properties interfere directly with the emotional experience of a subject, specifically as they address sensory modalities that are still hard to explore in virtual simulations due to technological constraints. Although the Presence Questionnaire was conceived to evaluate the sense of Presence, that is, the feeling of being "more or less compelled" by a virtual environment, it was considered as a valuable research tool to qualify a subjects' experience of a real environment because it helped in finding answers to the question: "how is it that a designed object/architecture space affects the emotions of (or is able to move) a user?"

The importance of the combined use of the PQ and the SAM chart also was reinforced by difficulties encountered in the course of the experiments with students. Sensors of the e-Health platform did not function consistently throughout the experiments, and performances with objects that demanded more movement interfered with the calibration of the sensors. For this reason, it was important to cross-reference data collected also with the SAM charts and the Presence Questionnaires to assess the emotions experienced by each subject/performer as accurately as possible. Even though the e-Health platform sensors presented such difficulties, the data collected were consistent with the results evaluated through the SAM charts and Presence Questionnaires in most cases. This suggests that for measuring emotions, it may be desirable to use biometric machinery, but it is not mandatory. Therefore, experiments with similar goals may be developed without sophisticated technological means, as the information collected with SAM charts and the Presence Questionnaires may be sufficient to measure rather comprehensively the emotions experienced by the subjects. This presents interesting opportunities as it allows performers to explore wider ranges of movements in the performances without being concerned with disconnecting sensors, and suggests that the experimental setting can be flexible, that is, not dependent on conditions built specifically for the experiment. Therefore, experiments with the goal of evaluating the emotional experience of a user in an architectural space can take place in existing environments and virtual simulations, facilitating the study of how subjects feel in such spaces, without compromising accuracy. As such, it would be possible and advantageous to integrate such a methodology in the design process, to evaluate the effectiveness of designed objects and architectural spaces in producing specific emotions or moods in a subject and, most interestingly, in analyzing how an existing built environment actually affects our bodies and, therefore, our minds. Such an analysis would not be focused on ergonomic factors in the strict sense, but rather on the psychophysiological effects of designed objects and spaces on the body and mind of the user. Hence, it would permit one to understand what could be improved in order to respond to both contemporary living requirements and basic biological demands. This way, architecture and design objects can be used to truly protect and nurture the emotional needs of the human body by consciously providing meaningful experiences to users.

Conclusions

Experimental results were effective in demonstrating that it is possible to consciously induce certain emotional states in a user or to analyze how specific environments affect users. Understanding this mechanism, we believe, is a useful way for becoming a better designer, especially nowadays that the understanding of human mind promises to be almost at hand's reach. One of the conclusions regarding the experiments described in this paper is that contemporary science still accepts that the human body is the most fine and precise evaluation tool of an object, a model, or an architectural or urban space. It is for this reason that it is important to include it in any experiments that aim to analyze the emotional experience of architectural space, and ideally this should happen in real space. As Mallgrave tells us, new knowledge is brought up every day in areas of research, such as neurosciences, but there still is a lot of uncertainty about the workings of the brain, especially regarding the field of emotional experience of architectural space. The research described in this paper left behind some possibilities for further work. For instance, there were no experiments undertaken in virtual settings. We consider that it would be scientifically useful to apply the same methodology to experiments in virtual settings, specifically to compare the emotional response of users in virtual simulations of existing architectural spaces with their responses in the real versions of such spaces.

References

Bradley, Margaret M., and Peter J. Lang. 1994. "Measuring Emotion: The Self-Assessment Manikin and the Semantic Differential." *Behaviour Therapy and Experimental Psychiatry* 25, no. 1: 49–59.

Damásio, António. 1999. *The Feeling of What Happens: Body and Emotions in the Making of Consciousness*. Orlando: Harcourt Books.

Eberhard, John Paul. 2009. *Brain Landscape: The Coexistence of Neuroscience and Architecture*. Oxford: Oxford University Press.

Ferreira, Maria da Piedade. 2016. "Embodied Emotions: Observations and Experiments in Architecture and Corporeality." PhD diss., FAULisboa, 2016.

Gallagher, Shaun. 2005. *How the Body Shapes the Mind*. New York: Oxford University Press.

Goldberg, RoseLee. 1988. *Performance Art: From Futurism to the Present*. London: Thames & Hudson.

Kim, Mi Jeong, Myung Eun Cho, and Jeong Tai Kim. 2015. "Measures of Emotion in Interaction for Health Smart Home." *IACSIT International Journal of Engineering and Technology* 7, no. 4: 10–12.

Lang, Peter J., Margaret M. Bradley, and Bruce N. Cuthbert. 1998. "Emotion, Motivation, and Anxiety: Brain Mechanisms and Psychophysiology." *Biological Psychiatry* 44, no. 12: 1248–63.

Lecoq, Jacques. 2006. *Theatre of Movement and Gesture*. New York: Routledge.

Lecoq, Jacques, and Jean Gabriel Carasso. 2001. *The Moving Body: Teaching Creative Theory*. New York: Routledge.

Mallgrave, Harry Francis. 2010. *The Architect Brain: Neuroscience, Creativity and Architecture*. Chichester: Wiley.

Vesalius, Andreas, Daniel Garrison, and Malcom Hast. 2003. *De Humani Corporis Fabrica*. Evanston, IL: Northwestern University.

Witmer, Bob, and Michael Singer. 1998. "Measuring Presence in Virtual Environments: A Presence Questionnaire." *Presence* 7, no. 3: 225–40.

Zeizel, John. 2006. *Inquiry by Design: Environment/Behavior/Neuroscience in Architecture, Interiors, Landscape, and Planning*. New York: W. W. Norton & Company.

Reciprocity and Interaction

Katharina Voigt
Technical University of Munich, Germany

Abstract — The process of future perception and appropriation of architectural situations contrasts with the process of their conception; design and interaction with the designed are directly interconnected. In a phenomenological understanding, the corporeality of the human body grants its access to the world; in order to perceive and recognize an object or space external to the body, the sensory body must extend to the object of interest in order to grasp its significance. An architectural space only appears to us as such if we include the palpable, tangible knowledge and memory of earlier movements. Contemporary dance reveals itself as key to a knowledgeable exploration of the sensorimotor experience of space and serves as a tool for a deeper understanding of the body-related architectural implications. Hence, movement in space is dependent on embodied experience and memory – one's corporeality serves as primary reference, questioning what or whom one refers to.

Architectural Space and Human Body

The attempts to grasp the interrelation of human and architecture have been various and undertaking multiple changes throughout the evolution of architectural history and theory, carrying along with deferring body schemes and space conceptions. Considering the human body, a basic measure and reference for architectural elements corresponds to an understanding of architecture as a solidified composition of proportion and geometry, mass, and space. Correspondingly, the bodies used as molds for architectural analogies were merely considered solid figures, in artificial poses, beyond any movement, depicted as statues resembling a building in size, form, or structure, assigned to architecture as figurine or element, scale figure, or caryatid. A static posture of the human body appears as structural mold for an architectural layout or serves as architectural element.

The Enlightenment changes of paradigm and cosmography, shifting the focus from geocentric to heliocentric, envisioning the individual as part of a larger picture, found a resembling in a different view on the interrelation of human and space. The human body thereafter was to be embedded into a larger-scale context. This attempt results in the question of how the body appears in the world and how it interrelates with its context. The body is contained within its life world – architecture is to be considered a vessel to the lively body. A change from static to kinesthetic understanding of space is to be observed in the invention of modern and contemporary dance from the academic ballet. In architecture the resolution of the regulated, determined spatial layout reveals with the introduction of the free floor plan in modernity. This further corresponds with new interrelating tendencies in philosophy and social studies, from which a rather qualitative evaluation of society, behavior, and community arose. Bernard Tschumi has fostered this matter in his architecture theoretical considerations, following the questions: "Can the geometrical spatial concept be replaced by a concept based on one's experience of space? Does the experience of space determine the space of experience?" (Tschumi 1994, 58). A question, which finds a relating counterpart in the ephemeral, kinesthetic and playful spatial installations of Wiliam Forsythe, which encourage the visitors to get engaged with the spatial interventions, adapt them, play with them, change position and perspective, and get out of balance and stability (fig. 1).

Fig. 1: William Forsythe, The Fact of Matter, 2009. Installation view, William Forsythe: Choreographic Objects, the Institute of Contemporary Art, Boston, 2018–19 (Photo: Liza Voll, © William Forsythe)

Procedural Interlacements

The interrelation of architecture and human body – other than convergence in measure or proportion – requires movement in the form of tangibility and a change of perspective. Leading to corporeal and spatial concepts, which oppose the understanding of architecture as a conception of form, proportion, and measure. The studies of Laban mark this changing point for dance, as he was the first to consider a theory on movement rather than on placement, from which body and space become interrelated counterparts, linked to experience through movement.

If the perceptual approach to the world is considered corporeal, perception requires action: "Perception is not something that happens to us, or in us. It is something we do. [...] To be a perceiver is to understand, implicitly, the effects of movement on sensory stimulation." (Noë 2006, 1) The perception of space appears as an embodied, enactive implication. Sensorimotor engagement with space and the inhabiting of architectures are dependent on corporeality, tangibility, and movement. The moving body becomes indispensable as access to the world and the extended corporeal sensorium connects the body with the things of the world: "For our perception and experience of spatial situations, the human body is indispensable to such an extent that 'there would be no space for me at all if I had no body' [Merleau-Ponty 1962, 102] [...] Kinesthetic sensations received through the body condition every perception. Our perceptions of our spatial surroundings must be regarded as a form of corporeal expansiveness. The corporeal sphere expands all the way to objects, and into the depth of the surrounding space" (Janson and Tigges 2014, 37–39). With the phenomenological coined concept of the life world, architecture becomes the framing condition for processes of action.

Considering the perception of spaces to be dependent on sensorimotor experience, architecture and contemporary dance intertwine as disciplinary counterparts. This evokes the suggestion of an interrelation of space perception and the perceptual space; the reach of awareness and the expansion of our individual corporeal space interdepend: "Architecture and movement condition one another reciprocally. The movements needed to perceive a building are dependent upon its spatial structure, while movements shape our perception of it. Our sensory perceptions encompass, in particular, the (proprioceptive) sense of position and the (kinesthetic) sense of movement" (Janson and Tigges 2014, 202).

The procedural interlacements of architecture and contemporary dance thus refer on the one hand to the respective understanding of space and body and the necessity of corporeality for experiencing space. On the other hand, they concern the design process of both disciplines: While the first consideration applies very substantially to space and dance, the second perspective draws significant importance to the work of Sasha Waltz, since it is particularly related to architecture in the process of its development, design, and concretion. Therefore, the artist and choreographer Sasha Waltz, her working method and oeuvre, define the core of this investigation. The dedication to the question of reference and interrelation refers to two different scales: First the general matter of reference, as the body within space either creates a reference point itself or – through perceptual expansion – it reaches out to objects and anchoring points of reference. Second, it raises the question of how to refer to a currently lively productive artist, her working method, and beliefs, as well as her oeuvre and work in progress.

The resembling of Waltz's working method and the creation process of an architect is tremendous: Starting with sketches as tool for communication at an early stage, reconsidering them and précising them throughout the further process, utilizing different scales, dimensions, and practices. As an architecture evolves from the fist abstract sketch through a reconsideration process, using further drawings, models, and mock-ups shifting back and forth in scale, Waltz's dance productions also evolve from this first abstraction through various states of tryouts – both spatially and motional – into the precision of the final work. "Drawings and notes that Waltz used to prepare, outline, and formulate her dance theatre works [...] demonstrated how methodologically Sasha Waltz deploys the methods of a visual artist, using gestural lines and her own sort of material painting to draft ideas about movement in space" (Riedel, Weibel, and Waltz 2014, 6). These characteristic drawing gestures are partly preserved into the final dance work (fig. 2).

Fig. 2: Impromptus 2004 by Sasha Waltz (© Sebastian Bolesch)

Like architecture, her projects are either developed in situ, within a specific context, or in the liberal realm of either studio or stage. Correspondingly to architecture they are either contextual or implemented as alienated pieces to a context. Waltz's oeuvre follows a strict division into "Dialogues" in situ and "Projects" as theater works (figs. 3 and 4).

Fig. 3: Dialog 09, Neues Museum Berlin, 2009, by Sasha Waltz (© Bernd Uhlig)

Fig. 4: noBody 2002 by Sasha Waltz (© Bernd Uhlig)

Further, she creates an in-between scale of body and space, as in the exhibition *Installations, Objects, Performances* at ZKM Karlsruhe (2014), where she brought installation objects to the museum, which either spoke for themselves, showing a contingent potential for activation and action, or were activated by dancers at times. These objects either derived from actual stage installations or were attributed to them, resembling the topic of a theater piece in a different scale (figs. 5 and 6).

Fig. 5: insideout 2003 by Sasha Waltz (© André Rival)

Fig. 6: Stammbaum by Sasha Waltz, exhibition view 2013, Sasha Waltz: Installations, Objects, Performances at ZKM Karlsruhe (© Martin Wagenhan and ZKM | Karlsruhe)

A practice, which is common in architecture as well, in terms of introducing a specific spatial appearance, preconceived in interior models, which can partially or fully be entered; large-scale models, which usually invite the spectator to interact, look, or move inside (fig. 7).

Fig. 7: Peter Zumthor, Model Kolumba, Art Museum of the Archdiocese of Cologne, 2007, exhibition view ground floor, Kunsthaus Bregenz (© Peter Zumthor, Kunsthaus Bregenz, photo: Markus Tretter)

Methodology: Coequal Consideration of Process and Result

This investigation is based on the thesis that contemporary dance and its procedures of corporeal experience and spatial exploration serve as a tool for the anticipation of the impact of architectural spaces in the design process. It therewith corresponds to Franz von Kutschera's understanding of movement possibilities' being the quintessence of spatial experience, as he describes the reciprocal interdependency of spatial configuration and figures of movement (see Kutschera 1998). The more precise principles of movement and bodily space perception are understood, the clearer future impact of architectural designs can be anticipated in the making. For the body in the state of injury and sickness, the effects of architectural spaces are already considered in various studies, whereas such investigations are still lacking for the body in well-being.

Different approaches and working methods are joined to form the methodological framework for this research: A humanist investigation on architecture theory and perception introduces the current status of perception studies. As focal points it addresses varying concepts for the interrelation of space and movement, phenomenological approaches to corporeality and being in the world, as well as the introduction of action and activation to spatial concepts. A phenomenological consideration of the interrelation of body, movement, and space perception is conducted. Waltz's working method and selected works are examined in the sense of a hermeneutic analysis. With a specific focus on the body-related impact of architectural spaces, the reconsideration of corporeal experience is taken into account through an own choreographic practice. Despite the involvement in choreography and dance, the investigation is lead with the expertise and from the perspective of an architect.

The reference to contemporary dance offers – from this perspective – the possibility to regard architectural space as a framework and prerequisite for movement, exploration, appropriation, and action and to examine the resonant relationship between spatial effect and experience. Elaborating the impacts of architecture and its body-related experience with the means of contemporary dance offers the possibility to consider a sensorimotor spatial experience already in the architectural design. The research question that underlies this work is: What insights into the body-related experience of space can be derived from Waltz's choreographic work and her working method and how can principles for a corporeality-related architectural design be derived from it? This corresponds to the acquaintance of phenomenological investigation, since it fosters these interdependencies of body, movement, and space – especially the current of French phenomenologists, as well as new phenomenological theories. According to Westphal, phenomenology plays a special role in the reflection upon space, and the rethinking of spaces, considering the world as staring point, which appears through bodily anchored sensation and corporeal movement (Westphal 2012, 15–16). Considering the being in the world not only a resonate interrelation of human and life world, the interaction and reference between bodies is also to be taken into account. The concept of poetics – especially in the sense Louppe introduced it – is of further reference to this interrelation: The concept of poetics serves the coequal approach to process and product. Louppe considers poetics a qualitative investigation, which aims to outline the sensual, atmospheric or tangible aspects of an artwork. She attributes the poetic approach to a different scheme for the division of labor than the traditional dispositive of sender-message-receiver. She assigns it the potential to open the realm of interaction with a piece of art, as constant wander between the perspective of discourse and practice, perception and implementation (see Louppe 1997). This approach offers the potential for a comparative consideration of dance and architecture in addition to an equal consideration of process and result.

Spatiality of the Body: Corporeality of Space

In the consecutive discussion to the panel of architectural space and human body, the matter of body and space was addressed in relation to sculpture. In contrast to the corporeality of dance, the focus of sculpture is on posing, defining, and materializing objects or bodies in space. The spatiality of the body is foremost irrelevant in that understanding that the sculptural body manifests a position in space creates a specific presence and focal point within it, but does not interfere with it in the sense of a subjective, corporeal interrelation. The impact it has on the space does not influence its being: Through its objectivity it contradicts the enactive, embodied interaction with its surrounding. The body as material physicality is referred to in Waltz's work *Körper* and it becomes most evident in the water basin from *Dido & Aeneas*, where the union of dancers in a containing space, the reciprocal influence of surrounding context – in this case, water – and body become implicit (fig. 8).

Fig. 8: Dido & Aeneas 2005, by Sasha Waltz (© Sebastian Bolesch)

Further it emphasizes the subjectivity of corporeal presence, which values the spatiality of the body to a significant extent. In regard to the body, any interaction with the world relies upon its corporeal spaciousness, be it through movement, expansion of the sensorium, or incorporation of the world into the body as a spatial container. Therewith the interest shifts from the corporeality of space to the spatiality of the body itself. Movement and action become the intertwining common ground for architectural space and human body. From this perspective the theoretical and artistic work of Franz Erhard Walther is an indispensable reference, focusing on the concept of work, body, space, and action: "Der stoffliche Bau begrenzt den Handlungsraum. [...] Der Raum entwickelt sich erst in der Handlung. Dabei fließen die inneren und äußeren Handlungen ineinander. [...] Mein Blick auf die Architektur veränderte sich. Warum sollte man diese nicht aus einer Handlung heraus denken." (The material construction limits the space for action. [...] The space develops only in the action. Thereby the inner and outer actions intertwine. [...] My view on architecture changed. Why not conceive it from an action?) (Walther 2003, 27–28).

Conclusions

The presented work argues that contemporary dance is capable of providing an in-depth knowledge of the principles of body-related spatial experience. It is subsequently assumed that the consideration of contemporary dance – explicitly the work of Sasha Waltz – examined from an architect's perspective, bares the potential to envision future spatial effects.

Taking the reciprocal influence of movement and architecture into account, the concept of space is set to disposition. It is not aimed for a dynamic or kinesthetic understanding of architectural spaces, but this research seeks to implement the potential of action and corporeality to the understanding of architecture. Referring to the work of Waltz, the appearance of architectural space changes tremendously through activation and interaction. The corporeal interference of dancers among each other and within architecture creates ephemeral spatial configurations – affected by the space, being influential for the space. Contemporary dance serves as a tool to highlight and amplify the effects architectural spaces have on the human body. It enables the anticipation of perspective corporeal experiences of architectural spaces in the design process. As a temporary form of artistic expression, contemporary dance offers the possibility of a perception-, experience- and event-oriented confrontation with specific architectural spaces.

References

Janson, Alban, and Florian Tigges. 2014. *Fundamental Concepts of Architecture*. Basel: Birkhäuser. Basel: Birkhäuser.

Kutschera, Franz von. 1998. *Ästhetik*. Berlin: de Gruyter.

Louppe, Laurence. 1997. *Poétique de la danse contemporaine*. Bruxelles: Contredanse.

Merleau-Ponty, Maurice. 1962 [1945]. *Phenomenology of Perception*. London: Routledge & K. Paul.

Noë, Alva. 2006. *Action in Perception*. Cambridge, MA: MIT Press.

Riedel, Christiane, Peter Weibel, and Yoreme Waltz, eds. 2014. *Sasha Waltz: Installations, Objects, Performances*, ZKM Karlsruhe. Berlin: Hatje Cantz.

Tschumi, Bernard. 1994. *Architecture and Disjunction*. Cambridge, MA: MIT Press.

Walther, Franz Erhard. 2003. *Architektur: Vernichtung des Raums*. Klagenfurth: Ritter Verlag.

Westphal, Kristin, ed. 2012. *Räume der Unterbrechung: Theater, Performance, Pädagogik*. Oberhausen: Athena Verlag.

Move to Design, Design to Move

Liselotte Vroman and Thierry Lagrange
Department of Architecture, KU Leuven, Belgium

Abstract — The research identifies a challenge to deepen our understanding of the concept of the embodied experience through practical experiments and aims to enrich our knowledge of spatial qualities. In the hypothesis put forward – drawn from philosopher and former dancer Maxime Sheets-Johnstone's (2011) movement theory – we suggest visualizing, drawing, and reflecting on human movement is a possible strategy to collect new insights on the topic. The paper describes, reflects, and evaluates one specific case, in which there is examined how we can gain better insights into the matter from the perspective of performance arts.

Introduction

This paper is a part of an ongoing design-driven research project in which we inquire the relationship between the human body and space and wherein movement is perceived as one of the most important actions to obtain deeper knowledge on the topic. The research is built upon several (self-)reflective actions within or at the border of the different disciplines (choreography, performance arts, architecture, geography, etc.).[1] In this paper we describe, reflect, and evaluate one specific accomplished action in the field of performance arts. First this action will be situated in a broader context and problem statement of the research, to continue with explaining how this action may fit in an overall method, to finally arrive at describing the condition in which the action took place and how it may contribute to a broader research field. In the last section we will discuss how the described action contributes to the research goals.

The Designed Versus the Built

Built architecture always has an influence on our entire body and all of our body senses (Pallasmaa 2007). In contrast, designed architecture – in the form of images and drawings – only affects our visual experience. This also applies to the architectural design process in which there are barely tools available to really understand the consequence of certain design decisions on the embodied experience, while the designer is considered to properly evaluate the elements and agencies that may determine this experience. Etymologically, design origins from the Italian word *disegnare*, meaning "to draw," which has a double connotation: to draw on paper and to draw forth an idea (Hill 2006). Acting upon this meaning, we could claim that drawing as well as the act of drawing have a prominent place within the discipline of architectural design. Drawing(s) is/are deployed as a thinking tool during a design process as well as to visualize and understand the designed space. The conventional drawing techniques within the discipline of architecture (plans, sections, elevations, and perspectives) usually do not go beyond this visual experience and fail in transmitting the multisensorial experience of the human body in the built architecture. The latter clarifies why it is really difficult or rather impossible to grasp the impact of architectural elements on our embodied experience. An architect has to rely on his/her own embodied knowledge and empathy, wherein sight acts as the most important sense to evaluate unbuilt designs. For this reason, sight is historically judged as the most noble sense within our Western culture (Pallasmaa 2007).

Urbanist and architect Paul Virilio (Virilio et al. 1994) notes that this purely visual way of designing often fails in creating multisensorial architecture, which go beyond a merely visual experience. He argues that "plans and sections reveal no indication of time"; they only represent a fixed state of the proposed geometry. They try to capture objects by using quantitative criteria rather than qualitative aspects.

Above all, we are constantly confronted with images and other visual experiences in our present society, which seems to paralyze somehow our awareness for our other senses. We could ask ourselves whether this phenomenon also increases the distance between our embodied experience and the physical space. Additionally, architectural design processes have been dominated by CAD systems since their introduction in the 1960s. The drawing of the unbuilt architecture is no longer limited to the boundaries of the paper, in which there is always a fixed scale between the body and the drawing. Boundaries are no longer limited to the edges of the sheet of paper but to the unlimited space of the screen. The ability of endless zooming in and out seems to distance our body and the sense of scale and impact even more. The American professor Scott Gartner summarizes this critical point as follows:

"The philosophical alienation of the body from the mind has resulted in the absence of embodied experience from almost all contemporary theories of meaning in architecture. [...] Experience, as it relates to understanding, seems reduced to a matter of the visual registration of coded messages – a function of the eye which might well rely on the printed page and dispense with the physical presence of architecture altogether. [...] Within this framework of

thought, the body and its experience do not participate in the constitution and realization of architectural meaning" (Gartner 1990, 83).

The aim of the research is to foster the understanding of the notion of embodied experience through the act of drawing, in which it is not about representing movement but rather about exposing spatial qualities. Moreover, we aim to derive design strategies originated from the new insights on embodied experience emerged during the course of this research.

Communication through Movement: Drawings, Notations, and Visualizations

The relationship body–space and the consequent embodied experience is approached from the idea that movement – similar to language – is also a means of communication, which may perhaps contain more elementary knowledge than language does. This hypothesis is based upon theory on movement from philosopher and former dancer Maxime Sheet-Johnstone (2011), wherein she states that movement is pre-linguistic and language post-kinetic in its nature. Based upon this statement she clarifies that particular experiences do not even fall into the limitations of language. Consequently, we could question how we may obtain an understanding of the embodied experience if language is not the appropriate medium to communicate about it. Through observation, capturing, and reflection on movement, we hope to gain new insights or at the very least to broaden our knowledge of the latter.

There exists a long history in human movement representation (Marey 1894; Muybridge 1955) as well as in movement notations (Eshkol and Wachmann 1958; Laban and Ullmann 2011; Brown 1975; Benesh and Benesh 1977; Halprin 1969), especially in the discipline of dance. Most of the movement notations were developed to make scores for choreographies, but also to archive, distribute, and analyze dance or body movements in general (Burrows 2000). Although the discipline of architecture is human-centered, these kind of notations or drawings are rather unknown in the field of architecture. Virilio stated that "Space is movement, it is the quality of a volume, and is therefore very difficult to note down" (Virilio et al. 1994, 5). Traditional plans and sections do not measure the aspect of time, while in dance notations both aspects are linked. Virilio believed that dance notations such as Labanotation could inspire architects to qualify space.

The exploration of drawing and visualization techniques for human movement is a main activity within this research. The intention is not to represent what movement is, but rather to expose hidden spatial qualities within the drawing or visualization. Moreover, we presume these movement drawings/visualizations may generate new insights on the matter of embodied experience and are rather deployed as language in order to communicate better about the concept. It is therefore much more about the action than about the final image that is created. The act of drawing/notating/visualizing human movement may reveal different things: on the one hand it shows how the drawer observes and experiences certain movements within a space; on the other, it may exhibit some visual qualities which are presumed to be connected with the quality of the movement or the spatial qualities. By translating the action of movement on paper, a basis on which to reflect appears. Reflection is also an important part of the research, which is explained further in the research method section.

Research Method

The method provided for carrying out the research is based on the learning circles of Kolb (1984). This method comes from educational science and departs from the fact that we learn from experience and reflection on the experiences. It is an iterative process, wherein repetition plays a crucial role. By repeating the learning process several times, the insights on the actions as well as on the proposed research questions became more founded. These learning circles are not exclusively situated at the level of the research but are extrapolated to two additional levels: those of the participants and those of the (self-reflective) practice (fig. 1).

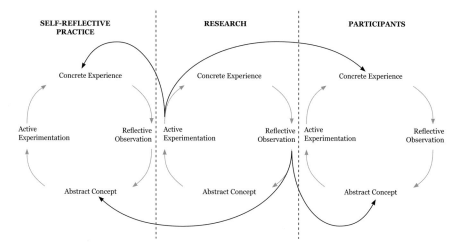

Fig. 1: Interwoven learning circles based on the experiential learning circle of Kolb (1984)
(Figure: authors)

The experiences from which we learn are not limited to the one discipline, namely architecture, but also extend to performance-related disciplines such as dance, performance arts, etc. The concrete experiences upon which we reflect depend on the learning level. At the level of the research this experience mainly exists of active reading on the subject, from which reflections and abstract concepts are created. At the level of the participant, these concrete experiences are more about moving and drawing. Video recordings, drawings, answers to questionnaires, etc., form here the basis for reflection, new insights, and development of abstract concepts. Whereas at the level of the (self-) reflective practice, the architectural design process (that is, imagining and drawing of spaces and objects) is the core activity of this learning circle. The reflection on this experience happens both during and after the process on the basis of self-reflective writings and drawings. With this approach we try to accumulate discipline-related experiential knowledge (Polanyi 1967; Biggs and Karlsson 2011) into new understandings for every concerned discipline.

Action of Participants

The action was set up with second-year bachelor degree performance arts students (a group consisting of twelve students) from KASK (School of Arts Ghent) and can be situated at the level of the participants of the before-mentioned interwoven learning cycles. This action happened during a conventional movement class (duration of 2.5 hours – 6 sessions), wherein the students learn about body awareness, body language, body spatiality, movement qualities, etc. This group of students have an affinity with movement and space, but are not trained to draw. From this point of view, it seems interesting to see how they draw very intuitively while having certain experiential knowledge of the drawn matter.

The research was introduced in the class as an extra layer of knowledge transfer with a focus on observation and (performative) drawing. The purpose of the action was to explore to what extent drawings from performance arts students could shed a different perspective on the matter of space, spatial qualities related to the physical space, and the embodied experience within that specific space.

Before starting each course, the group of students were introduced to the research topic through a short presentation about movement notations and visualizations.[2] A5 sketchbooks were handed out to draw their explorations during the weekly course. Furthermore, the students were only given the limited instruction to draw the movement in relation to the space without falling into a known technique such as a trajectory drawing in top view. Every course started with a warm-up session to free the body and the mind. Each separate session could be perceived as one learning cycle from which reflections lead to new insights for the following sessions. After warming up, the course started with improvisation on a specified movement quality concept introduced by the tutor Paola Bartoletti such as lightness, falling, spiraling, etc.[3] The number of students on stage differed from 1 to 12. Mostly half of the group was drawing while the others were performing. This led to a first series of drawings or rather notational explorations (see fig 2). Both the improvisations and the drawings are part of the concrete experience from the learning circles of the participants.

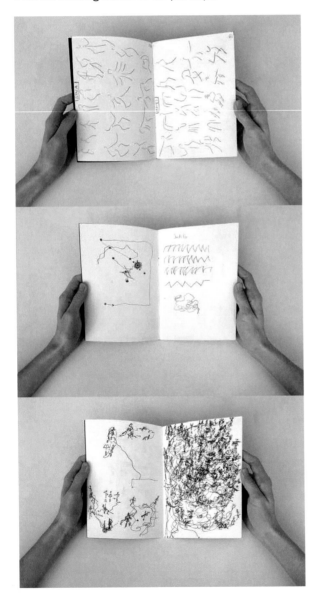

Fig. 2: Selection of first notational explorations, drawings courtesy of the participants
(Photos: authors)

At the end of each course there was a collective oral discussion and a questionnaire was sent to the students in order to reflect on the preceding actions. The following questions popped up from these reflections:

- How to divide the time between drawing and observing?
- What to draw and where to put a focus on: atmosphere, intention, emotion, time, space, trajectory, velocity ...? (notions derived from the reflections of the students)
- How to translate 4-D to 2-D?

As an attempt to provide an answer to the questions, the following concepts arose (fig. 3):

- drawing while performing or body performing while drawing
- drawing without looking at the paper
- drawing what is essential from your own perspective
- using the drawings from previous actions as a score for improvisation

These new concepts led again to new experiences and new drawings to reflect upon from which the process of the learning cycle repeats itself.

Fig. 3: Images from active experimentation of new concepts (Photos: authors)

One of the participants also indicated in her reflections that the physical space was greatly reduced by drawing on A5 size paper. A new space appeared on the size of the paper, which was created by the drawing of body movements in the physical space. From this insight we looked from a wider scope at the outcome – the actions and drawings – and identified they could be placed in an expandable matrix. The scale of the movement and the scale of the impact are placed in relation to each other, which makes it possible to situate the outcome within certain context. This matrix also has a third dimension, being the perspective from which the movement and the impact is approached (fig. 4). In addition, it makes it also possible to plan new upcoming actions in and outside the discipline of performance arts.

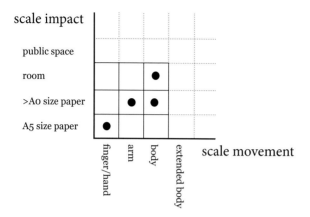

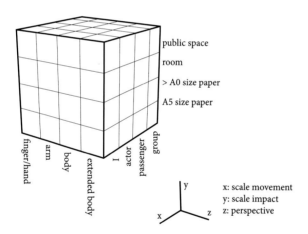

x: scale movement
y: scale impact
z: perspective

*Fig. 4: Expandable matrix in 2-D and 3-D
(Figure: authors)*

Conclusions

This paper shares some initial reflections and insights on the notion of embodied experience from the perceptive of performance artists. The described actions have led to an important foundation for further experimentation within the other two learning circles within this research project. The most important insights originated from these reflections is the layering between the paper space and the physical space, which also leads to the introduction of the expandable matrix. From observation, we could argue that the occurred space on paper probably communicates the embodied experience of the observer next to the embodied experience of the performer. From this act of drawing also initial concepts grew to deal with embodied experience within the domain of performance arts. In this way (performative) drawing was not only deployed as a tool to reflect on movement, but also to generate (or to design) movement. Analogously in the field of architecture, (performative) drawing could be a method to enhance our understanding of the embodied experience in regard to a specific place or space before intervening.

Apart from the different questions derived from the described action, we conclude that actions and reflections of performance students create a different perspective on the concept of embodied experience, both on observing and on understanding. Further sharpening on the actions, but also delineating the domain within the matrix in which we wish to interfere will lead to a better understanding of spatial qualities and embodied experience on different scales (hand, arm, body, and extended body).

Acknowledgments

We would like to thank Paola Bartoletti and her students for their collaboration and contribution to this paper.

References

Benesh, Rudolf, and Joan Benesh. 1977. *Reading Dance: The Birth of Choreology*. London: Souvenir Press.

Biggs, Michael, and Henrik Karlsson. 2011. *The Routledge Companion to Research in the Arts*. Oxon: Routledge.

Burrows, Jonathan. 2000. "Time, Motion, Symbol, Line." *Eye* 37, no. 10: 30–37.

Brown, Trisha. 1975. *Untitled (Locus)*, ink and graphite on paper, 8 pages, 5 pages 12 × 9. In Amanda Jane Graham. "Space Travel: Trisha Brown's Locus." *Art Journal Open* (blog). Accessed March 21, 2019. http://art-journal.collegeart.org/?p=7351.

Eshkol, Noa, and Avraham Wachmann. 1958. *Movement Notation*. London: Weidenfeld and Nicolson.

Gartner, Scott. 1990. "Corporeal Imagination: The Body as the Medium of Expression and Understanding in Architecture." In *The Architecture of the In-Between: Proceedings of the 78th ACSA Annual Conference*, 83–89. Washington, DC: Association of Collegiate Schools of Architecture.

Halprin, Lawrence. 1969. *The RSVP Cycles: Creative Processes in the Human Environment*. New York: Braziller.

Hill, Jonathan. 2006. "Drawing Research." *The Journal of Architecture* 11, no. 3: 329–33.

Hutchinson, Ann. 1970. *Labanotation or Kinetography Laban: The System of Analysing and Recording Movement*. London: Oxford University Press.

Kolb, David A. 1984. *Experiential Learning: Experience as the Source of Learning and Development*. 1st ed. Englewood Cliffs, NJ: Prentice Hall.

Laban, Rudolf, and Lisa Ullmann. 2011. *Choreutics*. Alton: Dance books.

Marey, Etienne-Jules. 1894. *Le mouvement*. Paris: Masson.

Muybridge, Eadweard. 1955. *The Human Figure in Motion*. New York: Dover Publications.

Pallasmaa, Juhani. 2007. *The Eyes of the Skin: Architecture and the Senses.* Chichester: Wiley.

Polanyi, Michael. 1967. *The Tacit Dimension*. London: Routledge and Kegan Paul.

Sheets-Johnstone, Maxine. 2011. *The Primacy of Movement*, exp. 2nd ed. Advances in Consciousness Research (AiCR) 82. Amsterdam: Philadelphia.

Virilio, Paul, Laurence Louppe, René Thom, Jean-Noel Laurenti, and Valérie Preston-Dunlop. 1994. *Traces of Dance: Choreographers' Drawings and Notations*. London: Dis Voir.

----

[1] This is a nonexhaustive list of disciplines. We could argue that this research borders all disciplines that in one way or another are occupied with space and human movement.

[2] Notations and (performative) drawings from Lucinda Childs, Rudolph Von Laban, Morgan O'Hara, Tony Orrico, Heater Hansen, Merce Cunningham, Trisha Brown, Anne Teresa De Keersmaecker, and Lawrence Halprin.

[3] Paola Bartoletti has a bachelor's degree in performing arts as well as a master's in drama. Paola is a teacher at the Academy of Drama in Ghent.

Biographies

Biographies of the Editors

Cornelie Leopold

is teaching and researching in the field of architectural geometry at FATUK, Technische Universität Kaiserslautern, Germany, in the position as academic director and head of the section Descriptive Geometry and Perspective. She received her degree in mathematics, philosophy, and German philology at University of Stuttgart, with specializations in geometry, aesthetics, and philosophy of science. She is a member of the editorial board of the *Nexus Network Journal*, the *Journal for Geometry and Graphics*, and of the scientific committee of the journal *Diségno*. She is the author and editor of several books, and has participated with lectures and reviews in many international conferences, journals, and book series. In 2017, she was a visiting professor at the Università Iuav di Venezia. Her research interests are: architectural geometry and design, visualization of architecture, development of spatial visualization abilities, and the philosophical background of architecture.

Christopher Robeller

leads the Digital Timber Construction group DTC at FATUK, Technische Univerität Kaiserslautern. He has previously worked as a postdoc at the Swiss National Centre of Competence in Research Digital Fabrication dfab at ETH Zurich, as a PhD assistant at the Timber Construction Laboratory IBOIS at EPFL Lausanne, and as a research associate at ICD Stuttgart. Christopher holds a doctor of sciences degree from the Swiss Federal Institute of Technology EPFL, and a professional diploma in architecture with distinction from the London Metropolitan University. His research in innovative timber structures, design for assembly, and digital fabrication is widely published in journals, books, conferences, and exhibitions, and has received awards such as the AAG 2014 best paper. The research has been implemented in experimental structures including the ICD/ITKE pavilion 2010, the 2013 IBOIS curved folded wood pavilion, and the 2018 X-fix Timberdome pavilion, as well as buildings such as the timber-folded plate structure for the 2017 Vidy Theater in Lausanne and the 2018 Multihalle Manternach.

Ulrike Weber

is an art historian educated at the Technische Universität Berlin and Humboldt University Berlin, Germany, and specialized in the fields of medieval architecture and architecture since the nineteenth century. She wrote her PhD dissertation on Modernism in England, researching London's Underground stations of the 1920s and 1930s in the context of architectural transfer within Europe. Therefor she received a scholarship of the County Berlin and the Deutsche Akademische Austauschdienst (DAAD) and was promoted by the Advancement of Science by VG Wort. Since 2009 she is teaching and researching at FATUK, Technische Universität Kaiserslautern, Germany. From 2012 to 2014 she led the research project Projekt Rheinland-Pfalz, focusing on the impact of regional potentials on architectural design. Currently she is concentrating her research on historical constructions, utopian architecture, architectural education, and the geometrical role during the Gothic period.

Biographies of the Authors

Samira Jama Aden
is an architect and design researcher at the research platform Bau Kunst
Erfinden, University of Kassel, Germany and a researcher at the ARC Centre
of Excellence in Exciton Science, Melbourne, Australia. She received her B.A.
at Aachen University of Applied Science and her M.Sc. in Architecture Design
Research at the University of Kassel. Her research concerns the development
of sustainable, highly innovative solar active building materials on an architectural scale. As an architect, she develops concepts and strategies for the
implementation of third-generation solar cells into structures and designs. Her
work combines the principles of renewable energy, sustainable architecture
and materials design with the aesthetic requirements for future buildings.
www.baukunsterfinden.org, www.excitonscience.com, www.samiraaden.com

Zuardin Akbar
is a research associate at the Department of Experimental and Digital
Design and Construction (EDEK), University of Kassel, Germany. He is originally from Indonesia, where he had the chance to study architecture with
strong craftsmanship influences. He holds a master of architecture degree
with distinction from the Bartlett School of Architecture, University College
London (UCL). He won an award from Sir Peter Cook for his graduation
project on high-resolution architectural computation. After the Bartlett,
he worked for Ai Build London in a collaborative project with Zaha Hadid
Design for a robotic 3-D-printed furniture series. In 2017 he moved back to
Southeast Asia and worked as a computational design researcher for the Advanced Architecture Lab at SUTD, Singapore. His current research focuses
on the development of multiscalar modeling and robotic fabrication methods
for a novel additive manufacturing using continuous solid wood fiber.
www.edek.uni-kassel.de

Udo Bach
is a professor at Monash University, the deputy director of the ARC Centre
of Excellence in Exciton Science, and an ANFF-VIC Technology Fellow at the
Melbourne Centre of Nanofabrication (MCN). He received his PhD from the
Swiss Federal Institute of Technology (EPFL, Switzerland) working in the research group of Prof. Michael Grätzel, and worked for three years in a technology start-up company in Dublin (Ireland). Subsequently he spent fifteen
months as a postdoc in the group of Prof. Paul Alivisatos at the University of
California, Berkeley (USA) before moving to Monash University in November

2005 to establish his own research group. He is involved in fundamental and applied research in the area of perovskite and dye-sensitized solar cells. www.udobach.com, www.excitonscience.com

Bahar Al Bahar

is an architect and designer specializing in computational design and robotic fabrication and founder of robo*craft*, based between Stuttgart, Germany, and Dubai, UAE. In 2017 Bahar completed his MSc in integrative technologies and architectural design research at the Institute for Computational Design and Construction at the University of Stuttgart, Germany, where he also worked as a research assistant on several projects of various materials, processes, and scales. Prior to his master's studies, Bahar worked as an independent designer and fabricator in Dubai, developing and realizing his own projects as well as projects of numerous other architects, artists, designers, and fabricators, and exhibiting works at venues including Emirates Palace and Dubai Opera. Through his practice robo*craft*, Bahar is currently developing his work, combining the digital and the analog, the material and the virtual, and following integrative processes, methods, and products for architectural and design manufacturing.

Miro Bannwart

is a Stuttgart-based architect focusing on the exploration of the potential of the application of wood in the contemporary architecture practice. Initially admiration for wooden structures pushed him to become a professional carpenter (EFZ 2009). However, a few years of hands-on experience in the profession and disenchantment with off-the-shelf solutions pushed him to study architecture at BFH/AHB Burgdort in Bern. His special focus lies in the possibilities of applications of computational tools in the design and assembly processes of complex-geometry timber structures. He initiated the construction of the experimental Gravitational Pavilion, exploring the interdependence of complexity and buildability in free-form structures. Currently Miro is deepening his skills in robotic fabrication of timber structures by participating in the ITECH (Integrative Technologies Architectural Design Research) master's program at the University of Stuttgart. He deeply believes that wood and the combination of traditional methods and computational design workflows are the future of architecture and that they will play a crucial part in answering contemporary sustainability challenges.

Simon Bechert

is a structural engineer and research associate at the Institute of Building Structures and Structural Design (ITKE) at the University of Stuttgart. His research focuses on the development of building systems, connection strategies, and integral structural design processes for segmented timber shell structures. Simon researches structurally informed lightweight timber plate structures within projects that explore advanced computational design strategies for resource-effective and robotically fabricated building systems. Applying this research, he led the structural design effort of innovative lightweight structures such as the Wood Pavilion for the Bundesgartenschau 2019 in Heilbronn (Germany) and the Urbach Tower at the Landesgartenschau 2019 in Urbach (Germany). As an author, Simon has published in international journals and conference proceedings, and given lectures at numerous international conferences in architectural design and structural engineering.

Michal Berkowitz

is a postdoctoral researcher at the Chair for Research on Learning and Instruction at ETH Zurich. She studied psychology at Tel-Aviv University and began her career in clinical psychology. She later moved on to research in cognitive psychology and obtained her doctoral degree in 2017 at the Chair for Research on Learning and Instruction at ETH Zurich. Her research focuses on cognitive predictors of advanced STEM achievements, the role of spatial ability in STEM learning in general, and the link between spatial ability and mathematics in particular. She has also studied links between working memory, cognitive abilities, and academic achievements among higher-education STEM students.

Stefan Böhm

studied electrical engineering and automation at the Technische Universität Darmstadt. He received his doctorate in mechanical engineering at the RWTH Aachen with the dissertation "Simulation and Modeling of the Electron Beam Welding Process under Consideration of Electron Reflection and Scattering." In 2003 he became the head of the Chair for Micro Joining at the Technische Universität Braunschweig. Since 2010 he is the head of the Department of Cutting and Joining Manufacturing Processes at the University of Kassel. One of his research focuses is the use of wood as a technical material in mechanical and civil engineering. Here both the production of wood-based multimaterial systems and the joining to structures are of interest. www.tff-kassel.de

Sigrid Brell-Cokcan

cofounded the Association for Robots in Architecture in 2010 with the goal of making industrial robots accessible to the creative industry. Toward that goal, the Association is developing innovative software tools such as KUKA|prc (parametric robot control) and initialized the Rob|Arch conference series on robotic fabrication in architecture, art, and design. Robots in Architecture is a KUKA System Partner and has been validated as a research institution by national and international research agencies such as the European Union's FP7 program. Recently, Sigrid founded the Chair for Individualized Production in Architecture (IP) at RWTH Aachen University and a new scientific journal on construction robotics in cooperation with euRobotics. Her work has been widely published in peer-reviewed scientific journals, international proceedings, and books, as well as being featured in formats such as *Wired*, *Gizmodo*, FAZ, and RBR.

Oliver Bucklin

is a research associate and doctoral candidate at the Institute for Computational Design and Construction at the University of Stuttgart. Oliver holds a master in architecture degree from the Harvard Graduate School of Design, as well as a bachelor of fine arts degree in ceramics from the University of Washington. Experience at the Harvard Center for Green Buildings and Cities led to an interest in scientific approaches to architectural design. Current research investigates embedded electronics and custom mechanics, including mobile robotics and integrating computational intelligence in industrial processes. He has had extensive experience in the United States in general construction and woodworking, and is currently involved in the Performative Wood group at the ICD.

Lucas Büscher

is a horticulturist and studied landscape architecture and landscape planning at the University of Kassel. Since 2015 he is a research assistant, PhD student, and lecturer in the Department of Landscape Architecture/Technology, University of Kassel. He is an elected member of the Directorate of the Institute for Landscape Architecture and Landscape Planning since 2017; in 2019 he cofounded the research center Klimadynamik, Raum + Objekt (KliRO). His research on concrete habitat focuses on the functionalization of concrete in context of vertical green, targeted vegetation, and vegetation dynamic on extreme sites and substrate development. Under the premise of sustainable planning, his research interests focus on technology and construction in landscape architecture, climate, and object, vegetation on extreme sites, and the aesthetics of synergies: the transfer of everyday infrastructure and technical necessity into spatial and design quality ranking.

Corneel Cannaerts

is an architect and postdoctoral researcher interested in the impact of emerging technologies on the culture and practice of architecture. He has obtained a master's in architectural engineering from the University of Ghent in 2004 and a PhD in architecture from SIAL, RMIT University Melbourne in 2015. He is currently researching and lecturing at the KU Leuven Faculty of Architecture. He was a guest researcher at the Architectural Robotics and Computation Lab of the Aarhus School of Architecture in 2017. His research and work have been presented, published, and exhibited and he has lectured and taught workshops internationally. He cofounded MMlab, a digital fabrication lab at KU Leuven Faculty of Architecture, and is a member of the fieldstations network, a nonprofit organization exploring models for architecture in the Anthropocene and the technosphere.

Luigi Cocchiarella
is associate professor at the Department of Architecture and Urban Studies (DASTU) of the Politecnico di Milano. His research lines deal with history, methods, and techniques of geometric and graphic representation of space and their applications to the architectural design processes, with special re-gard to projective methods and their links with digital graphics procedures, including the educational implications in terms of teaching and learning goals. He teaches at the School of Architecture, Urban Planning, Construc-tion, Engineering (AUIC), and he is a member of the Teaching Board of the PhD program in architectural, urban and interior design at the Politecnico di Milano, where he is also responsible for Erasmus Exchanges with European and extra-EU universities. His portfolio includes more than 150 publications, including books, articles on scientific reviews, papers in proceedings, and editorship of volumes.

Renate Delucchi Danhier
is a linguist and holds a PhD from Heidelberg University. In her thesis she compared the organization of spatial information in Spanish and German route directions. She studied linguistics and archaeology, majoring in Egyp-tology. Her interest in dead languages such as Middle Egyptian has shifted in the last years to conlangs such as Quenya and Dothraki. She currently teaches linguistics at the TU Dortmund University and is part of the team of the Psycholinguistics Laboratories. In her research she explores language relativity effects and the mental management of different expertise (native language, profession, etc.). She enjoys developing new experimental para-digmata (mainly using eye-tracking) and has specialized in the use of novel visualizations for multidimensional analysis of linguistic data. She lives in Dortmund surrounded by *tsundoku* – a big pile of unfinished books.

Martin Dembski
displayed interest – and talent – for art, design, and nature. In his design-driven architectural studies at the Bauhaus University Weimar he was able to refine and expand his skills. Here he specialized in complex geometries;

adaptive, parametric, and generative systems, CAD, and CAAD, as well as digital analysis and simulation techniques. As a research assistant at the Bauhaus University Weimar in the professorships of computer science in architecture under the direction of Prof. Dr.-Ing. Dirk Donath and Vertr.-Prof. Dr.-Ing. Reinhard König and structural engineering under the direction of Prof. Dr.-Ing. Jürgen Ruth he gained insights into research and accumulated experience as a teacher. After completing his studies in 2014, he became a member of the research project fhoch3 at the University of Applied Sciences Leipzig, which was successfully completed in 2016, and is currently assigned to the research project ReFlexRoof.

Christian Derix
is a principal of Woods Bagot and the Global Leader of SUPERSPACE, the design research agency of Woods Bagot. SUPERSPACE develops human-centric spatial environments simulating user experience employing data analysis, cognitive science, and machine learning. SUPERSPACE has been a pioneer in computational design since 2004, when Derix set up the first global professional computational design group, at Aedas in London, to focus on users and spatial design. The work of the group won awards in various domains such as the 2010 President's Medal commendation of the Royal Institute of British Architects (RIBA) for Research in Practice for its Open Framework for Spatial Simulation or the 2011 Compasso d'Oro Honorary Mention for the interactive and generative web-based furniture system called VITA.
Derix holds a PhD from the TU Wien and has been teaching at various European universities, completing visiting professorships at the Technical University of Munich, Germany, and University of Sheffield, United Kingdom. In 2002 he helped to establish the Centre for Evolutionary Computing in Architecture (CECA) at the University of East London with Paul Coates.

Cristoph Dijoux
completed his master's in structural engineering at the HTWK Leipzig in 2015, supplementing it with an internship at ifb-berlin and one year of international experience in Istanbul. Since then he has been working for FLEX on experiments with timber construction for the current scientific collaboration of Prof. Dr.-Ing. Alexander Stahr at the HTWK Leipzig, and has worked for two years on the successfully completed MVK – micro offset node project. He is currently a doctoral student and is researching with Prof. Dr.-Ing. Peer Haller (Technische Universität Dresden) and Prof. Dr.-Ing. Alexander Stahr (HTWK Leipzig) on shell structures in timber construction.

José Pinto Duarte

holds a professional degree in architecture from the Technical University of Lisbon, Portugal, a master's degree in design methods, and a PhD in design and computation from the Massachusetts Institute of Technology, USA. Currently, he is Chair in Design Innovation and director of the Stuckeman Center for Design Computing at Penn State University, USA. He was dean and professor at the Faculty of Architecture, University of Lisbon, and President of eCAADe – Education and Research in Computer-aided Architectural Design in Europe. The main focus of his research is the use of new technologies as conceptual tools in architectural, urban, and product design.

Beatrix Emo

is a practicing architect and director of Spatialist Arch. She holds a PhD from the Bartlett School of Architecture, University College London, in which she explored how individuals experience urban spaces. She is currently a lecturer at the Chair of Cognitive Science, ETH Zurich, an interdisciplinary group where she leads the focus on how people interact with the environment. Her interests lie in urban design, space syntax, and spatial cognition. She has experience conducting behavioral experiments in real and virtual environments, and works with augmented reality tools such as HoloLens. Beatrix is a recipient of the ETH Career Seed Grant for the project Human-Centered Urban Design: Analyzing Pedestrians' Perceived Density of Public Space. She is guest lecturer at the Institute for the History and Theory of Architecture (gta), ETH Zurich, at the Bartlett School of Architecture, UCL, and at the Faculty of Architecture (fatuk), Technische Universität Kaiserslautern.

Philipp Eversmann

is a registered architect in Munich and a professor at the University of Kassel, where he directs the Department of Experimental and Digital Design and Construction (EDEK). He was head of Education at the National Center of Competence in Research NCCR Digital Fabrication at ETH Zurich, where he created a new master's program focused on robotic technologies in architecture. As a visiting professor, he directed architectural research classes at the EPF Lausanne, at the Ecole Spéciale d'Architecture in Paris, and at the Technical University of Munich. He is an architect with a wide range of interdisciplinary experiences through his collaboration in various large-scale projects with architecture practices in France and Germany. In his independent practice, he explores digital design principles in a range of different projects, competitions, and structures. His work is based on establishing spatial connections by combining systems of associative geometry with effects of architectural perception and computational fabrication technology. www.edek.uni-kassel.de, www.eversmann.fr

Maria da Piedade Ferreira

is an award-winning architect and researcher. Her research is focused on the topic of human-centered design, particularly on the connections between architecture, art, neuroscience, and cognitive science. Her PhD thesis, "Embodied Emotions: Observations and Experiments in Architecture and Corporeality" presents the foundations of her research and coins her concept of corporeal architecture. Her work has been published and presented in international journals and venues, such as the Academy for Neuroscience and Architecture (ANFA) 2016 conference. Her practice is continued in academia and focused on developing corporeal awareness in future architects/designers, raising consciousness about how the built environment directly shapes our body/mind and how design can be used to promote health and feelings of well-being. Since 2019, she is the founder of the collaborative design platform Corporeal Architecture. https://corporeal.persona.co

Augusto Gandia

received his diploma in architecture urbanism at the University of Mendoza, Argentina. He received a grant for further studies from the DAAD that allowed the completion of a master of science degree in media-architecture at the Bauhaus-University Weimar, Germany. He has worked for different architecture offices around the world, including Argentina, the United States, Spain, and Germany. After briefly collaborating at Design-to-Production in Stuttgart, he joined Gramazio Kohler Research and ETH Zurich to support the project Aerial Constructions and later as a PhD researcher of the NCCR Digital Fabrication as part of the project Robotic Fabrication Simulation for Spatial Structures. His investigation focuses on the relationship between computational design and the previsualization of architectural fabrication processes, more specifically, on the development of simulation-based computational methods and tools for supporting the fabrication-aware design of robotically assembled structures with discrete elements.

Federico Garrido

studied architecture at FADU-UBA in Buenos Aires, Argentina. He also attended postgraduate master studies in advanced architectural design at the FADU-UBA, where he held scholarships and several teaching and research positions in graduate and postgraduate programs. From 2014 to 2018 he held a DAAD research scholarship pursuing a PhD at the Technische Universität Kaiserslautern with a thesis entitled "Innovative Design Strategies: The Case of Eclectic Architecture in Buenos Aires, 1880–1930" focusing on the relationship between manufacturing techniques and design strategies during the nineteenth century and its reinterpretation under the light of contemporary digital tools. Since 2014 he collaborates with the research project

Rokokorelevanz (Prof. Lucas Merx) and Joost Meyer at the Chair for Visual Arts at RWTH Aachen exploring the role of manual and digital tools in architecture and design, with a strong emphasis on digital modeling, algorithmic design, and digital fabrication tools.

Dominga Garufi
is an architect and designer committed to integrate construction industry, innovation in material research, and computational design strategies in architecture. She graduated from the ITECH master's program at the University of Stuttgart in 2017 and from the SED master's program at the AA in London in 2015, after completing her bachelor studies in architecture and construction engineering in Italy. Dominga worked at Wilkinson Eyre Architects and Hawkes Architects in England, and also as an architect with a focus on BIM coordination at HPP Architekten in Stuttgart. In 2018 she taught the workshop "Fibrous Timber Joints" at the *Smart Geometry* conference at the University of Toronto. She is currently working as an architect at Werner Sobek Design in Stuttgart.

Andri Gerber
is an architectural and planning historian and an urban metaphorologist. He studied architecture at the ETH Zurich and was a project architect and project manager for Peter Eisenman in New York. In 2008 he received his doctorate from the ETH Zurich, for which he was awarded the ETH Medal. From 2008 to 2011 he was an assistant professor at the Ecole spéciale d'architecture in Paris. Since 2011 he has been a lecturer and since 2017 a professor in urban planning history at the Zurich University of Applied Sciences (ZHAW). He completed his habilitation in 2016 at the ETHZ's gta Institute, funded by an SNSF Ambizione Scholarship. Gerber has been a visiting professor and is private lecturer at the ETHZ since August 2017. His research interest turns around space and metaphors, specifically from a cognitive perspective.

Jürgen Graf
is a registered engineer and has been a professor of structural engineering and material at the Department of Architecture at the Technische Universität Kaiserslautern, Germany since 2013. He is a founding member and the spokesman of the research institute T-Lab Timber Architecture and Wood Materials. He studied civil engineering and received his doctoral degree in 2002 with a thesis about design and construction of translational net shells at the University of Stuttgart. He was a professor of building technology and structural engineering at the University of Applied Sciences Munich in 2012. Jürgen Graf's research, teaching, and practice concentrates on sufficient timber construction methods.

Fabio Gramazio

is an architect with multidisciplinary interests ranging from computational design and robotic fabrication to material innovation. In 2000 he founded the architecture practice Gramazio & Kohler in conjunction with his partner Matthias Kohler, where numerous award-wining designs have been realized. Current projects include the design of the Empa NEST research platform, a future living and working laboratory for sustainable building construction. Opening also the world's first architectural robotic laboratory at ETH Zurich, Gramazio Kohler Research has been formative in the field of digital architecture, setting precedents and de facto creating a new research field merging advanced architectural design and additive fabrication processes through the customized use of industrial robots. This ranges from 1:1 prototype installations to the design of robotically fabricated high-rises. His recent research is outlined and theoretically framed in the book *The Robotic Touch: How Robots Change Architecture* (Park Books, 2014).

Charlott Greub

is an artist, architect, and urban designer, educated at the Kunstakademie Düsseldorf, Germany, who had received many fellowships and awards, among them the Cité des Arts Paris, France, and the Akademie Schloss Solitude, Stuttgart, Germany. Her work has been exhibited at Gallery Aedes Berlin; the German Architecture Museum DAM, Frankfurt; and the Lehmbruck Museum Duisburg, Germany. Currently, she is as an assistant professor for architecture at North Dakota State University in Fargo, USA. Previously she taught design studios in architecture and art at the University of Utah, USA; the Bauhaus University in Weimar, Germany; and the Graz University of Technology, Austria. She is licensed as an architect in Germany since 1993 and has practiced internationally as an architect in New York City (USA), Maastricht (Netherlands), and Berlin (Germany). Since 2015 she is a PhD candidate at the RWTH University in Aachen, Germany, where she conducts research about the pavilion as a new genre between art and architecture.

Abel Groenewolt

studied architecture and building technology at Eindhoven University of Technology. After having received his MSc degree, he worked at K2S Architects and at Sarc Architects in Helsinki as well as in his own practice, completing projects in both Finland and the Netherlands. He has employed computational methods in various design projects and developed multiple custom design tools. Through postgraduate studies at ETH Zurich, he further explored computation as an architectural design tool. Before joining the Institute for Computational Design and Construction at the University of Stuttgart in 2015, Abel worked as a researcher at the Chair of Architecture and

Building Systems at ETH Zurich, developing and employing computational design tools to analyze and optimize various energy-related building systems. He also worked as a plug-in developer for Design-to-Production. Currently, his research focuses on the development and analysis of segmented timber shell structures.

Jannis Heise

is an industrial engineer who studied at Ostfalia University of Applied Science Wolfsburg, Germany, and the University of Kassel, Germany. Since 2017 he is part of the Department for Cutting and Joining Manufacturing Processes, University of Kassel. At the institute he conducts research in the field of wood-based multimaterial systems and micro joining of wood with narrow cross sections. Within the scope of his activity, Heise is part of the cooperative research project TETHOK – Textile Tectonics for Wood Construction among six departments at the University of Kassel in the fields of architecture, civil engineering, and mechanical engineering.

Matthias Helmreich

is an architect and currently a research assistant at the Chair of Architecture and Digital Fabrication at ETH Zurich. His research includes the development of computational design and fabrication tools in virtual reality and the implementation of robots in the prefabrication of large-scale timber structures. At Gramazio Kohler Research Matthias has worked on numerous research projects including Spatial Timber Assemblies, Robotic Cosmogony, and currently the acoustic walls at Basler Hofmann. He supervises postgraduate students in the associated research fields and has recently led a seminar week at ETH on virtual reality in architecture and construction. Matthias has been educated at the HBC Biberach, Tsinghua University Beijing, and the University of Stuttgart and has completed his postgraduate at ETH Zurich with a specialization in architecture and digital fabrication in 2016. Professionally he has worked as an architect at MAD Office in Beijing, China, and at Gramazio Kohler Architects in Zurich, Switzerland.

Michael Hensel

Univ. Prof. Dr. Michael U. Hensel is an architect. He codirects OCEAN Architecture | Environment with Dr. Defne Sunguroğlu Hensel. He was founding and acting chairman of OCEAN – Design Research Association and OCEAN | SEA – Sustainable Environment Association, and a board member of BIONIS – the Biomimetics Network for Industrial Sustainability. Since 2018 he is professor at the TU Wien, where he heads the Department for Digital Architecture and Planning. He taught at the Architectural Association School of Architecture in London, Rice University, the Technical University of Munich (where he was an honorary fellow at the Institute of Advanced Study), and he was founding and acting director of the Research Centre for Architecture and Tectonics at the Oslo School of Design. He has authored and edited numerous books including *Performance-oriented Architecture* (Wiley, 2013), *Grounds and Envelopes*, with Jeffrey P. Turko (Routledge, 2015), *The Changing Shape of Practice* (2016), and *The Changing Shape of Architecture* (2019), both with Fredrik Nilsson.

Holger Hoffmann
is a registered architect and founder of one fine day. office for architectural design, based in Düsseldorf, Germany. He holds a professorship for techniques of representation and design at the University of Wuppertal since 2011. From 2007 to 2011 he led the Department for Digital Design at the University of Applied Sciences in Trier, Germany. Holger gained professional expertise at UNStudio, Amsterdam, (2002–2008) and Bolles+Wilson, Münster (2000–2001). He received a postgraduate diploma in 2004 from the Städelschule (SAC), Frankfurt, and he holds a professional degree in architecture from the Münster School of Architecture (MSA), Germany. Before studying architecture, he worked for two years as a mason apprentice. His work has been published and exhibited internationally, and he has been awarded with, among others, a scholarship by the Konrad Adenauer Stiftung and the Taut Preis 2005 of the German Architects Chamber. He is a member of the Bund Deutscher Architekten (BDA).

Christoph Hölscher
is a full professor of cognitive science in the D-GESS at ETH Zurich since 2013, with an emphasis on applied cognitive science. Since 2016 Christoph has been a principal investigator at the Singapore ETH Center (SEC) Future Cities Laboratory, heading a research group on Cognition, Perception and Behavior in Urban Environments. He holds a PhD in psychology from the University of Freiburg, and has served as honorary senior research fellow at UCL, Bartlett School of Architecture, and as a visiting professor at Northumbria University Newcastle. He has several years of industry experience in human-computer interaction and usability consulting. The core mission of his research groups in Zurich and Singapore is to unravel the complex interaction of humans and their physical, technical, and social environment with an emphasis on cognitive processes and task-oriented behavior.

David Jenny
is an architect and designer with a strong background in digital fabrication and computational methods. He holds a bachelor of science in architecture from the EPF Lausanne (study exchange at the University of Tokyo) and a master

of science in architecture from ETH Zurich, where his diploma project on algorithmic methods for housing design was awarded with the SIA master prize. He has worked in several architectural offices in Switzerland and Japan and as a researcher at the Future Cities Laboratory in Singapore. Since 2015 he has been a research assistant at Gramazio Kohler Research, teaching courses in the Master of Architecture curriculum and since 2016 leading the teaching projects of the postgraduate program MAS ETH in digital fabrication.

Muhammad Kalim Kashif
is a postdoctoral fellow at Monash University, Australia, in the research group of Prof. Udo Bach. His research focuses on the design and synthesis of electroactive materials and toward the fundamental understanding of their charge transport properties and subsequent applications in energy devices. Dr. Kashif did his PhD under the supervision of Prof. Udo Bach and the late Prof. Leone Spiccia. He did his MPhil studies under the supervision of Prof. Shahid Hameed at Quaid-i-Azam University, Pakistan. www.udobach.com, www.excitonscience.com

Reiner Klopfer
studied wood engineering at the Faculty of Architecture, Engineering, and Conservation in Hildesheim, graduating in 1995. After seven years working as an scientific assistant at the Deutsches Zentrum für Handwerk und Denkmalpflege e.V in Fulda, he founded his own expert office, holzansicht, in 2002. In 2001 the Chamber of Industry and Commerce officially appointed and attested him as technical expert for wood damage and wood protection. He is a member of the International Association for Science and Technology of Building Maintenance and Monuments Preservation (WTA) and contributes his experience in various working groups. Since 2008 he has taught as an assistant lecturer in the master's degree course "Old Building Renovation" at the Karlsruhe Institute of Technology (KIT). Since 2014 he works as technical assistant at the Faculty of Architecture, Structure and Material at the Technische Universität Kaiserslautern, Germany. His work focuses on hardwood research, modified wood, and the monitoring of weathered wooden structures.

Heike Klussmann
is a professor of art and architecture at the University of Kassel, where she directs the Bau Kunst Erfinden research group, which is dedicated to the development of innovative materials systems at the convergence of art, architecture, and new technologies. She has taught and conducted research at numerous institutions including the Art Center College of Design, Pasadena (USA), Monash University, Melbourne (AUS), and the ARC Centre of Excellence in Exciton Science, and has received numerous international awards,

among others the iF Material Gold Award for outstanding materials research and design achievement, the German Design Prize, the World Architecture Award, the Design Plus Award, the International Tunnelling and Underground Space Award, and the Higher Education Prize for Teaching Excellence. Furthermore, she conceived the overall concept for the new metro Wehrhahn Line in Düsseldorf with six unique stops in collaboration with netzwerkarchitekten, where art, architecture, and engineering are inseparably bound to one another. www.baukunsterfinden.org, www.excitonscience.com

Jan Knippers

was born in Düsseldorf and completed his academic studies of structural engineering at the Technische Universität Berlin in 1992 with the award of a PhD. After that he worked for a few years in an internationally recognized engineering firm. Since 2000 he is head of the Institute for Building Structures and Structural Design (ITKE) at the Faculty for Architecture and Urban Design at the University of Stuttgart. In 2001 he cofounded, together with Thorsten Helbig in Stuttgart, Knippers Helbig Advanced Engineering; and in 2018 Jan Knippers Ingenieure. Knippers focuses on efficient structural design for international and architecturally demanding construction projects involving solid timber, steel, and glass constructions. He specializes in the design of complex-shaped and highly efficient roof and facade structures, as well as in research and development on the use of fiber-based materials and biomimetic structures in architecture.

Daniel Kohl

is an industrial engineer and economist who studied the key aspects of quality and process management, supply chain management, private and public management, and material engineering at the University of Kassel. Since February 2011 he works at the Department for Cutting and Joining Manufacturing Processes at the University of Kassel. Here he focuses on research in wood-based multimaterial systems and adequate joining techniques. He initiated and managed several projects on these topics and is the actual head of the Division of Wood-based Materials. In addition, he is a private lecturer for different courses at universities and external institutions. Furthermore, Daniel Kohl has practical experience with the introduction and implementation possibilities of Six Sigma in small and medium-sized enterprises as well as in management consultancy and training. www.tff-kassel.de

Matthias Kohler

is an architect with multidisciplinary interests ranging from computational design and robotic fabrication to material innovation. In 2000 he founded the architecture practice Gramazio & Kohler in conjunction with his partner

Fabio Gramazio, where numerous award-wining designs have been realized. Current projects include the design of the Empa NEST research platform, a future living and working laboratory for sustainable building construction. Opening also the world's first architectural robotic laboratory at ETH Zurich, Gramazio Kohler Research has been formative in the field of digital architecture, setting precedents and de facto creating a new research field merging advanced architectural design and additive fabrication processes through the customized use of industrial robots. This ranges from 1:1 prototype installations to the design of robotically fabricated high-rises. His recent research is outlined and theoretically framed in the book *The Robotic Touch: How Robots Change Architecture* (Park Books, 2014). From 2014 to 2017 Matthias Kohler was director of the National Centre of Competence in Research (NCCR) Digital Fabrication.

Toni Kotnik

is a professor of design of structures at Aalto University in Helsinki, Finland. He studied architecture, mathematics, and computational design in Germany, Switzerland, and the United States and received his doctoral degree from the University of Zurich. Before joining Aalto, he taught among others at the ETH in Zurich, the Architectural Association in London, the Institute for Experimental Architecture at the University of Innsbruck, and the Singapore University of Technology and Design. He has been lecturing at universities worldwide as well as at museums like the Guggenheim in Bilbao or the Museum of Modern Art in New York. His practice and research work has been published and exhibited internationally, including at the Venice Biennale, and is centered on the integration of knowledge from science and engineering into architectural design thinking and the exploration of organizational principles and formal methods as a design driver at the intersection of art and science.

Bettina Kraus

studied architecture at the ETH Zurich, the Berlin University of the Arts, and the University of Stuttgart from which she received her diploma in 1996. From 1997 to 2012 she worked with Wiel Arets Architects, initially in Maastricht. She became a partner in 2000 and was put in charge of setting up a new office in Amsterdam. In 2013 she moved back to Germany to cofound the architectural practice Thomas Baecker Bettina Kraus in Berlin. She was an assistant professor at the Berlin University of the Arts between 2004 and 2010. After that, she was in charge of the design program at the Berlin Studio of Northeastern University between 2011 and 2014. Thereafter until 2017 she headed the Chair of Architectural Design and Building in Context at the BTU Cottbus. In this connection the publication *Werkstücke: Making*

Objects into Houses was released. Since 2017 she has led the Chair of Architectural Design and Construction at the Technische Universität Berlin.

Andreas Kretzer

studied architecture at the Technical University of Munich and scenography at the University of Television and Film Munich. After teaching at the Technische Universität Darmstadt and a professorship at the Technische Universität Kaiserslautern from 2011 to 2017, Andreas Kretzer is a visiting professor at the Technical University of Munich and a professor at the Faculty of Architecture and Design at the University of Applied Sciences Stuttgart. The community center in the refugee shelter Spinelli Mannheim that was built in 2016 as a design-build project with students from TU Kaiserslautern by the consortium Krötsch Graf Kretzer was nominated for the DAM Prize 2018 – Shortlist and the European Union Prize for Contemporary Architecture – Mies van der Rohe Award 2019, and was awarded the Students of the Year 2017, Heinze Architekten AWARD 2017 – Young Talent Award, The Erskine Award 2017, and the Prize for Timber Construction Baden-Württemberg 2018 – Special Prize Building Culture.

Oliver David Krieg

is an expert in computational design and digital fabrication in architecture. As Chief Technology Officer at Intelligent City in Vancouver, Canada, and doctoral candidate at the Institute for Computational Design and Construction at the University of Stuttgart, Germany, his work aims to enable reciprocities among design, technology, and materiality in order to reconceptualize how architecture can be designed, fabricated, and constructed. With a profound interest in computational design processes and robotic fabrication in architecture, Oliver has led and participated in several research and built projects around the world that explore new potentials in timber construction. He recently joined LWPAC and Intelligent City for the development of bespoke digital design and manufacturing methods for multistory, high-rise timber construction. In 2018 he founded the design label and explorative platform odk.design.

Stefan Krötsch

is a certified architect and cofounder of the Munich-based architectural office Braun Krötsch Architekten. He is a professor for construction and architectural design at the University of Applied Sciences in Constance since 2018. He studied architecture at the Technical University of Munich and received his diploma in 2001. From 2008 to 2014 he worked as an academic council at the Professorship of Architectural Design and Timber Construction, Prof. Hermann Kaufmann, Technical University of Munich.

From 2015 to 2018 he led the newly founded Department of Tectonics in Timber Construction, Faculty of Architecture at the Technische Universität Kaiserslautern. Together with Hermann Kaufmann and Stefan Winter he is coauthor of the 2017 published *Manual of Multi-Storey Timber Construction*.

Stefan Kurath

is professor for architecture and design in the School of Architecture and is head of the Institute of Urban Landscape at ZHAW, together with Regula Iseli. He studied architecture at universities in Switzerland and the Netherlands. In 2010 he received a doctoral degree at HafenCity University in Hamburg (summa cum laude). He has published several books and articles about architecture, urban design, and urban cultures. Together with Peter Jenni he was the winner of the CS-ZHAW Award for best teaching in 2013. In addition to his scientific research, he leads his own practice for architecture and urban design: urbaNplus/Stefan Kurath/GmbH in Zurich, and he is a partner at Iseppi-Kurath GmbH in Grison.

Thierry Lagrange

is the coordinator of the Master of Architecture program of the KU Leuven Faculty of Architecture, where he teaches architectural design in his master dissertation studio (together with Prof. Johan Van Den Berghe), which is an incubator for doctoral research out of which a number of PhDs have been initiated. Together with Dr. Dimitri Vangrunderbeek he teaches architectural design in his experimental studio The Double Look – Abstraction. He works as a researcher in the field of New Spatialities at the KU Leuven Department of Architecture, where he founded the research group The Drawing and the Space with Prof.dr.arch. Jo Van Den Berghe (www.thedrawingandthespace. info). In his current design-driven research he is developing new spatialities, so-called analogous spaces, wherein intangible and mental elements become explicit. Graduated from University of Ghent, MSc in civil engineering architecture and obtained a PhD ("Look Here Now: Mapping Design Trajectories") in 2013 at the Faculty of Architecture KU Leuven. He is a practitioner-architect in Belgium since 1997 (www.alt-architectuur.be) and a photographer (www.thierrylagrange.com).

Samuel Leder

is currently a doctoral candidate at the Institute for Computational Design and Construction (ICD) through the Cluster of Excellence: Integrative Computational Design and Construction for Architecture (IntCDC) at the University of Stuttgart. He holds a bachelor of design in architecture, summa cum laude, as well as a bachelor of applied science in systems science and engineering, magna cum laude, from Washington University in St. Louis.

He received an MSc in architecture with distinction through the Integrative Technologies and Architectural Design Research (ITECH) program at the University of Stuttgart, during which he was a recipient of both the German Academic Exchange Service (DAAD) Award for Outstanding Achievement and the Deutschlandstipendium. Professionally, Sam has worked as a junior architect in Munich, Germany, and as a designer at a graphic design/branding firm outside of San Francisco, CA.

Luyi Liu

graduated in 2006 from the Department of Architecture, Harbin Institute of Technology, China. She has more than seven years of professional experience in China as an architect. Now she is PhD student at the Department of Architecture and Urban Studies (DASTU) of the Politecnico di Milano, Italy. Her research lines deal with the history and methods of ancient Chinese spatial phenomena, seeking to reveal some misunderstood and ignored cognitions and techniques, and their applications to general contemporary landscape architecture, and urban and interior design.
She has authored essays published both in international conferences and magazines. In September 2017 Luyi was invited to take part in Beijing Design Week to exhibit her work "From Vitruvius to 3-D Printing: Customized Tea House Design."

Achim Menges

is a registered architect and professor at the University of Stuttgart where he is the founding director of the Institute for Computational Design (ICD). He has also been a visiting professor in architecture at Harvard University's Graduate School of Design from 2009 to 2015. He graduated with honors from the AA School of Architecture in London, where he subsequently taught as studio master of the Emergent Technologies and Design Graduate Program from 2002 to 2009, as visiting professor from 2009 to 2012, and as unit master of Diploma Unit 4 from 2003 to 2006. Achim Menges's research and practice focuses on the development of integrative design processes at the intersection of morphogenetic design computation, biomimetic engineering, and digital fabrication. His projects and design research have received numerous international awards, and have been published and exhibited worldwide.

Barbara Mertins

is a full professor of German linguistics, with a focus on experimental linguistics and psycholinguistics at the TU Dortmund University. In her research, she uses eye-tracking and the EEG method to study the effects of language and expertise on cognition in language production and comprehension of monolingual and multilingual speakers. She is interested in conceptual learning and restructuring, the relation between memory, visual attention, and language, spatial perception, language pathology, and structure of bilingual and multilingual mental lexicon. Prof. Mertins is head of the Psycholinguistics Laboratories at TU Dortmund University (https://url.tu-dortmund.de/psycho-linguistics-laboratories).

Holger Mertins

is an architect and researcher at the Chair of Architectural Construction of TU Dortmund University. His focus is on empirical research of spatial perception in architecture. He uses eye-tracking and the EEG method to study the effects of architectural expertise on cognition in spatial perception. In his professional career as an architect he has worked on projects such as the Museum Folkwang, Essen; Statoil Headquarters, Oslo; and the State Parliament of Lower Saxony, Hannover. At the TU Dortmund University he is part of the interdisciplinary project Space, Language, Cognition, which is a cooperation between the Chair of Architectural Construction and the Psycholinguistics Laboratories. The cooperation aims at a deeper understanding of visual attention and language in an architectural context.

Joost Meyer

studied sculptural design at FH Aachen, Germany. This was accompanied by long-term work stays for stone sculpting in Harare, Zimbabwe, and Split, Croatia. For ten years he was an art director in a design bureau in Aachen. Since 2011 he is scientific assistant at the Chair for Visual Arts, RWTH Aachen University, where he combines his artistic background and experience with scientific research focusing on the interaction of manual techniques and craftsmanship and digital design procedures. Meyer explores the possibilities offered by digitalized design and fabrication tools, and sees a gradual elimination of analog and digital methods as opposing concepts. The design strategy should rather be a conscious decision for a method or combination of methods. In his PhD project "Modeling in the Field of Tension between Manual and Digital Methods: Comparative Investigation Using the Example of 'Digital Me,' a Self-portrait Study in Lecture for Sculptural Design," he traces reflective processes of students during and after their work.

Rebecca A. Milhuisen

is a research associate at Monash University (Australia). She received her PhD in 2018 working in the research group of Prof. Udo Bach, focusing on novel redox active materials for their application in thin-film solar cells. www.udobach.com, www.excitonscience.com

Nandini Oehlmann

graduated in architecture in 2013 after studying at the Berlin University of the Arts and the Istanbul Technical University. She has been academic assistant at the Chair of Architectural Design and Building in Context at the Brandenburg University of Technology Cottbus-Senftenberg since 2014 and at the Chair of Architectural Design and Construction at the Technische Universität Berlin since 2018. In this connection the publication *Werkstücke: Making Objects into Houses* was released. She has been a doctoral candidate at the Berlin University of the Arts since 2017, researching embodied knowledge in architectural design. Furthermore, she is working in architectural practice. Her focus lies on private housing and made-to-measure interiors.

Tomas Ooms

studied architecture (1995), literature (1996), research methods (2009), and music (2016). He is founding partner of STUDIO TUIN en WERELD (a&t architects, Antwerp, BE) and is academic promotor of the master dissertation design studio at the master of science program in architecture at the Faculty of Architecture at KU Leuven. His ongoing PhD research, "Yard and World: To Draw a Distinction: On the Form of Re-Entry: A Practice Between: Yard and World" is a practice-based architectural inquiry into the liminal and investigates space as relationships. As project and team member he collaborated in several international research projects and won international scholarships, awards, and competitions. He participated in international exhibitions and performances. Besides being a practicing architect, he is a composer and performing musician. He is the lead architect of the project discussed in the article in this publication.

Mathias Peppler

studied architecture at the Karlsruher Institute of Technology and at the University of East London, graduating in 2008. After working for different architecture offices in Basel and Berlin he became academic assistant at the Chair of Architectural Design and Building in Context at the Brandenburg University of Technology Cottbus in 2011. He has been running his own office, MATA Architekten, in Berlin since 2012. Together with his partner Markus Tauber, their emphasis lies in building conversions.

Roman Polster

is an urban planner and research associate at the research group Bau Kunst Erfinden, University of Kassel, Germany, which is dedicated to the development of innovative materials systems at the convergence of art, architecture, and new technologies. His research centers on architectural engineering and the development of smart materials for the building and construction industry. In his PhD thesis he focuses on the functionalization of concrete and concrete surfaces in the context of vertical green and targeted greening. www.baukunsterfinden.org

Viktor Poteschkin

Dipl.-Ing. Viktor Poteschkin is an architect. He studied architecture at the Technische Universität Kaiserslautern, Germany and after the successful completion of the Participatory Student Building Project Spinelli Mannheim and subsequent graduation, he was invited to work as a scientific assistant at the Faculty of Architecture, Structure and Material, led by Prof. Dr.-Ing. Jürgen Graf, to research the recycling potential of cross-laminated timber (CLT) production waste and ways of incorporating this material into new composite structures. After completing the assignment and leaving the university, he is currently pursuing his architectural career.

Wigbert Riehl

is a horticulturist, self-employed landscape architect, and founding shareholder of Riehl Bauermann und Partner, Landscape Architects, Kassel. He is a professor for landscape architecture/technology and from 2017 director of the Institute of Landscape Architecture and Planning, Faculty 06, University of Kassel. He is cofounder of the research center Klimadynamik, Raum + Objekt (KliRO) in 2019. His research priority is sustainability in landscape architecture with a focus on experimental techniques and construction methods, low-tech building methods and recycling, rainwater management and systems as well as greening support areas such as for vertical farming and rooftop gardening.

Eike Roswag-Klinge

Prof. Roswag-Klinge is founder and head of Chair of the Natural Building Lab at Technische Universität Berlin as well as coinitiator of ZRS Architekten Ingenieure. With his teams he undertakes research, planning, and realization projects in diverse global contexts with a focus on holistic, climate-adaptive design solutions that allow the reduction of technology. The focus of current research is the development of healthy low-tech building shells that can control humidity levels through the use of natural building materials such as earth and timber, as well as the development of circular construction elements. As cofounder of the DieNachwachsendeStadt Network, he pursues the resource-positive development and densification of urban contexts with a focus on Berlin. Roswag-Klinge and ZRS have been recognized by a number of international prizes and awards including the Aga Kahn Award for Architecture 2007, the KAIROS European Kulturpreis 2015, the Holcim Award in Gold 2011 Asia-Pacific, and the BDA-Preis Berlin.

Ansgar Schulz

studied architecture at RWTH Aachen University and the ETSA de Madrid from 1985 to 1992. He has been a member of Schalke 04 since 1990. He founded the architecture firm Schulz und Schulz, headquartered in Leipzig, with his brother Benedikt in 1992. He was appointed to the Association of German Architects in 2002 and to the Deutscher Werkbund Berlin in 2015. He was appointed to the Convention of the Federal Foundation for the Culture of Building in 2010, 2016, and 2018. Since 2016 he has been a member of the scientific advisory board of the German Institute for Urban Design. From 2002 to 2004 he was an instructor at the Karlsruhe Institute of Technology. Together with his brother he was cochair in Building Construction at the Faculty of Architecture and Civil Engineering at the TU Dortmund University from 2010 to 2018. He has been a professor for architectural design and construction at the Faculty of Architecture at the Technische Universität Dresden since 2018.

Benedikt Schulz

studied architecture at RWTH Aachen University and the Universidad Católica Nuestra Señora de la Asunción in Paraguay from 1988 to 1994. He has been a member of Schalke 04 since 1990. He founded the architecture firm Schulz und Schulz, headquartered in Leipzig, with his brother Ansgar in 1992. He was appointed to the Association of German Architects in 2002. In 2010 he was appointed to the Saxon Academy of Arts, and in 2015 to the Deutscher Werkbund Berlin. Since 2016 he has been a member of the scientific advisory board of the German Institute for Urban Design. He worked as a research assistant at RWTH Aachen from 1995 to 1996, and was an instructor at the Karlsruhe Institute of Technology from 2002 to 2004. Together with his brother he was cochair in Building Construction at the Faculty of Architecture and Civil Engineering at the TU Dortmund University from 2010 to 2018. He has been a professor for architectural design and construction in the Faculty of Architecture at the Technische Universität Dresden since 2018.

Isabell Schütz

earned her master of science in architecture at RWTH Aachen University in 2012. After two years working as an architect in Stuttgart, she started her academic work at the Technische Universität Darmstadt. At the Department of Design and Building Construction lead by Prof. Dipl.-Ing. M.Arch. Felix Waechter, she takes on a variety of tasks in teaching, research, and university self-government. In her undergraduate classes she can incorporate her experience as a skilled draftsman. Her advanced seminars cover architectural theory, typology, and innovative concepts of construction. As part of her dissertation, she is researching the German settlements in the œuvre of Richard Neutra.

Tobias Schwinn

is a lecturer (Akademischer Rat) at the Institute for Computational Design and Construction (ICD) at University of Stuttgart, Germany. In research and teaching, he is focusing on behavior-based approaches for integrating robotic fabrication and architectural design in the context of segmented shell structures. As head of Research and Research Infrastructure, he is also in charge of research infrastructure, such as the Robolab and the Computational Construction Laboratory in Wangen. Prior to joining the ICD, he worked as a senior designer for Skidmore, Owings and Merrill in New York and London, applying computational approaches at various design stages. Tobias studied architecture at the Bauhaus-University in Weimar, Germany, and at the University of Pennsylvania in Philadelphia. He received his diploma-engineering degree in 2005.

Wenchang Shi

studied lightweight engineering and polymer technology at the Technische Universität Dresden. After successful completion of the master thesis with the title "Creation of a database-based calculation tool for the determination of laminate characteristics using test data," he was invited by Prof. Dr.-Ing. Jürgen Graf at the Faculty of Architecture (fatuk), Technische Universität Kaiserslautern to work as a scientific assistant and to research the recycling potential of cross laminated timber (CLT) production waste and ways of incorporating this material into new composite structures.

Steffi Silbermann

is a product designer and research associate at the research group Bau Kunst Erfinden, University of Kassel, Germany. She received her diploma from Weißensee Kunsthochschule Berlin, where she developed the idea to use woven traditional willow withes for a variation of plywood. In her PhD thesis Steffi Silbermann focuses on the development of a solid-wood willow monofil and textile constructions out of it for building materials. At the research group Bau Kunst Erfinden, University of Kassel, Steffi Silbermann has initiated several research projects, among others the joint research projects FLIGNUM – Continous solid-wood fibre and TETHOK – Textile Tectonics for Wood Construction. They aim to develop a monofil made of solid wood which can be used to create technical textiles for building. In her design practice she collaborates with Oderbruch Museum Altranft – Werkstatt für ländliche Kultur that explores the transformation of the cultural heritage of the region into its present and future. www.steffisilbermann.de, www.baukunsterfinden.org, www.oderbruchmuseum.de

Alexander Stahr

holds a PhD in civil engineering and has been a professor of structural engineering at the University of Applied Sciences HTWK in Leipzig since 2010. The main purpose of his teaching, with its key aspect being architectural structures, is to convey an understanding for the flow of forces in construction via (the visual) methods of graphical structural engineering and the use of digital parametric tools. Stahr is the initiator and creative director of FLEX, which is in equal parts an interdisciplinary team of professional researchers and a platform for technically driven, ambitious student projects. In consideration of the ever increasing responsibility the building industry has in regard to the use of material resources, the main research efforts of this group of architects and civil and industrial engineers focuses on the design and development of innovative strategies and the cost and resource efficiency of structures on the basis of consistent digital process chains.

Elsbeth Stern

is professor of learning and instruction at ETH Zurich since 2006, where she is heading the teacher education program. For the past thirty years, her research has focused on learning in science and mathematics from the perspective of cognitive psychology. After completing her doctorate at the University of Hamburg in 1986, Elsbeth worked at the Max-Planck Institute for Psychological Research in Munich, and in 1994 became professor for educational psychology at the University of Leipzig. In 1997 she moved to the Max-Planck Institute for Human Development in Berlin. She has published several books and more than 150 articles, with many of them in high-ranking international scientific journals. She has been on the editorial board of a number of journals, including *Science*. In addition to her scientific research, she is well known for her contributions on educational topics to a broader public. For these activities, she was awarded the Franz-Weinert Prize from the German Society of Psychology in 2018.

Shilong Tan

is currently a doctoral student at the Politecnico di Milano, Milan, Italy. Shilong graduated with a master's degree in architecture from the Politecnico di Milano. He is an architect at Stefano Boeri Studio since 2014. His doctoral research focuses on immersive space in museums and smart technology in architecture design.

Andreas Thoma

is a research assistant at the Professorship for Architecture and Digital Fabrication, Gramazio Kohler Research, at ETH Zurich. Prior to Zurich, he worked at Herzog & de Meuron's Digital Technologies group in Basel.

During his time at Gramazio Kohler Research he has co-led the projects Iridescence Print, Rock Print, and Spatial Timber Assemblies. In 2017 Rock Print was awarded the Ars Electronica STARTS Prize. He holds a master of science in architecture from ETH Zurich and a bachelor of science in architecture from the Bauhaus-University Weimar. His work has been exhibited at the Palais de Tokyo in Paris, Chicago Architecture Biennial, Museum of Digital Art in Zurich, and the Swiss Institute in Rome. Currently he is focused on scaling up digital fabrication techniques with industrial robots while using wood as the main constructive material. This work is highlighted in both the Spatial Timber Assemblies contribution to the DFAB HOUSE project and the Gradual Assemblies project in Rome.

Katharina Voigt

studied architecture at HCU Hamburg, TUM Munich, and KTH Stockholm; she attended the curatorial seminar *Choreographing a Context* at DOCH Stockholm. Among others, she worked with Heim Kuntscher Architekten und Stadtplaner BDA and Stölken Schmidt Architekten BDA. Since 2016 she is a research associate at the Chair of Architectural Design and Conception, Technical University of Munich. Her scientific research focuses on the corporeal and body-related experience of architectural spaces. Her investigation "Sterbeorte," on the spatial-, body-, and experience-related phenomenology of adequate architectures for the dying, will be published in 2020. Her recent research addresses the interrelation of architecture, perception, and contemporary dance, with the doctoral project "Aktionsräume – über das dynamische Moment architektonischer Räume am Beispiel des Werkes von Sasha Waltz." Further, she works as a choreographer, developing site-specific and architecture-related performances.

Georg Vrachliotis

is professor of architecture theory and director of the architecture collection (saai | Südwestdeutsches Archiv für Architektur und Ingenieurbau) at the Karlsruhe Institute of Technology. He was Dean of the KIT Faculty of Architecture from 2016 to 2019. He previously taught and conducted research at the Institute for the History and Theory of Architecture (gta) at the ETH Zurich. He studied architecture at the Berlin University of the Arts and did his PhD at the ETH Zurich. He was a visiting researcher at the UC Berkeley Department of Architecture in California. From 2006 to 2010 he was a guest lecturer on architecture theory at the TU Wien. He is a member of the advisory board of the magazine *ARCH+*. He is a coeditor and coauthor of many books and (co-)curated several exhibitions: *Fritz Haller: Architect and Researcher* at the SAM Swiss Architecture Museum in 2014 in collaboration with the Institute for History and Theory (gta) at ETH Zurich; *Frei Otto: Thinking by Modeling* at ZKM | Center for Art and Media Karlsruhe (2016/17); and *Sleeping Beauty: Reinventing Frei Otto's Multihalle* on the occasion of the 16th International Architecture Exhibition of the Venice Biennale in 2018. Currently, he is working on an exhibition at Yale School of Architecture (2020).

Liselotte Vroman

obtained a master's degree in architecture in 2010 and worked for five years as a practicing architect. Since 2016 she is a full-time doctoral researcher and teacher at the KU Leuven Faculty/Department of Architecture and is part of the research group "The Drawing and the Space" (www. thedrawingandthespace.info). Her academic activities mainly focus on topics concerning the relationship between the human body and the built environment. Specifically, she has an interest in movement and the associated embodied experience. This interest mainly arose during her second master's and was nurtured by the proximity of her sister Laura Vanhulle (https://www. vanhulledancetheatre.com/), a contemporary dancer based in the UK. She also devoted her master's thesis to this theme, in which the first seeds of her current PhD project were sown. In the PhD project, supervised by Thierry Lagrange, she explores how a better understanding of the notion of embodied spatial experience can be generated by means of experimental mapping techniques and how designers can deal with it in their design processes.

Hans Jakob Wagner

is a research associate and PhD candidate at the Institute for Computational Design and Construction (ICD) at the University of Stuttgart with a focus on robotic fabrication and lightweight wood building systems. He graduated from the ITECH master's program at the University of Stuttgart in 2017 after acquiring a BSc in architecture at the Vienna University of Technology. During his studies he worked in renowned architectural offices in Paris and Vienna and as a student assistant at both the TU Wien and the University of Stuttgart. He assumed a leading role as student coordinator for the ICD/ ITKE Research Pavilion 2016/17 and oversaw the development of the robotic fabrication platform for the BUGA Wood Pavilion 2019. He taught the workshop "Fibrous Joints for Lightweight Timber Shells" at the *Smart Geometry* 2018 conference in Toronto and is adviser of several master theses within the ITECH master's program.

Ramon Weber

is a research assistant at the Massachusetts Institute of Technology MIT Media Lab in the Mediated Matter Group. Working with experimental fabrication platforms and digital building technologies, he is investigating how computational design and robotics can impact future architecture. He received his master's degree in integrative technologies and architectural design research with distinction from the University of Stuttgart and holds a bachelor's in architecture from ETH Zurich, where he conducted research at the Block Research Group, the Institute for Computational Design and Construction (ICD), and the Institute of Building Structures and Structural Design (ITKE), and was a designer at the lightweight composite construction company FibR. He previously worked for Zaha Hadid Architects in London, where he was involved in projects across all scales and design research in the in-house ZHA|CODE research group.

Christian Weisgerber

studied civil engineering with a focus on structural engineering at the Technische Universität Kaiserslautern. As a student he was involved in several research projects at the Department of Concrete Structures and Building Constructions where he also wrote his diploma thesis. Since 2016, he has been teaching the basics of supporting structures to students of the first four semesters as a scientific assistant at the Faculty of Architecture of the Technische Universität Kaiserslautern. During his time as an assistant he has extended his knowledge by studying and researching timber constructions. Beside his teaching activity he is engaged in research on the subject of efficient and resource-saving structural solutions. These aims are implemented by optimizing construction designs and using highly loadable yet sustainable timber and timber-concrete composite structures.

Dylan Marx Wood

is a research group leader at the Institute for Computational Design and Construction at the University of Stuttgart. At ICD, Dylan leads the Institute's research on programmable materials with an emphasis on shape-changing bio-based material systems. His current research focuses on developing intelligent design and fabrication principles for "smart" self-shaping materials as a form of material robotics that can be applied in building systems, construction, and manufacturing. His doctoral research on self-shaping wood building components is funded by Innosuisse (the Swiss Innovation Agency) and the GETTYLAB. He holds an ITECH MSc with distinction from the University of Stuttgart, and a bachelor's in architecture, magna cum laude from the University of Southern California. Professionally he has worked as a designer and computational fabrication specialist at Barkow Leibinger Architects in Berlin, Germany, and DOSU Studio Architects in Los Angeles, CA.

Yuxin Yang

is currently a doctoral student at the Politecnico di Milano, Italy. She graduated with a master's degree in fashion system design at the Politecnico di Milano. Her doctoral research focuses on design and cultural heritage.

Index of Authors

RCA 2018

International Conference on Cross-Disciplinary Collaboration
27–28 September 2018, Faculty of Architecture, TU Kaiserslautern,
Germany

The RCA Conference (https://rca2018.architektur.uni-kl.de) was only possible with the help and support by the following people and organizations:

Conference Chairs

Maria da Piedade Ferreira
Cornelie Leopold
Christopher Robeller
Peter Spitzley
Ulrike Weber

Scientific Committee

Bayer, Dirk – TU Kaiserslautern, Germany
Beirao, Jose Nuno – FAU Lisbon, Portugal
Blancafort, Jaume – ETSAE, Cartagena, Spain
Brandt, Stefanie – STEPHANIE BRANDT Studio, Germany
Braumann, Johannes – UFG Linz, Austria
Dähne, Chris – TU Darmstadt, Germany
Darling, Elizabeth – Oxford Brooks, UK
Dillenburger, Benjamin – ETH Zürich, Switzerland
Friedrich, Eva – Google San Francisco, USA
Graf, Jürgen – TU Kaiserslautern, Germany
Graff, Uta – TU München, Germany
Hagen, Hans – TU Kaiserslautern, Germany
Hagg, Catharina – TU Berlin, Germany
Hauser, Susanne – UdK Berlin, Germany
Henriques, Goncalo Castro – Unifederal, Rio de Janeiro, Brasil
Hild, Andreas – TU München, Germany
Kern, Heike – TU Kaiserslautern, Germany
Krötsch, Stefan – Hochschule Konstanz, Germany
Langenhan, Christoph – TU München, Germany
Lindenberg, Katharina – Berner Fachhochschule, Switzerland
Paio, Alexandra – ISCTE, Lisbon, Portugal
Palti, Itai – Bartlett, UCL, UK
Palz, Norbert – UdK Berlin, Germany

Pogacnik, Marco - IUAV Venezia, Italy
Ruskowski, Martin - TU Kaiserslautern/DFKI, Germany
Schindler, Christoph - Hochschule Luzern, Switzerland
Schubert, Gerhard - TU München, Germany
Schwinn, Tobias - Uni Stuttgart, Germany
Sedrez, Maycon - TU Braunschweig, Germany
Sousa, José Pedro - FAUP Porto, Portugal
Spaeth, A. Benjamin - Cardiff, UK
Stavric, Milena - TU Graz, Austria
Sunguroglu Hensel, Defne - TU München, Germany
Symeonidou, Ioanna - AUTH, Greece
Tersluisen, Angèle - TU Kaiserslautern, Germany
Vrachliotis, Georg - KIT Karlsruhe, Germany
Wang, Xiaohong - CAFA Bejing, China
Winkels, Andreas - TH Bingen, Germany
Zupancic, Tadeja - UL-FA, Slovenja

Organization
Dagmar Häßel, Silke Wienands, Falk Ahlhelm, Heinrich Geißendörfer, Daniel
Jeffrey Köhler, Yolanda Guastaferro Marcano, Lea Schön, Lukas Wasem,
Viyaleta Zhurava

Graphic Design
Florian Budke

Sponsored by

 Deutsche Forschungsgemeinschaft
German Research Foundation

 Fachbereich Architektur
Technische Universität
Kaiserslautern

Project management: Nora Kempkens
Production: Heike Strempel, Bettina Chang
Layout, cover design and typesetting: Falk Kuckert, leisundkuckert.de

Paper: Magno Volume, 135 g/m²
Lithography: bildpunkt Druckvorstufen GmbH
Printing: optimal media GmbH

Library of Congress Control Number: 2019953727

Bibliographic information published by the German National Library
The German National Library lists this publication in the Deutsche Nation-
albibliografie; detailed bibliographic data are available on the Internet at
http://dnb.dnb.de.

ISBN 978-3-0356-2014-6

e-ISBN (PDF) 978-3-0356-2023-8

© 2020 Birkhäuser Verlag GmbH, Basel
P.O. Box 44, 4009 Basel, Switzerland
Part of Walter de Gruyter GmbH, Berlin/Boston

9 8 7 6 5 4 3 2 1   www.birkhauser.com